The Governance of China

III

XI JINPING

The Governance of China

III

FOREIGN LANGUAGES PRESS

First Edition 2020
Fourth Printing 2023

All rights reserved. No part of this publication may be reproduced, stored in a retrieval system, or transmitted in any form or by any means, electronic, mechanical, photocopying, recording, scanning, or otherwise, except as expressly permitted by law, without the prior written permission of the Publisher.

ISBN 978-7-119-12411-7
© Foreign Languages Press Co. Ltd, Beijing, China, 2020
Published by Foreign Languages Press Co. Ltd
24 Baiwanzhuang Road, Beijing 100037, China
http://www.flp.com.cn
Email: flp@CIPG.org.cn
Distributed by China International Book Trading Corporation
35 Chegongzhuang Xilu, Beijing 100044, China
P.O. Box 399, Beijing, China
Printed in the People's Republic of China

Publisher's Note

The 19th National Congress of the Communist Party of China (CPC) in 2017 recognized Xi Jinping Thought on Socialism with Chinese Characteristics for a New Era as the latest milestone on the road that the CPC will follow for the foreseeable future, and has since written it into the CPC Constitution. At the First Session of the 13th National People's Congress in 2018, the Constitution of the People's Republic of China was also amended to include this thought. These represented timely updates to the guiding philosophy of the Party and the country.

Embodying Marxism in contemporary China and in the 21st century, Xi Jinping Thought on Socialism with Chinese Characteristics for a New Era is the banner of the CPC in the new era. It steers the political and social activities of the country, and is a guide to action for the rejuvenation of the Chinese nation. The thought has also contributed a Chinese perspective and Chinese ideas to building a global community of shared future.

Since the 19th CPC National Congress, guided by this thought and remaining true to the Party's original aspiration and founding mission, the CPC Central Committee, with Xi Jinping as its core, has fully considered the overall goal of national rejuvenation and the international situation in a context of change at a level unseen in a century, and has coordinated efforts on the great struggle, the great project, the great cause and the great dream. The CPC Central Committee has handled with composure a complex situation, with clearly increasing risks and challenges both at home and abroad. It has furthered reform and opening up, fought for the final victory in building a moderately prosperous society in all respects, and achieved new breakthroughs in all undertakings of the Party and the country. China has also made a major contribution to world peace and development.

The first and second volumes of *Xi Jinping: The Governance of China* have received an enthusiastic response from China and other parts of the world. Since the 19th CPC National Congress, Xi Jinping has put forward many original ideas drawn from his experiences in state governance in the new era, charting the course in line with the times and further enriching the theoretical base of the Party. To help officials and the public understand and apply Xi Jinping Thought on Socialism with Chinese Characteristics for a New Era, to strengthen their commitment to the Four Consciousnesses, the Four-sphere Confidence and the Two Upholds, and also to help the international community gain a full appreciation of the thought and the reasons for the success of the CPC, Marxism and Chinese socialism, the Publicity Department of the CPC Central Committee and the State Council Information Office, with the support of the Research Institute of Party History and Literature of the CPC Central Committee and China International Publishing Group, have compiled a third volume of *Xi Jinping: The Governance of China*.

This volume contains a compilation of 92 of Xi Jinping's spoken and written works from October 18, 2017 to January 13, 2020, along with 41 photographs. It is divided into 19 sections by topic, with the articles in each section arranged in chronological order. For ease of reading, notes are to be found at the end of relevant articles.

CONTENTS

Secure a Decisive Victory in Building a Moderately Prosperous Society in All Respects and Strive for the Great Success of Socialism with Chinese Characteristics for a New Era
October 18, 2017   1

Thought on Socialism with Chinese Characteristics for a New Era

New Requirements for Chinese Socialism in the New Era
October 25, 2017   83

Fully Implement the Thought on Socialism with Chinese Characteristics for a New Era
October 25, 2017   85

New Era, New Initiatives, New Achievements
October 25, 2017   87

Continue the Great Historic Struggle
January 5, 2018   91

Broader Dimensions for Marxism in Contemporary China and the 21st Century
May 4, 2018   96

Focus on Our Tasks – Bear in Mind the National Goal and Changing Conditions
May 21, 2019   99

Speech at the Celebration of the 70th Anniversary of the Founding of the PRC
October 1, 2019   100

Overall CPC Leadership

Strengthen Commitment to the Four Consciousnesses, the Four-Sphere Confidence, and the Two Upholds
October 25, 2017-May 31, 2019   105

Maximize the Institutional Strength of CPC Leadership
February 26, 2018   112

Initiative and Resolve in Reinforcing the Party's Political Foundations
June 29, 2018   114

Ensure the Two Upholds in Central Party and Government Departments
July 9, 2019   124

State System and National Governance

Improve the Functions of Party and State Institutions
July 5, 2019 — 129

Note to the Decision of the CPC Central Committee on Upholding and Improving Chinese Socialist System and Modernizing State Governance
October 28, 2019 — 134

Uphold and Improve the Chinese Socialist System and Modernize State Governance
October 31, 2019 — 143

People-Centered Development

A Better Life for All Our People
November 30, 2017 — 159

The People Are Our Greatest Strength in Governance
March 1, 2018-December 27, 2019 — 161

Always Put the People First
March 20, 2018 — 165

Never Fail the People
March 22, 2019 — 170

Poverty Elimination and a Moderately Prosperous Society

Complete the Work of Building a Moderately Prosperous Society in All Respects
October 25, 2017 — 173

A New Chapter in the Fight Against Poverty
February 12, 2018 — 175

Win the Battle Against Poverty
February 12, 2018 — 182

Deliver the Two Assurances and Three Guarantees
April 16, 2019 — 188

Further Reform

Follow the Guidance of the Third Plenary Session of the 19th CPC Central Committee
February 28, 2018 — 195

Deeper Reform Requires Greater Resolve
July 6, 2018-November 26, 2019 — 209

Valuable Experience from 40 Years of Reform and Opening Up
December 18, 2018   *213*

All-Round Opening Up

China Will Open Even Wider
April 10, 2018   *227*

Roll Out Free Trade Ports
April 13, 2018   *232*

For a Global Economy – Open, Innovative and Inclusive
November 5, 2018   *235*

Open Up and Cooperate Towards a Shared Future
November 5, 2019   *245*

Risk Management

Ensure Absolute Party Leadership over National Security
April 17, 2018   *253*

Be Alert to Risks
January 21, 2019   *256*

Meet Challenges Head-On
September 3, 2019   *263*

High-Quality Development

Enrich the Thought on the Socialist Economy in the New Era
December 18, 2017   *269*

China's Economy: From High-Speed Growth to High-Quality Development
December 18, 2017   *277*

Accelerate Economic Modernization
January 30, 2018   *281*

Speed Up China's Maritime Development
March 8, 2018-October 15, 2019   *285*

Make China a Global Center for Science and Innovation
May 28, 2018   *287*

Promote Rural Revitalization
September 21, 2018   *299*

Boost the Private Sector
November 1, 2018   *309*

Coordinated Quality Development Across Regions
August 26, 2019   *316*

Socialist Democracy

Constitutional Safeguards for Chinese Socialism in the New Era
January 19, 2018 — 327

Advance the Rule of Law Under Chinese Socialism
August 24, 2018 — 331

Protect and Promote Human Rights in the Chinese Context
December 10, 2018 — 337

Enhance Local Legislation and Supervision
July 2019 — 339

Consolidate Socialist Consultative Democracy
September 20, 2019 — 341

Heighten a Sense of Chinese Identity
September 27, 2019 — 351

Chinese Culture

Enhance Cyber Capabilities Through Innovation
April 20, 2018 — 357

Public Communication in the New Era
August 21, 2018 — 362

Accelerate Media Integration
January 25, 2019 — 369

A Nation Must Have a Soul
March 4, 2019 — 375

Raise Students' Awareness of the Thought on Socialism with Chinese Characteristics for a New Era
March 18, 2019 — 382

Carry On the Legacy of the May 4th Movement, and Be Worthy of the New Era
April 30, 2019 — 387

The People's Wellbeing

Continue the "Toilet Revolution"
November 2017 — 395

Bring a Sense of Gain, Happiness and Security to the People
December 2017-November 3, 2019 — 396

Remove Institutional Barriers to Educational Development
September 10, 2018 — 401

Safeguard Political Security, Social Order and Peaceful Lives
January 15, 2019 — 408

Harmony Between Humanity and Nature

Principles to Apply in Protecting the Eco-Environment
May 18, 2018   *417*

Win the Battle Against Pollution
May 18, 2018   *425*

Build a Green and Beautiful Homeland for All
April 28, 2019   *434*

Major Goals for Eco-Conservation and Quality Development of the Yellow River Basin
September 18, 2019   *438*

The People's Armed Forces

Strengthen the Party's Leadership and Organizations in the Military
August 17, 2018   *445*

Improve the Socialist Military Policy Framework with Chinese Characteristics
November 13, 2018   *450*

Be Combat Ready Under the New Conditions
January 4, 2019   *454*

Hong Kong, Macao and China's Peaceful Reunification

Promote Development in Hong Kong and Macao as Part of China's Overall Development
November 12, 2018   *459*

Strive for China's National Rejuvenation and Peaceful Reunification
January 2, 2019   *468*

Speech on the 20th Anniversary of Macao's Return to China and the Inauguration of the Fifth-Term Government of the Macao Special Administrative Region
December 20, 2019   *478*

China's Diplomacy as a Major Country

China's Diplomacy in the New Era
December 28, 2017   *489*

Strengthen CPC Central Committee Leadership over Foreign Affairs
May 15, 2018   *493*

Break New Ground in China's Major-Country Diplomacy
June 22, 2018   *495*

A Global Community of Shared Future

Meet the People's Expectation for a Better Life
December 1, 2017 — 503

Carry Forward the Shanghai Spirit; Build a Community of Shared Future
June 10, 2018 — 510

The Role of the BRICS in Building a Global Community of Shared Future
July 25, 2018 — 516

Towards a Stronger China-Africa Community of Shared Future
September 3, 2018 — 521

Define an Effective Approach to Global Economic Governance
November 17, 2018 — 529

Endeavor to Shape the Future of Humanity
March 26, 2019 — 535

Build a Maritime Community of Shared Future
April 23, 2019 — 538

Create an Asian Community of Shared Future Through Mutual Learning
May 15, 2019 — 540

Work Together for a High-Quality World Economy
June 28, 2019 — 548

The Belt and Road Initiative

Open a Path to Cooperation Across the Pacific
January 22, 2018 — 555

Strengthen Cooperation to Advance the Belt and Road Initiative
July 10, 2018 — 556

Ensure that Belt and Road Cooperation Delivers Solid Outcomes
August 27, 2018 — 562

Promote High-Quality Belt and Road Cooperation
April 26, 2019 — 566

Self-Reform of the CPC

Never Forget Where We Started
October 31, 2017 — 575

Say No to Form over Substance and Reject Bureaucratism
December 2017-January 11, 2019 — 578

Strengthen Party Self-Governance as an Ongoing Mission
January 11, 2018 — 584

Strengthen the Party and Its Organizational Line in the New Era
July 3, 2018 — 597

Cultivate Officials with Firm Conviction, Political Commitment,
  Professional Competence, and Proper Conduct
  March 1, 2019   *601*

Goals of the Aspiration and Mission Education Campaign
  May 31, 2019   *607*

Stay True to the Party's Original Aspiration and Founding Mission and
  Carry Out Self-Reform
  June 24, 2019   *614*

Remain True to Our Original Aspiration and Founding Mission –
  An Ongoing Campaign
  January 8, 2020   *623*

Strengthen Discipline and Scrutiny over the Exercise of Power
  January 13, 2020   *632*

Index   *639*

Secure a Decisive Victory in Building a Moderately Prosperous Society in All Respects and Strive for the Great Success of Socialism with Chinese Characteristics for a New Era*

October 18, 2017

Comrades,

On behalf of the 18th Central Committee of the Communist Party of China, I will now deliver a report to the 19th National Congress.

The 19th National Congress of the Communist Party of China is a meeting of great importance taking place during the decisive stage in building a moderately prosperous society in all respects and at a critical moment as socialism with Chinese characteristics has entered a new era.

The theme of the Congress is: Remain true to our original aspiration and founding mission, hold high the banner of socialism with Chinese characteristics, secure a decisive victory in building a moderately prosperous society in all respects, strive for the great success of socialism with Chinese characteristics for a new era, and work tirelessly to realize the Chinese Dream of national rejuvenation.

Never forget why you started, and you can accomplish your mission. The original aspiration and mission of Chinese Communists is to seek happiness for the Chinese people and rejuvenation for the Chinese nation. This original aspiration, this mission, is what inspires Chinese Communists to advance. In our Party, each and every

---

* Report to the 19th National Congress of the Communist Party of China.

one of us must always breathe the same air as the people, share the same future, and stay truly connected to them. The aspirations of the people to live a better life must always be the focus of our efforts. We must keep on striving with endless energy towards the great goal of national rejuvenation.

Both China and the world are in the midst of profound and complex changes. China is still in an important period of strategic opportunity for development; the prospects are bright but the challenges are severe. All comrades must aim high and look far, be alert to dangers even in times of calm, have the courage to pursue reform and break new ground, and never become hardened to change or inactive. We will unite the Chinese people of all ethnic groups and lead them to a decisive victory in building a moderately prosperous society in all respects and in the drive to secure the success of socialism with Chinese characteristics for a new era.

I. The Past Five Years: Our Work and Historic Change

The five years since the 18th National Congress have been a truly remarkable five years in the course of the development of the Party and the country. Outside China, we have been confronted with sluggish global economic recovery, frequent outbreaks of regional conflicts and disturbances, and intensifying global issues. At home, we have encountered profound changes as China has entered a new normal in economic development. We have upheld the underlying principle of pursuing progress while ensuring stability, risen to challenges, pioneered and pushed ahead, and made historic achievements in reform, opening up, and socialist modernization.

To put the guiding principles from the 18th National Congress into action, the Party Central Committee has held seven plenary sessions. There, decisions and plans were made on issues of major importance, from reforming the institutions and transforming the functions of government to deepening reform in all areas, advancing law-based governance, formulating the 13th Five-year Plan, and seeing governance over the Party is exercised fully and with rigor. In the past five years, we have implemented the Five-sphere Integrated Plan[1] and the Four-pronged Comprehensive Strategy[2], fulfilled the goals of the 12th Five-year Plan, and made smooth progress in implementing the 13th Five-year Plan. On all fronts new advances have been made for the cause of the Party and the country.

We have made major achievements in economic development.

We have remained committed to the new development philosophy, adopted the right approach to development, and endeavored to transform the growth model. The result has been a constant improvement in the quality and effect of development. The economy has maintained a medium-high growth rate, making China a leader among the major economies. With the gross domestic product rising from RMB54 trillion to RMB80 trillion, China has maintained its position as the world's second largest economy and contributed more than 30 percent of global economic growth. Supply-side structural reform has made further headway, bringing a steady improvement in the economic structure.

Emerging industries like the digital economy are thriving; the construction of high-speed railways, highways, bridges, ports, airports, and other types of infrastructure has picked up pace. Agricultural modernization has steadily advanced, with annual grain production reaching 600 million tons. The rate of urbanization has risen by an annual average of 1.2 percentage points, and more than 80 million people who have moved from rural to urban areas have gained permanent urban residency. Regional development has become more balanced; the Belt and Road Initiative[3], the coordinated development of the Beijing-Tianjin-Hebei Region, and the development of the Yangtze River Economic Belt have all made notable progress. Through devoting great energy to implementing the innovation-driven development strategy, we have seen much accomplished towards making China a country of innovators, with major advances made in science and technology, including the successful launch of *Tiangong-2* space lab, the commissioning of the deep-sea manned submersible

Jiaolong and of the five-hundred-meter aperture spherical telescope (FAST) *Tianyan*, the launch of the dark matter probe satellite *Wukong* and the quantum science satellite *Mozi*, and the test flight of the airliner C919. Construction on islands and reefs in the South China Sea has seen steady progress. The new institutions of the open economy have been steadily improved. China now leads the world in foreign trade, outbound investment, and foreign exchange reserves.

We have made major breakthroughs in deepening reform.

We have taken comprehensive steps to deepen reform swiftly but steadily, and worked with resolve to remove institutional barriers in all areas. We have taken moves across the board, achieved breakthroughs in many areas, and made further progress in reform. We have pursued reform in a more systematic, holistic, and coordinated way, increasing its coverage and depth. Thanks to the launch of over 1,500 reform measures, breakthroughs have been made in key areas, and general frameworks for reform have been established in major fields. The system of socialism with Chinese characteristics has been further improved, with notable progress made in modernizing China's system and capacity for governance. Throughout society, development is full of vitality and is driven by greater creativity.

We have taken major steps in developing democracy and the rule of law.

We have actively developed socialist democracy and advanced law-based governance. We have stepped up institution building across the board to ensure that the Party's leadership, the people's position as masters of the country, and law-based governance form an indivisible whole; and we have continuously improved the institutions and mechanisms by which the Party exercises leadership. Steady progress has been made in enhancing socialist democracy; intra-Party democracy has been expanded, and socialist consultative democracy is flourishing. The patriotic united front[4] has been consolidated and developed, and new approaches have been adopted for work related to ethnic and religious affairs. Further progress has been made in ensuring our legislation is sound, law enforcement is strict, the administration of justice is impartial, and the law is observed by everyone. Our efforts to build a country, government, and society based on the rule of law are mutually reinforcing; the system of distinctively Chinese socialist rule of law has been steadily improved; and public awareness of the rule of law has risen markedly. Good progress has been made in piloting the reform of the national supervision system, and effective measures have been taken to reform the system of government administration and the judicial system, and to develop systems to apply checks and oversight over the exercise of power.

We have made significant advances on the theoretical and cultural fronts.

We have strengthened Party leadership over ideological work and explored new ground in advancing Party-related theories. The importance of Marxism as a guiding ideology is better appreciated. Socialism with Chinese characteristics and the Chinese Dream have been embraced by our people. The core socialist values[5] and fine traditional Chinese culture are alive in the people's hearts. Initiatives to improve public etiquette and ethical standards have proved successful. Public cultural services have been improved; art and literature are thriving, and cultural programs and industries are going strong. The development, administration, and functioning of internet services have been enhanced. Fitness-for-all programs and competitive sports have seen extensive development. Our country's underlying values hold greater appeal than ever before, and the wave of positive energy felt throughout society is building. We, the Chinese people, have greater confidence in our own culture. China's cultural soft power and the international influence of Chinese culture have increased significantly. There is greater unity in thinking both within the Party and throughout society.

We have steadily improved living standards.

Our vision of making development people-centered has been actioned, a whole raft of initiatives to benefit the people has seen implementation, and the people's sense of fulfillment has grown stronger. Decisive progress has been made in the fight against poverty: More than 60 million people have been lifted out of poverty, and the poverty headcount ratio has dropped from 10.2 percent to less than 4 percent. All-round progress has been made in education, with remarkable advances made in the central and western regions and in rural areas. Employment has registered steady growth, with an average of over 13 million urban jobs created each year. Growth of urban and rural personal incomes has outpaced economic growth, and the middle-income group is expanding. A social security system covering both urban and rural residents has taken shape; both public health and medical services have improved markedly. Solid progress has been made in building government subsidized housing projects to ensure basic needs are met. Social governance systems have been improved; law and order has been maintained; and national security has been fully enhanced.

We have made notable progress in building an eco-civilization.

We have devoted serious effort to the eco-environment. As a result, the entire Party and the whole country have become more conscious about and active in pursuing green development, and there has been a clear shift away from the tendency to neglect ecological and environmental protection. Efforts to develop a system of institutions for building an eco-civilization have been accelerated; the system of functional zoning has been steadily improved; and progress has been made in piloting the national park system. Across-the-board efforts to conserve resources have seen encouraging progress; the intensity of energy and resource consumption has been significantly reduced. Smooth progress has been made in major eco-environmental conservation and restoration projects; and forest coverage has been increased. Ecological and environmental governance has been significantly strengthened, leading to marked improvements in the environment. Taking a driving seat in international cooperation to respond to climate change, China has become an important participant, contributor, and torchbearer in the global endeavor for eco-civilization.

We have initiated a new stage in strengthening and revitalizing the armed forces.

With a view to realizing the Chinese Dream and the dream of building a powerful military, we have developed a strategy for the military under new circumstances, and have made every effort to modernize national defense and the armed forces. We convened the Gutian Conference on Military Political Work to revive and pass on the proud traditions and fine conduct of our Party and our armed forces, and have seen a strong improvement in the political ecosystem of the people's forces. Historic breakthroughs have been made in reforming national defense and the armed forces: A new military structure has been established with the Central Military Commission exercising overall leadership, the theater commands responsible for military operations, and the services focusing on developing capabilities. This represents a revolutionary restructuring of the organization and the services of the people's armed forces. We have strengthened military training and war preparedness, and undertaken major missions related to the protection of maritime rights, countering terrorism, maintaining stability, disaster rescue and relief, international peacekeeping, escort services in the Gulf of Aden, and humanitarian assistance. We have stepped up weapons and equipment development, and made major progress in enhancing military preparedness. The people's armed forces have taken solid strides on the path of building a powerful military with Chinese characteristics.

We have made fresh progress in work related to Hong Kong, Macao, and Taiwan.

We have fully and faithfully implemented the principle of "one country, two systems", and ensured that the central government exercises its overall jurisdiction over Hong Kong and Macao as mandated by China's Constitution and the basic laws of the two special administrative regions. We have thus boosted exchanges and cooperation between the mainland and the two regions and maintained prosperity and stability in Hong Kong and Macao. We have upheld the one-China principle and the 1992 Consensus[6], promoted the peaceful development of cross-Straits relations, strengthened cross-Straits economic and cultural exchanges and cooperation, and held a historic meeting between the leaders of the two sides. We have responded as appropriate to the political developments in Taiwan, resolutely opposed and deterred separatist elements advocating "Taiwan independence", and vigorously safeguarded peace and stability in the Taiwan Straits.

We have made further progress in China's diplomacy on all fronts.

We have made all-round efforts in the pursuit of major-country diplomacy with Chinese characteristics, thus advancing China's diplomatic agenda in a comprehensive, multilevel, multifaceted way and creating a favorable external environment for China's development. We have jointly pursued the Belt and Road Initiative, initiated the Asian Infrastructure Investment Bank, set up the Silk Road Fund, and hosted the First Belt and Road Forum for International Cooperation, the 22nd APEC Economic Leaders' Meeting, the G20 2016 Summit in Hangzhou, the BRICS Summit in Xiamen, and the Fourth Summit of the Conference on Interaction and Confidence Building Measures in Asia. China champions the development of a global community of shared future, and has encouraged the evolution of the global governance system. With this we have seen a further rise in China's international influence, ability to inspire, and power to shape; and China has made great new contributions to global peace and development.

We have achieved remarkable outcomes in ensuring full and strict governance over the Party.

We have made sweeping efforts to strengthen the Party and its leadership, and taken strong action to transform lax and weak governance over the Party. We encourage all Party members to hold the Party Constitution in great esteem. We urge them to strengthen their consciousness of the need to maintain political commitment, think in terms of the general picture, follow the core leadership of the CPC Central Committee, and act in accordance with its requirements, and to uphold the authority of the Central Committee and its centralized, unified leadership. We have tightened political discipline and rules to ensure that political responsibility for governance over the Party is fulfilled at every level of the Party organization.

We have committed to "examining ourselves in the mirror, tidying our attire, taking a bath, and treating our ailments", launched activities to see members command and act on the Party's mass line[7], and initiated a campaign for the observance of the Three Guidelines for Ethical Behavior and Three Basic Rules of Conduct[8]. We have regularized and institutionalized the requirement for all Party members to have a solid understanding of the Party Constitution, Party regulations, and related major policy addresses, and to meet Party standards. As a result, the ideals and convictions of all Party members have been strengthened and their Party consciousness is deeper. We have adopted standards fitting for a new era to assess the caliber of officials, and achieved a notable improvement in the way officials are selected and appointed. Further advances have been made in the reform of the institutional framework for strengthening the Party, and continuous improvements have been made to the system of Party regulations.

We have given top priority to ensuring compliance with Party discipline, and tackled the prominent problems that prompt the strongest public reaction and that threaten to erode the very foundation of the Party's governance. We have adopted the Eight Rules[9] on improving Party and government conduct, taken tough action against the practice of favoring form over substance, bureaucratism, hedonism, and extravagance, and staunchly opposed privilege seeking. Disciplinary inspections have cut like a blade through corruption and misconduct; they have covered every Party committee in all departments at the central and provincial levels. No place has been out of bounds, no ground left unturned, and no tolerance shown in the fight against corruption. We have taken firm action to "take out tigers", "swat flies", and "hunt down foxes". The goal of creating a deterrent against corruption has been initially attained; the cage of institutions that prevents corruption has been strengthened; and moral defenses against corruption are in the making. The anti-corruption campaign has built into a crushing tide, and is being consolidated and developed.

The achievements of the past five years have touched every area and broken new ground; the changes in China over the past five years have been profound and fundamental. For five years, our Party has demonstrated tremendous political courage and a powerful sense of mission as it has developed new ideas, new thinking, and new strategies, adopted a raft of major principles and policies, launched a host of major initiatives, and pushed ahead with many major tasks. We have solved many tough problems that were long on the agenda but never resolved, and accomplished many things that were wanted but never done. With this, we have prompted historic shifts in the cause of the Party and the country. These historic changes will have a powerful and far-reaching effect on the development of this cause.

Over the past five years, we have acted with courage to confront major risks and tests facing the Party and to address prominent problems within the Party itself. With firm resolve, we have tightened discipline and improved Party conduct, fought corruption and punished wrongdoing, and removed serious potential dangers in the Party and the country. As a result, both the intra-Party political atmosphere and the political ecosystem of the Party have improved markedly. The Party's ability to innovate, power to unite, and energy to fight have all been significantly strengthened; Party solidarity and unity have been reinforced, and our engagement with the people has been greatly improved. Revolutionary tempering has made our Party stronger, and it now radiates with great vitality. With this, efforts to develop the cause of the Party and the country have gained a strong political underpinning.

But we must be very clear: There are still many inadequacies in our work and many difficulties and challenges to face. The main ones are as follows.

Some acute problems caused by unbalanced and inadequate development await solutions; and the quality and effect of development are not what they should be. China's ability to innovate needs to be stronger, the real economy awaits improvement, and we have a long way to go in protecting the environment.

In work on public wellbeing there are still many areas where we fall short; and poverty alleviation remains a formidable task. There are still large disparities in development between rural and urban areas, between regions, and in income distribution; and our people face many difficulties in employment, education, health care, housing, and elderly care.

Civic awareness needs further improvement. Social tensions and problems are intertwined, much remains to be done in seeing the country's governance is based on law, and China's system and capacity for governance need to be further strengthened. Ideological struggle is still complicated, and in national security we face new developments. Some reform plans and major policies and measures need to be better implemented. Many dimensions of strengthening the Party remain weak. These are all problems that demand our full attention.

The achievements of the past five years are the result of the strong leadership of the Party Central Committee, and, more importantly, the result of all Party members and all the Chinese people pulling together in their pursuit. On behalf of the Central Committee of the Communist Party of China, I express our heartfelt thanks to the people of all ethnic groups, to all other political parties, to the people's organizations, and to patriotic figures from all sectors of society, to our fellow countrymen and women in the Hong Kong and Macao special administrative regions and in Taiwan, to overseas Chinese, and to all our friends from around the world who have shown understanding and support for China's modernization.

Comrades,

In the early days of reform and opening up, the Party made a clarion call for us to take a path of our own and build socialism with Chinese characteristics. Since that time, the Party has united and led all the Chinese people in a tireless struggle, propelling China into a leading position in terms of economic and technological strength, defense capabilities, and composite national strength. China's international standing has risen as never before. Our Party, our country, our people, our forces, and our nation have changed in ways without precedent. The Chinese nation, with an entirely new posture, now stands tall and firm in the East.

With decades of hard work, socialism with Chinese characteristics has crossed the threshold into a new era. This is a new historic juncture in China's development.

This is what socialism with Chinese characteristics entering a new era means:

The Chinese nation, which since modern times began had endured so much for so long, has achieved a tremendous transformation: It has stood up, become better off, and grown in strength; it has come to embrace the brilliant prospects of rejuvenation. It means that scientific socialism is full of vitality in 21st century China, and that the banner of socialism with Chinese characteristics is now flying high and proud for all to see. It means that the path, the theory, the system and the culture of socialism with Chinese characteristics have kept developing, blazing a new trail for other developing countries to achieve modernization. It offers a new option for other countries and nations who want to speed up their development while preserving their independence; and it offers Chinese wisdom and a Chinese approach to solving the problems facing humanity.

This new era will be an era of building on past successes to further advance our cause, and of continuing in a new historic context to strive for the success of socialism with Chinese characteristics. It will be an era of securing a decisive victory in building a moderately prosperous society in all respects, and of moving on to all-out efforts to build a great modern socialist country. It will be an era for the Chinese people of all ethnic groups to work together and work hard to create a better life for themselves and ultimately achieve common prosperity for everyone. It will be an era for all of us, the sons and daughters of the Chinese nation, to strive with one heart to realize the Chinese Dream of national rejuvenation. It will be an era that sees China moving closer to center stage and making greater contributions to humanity.

As socialism with Chinese characteristics has entered a new era, the principal challenge facing Chinese society has evolved. What we now face is the gap between unbalanced and inadequate development and the ever-growing expectation of the people for a better life. China has seen the basic needs of over a billion people met, has basically made it possible for people to live decent lives, and will soon bring the building of a moderately prosperous society to a successful completion. The requirements of the people to live better lives are increasingly broad. Not only have their material and cultural needs grown; their demands for democracy, rule of law, fairness and justice, security, and a better environment are increasing. At the same time, China's overall productive forces have significantly improved and in many areas our production capacity leads the world. The more prominent problem is that our development is unbalanced and inadequate. This has become the main constraining factor in meeting the people's increasing expectation for a better life.

We must recognize that the evolution of the principal challenge facing Chinese society represents a historic shift that affects the whole landscape and that creates many new demands for the work of the Party and the country. Building on continued efforts to sustain development, we must devote great energy to addressing development's imbalances and inadequacies, and push hard to improve the quality and effect of development. With this, we will be better placed to meet the ever-growing economic, political, cultural, social, and ecological needs of our people, and to promote well-rounded human development and all-round social progress.

We must recognize that the evolution of the principal challenge facing Chinese society does not change our assessment of the present stage of socialism in China. The basic dimension of the Chinese context – that our country is still and will long remain in the primary stage of socialism – has not changed. China's international status as the world's largest developing country has not changed. The whole Party must be completely clear about this fundamental dimension of our national context, and must base our work on this most important reality – the primary stage of socialism. We must remain fully committed to the Party's basic line as the source that keeps the Party and the country going and that brings happiness to the people. We must lead and unite the Chinese people of all ethnic groups in fulfilling the central task of economic development. We must uphold the Four Cardinal Principles[10], continue to reform and open up, be self-reliant, hardworking, and enterprising, and strive to build China into a great modern socialist country that is prosperous, strong, democratic, culturally advanced, harmonious, and beautiful.

Comrades,

Chinese socialism's entrance into a new era is, in the history of the People's Republic of China and the history of the Chinese nation, of tremendous importance. In the history of international socialism and the history of human society, it is of tremendous importance. Our entire Party should develop unshakable confidence, work hard and work well to see socialism with Chinese characteristics display even stronger vitality.

II. The New Era: The Historic Mission of the Communist Party of China

A hundred years ago, the salvoes of the October Revolution brought Marxism-Leninism to China. In the scientific truth of Marxism-Leninism, Chinese progressives saw a solution to China's problems. With the advent of modern times, Chinese society became embroiled in intense upheavals; this was a time of fierce struggle as the Chinese people resisted feudal rule and foreign aggression. It was in the midst of this, in 1921, as Marxism-Leninism was integrated with the Chinese workers' movement, that the Communist Party of China was born. From that moment on, the Chinese people have had in the Party a backbone for their pursuit of national independence and liberation, of a stronger and more prosperous country, and of their own happiness; and the mindset of the Chinese people has changed, from passivity to taking the initiative.

With a history dating back more than 5,000 years, our nation created a splendid civilization, made remarkable contributions to humanity, and became one of the world's great nations. But with the Opium War of 1840, China was plunged into the darkness of domestic turmoil and foreign aggression; its people, ravaged by war, saw their homeland torn apart, and lived in poverty and despair. With tenacity and heroism, countless dedicated patriots fought, pressed ahead against the odds, and tried every possible means to seek the nation's salvation. But despite their efforts, they were powerless to change the nature of society in old China and the plight of the Chinese people.

National rejuvenation has been the greatest dream of the Chinese people since modern times began. At its founding, the Communist Party of China made realizing communism its highest ideal and its ultimate goal, and shouldered the historic mission of national rejuvenation. In pursuing this goal, the Party has united the Chinese people and led them through arduous struggles to epic accomplishments.

Our Party was deeply aware that, to achieve national rejuvenation, it was critical to topple the three mountains of imperialism, feudalism, and bureaucrat-capitalism that were oppressing the Chinese people, and realize China's independence, the people's liberation, national reunification, and social stability. Our Party united the people and led them in embarking on the right revolutionary path, using rural areas to encircle the cities and seizing state power with military force. We completed the New Democratic Revolution through 28 years of painful struggle, and founded the People's Republic of China in 1949, thus marking China's great transition from a millennia-old feudal autocracy to a people's democracy.

Our Party was deeply aware that, to achieve national rejuvenation, it was essential to establish an advanced social system that fits China's reality. It united the people and led them in completing socialist revolution, establishing socialism as China's basic system, and advancing socialist construction. This completed the broadest and most profound social transformation in the history of the Chinese nation. It created the fundamental political conditions and the institutional foundation for achieving all development and progress in China today. Thus was made a great transition: The Chinese nation reversed its fate from the continuous decline of modern times to steady progress towards prosperity and strength.

Our Party was deeply aware that, to achieve national rejuvenation, it was imperative to follow the tide of the times, respond to the wishes of the people, and have the courage to reform and open; and this awareness created a powerful force for advancing the cause of the Party and the people. Our Party united the people and led them in launching the great new revolution of reform and opening up, in removing all ideological and institutional barriers to our country and nation's development, and in embarking on the path of socialism with Chinese characteristics. Thus was China able to stride ahead to catch up with the times.

Over the past 96 years, to accomplish the historic mission of national rejuvenation, whether in times of weakness or strength, whether in times of adversity or smooth sailing, our Party has never forgotten its founding mission, nor wavered in its quest. It has united the people and led them in conquering countless challenges, making enormous sacrifices, meeting setbacks squarely, and courageously righting wrongs. Thus we have, time and again, overcome the seemingly insurmountable and created miracle upon miracle.

Comrades,

Today, we are closer to, and more confident and capable than ever before of making the goal of national rejuvenation a reality.

As the Chinese saying goes, the last leg of a journey marks the halfway point. Achieving national rejuvenation will be no walk in the park; it will take more than drum beating and gong clanging to get there. Every one of us in the Party must be prepared to work even harder towards this goal.

Realizing our great dream demands a great struggle. It is in the movement of contradictions that a society advances; where there is contradiction there is struggle. If our Party is to unite and lead the people to effectively respond to major challenges, withstand major risks, overcome major obstacles, and address major contradictions, it must undertake a great historic struggle with many new features. All thinking and behavior in the vein of pleasure seeking, inaction and sloth, and problem avoidance are unacceptable.

Every one of us in the Party must do more to uphold Party leadership and the Chinese socialist system, and resolutely oppose all statements and actions that undermine, distort, or negate them. We must do more to protect our people's interests, and firmly oppose all moves that damage their interests or put distance between the Party and the people. We must do more to channel our energies towards the contemporary current of reform and innovation, and resolve to address deep-rooted problems. We must do more to safeguard China's sovereignty, security, and development interests, and staunchly oppose all attempts to split China or undermine its ethnic unity and social harmony and stability. We must do more to guard against all kinds of risk, and work determinedly to prevail over every political, economic, cultural, social, and natural difficulty and challenge.

Every Party member must fully appreciate the long-term, complex, and onerous nature of this great struggle; we must be ready to fight, build our ability, and keep striving to secure new victories in this great struggle.

Realizing our great dream demands a great project. This project is the great new project of strengthening the Party that is building momentum. As history has shown and will continue to testify, without the leadership of the Communist Party of China, national rejuvenation would be just wishful thinking. To remain the vanguard of the times, the backbone of the nation, and a Marxist governing party, our Party must always hold itself to the highest standards. Every Party member must be more actively involved in enhancing Party consciousness, and demonstrate commitment to Party principles. We must have the courage to face problems squarely, be braced for the pain, act to remove whatever undermines the Party's integrity and advanced nature, and rid ourselves of any virus that erodes the Party's health. We must keep on strengthening the Party's ability to lead politically, to guide through theory, to organize the people, and to inspire society, thus ensuring that the Party's great vitality and strong ability are forever maintained.

Realizing our great dream represents a great cause. Socialism with Chinese characteristics has been the focus of all of the Party's theories and practice since reform and opening up began. It is the fundamental achievement of our Party and our people made through countless hardships at enormous cost. The path of socialism with Chinese characteristics is the only path to socialist modernization and a better life for the people. The theory of socialism with Chinese characteristics is the right theory to guide the Party and people to realize national rejuvenation. The system of socialism with Chinese characteristics provides the fundamental institutional guarantee for progress and development in contemporary China. The culture of socialism with Chinese characteristics is a powerful source of strength that inspires all members of the Party and the people of all ethnic groups in China. Our whole Party must strengthen our confidence in the path, theory, system and culture of socialism with Chinese characteristics. We must neither retrace our steps to the rigidity and isolation of the past, nor take the wrong turn by changing our nature and abandoning our system. We must maintain our political orientation, do the good solid work that sees our country thrive, and continue to uphold and develop socialism with Chinese characteristics.

This great struggle, great project, great cause, and great dream are closely connected, flow seamlessly into each other, and are mutually reinforcing. Among them, the great new project of strengthening the Party plays the decisive role. All work to advance this project must go hand in hand with the struggle, the cause, and the dream. We must see that as history progresses and the world undergoes profound changes, the Party remains always ahead of the times; that as history progresses and we respond to risks and tests at home and abroad, the Party remains always the backbone of the nation; and that as history progresses and we continue to uphold and develop socialism with Chinese characteristics, the Party remains always a powerful leadership core.

Comrades,

Our mission is a call to action; our mission steers the course to the future. We must live up to the trust the people have placed in us and prove ourselves worthy of history's choice. In the great endeavor of building socialism with Chinese characteristics in the new era, let us get behind the strong leadership of the Party and engage in a tenacious struggle. Let all of us, the sons and daughters of the Chinese nation, come together, keep going, and create a mighty force that enables us to realize the Chinese Dream.

III. The Thought on Socialism with Chinese Characteristics for a New Era and the Basic Policy

Since our 18th National Congress, changes both in and outside China, and the progress made in all areas of China's endeavors, have presented us with a profound question – the question of an era. Our answer must be a systematic combination of theory and practice and must address what kind of socialism with Chinese characteristics the new era requires us to uphold and develop, and how we should go about doing it. This involves fundamental issues like the overarching objective, task, plan, and strategy for upholding and developing socialism with Chinese characteristics in the new era; like the direction, model, and driving force of development, and the strategic steps, external conditions, and political guarantees. In addition, to uphold and develop socialism with Chinese characteristics, we should, based on new practice, undertake theoretical analysis and produce policy guidance on the economy, political affairs, rule of law, science and technology, culture, education, the wellbeing of our people, ethnic and religious affairs, social development, the eco-environment, national security, defense and the armed forces, the principle of "one country, two systems" and national reunification, the united front, foreign affairs, and the strengthening of the Party.

In answering this question, our Party has been guided by Marxism-Leninism, Mao Zedong Thought[11], Deng Xiaoping Theory[12], the Theory of Three Represents[13], and the Scientific Outlook on Development[14]. It has continued to free our minds, seek truth from facts, move with the times, and apply a realistic and pragmatic approach. In answering this question, our Party has continued to uphold dialectical and historical materialism; has considered carefully the new conditions of the era and the new requirements of practice; and has adopted an entirely new perspective to deepen its understanding of the laws that underlie governance by a communist party, the development of socialism, and the evolution of human society. It has worked hard to undertake theoretical explorations, and has achieved major theoretical innovations, ultimately giving shape to the Thought on Socialism with Chinese Characteristics for a New Era.

The Thought on Socialism with Chinese Characteristics for a New Era makes the following things clear:

– It makes clear that the overarching task of upholding and developing socialism with Chinese characteristics is to realize socialist modernization and national rejuvenation, and, that on the basis of finishing the building of a moderately prosperous society in all respects, a two-step approach should be taken to build China into a great modern socialist country that is prosperous, strong, democratic, culturally advanced, harmonious, and beautiful by the middle of the century.

– It makes clear that the principal challenge facing Chinese society in the new era is the gap between unbalanced and inadequate development and the ever-growing expectation of the people for a better life. We must therefore continue commitment to our people-centered philosophy of development, and work to promote well-rounded human development and common prosperity for everyone.

– It makes clear that the overall plan for building socialism with Chinese characteristics is the Five-sphere Integrated Plan, and the overall strategy is the Four-pronged Comprehensive Strategy. It highlights the importance of fostering stronger confidence in the path, theory, system and culture of socialism with Chinese characteristics.

– It makes clear that the overall goal of in-depth reform in every field is to improve and develop the system of socialism with Chinese characteristics and modernize China's governance system and capacity.

– It makes clear that the overall goal of comprehensively advancing law-based governance is to establish a system of socialist rule of law with Chinese characteristics and build a country of socialist rule of law.

– It makes clear that the Party's goal of building a strong military in the new era is to build the people's forces into world-class forces that obey the Party's command, can fight and win, and maintain excellent conduct.

– It makes clear that major-country diplomacy with Chinese characteristics aims to foster a new type of international relations and build a global community of shared future.

– It makes clear that the defining feature of socialism with Chinese characteristics is the leadership of the Communist Party of China; the greatest strength of the system of socialism with Chinese characteristics is the leadership of the Communist Party of China; the Party is the highest force for political leadership. It sets forth the general requirements for strengthening the Party in the new era and underlines the importance of reinforcing the Party's political foundations.

The Thought on Socialism with Chinese Characteristics for a New Era builds on and further enriches Marxism-Leninism, Mao Zedong Thought, Deng Xiaoping Theory, the Theory of Three Represents, and the Scientific Outlook on Development. It represents the latest achievement in adapting Marxism to the Chinese context and encapsulates the practical experience and collective wisdom of our Party and the people. It is an important component of the theory of socialism with Chinese characteristics, and a guide to action for all our members and all the Chinese people as we strive to achieve national rejuvenation. This Thought must be adhered to and steadily developed on a long-term basis.

Everyone in the Party should develop a good grasp of the essence and rich implications of the Thought on Socialism with Chinese Characteristics for a New Era and fully and faithfully apply it in all our work.

1. Ensuring Party leadership over all work

The Party exercises overall leadership over all areas of endeavor in every part of the country. We must strengthen our consciousness of the need to maintain political commitment, think in terms of the general picture, follow the core leadership of the Central Committee, and act in accordance with its requirements. We must work harder to uphold the authority and centralized, unified leadership of the Central Committee, and closely follow the Central Committee in terms of our thinking, political orientation, and actions. We must improve the institutions and mechanisms for upholding Party leadership, remain committed to the underlying principle of pursuing progress while ensuring stability, and ensure coordinated implementation of the Five-sphere Integrated Plan and the Four-pronged Comprehensive Strategy. We must strengthen the Party's ability and resolve to chart our course, craft overall plans, design policy, and promote reform; and we must ensure the Party always provides overall leadership and coordinates the efforts of all involved.

2. Committing to a people-centered approach

The people are the creators of history; they are the fundamental force that determines our Party and country's future. We must ensure the principal status of the people, and adhere to the Party's commitment to serving the public good and exercising power in the interests of the people. We must observe the Party's fundamental purpose of wholeheartedly serving the people, and put into practice the Party's mass line in all aspects of governance. We must regard as our goal the people's aspirations to live a better life, and rely on the people to move history forward.

3. Continuing to comprehensively deepen reform

Only with socialism can we save China; only with reform and opening can we develop China, develop socialism, and develop Marxism. We must uphold and improve the system of socialism with Chinese characteristics and continue to modernize China's system and capacity for governance. We must have the determination to get rid of all outdated thinking and ideas and all institutional ailments, and to break through the blockades of vested interests. We should draw on the achievements of other civilizations, develop a set of institutions that are well-conceived, fully built, procedure-based, and efficiently functioning, and do full justice to the strengths of China's socialist system.

4. Adopting a new vision for development

Development is the underpinning and the key for solving all our country's problems; our development must be sound development. We must pursue with firmness of purpose the vision of innovative, coordinated, green, and open development that is for everyone. We must uphold and improve China's basic socialist economic system and socialist distribution system. We must be resolute in consolidating and developing the public sector; and we must be resolute in encouraging, supporting, and guiding the development of the non-public sector. We must see that the market plays the decisive role in resource allocation, the government plays its role better, and new industrialization, IT application, urbanization, and agricultural modernization go hand in hand. We must actively participate in and promote economic globalization, develop an open economy of higher standards, and continue to increase China's economic power and composite strength.

5. Seeing that the people are the masters of the country

Commitment to the unity of the Party's leadership, the people's position as masters of the country, and law-based governance is a natural element of socialist political advancement. We must keep to the path of socialist political advancement with Chinese characteristics; uphold and improve the system of people's congresses, the system of Party-led multiparty cooperation and political consultation, the system of regional ethnic autonomy, and the system of community-level self-governance; and consolidate and develop the broadest possible patriotic united front. We should develop socialist consultative democracy, improve our democratic institutions, diversify our forms of democracy, and establish more democratic channels. We must see to it that the principle of the people as masters of the country is put into practice in China's political and social activities.

6. Ensuring every dimension of governance is law-based

Law-based governance is an essential requirement and important guarantee for socialism with Chinese characteristics. We must exercise Party leadership at every point in the process and over every dimension of law-based governance, and be fully committed to promoting socialist rule of law with Chinese characteristics. We must improve the Chinese socialist system of laws, at the heart of which is the Constitution; establish a Chinese system of socialist rule of law; build a socialist country based on the rule of law; and develop Chinese socialist rule of law theory.

We must pursue coordinated progress in law-based governance, law-based exercise of state power, and law-based government administration, and promote the integrated development of rule of law for the country, the government, and society. We must continue to promote a combination of rule of law and rule of virtue, and combine law-based governance of the country and rule-based governance over the Party. We must further the reform of the judicial system, and strengthen awareness of the rule of law among all our people while also enhancing their moral integrity.

7. Upholding the core socialist values

Cultural confidence represents a fundamental and profound force that sustains the development of a country and a nation. We must uphold Marxism, firm up and further build the ideal of communism and a shared ideal of socialism with Chinese characteristics, and nurture and practice the core socialist values, while making continued and greater efforts to maintain the initiative and ensure we have our say in the realm of ideology. We must promote the creative evolution and development of fine traditional Chinese culture, see our revolutionary culture remains alive and strong, and develop an advanced socialist culture. We should cherish our cultural roots, draw on other cultures, and be forward-thinking. We should do more to foster a Chinese spirit, Chinese values, and Chinese strength to provide a source of cultural and moral guidance for our people.

8. Ensuring and improving living standards through development

The wellbeing of the people is the fundamental goal of development. We must do more to improve the lives and address the concerns of the people, and use development to strengthen areas of weakness and promote social fairness and justice. We should make steady progress in ensuring people's access to childcare, education, employment, medical services, elderly care, housing, and social assistance. We will intensify poverty alleviation, see that all our people have a greater sense of fulfillment as they contribute to and gain from development, and continue to promote well-rounded human development and common prosperity for everyone. We will continue the Peaceful China initiative, strengthen and develop new forms of social governance, and ensure social harmony and stability. We must work hard to see that our country enjoys enduring peace and stability and our people live and work in contentment.

9. Ensuring harmony between human and nature

Building an eco-civilization is vital to sustaining the Chinese nation's development. We must realize that lucid waters and lush mountains are invaluable assets and act on this understanding, implement our fundamental national policy of conserving resources and protecting the environment, and cherish the environment as we cherish our own lives. We will adopt a holistic approach to conserving our mountains, rivers, forests, farmlands, lakes, and grasslands, implement the strictest possible systems for environmental protection, and develop eco-friendly growth models and ways of life.

We must pursue a model of sustainable development featuring increased production, higher living standards, and healthy ecosystems. We must continue the Beautiful China initiative to create good working and living environments for our people and play our part in ensuring global ecological security.

10. Pursuing a holistic approach to national security

We should ensure both development and security and be ever ready to protect against potential dangers in time of peace. This is a major principle underlying the Party's governance. We must put national interests first, take protecting our people's security as our mission and safeguarding political security as a fundamental task, and ensure both internal and external security, homeland and public security, traditional and non-traditional security, and China's own and common security. We will improve our systems and institutions and build additional capacity for national security, and resolutely safeguard China's sovereignty, security, and development interests.

11. Upholding absolute Party leadership over the people's armed forces

Building people's forces that obey the Party's command, can fight and win, and maintain excellent conduct is strategically important to achieving the Two Centenary Goals[15] and national rejuvenation. To realize the Party's goal of building a powerful military in the new era, we must fully implement the fundamental principles and systems of Party leadership over the military, and see that the Party's thinking on strengthening the military for the new era guides work to build national defense and the armed forces. We must continue to enhance the political loyalty of the armed forces, strengthen them through reform and technology, and run them in accordance with the law. We must place greater focus on combat, encourage innovation, build systems, increase efficacy and efficiency, and further civil-military integration.

12. Upholding the principle of "one country, two systems" and promoting national reunification

Maintaining lasting prosperity and stability in Hong Kong and Macao and achieving China's full reunification are essential to realizing national rejuvenation. We must ensure both the central government's overall jurisdiction over the Hong Kong and Macao special administrative regions and a high degree of autonomy in the two regions. We should ensure that the principle of "one country, two systems" remains unchanged, is unwaveringly upheld, and in practice is not bent or distorted. We must uphold the one-China principle and the 1992 Consensus, promote the peaceful development of cross-Straits relations, deepen economic cooperation and cultural exchanges between the two sides of the Straits, and encourage fellow Chinese on both sides to oppose all separatist activities and work together to realize China's national rejuvenation.

13. Building a global community of shared future

The dream of the Chinese people is closely connected with the dreams of the peoples of other countries; the Chinese Dream can be realized only in a peaceful international environment and under a stable international order. We must keep in mind both the internal and the international situation, stay on the path of peaceful development, and continue to pursue a mutually beneficial strategy of opening up. We will uphold justice while pursuing shared interests, and will foster new thinking on common, comprehensive, cooperative, and sustainable security. We will pursue open, innovative, and inclusive development that benefits everyone; boost cross-cultural exchanges characterized by harmony within diversity, inclusiveness, and mutual learning; and cultivate ecosystems based on respect for nature and green development. China will continue its efforts to safeguard world peace, contribute to global development, and uphold international order.

14. Exercising full and rigorous governance over the Party

To have the courage to carry out self-reform and conduct strict self-governance: This is the most distinctive part of our Party's character. We must uphold the Party Constitution as our fundamental rules, reinforce the political foundations as our priority, buttress our ideological commitment, strengthen our systems, and increase Party competence in all respects. We must focus on oversight over the "key few", by which we mean leading officials, and see that the Three Guidelines for Ethical Behavior and Three Basic Rules of Conduct are observed.

We must uphold democratic centralism, ensure that intra-Party political activities are carried out in earnest, impose strict Party discipline, and strengthen internal oversight. We must develop a positive and healthy political culture in the Party and improve the Party's political ecosystem, resolutely correct misconduct in all its forms, and show zero tolerance for corruption. We will continue to strengthen the Party's ability to cleanse, improve, and reform itself, and forever maintain its close ties with the people.

The above 14 points form the basic policy that underpins our endeavors to uphold and develop socialism with Chinese characteristics in the new era. All our members must fully implement the Party's underlying theories, basic guidelines, and fundamental principles so as to better steer the development of the Party and people's cause.

Just as there are no bounds to practice, there is no end to theoretical innovation. The world is changing with every second, every moment; and China, too, is changing with every second, every moment. We must ensure our theory evolves with the times, deepen our appreciation of objective laws, and advance our theoretical, practical, institutional, cultural, and other innovations.

Comrades,

The era is the mother of thought; practice is the fount of theory. If we respond to the call of our times and have the courage to uphold truth and correct errors, the Marxism of 21st century China will, without a doubt, emanate a more mighty, more compelling power of truth.

IV. Securing a Decisive Victory in Building a Moderately Prosperous Society in All Respects and Embarking on a Journey to Fully Build a Modern Socialist China

After adopting the policy of reform and opening up, our Party laid out the three-step strategic plan for modernization[16] in China. The first two – ensuring that people's basic needs are met and that their lives are generally decent – have been accomplished ahead of time. Building on this, our Party then developed the vision that by the time we celebrate our centenary, we will have developed our society into a moderately prosperous one with a stronger economy, greater democracy, more advanced science and education, thriving culture, greater social harmony, and a better quality of life. After this, with another 30 years of work, and by the time we celebrate the centenary of the People's Republic of China, we will have basically achieved modernization and turned China into a modern socialist country.

The period between now and 2020 will be decisive in finishing the building of a moderately prosperous society in all respects. We must follow the requirements on building this society set out at our 16th, 17th, and 18th national congresses, act in response to the evolution of the principal challenge in Chinese society, and promote coordinated economic, political, cultural, social, and eco-environmental progress. We must show firm resolve in implementing the strategy for invigorating China through science and education, the strategy on developing a quality workforce, the innovation-driven development strategy, the rural revitalization strategy, the coordinated regional development strategy, the sustainable development strategy, and the civil-military integration strategy. We must focus on priorities, address inadequacies, and shore up points of weakness. In this regard, I want to stress that we must take tough steps to forestall and defuse major risks, carry out targeted poverty alleviation, and prevent and control pollution, so that the moderately prosperous society we build earns the people's approval and stands the test of time.

The period between the 19th and the 20th national congresses is the period in which the timeframes of the Two Centenary Goals converge. In this period, not only must we finish building a moderately prosperous society in all respects and achieve the First Centenary Goal; we must also build on this achievement to embark on a new journey towards the Second Centenary Goal of fully building a modern socialist country.

Based on a comprehensive analysis of the international and domestic environments and the conditions for China's development, we have drawn up a two-stage development plan for the period from 2020 to the middle of this century.

In the first stage from 2020 to 2035, we will build on the foundation created by the moderately prosperous society with a further 15 years of hard work to see that socialist modernization is basically realized. The vision is that by the end of this stage, the following goals will have been met:

– China's economic and technological strength has increased significantly. China has become a global leader in innovation.

– The rights of the people to participate and to develop as equals are adequately protected. The rule of law for the country, the government, and society is basically in place. Institutions in all fields are further improved; the modernization of China's system and capacity for governance is basically achieved.

– Social etiquette and civility are significantly enhanced. China's cultural soft power has grown much stronger; Chinese culture has greater appeal.

– People are leading more comfortable lives, and the size of the middle-income group has grown considerably. Disparities in urban-rural development, in development between regions, and in living standards are significantly reduced; equitable access to basic public services is basically ensured; and solid progress has been made towards prosperity for everyone.

– A modern social governance system has taken shape, and society is full of vitality, harmonious, and orderly.

– There is a fundamental improvement in the environment; the goal of building a Beautiful China is basically attained.

In the second stage from 2035 to the middle of the 21st century, having basically achieved modernization, we will work hard for a further 15 years and develop China into a great modern socialist country that is prosperous, strong, democratic, culturally advanced, harmonious, and beautiful. By the end of this stage, the following goals will have been met:

– New heights are reached in every dimension of material, political, cultural and ethical, social, and eco-environmental progress.

– Modernization of China's system and capacity for governance is achieved.

– China has become a global leader in terms of composite national strength and international influence.

– Common prosperity for everyone is basically achieved.

– The Chinese people enjoy happier, safer, and healthier lives.

The Chinese nation will become a proud and active member of the community of nations.

Comrades,

This is our strategic vision for developing socialism with Chinese characteristics in the new era: Finish building a moderately prosperous society in all respects, move on to basically realizing modernization, and then turn to making China a great modern socialist country in every dimension. We must work with resolve and tenacity, and strive to write a brilliant chapter on our new journey to socialist modernization.

V. Applying a New Vision of Development and Developing a Modernized Economy

To deliver on the Two Centenary Goals, realize the Chinese Dream of national rejuvenation, and steadily improve our people's lives, we must continue to pursue development as the Party's top priority in governance; we must unleash and develop productive forces, continue reforms to develop the socialist market economy, and promote sustained and sound economic growth.

China's economy has been transitioning from a phase of rapid growth to a stage of high-quality development. This is a pivotal period for transforming our growth model, improving our economic structure, and fostering new drivers of growth. It is imperative that we develop a modernized economy. This is both an urgent requirement for getting us smoothly through this critical transition and a strategic goal for China's development. We must put quality first and give priority to performance. We should pursue supply-side structural reform as our main task, and work hard for better quality, higher efficiency, and more robust drivers of economic growth through reform. We need to raise total factor productivity and accelerate the building of an industrial system that promotes coordinated development of the real economy with technological innovation, modern finance, and human resources. We should endeavor to develop an economy with more effective market mechanisms, dynamic micro-entities, and sound macro-regulation. This will steadily strengthen the innovation capacity and competitiveness of China's economy.

1. Furthering supply-side structural reform

In developing a modernized economy, we must focus on the real economy, give priority to improving the quality of the supply system, and enhance our economy's strength in terms of quality.

We will work faster to build China into a manufacturer of quality and develop advanced manufacturing, promote further integration of the internet, big data, and artificial intelligence with the real economy, and foster new growth areas and drivers of growth in medium-high end consumption, innovation-driven development, the green and low-carbon economy, the sharing economy, modern supply chains, and human capital services. We will help traditional industries to upgrade and accelerate development of modern service industries to elevate them to international standards. We will move Chinese industries up to the medium-high end of the global value chain, and foster a number of world-class advanced manufacturing clusters.

We will strengthen infrastructure networks for water conservancy, railways, highways, waterways, aviation, pipelines, power grids, information, and logistics. We will continue efforts to cut overcapacity, reduce excess inventory, deleverage, lower costs, and strengthen areas of weakness, and work to achieve a dynamic balance between supply and demand by improving the allocation of available resources and increasing high-quality supply.

We will inspire and protect entrepreneurship, and encourage more entities to engage in innovation and businesses. We will build an educated, skilled, and innovative workforce, foster respect for model workers, promote quality workmanship, and see that taking pride in labor becomes a social norm and seeking excellence is valued as a good work ethic.

2. Making China a country of innovators

Innovation is the primary driving force behind development; it is the strategic foundation for building a modernized economy.

We should aim for the frontiers of science and technology, strengthen basic research, and make major breakthroughs in pioneering basic research and groundbreaking and original innovations. We will strengthen basic research in applied sciences, launch major national science and technology projects, and prioritize innovation in key generic technologies, cutting-edge frontier technologies, modern engineering technologies, and disruptive technologies. These efforts will provide powerful support for building China's strength in science and technology, product quality, aerospace, cyberspace, and transport, and for building a digital China and a smart society.

We will improve our national innovation system and boost our strategic scientific and technological strength. We will further reform the management system for science and technology, and develop a market-oriented system for technological innovation in which enterprises are the main players and synergy is created through the joint efforts of enterprises, universities, and research institutes. We will support innovation by small and medium-sized enterprises and encourage the application of advances in science and technology.

We will foster a culture of innovation, and strengthen the creation, protection, and application of intellectual property. We should cultivate a large number of world-class scientists and technologists in strategically important fields, scientific and technological leaders, and young scientists and engineers, as well as high-performing innovation teams.

3. Pursuing a rural revitalization strategy

Issues relating to agriculture, rural areas, and rural people are fundamental to China as they directly concern our country's stability and our people's wellbeing. Addressing these issues should have a central place on the work agenda of the Party, and we must prioritize the development of agriculture and rural areas. To build rural areas with thriving businesses, pleasant living environments, social etiquette and civility, effective governance, and prosperity, we need to put in place sound systems, mechanisms, and policies for promoting integrated urban-rural development, and speed up the modernization of agriculture and rural areas.

We will consolidate and improve the basic rural operation system, advance reform of the rural land system, and improve the system for separating the ownership rights, contract rights, and management rights for contracted rural land. Rural land contracting practices will remain stable and unchanged on a long-term basis; the current round of contracts will be extended for another 30 years upon expiration. We will press ahead with reform of the rural collective property rights system, safeguard the property rights and interests of rural people, and strengthen the collective economy.

We must ensure China's food security so that we always have control over our own food supply. We will establish industrial, production, and business operation systems for modern agriculture, and improve the systems for supporting and protecting agriculture. We will develop appropriately scaled agricultural operations of various forms, cultivate new types of agribusiness, improve specialized agricultural services, and encourage small rural households to become involved in modern agriculture.

We will integrate the primary, secondary, and tertiary industries in rural areas, support and encourage employment and business startups there, and open up more channels to increase rural incomes. We will strengthen basic services in rural communities, and improve the rural governance model which combines self-governance, rule of law, and rule of virtue. We will train professional rural service personnel who have a good knowledge of agriculture, love our rural areas, and care about rural people.

4. Implementing the coordinated regional development strategy

We will devote more energy to speeding up the development of old revolutionary base areas, areas with large ethnic minority populations, border areas, and poor areas. We will strengthen measures to reach a new stage in the large-scale development of the western region; deepen reform to accelerate the revitalization of old industrial bases in the northeast and other parts of the country; help the central region rise by tapping into local strengths; and support the eastern region in taking the lead in pursuing optimal development through innovation. To this end, we need to put in place new, effective mechanisms to ensure coordinated development of different regions.

We will create networks of cities and towns based on city clusters, enabling the coordinated development of cities of different sizes and small towns, and speed up work on granting permanent urban residency to people who move from rural to urban areas. We will relieve Beijing of functions nonessential to its role as the capital and use this effort to drive the coordinated development of the Beijing-Tianjin-Hebei Region; and we will develop forward-looking plans and adopt high standards for building the Xiongan New Area. We will facilitate the development of the Yangtze River Economic Belt by promoting well-coordinated environmental conservation and avoiding excessive development. Support will be given to resource-depleted areas in their economic transformation. We will accelerate development in the border areas, and ensure their stability and security. We will pursue coordinated land and marine development, and step up efforts to build China into a strong maritime country.

5. Accelerating efforts to improve the socialist market economy

In our economic reforms, we must concentrate on improving the property rights system and ensuring the market-based allocation of factors of production, so that property rights act as effective incentives. We should ensure free flows of factors, flexible prices, fair and orderly competition, and that business survival is determined by competition.

We will improve the systems for managing different types of state assets, and reform the system of authorized operation of state capital. In the state-owned sector, we will step up improved distribution, structural adjustment, and strategic reorganization. We will work to see that state assets maintain and increase their value; we will support state capital in becoming stronger, doing better, and growing bigger, and take effective measures to prevent the loss of state assets. We will further reform state-owned enterprises, develop mixed-ownership economic entities, and turn Chinese enterprises into world-class, globally competitive firms. We will introduce a negative list for market access nationwide, sort through and do away with regulations and practices impeding the development of a unified market and fair competition, support the growth of private businesses, and stimulate the vitality of various market entities.

We will deepen reforms in the business sector, break administrative monopolies, preclude the forming of market monopolies, speed up the reform of market-based pricing of factors of production, relax control over market access in the service sector, and improve market oversight mechanisms. We will develop new methods to improve macro-regulation, give full play to the strategic guidance of national development plans, and improve mechanisms for coordinating fiscal, monetary, industrial, regional, and other economic policies.

We will improve systems and mechanisms for stimulating consumer spending, and leverage the fundamental role of consumption in promoting economic growth. We will further reform the investment and financing systems, and enable investment to play a crucial role in improving the supply structure.

We will expedite the creation of a modern public finance system, and establish a fiscal relationship between the central and local governments built upon clearly defined powers and responsibilities, appropriate financial resource allocation, and greater balance between regions.

We will put in place a comprehensive, procedure-based, transparent budget system that uses well-conceived standards and imposes effective constraints; and we will implement performance-based management nationwide.

We will deepen reform of the taxation system, and improve the local tax system. We will deepen institutional reform in the financial sector, make it better serve the real economy, increase the proportion of direct financing, and promote the healthy development of a multi-level capital market.

We will improve the framework of regulation underpinned by monetary policy and macro-prudential policy, and see that interest rates and exchange rates become more market-based. We will improve the financial regulatory system to forestall systemic financial risks.

6. Making new ground in pursuing opening up on all fronts

Openness brings progress, while self-imposed isolation leaves one behind. China will not close its door to the world; we will only become more and more open.

We should pursue the Belt and Road Initiative as a priority, give equal emphasis to "bringing in" and "going global", follow the principle of achieving shared growth through discussion and collaboration, and increase openness and cooperation in building innovation capacity. With these efforts, we hope to make new ground in opening China further through links running eastward and westward, across land and over sea.

We will expand foreign trade, develop new models and new forms of trade, and turn China into a trader of quality. We will adopt policies to facilitate high-standard free trade and investment; we will implement the system of pre-establishment national treatment plus a negative list across the board, significantly ease market access, further open the service sector, and protect the legitimate rights and interests of foreign investors. All businesses registered in China will be treated equally.

We will improve the balance in opening our different regions, and open the western region wider. We will grant more powers to pilot free trade zones to conduct reform, and explore the opening of free trade ports. We will develop new ways of making outbound investments, promote international cooperation on production capacity, form globally-oriented networks of trade, investment and financing, production, and services, and build up our strengths for international economic cooperation and competition.

Comrades,

Unlocking and developing the productive forces is a fundamental task of socialism. We must inspire creativity and vitality throughout society, and strive to achieve better quality, more efficient, fairer, and more sustainable development.

VI. Improving the Systems to Ensure the People's Position as Masters of the Country and Socialist Democracy

China is a socialist country of people's democratic dictatorship under the leadership of the working class based on an alliance of workers and farmers; it is a country where all power of the state belongs to the people. China's socialist democracy is the broadest, most genuine, and most effective democracy to safeguard the fundamental interests of the people. The very purpose of developing socialist democracy is to give full expression to the will of the people, protect their rights and interests, spark their creativity, and provide systemic and institutional guarantees to ensure the people's position as masters of the country.

The path of socialist political advancement with Chinese characteristics is the logical outcome of the evolution of history, theory, and practice as the Chinese people have long been engaged in struggles since the advent of modern times. It is a requisite for maintaining the very nature of the Party and fulfilling its fundamental purpose.

No two political systems are entirely the same, and a political system cannot be judged in abstraction without regard for its social and political context, its history, and its cultural traditions. No one political system should be regarded as the only choice; and we should not mechanically copy the political systems of other countries.

We must always uphold and steadily strengthen China's socialist democracy, make active and prudent efforts to advance the reform of the political system, and improve the institutions, standards, and procedures of socialist democracy. We should ensure that people participate, in accordance with the law and in various ways and forms, in the management of state, economic, cultural, and social affairs, and consolidate and enhance political stability, unity, and vitality.

1. Upholding the unity of the Party's leadership, the people's position as masters of the country and law-based governance

The Party's leadership is the fundamental guarantee for ensuring that the people are the masters of the country and governance in China is law-based; that the people are the masters of the country is an essential feature of socialist democracy; and that law-based governance is the basic way for the Party to lead the people in governing the country. These three elements are integral components of socialist democracy.

In China's political life, our Party exercises leadership. Strengthening the centralized, unified leadership of the Party on the one hand and, on the other, supporting the people's congresses, governments, committees of the Chinese People's Political Consultative Conference (CPPCC), courts, and procuratorates in performing their functions and playing their roles in accordance with the law and their charters, form a unified pair.

We will improve the way the Party exercises leadership and governance to ensure that it leads the people in effectively governing the country. We will expand the people's orderly political participation to see that in accordance with the law they engage in democratic elections, consultations, decision-making, management, and oversight. We should uphold the unity, sanctity, and authority of China's legal system, and strengthen legal protection for human rights to ensure that the people enjoy extensive rights and freedoms as prescribed by law. We should both consolidate government and improve the institutions of democracy at the primary level to ensure the people's rights to be informed, to participate, to be heard, and to oversee.

We will improve mechanisms for law-based decision-making, and put in place mechanisms for the exercise of power that ensure sound decision-making, resolute execution, and effective oversight. Officials at all levels must deepen their understanding of democracy, be democratic in their conduct, willingly accept public oversight, and perform as they should in their role as public servants.

2. Strengthening institutional guarantees to ensure the people are the masters of the country

We must always uphold and steadily improve the system of people's congresses, a political system fundamental to the Party's leadership, the people's position as masters of the country, and law-based governance. We should support and ensure the people's exercise of state power through people's congresses.

We should see to it that people's congresses and their standing committees play the leading role in lawmaking, and improve the organizational and working systems of people's congresses to support and ensure the exercise of their statutory powers of enacting laws and regulations, conducting oversight, making decisions, and appointing and removing officials. We should give better play to the role of deputies to people's congresses, and enable people's congresses at all levels and their standing committees to fully perform their functions as stipulated in the Constitution and the law, and to truly represent the people and maintain close ties with them. We should improve the setup of special committees of people's congresses and the composition of their standing committees and special committees.

3. Giving play to the important role of socialist consultative democracy

The essence of the people's democracy is that the people get to discuss their own affairs. Consultative democracy is an important way of effecting Party leadership and a model and strength unique to China's socialist democracy. We will advance extensive, multilevel, and institutionalized development of consultative democracy, and adopt a coordinated approach to promoting consultation carried out by political parties, people's congresses, government departments, CPPCC committees, people's organizations, communities, and social organizations. We will strengthen the institutions of consultative democracy and develop complete procedures and practices to enable the people's broad, continuous, and intensive participation in day-to-day political activities.

The CPPCC, as a distinctive Chinese political institution, is a major channel for socialist consultative democracy, and its committees are specialist consultative bodies. The CPPCC committees should focus on the Party and the country's key tasks. With the themes of unity and democracy in mind, they should exercise consultative democracy throughout the whole process of political consultation, democratic oversight, and participation in the deliberation and administration of state affairs; and they should improve the content and forms of consultation and deliberation to build consensus and promote unity. They should strengthen democratic oversight, focusing on the implementation of the major principles, policies, decisions, and plans of the Party and the state. They should better represent the different social sectors and strengthen the competence of their members.

4. Advancing law-based governance

Advancing law-based governance in all fields is a profound revolution in China's governance. We must promote the rule of law and work to ensure sound lawmaking, strict law enforcement, impartial administration of justice, and the observance of law by everyone. A central leading group for advancing law-based governance in all areas will be set up to exercise unified leadership over the initiative to build rule of law in China. We will strengthen implementation of the Constitution and enhance oversight to ensure compliance with the Constitution, advance constitutionality review, and safeguard the authority of the Constitution. We will carry out lawmaking in a well-conceived and democratic way and in accordance with the law, so that good laws are made to promote development and ensure good governance. We will govern by rule of law, promote law-based government administration, and see that law is enforced in a strict, procedure-based, impartial, and non-abusive way. We will carry out comprehensive and integrated reform of the judicial system and enforce judicial accountability in all respects, so that the people can see in every judicial case that justice is served.

We will redouble efforts to raise public awareness of the law, develop a socialist culture of rule of law, and increase public awareness of the principle underlying rule of law that the Constitution and the law are above everything else and that everyone is equal before the law. Every Party organization and every Party member must take the lead in respecting, studying, observing, and applying the law. No organization or individual has the power to overstep the Constitution or the law; and no one is allowed in any way to override the law with his or her own orders, place his or her authority above the law, violate the law for personal gain, or abuse the law.

5. Deepening reform of Party and government institutions and the system of government administration

We will adopt a comprehensive approach to the setup of Party and government institutions, and ensure that powers are designated properly and functions and duties are defined clearly both for the institutions themselves and their internal bodies. We will use staffing resources in a coordinated way, develop a sound system of administration, and improve the organic law for state institutions. The government needs to transform its functions, further streamline administration and delegate powers, develop new ways of regulation and supervision, and strengthen its credibility and administrative capacity, building itself into a service-oriented government able to satisfy the needs of the people.

More decision-making power should be given to governments at and below the provincial level, and ways should be explored to merge Party and government bodies with similar functions at the provincial, city, and county levels or for them to work together as one office while keeping separate identities. We will deepen the reform of public institutions to see that they focus on serving public interests, relieve them of government functions, keep them away from business activities, and let them run their own day-to-day operations while maintaining supervision over them.

6. Consolidating and developing the patriotic united front

The united front is important to the success of the Party's cause, and we must maintain a long-term commitment to it. We must uphold the banner of patriotism and socialism, strive to achieve great unity and solidarity, balance commonality and diversity, and expand common ground and the convergence of interests. In handling its relationships with other Chinese political parties, the Communist Party of China is guided by the principles of long-term coexistence, mutual oversight, sincerity, and sharing the rough times and the smooth, and it supports these parties in performing their duties in accordance with the requirements of the Chinese socialist system for their participation in governance.

We will fully implement the Party's policies concerning ethnic groups, heighten public awareness of ethnic unity and progress, and create a keen sense of identity of the Chinese nation. We will encourage more exchanges and interactions among different ethnic groups, helping them remain closely united like the seeds of a pomegranate that stick together, and work jointly for common prosperity and development.

We will fully implement the Party's basic policy on religious affairs, uphold the principle that religions in China must be Chinese in orientation and provide active guidance to religions so that they can adapt themselves to socialist society. We will encourage intellectuals who are not Party members and people belonging to new social groups to play important roles in building socialism with Chinese characteristics. We should form a new type of cordial and clean relationship between government and business, promote healthy growth of the non-public sector of the economy, and encourage those working in this sector to achieve success. We will maintain extensive contacts with overseas Chinese nationals, returned Chinese and their relatives and unite them so that they can join our endeavors to rejuvenate the Chinese nation.

Comrades,

The political system of socialism with Chinese characteristics is a great creation of the Communist Party of China and the Chinese people. We have every confidence that we can give full play to the strengths and distinctive features of China's socialist democracy, and make China's contribution to the political advancement of humanity.

VII. Building Stronger Cultural Confidence and Helping Socialist Culture to Flourish

Culture is a country and nation's soul. Our country will thrive only if our culture thrives, and our nation will be strong only if our culture is strong. Without full confidence in our culture, without a rich and prosperous culture, the Chinese nation will not be able to rejuvenate itself. We must develop a socialist culture with Chinese characteristics, inspire the cultural creativity of our whole nation, and develop a great socialist culture in China.

Socialist culture with Chinese characteristics is derived from China's fine traditional culture, which was born of the Chinese civilization and nurtured over more than 5,000 years; it has grown out of the revolutionary and advanced socialist culture that developed over the course of the Chinese people's revolution, construction, and reform under the Party's leadership; and it is rooted in the great practice of socialism with Chinese characteristics.

To develop socialist culture with Chinese characteristics means developing a socialist culture for our nation – a culture that is sound and people-oriented, that embraces modernization, the world, and the future, and that both promotes socialist material wellbeing and raises socialist cultural-ethical standards. In developing this culture, we must follow the guidance of Marxism, base our efforts on Chinese culture, and take into account the realities of contemporary China and the conditions of the present era. We should ensure that this culture serves the people and serves socialism. We should follow the principle of letting a hundred flowers bloom and a hundred schools of thought contend, and encourage creative transformation and development, so as to add new luster to Chinese culture.

1. Holding firmly the leading position in ideological work

Ideology determines the direction a culture should take and the path it should follow as it develops. We must continue to adapt Marxism to China's conditions, keep it up-to-date, and enhance its popular appeal. We will develop socialist ideology that has the ability to unite and the power to inspire the people to embrace shared ideals, convictions, values, and moral standards. We will better arm ourselves with theory and increase the public appeal of the Thought on Socialism with Chinese Characteristics for a New Era. We will work harder to study and develop Marxist theory, work faster to develop philosophy and social sciences with Chinese characteristics, and develop new types of think tanks with distinctive Chinese features.

We will maintain the right tone in public communication, give priority to improving means of communication and to creating new ones, and strengthen the penetration, guidance, influence, and credibility of the media. We will provide more and better online content and put in place a system for integrated internet management to ensure a clean cyberspace. We will implement the system of responsibility for ideological work, and further consolidate our positions and improve management in this field. We will distinguish between matters of political principle, issues of understanding and thinking, and academic viewpoints, but we must oppose and resist various erroneous views with a clear stand.

2. Cultivating and observing the core socialist values

The core socialist values represent the contemporary Chinese spirit and are a crystallization of the values shared by all Chinese people.

We will focus on fostering a new generation capable of shouldering the mission of national rejuvenation; we will offer them better guidance, expose them to practice, and provide institutional guarantees. We will draw on the core socialist values to guide education, efforts to raise cultural-ethical standards, and the creation, production, and distribution of cultural and intellectual products, and see that all areas of social development are imbued with these values and that they become part of people's thinking and behavior. To this end, we will encourage extensive public involvement, making our officials take the lead and starting with families and children.

We will draw on China's fine traditional culture, keep alive and develop its vision, concepts, values, and moral norms, and do so in a way that responds to the call of our era. With this we will see that Chinese culture maintains its appeal and evolves with the times.

3. Raising intellectual and moral standards

When the people have ideals, their country will have strength, and their nation will have a bright future. We will help our people raise their political awareness and moral standards, foster appreciation of fine culture, and enhance social etiquette and civility.

We will undertake extensive public awareness activities to help the people develop firm ideals and convictions, build their awareness of socialism with Chinese characteristics and the Chinese Dream, foster a Chinese ethos and a readiness to respond to the call of our times, strengthen the guiding role of patriotism, collectivism, and socialism, and see that the people develop an accurate understanding of history, ethnicity, country, and culture. We will launch a civic morality campaign to raise public ethical standards, and enhance work ethics, family virtues, and personal integrity. We will encourage our people to strive for excellence and to develop stronger virtues, respect the elderly, love families, and be loyal to the country and the people.

We will improve and strengthen our ideological and political work, and launch initiatives to raise the public's cultural-ethical standards. We will promote the spirit of science and make scientific knowledge widely attainable; we will work to see the back of outdated social mores and to promote good and up-to-date practices and trends; and we will resist the corrosive influence of backward and decadent culture. We will build credibility, institutionalize volunteer services, and heighten people's sense of social responsibility, awareness of rules, and sense of dedication.

4. Seeing socialist literature and art thrive

Socialist literature and art are for the people: Writers and artists should take a people-centered approach and draw inspiration from everyday life and the experiences of the people to produce works that do justice to our times. We encourage them to create fine works that are thought provoking and of a high artistic standard, that reflect real life, and that extol our Party, our country, our people, and our heroes.

We will foster democracy in academic research and artistic pursuits, and encourage originality and experimentation with new approaches in the creation of literature and art. We encourage the cultivation of fine tastes, style, and a sense of responsibility, and reject vulgarity and kitsch in literary and artistic creation. We will strengthen the professional standards of artists and writers to see the emergence of a large number of eminent figures who have moral integrity and outstanding artistic appeal, and creators of inspiring works.

5. Promoting cultural programs and industries

To meet the people's new aspirations for a better life, we must provide them with rich intellectual nourishment. We need to deepen structural reform of the cultural sector, improve the cultural management system, and accelerate the establishment of systems and mechanisms that put social benefits first while pursuing economic returns. We will improve the public cultural service system, carry out public-interest cultural programs, and launch more popular cultural activities. We will strengthen protection and utilization of cultural relics, and better preserve and carry forward our cultural heritage.

We will improve modern systems for cultural industries and markets, explore new mechanisms for cultural production and operation, improve economic policy on the cultural sector, and develop new forms of business in this sector. We will carry out extensive fitness-for-all programs, speed up efforts to build China into a country strong in sport, and make smooth preparations for the 2022 Beijing Winter Olympic Games and Paralympic Games. We will strengthen people-to-people and cultural exchanges with other countries, giving prominence to Chinese culture while also drawing on other cultures. We will improve our capacity for engaging in international communication so as to tell China's stories well, present a true, multidimensional, and panoramic view of China, and enhance our country's cultural soft power.

Comrades,

Since its founding, the Communist Party of China has actively guided and promoted China's advanced culture while keeping China's fine traditional culture alive and strong. Today, we Chinese Communists and the Chinese people should and can shoulder our new cultural mission, make cultural creations through practice, and promote cultural progress along with history.

VIII. Growing Better at Ensuring and Improving People's Wellbeing and Strengthening and Developing New Approaches to Social Governance

Everyone in the Party must keep firmly in mind that the nature of a political party and of a government is determined by those whom they serve. To lead the people to a better life is our Party's abiding goal. We must put the people's interests above all else, see that the gains of reform and development benefit all our people in a fair way, and strive to achieve shared prosperity for everyone.

As we work to ensure and improve people's wellbeing, we must focus on the most pressing, most immediate issues that concern the people the most. We will do everything in our capacity and work away, issue by issue, year in and year out. We will see that everyone performs their duties and shares in the benefits. We will see basic needs are met, prioritize key areas, improve institutions, and guide public expectations. We will improve public services, ensure people's basic quality of life, and keep up with people's ever-growing desire for a better life. We will continue to promote social fairness and justice, develop effective social governance, and maintain public order. With this we should see that our people will always have a strong sense of fulfillment, happiness, and security.

1. Giving priority to developing education

Strengthening education is fundamental to our pursuit of national rejuvenation. We must give priority to education, further reform in education, speed up its modernization, and develop education that people are satisfied with. We should fully implement the Party's education policy, foster virtue through education, enhance our students' well-rounded development, promote fairness in education, and nurture a new generation of capable young people who have a good and all-round moral, intellectual, physical, and aesthetical grounding and are well-prepared to join the socialist cause.

We will promote the coordinated development of compulsory education in urban and rural areas, while giving particular attention to rural areas. We will improve preschool education, special needs education, and online education, make senior secondary education universally available, and strive to see that each and every child has fair access to good education.

We will improve the system of vocational education and training, and promote integration between industry and education and cooperation between enterprises and colleges. We will move faster to build Chinese universities into world-class universities and develop world-class disciplines as we work to bring out the full potential of higher education. We will improve the system of financial aid to students, and work to see that the vast majority of the new members of the urban and rural labor force have received senior secondary education, and that more and more of them receive higher education. We will support the well-regulated development of private schools. We will strengthen the professional ethics and competence of teachers, and encourage public respect for educators and public support for education. We will improve continuing education, step up efforts to build a learning society, and promote the well-rounded development of all our people.

2. Improving the quality of employment and raising incomes

Employment is pivotal to people's wellbeing. We must give high priority to employment and pursue a proactive employment policy, striving to achieve fuller employment and create better quality jobs. We will launch large-scale vocational skills training programs, give particular attention to tackling structural unemployment, and create more jobs by encouraging business startups. We will provide extensive public employment services to open more channels for college graduates and other young people as well as migrant rural workers to find jobs and start their own businesses. We must remove institutional barriers that block the social mobility of labor and talent, and ensure that every one of our people has the chance to pursue a career through hard work. We will improve mechanisms for joint discussion and mediation involving government, trade unions, and employers in an effort to ensure harmonious labor relations.

We will continue to follow the principle of distribution according to one's work while improving our institutions and mechanisms for distribution based on factors of production, so as to make income distribution fairer and more orderly. We will encourage people to make their money through hard work and legal means. We will expand the size of the middle-income group, increase income for people on low incomes, adjust excessive incomes, and prohibit illicit income. We will work to see that individual incomes grow in step with economic development, and that pay rises in tandem with increases in labor productivity. We will expand the channels for people to make work-based earnings and property income. We will see that government plays its function of adjusting redistribution, move faster to ensure equitable access to basic public services and narrow the gaps in incomes.

3. Strengthening the social security system

We will act on the policy requirements to help those most in need, to build a tightly woven safety net, and to build the necessary institutions, as we work to develop a sustainable multitiered social security system that covers the entire population in both urban and rural areas, with clearly defined rights and responsibilities, and support that hits the right level. We will work to see that everyone has access to social security. We will improve the basic pension schemes for urban employees and for rural and non-working urban residents, and quickly bring pension schemes under national unified management.

We will improve the unified systems of basic medical insurance and serious disease insurance for rural and non-working urban residents, and improve unemployment insurance and work-related injury insurance. We will establish a unified national platform for social security services. We will promote the coordinated development of the social assistance systems for urban and rural residents, and improve the subsistence allowances system.

We must adhere to the fundamental national policy of gender equality, and protect the legitimate rights and interests of women and minors. We will improve our systems for social assistance, social welfare, charity, and entitled groups' benefits and services. We will improve the system for supporting and caring for children whose parents are working in cities, women, and elderly people in rural areas. We will develop programs for people with disabilities and work to provide better rehabilitation services for them.

We must not forget that housing is for living in, not for speculation. With this in mind, we will move faster to put in place a housing system that ensures supply through multiple sources, provides housing support through multiple channels, and encourages both housing purchase and renting. This will put us in a better position to meet the housing needs of all of our people.

4. Winning the battle against poverty

Seeing that poor people and poor areas will enter the moderately prosperous society together with the rest of the country is a solemn promise made by our Party. We should mobilize the energies of our whole Party, our whole country, and our whole society, and continue to implement targeted poverty reduction and alleviation measures. We will operate on the basis of a working mechanism whereby the central government makes overall plans, provincial-level governments take overall responsibility, and city and county governments ensure implementation; and we will strengthen the system for making heads of Party committees and governments at each level assume the overall responsibility for poverty alleviation.

We will continue to advance poverty reduction drawing on the joint efforts of government, society, and the market. We will pay particular attention to helping people increase confidence in their own ability to lift themselves out of poverty and see that they can access the education they need to do so. We will strengthen collaboration on poverty alleviation between the eastern and western regions; and we will provide focused assistance to areas of extreme poverty. We must ensure that by the year 2020, all rural residents living below the current poverty line have been lifted out of poverty, and poverty is eliminated in all poor counties and regions. Poverty alleviation should reach those who truly need it and deliver genuine outcomes.

5. Carrying out the Healthy China initiative

A healthy population is a key mark of a prosperous nation and a strong country. We will improve the national health policy, and ensure the delivery of comprehensive lifecycle health services for our people. We will deepen reform of the medicine and health care system, establish distinctive Chinese systems for providing basic health care, medical insurance, and quality and efficient health care services, and develop a sound modern hospital management system.

We will improve community-level health care services, and strengthen the ranks of general practitioners. We will put an end to the practices of hospitals funding their operations with profits from overpriced drugs, and improve the system for medicine supply.

With emphasis on prevention, we will carry out extensive patriotic health campaigns, promote healthy and positive lifestyles, and prevent and control major diseases. We will initiate a food safety strategy to ensure that people have peace of mind about what they are putting on their plates. We will support both traditional Chinese medicine and Western medicine, and ensure the preservation and development of traditional Chinese medicine. We will support the development of private hospitals and health-related industries.

We will work to ensure that our childbirth policy meshes with related economic and social policies, and carry out research on the population development strategy. As we respond proactively to population aging, we will adopt policies and foster a social environment in which senior citizens are respected, cared for, and live happily in their later years. We will provide integrated elderly care and medical services, and accelerate the development of old-age programs and industries.

6. Establishing a social governance model based on collaboration, participation, and common interests

We will step up institution building in social governance and improve the law-based social governance model under which Party committees exercise leadership, government assumes responsibility, non-governmental actors provide assistance, and the public get involved. We will strengthen public participation and rule of law in social governance, and make such governance smarter and more specialized.

We will improve mechanisms for preventing and defusing social tensions, and properly handle problems among the people. We will promote safe development, and raise public awareness that life matters most and that safety comes first; we will improve the public safety system and the responsibility system for workplace safety; we will take resolute measures to prevent serious and major accidents, and build up our capacity for disaster prevention, mitigation, and relief.

We will accelerate development of the crime prevention and control system, combat and punish in accordance with the law all illegal and criminal activities such as pornography, gambling, drug abuse, gang violence, kidnapping, and fraud, and protect people's personal rights, property rights, and right to dignity. We will improve the system of public psychological services, and cultivate self-esteem, self-confidence, rationality, composure, and optimism among our people. We will strengthen the system for community governance, shift the focus of social governance to the community level, leverage the role of social organizations, and see that government's governance efforts on the one hand and society's self-regulation and residents' self-governance on the other reinforce each other.

7. Effectively safeguarding national security

National security is the cornerstone of peace and stability of our country, and safeguarding it is in the fundamental interests of the Chinese people of all ethnic groups. We will improve our national security strategy and policy, guarantee China's political security, and take coordinated steps to ensure security in all areas. We will improve our national security system, strengthen legal measures to enhance national security, and enhance our capacity for forestalling and fending off security risks. We must rigorously protect against and take resolute measures to combat all acts of infiltration, subversion, and sabotage, as well as violent and terrorist activities, ethnic separatist activities, and religious extremist activities. We will strengthen efforts to raise awareness of national security among all Party members and all the people, and create a strong synergy of the whole society to safeguard national security.

Comrades,

Meeting the fundamental interests of all our people is the ultimate yardstick for judging all the work of our Party. The issues of concern to the people, be they big or small, should be handled with utmost care and attention. We must start by addressing issues of public concern, start by delivering the outcomes that satisfy public needs, and work without rest to lead our people in pursuing a better life.

IX. Speeding Up Reform of the System for Developing an Eco-Civilization, and Building a Beautiful China

Man and nature form a community of life; we, as human beings, must respect nature, follow its ways, and protect it. Only by observing the laws of nature can humanity avoid costly blunders in its exploitation. Any harm we inflict on nature will eventually return to haunt us. This is a reality we have to face.

The modernization that we pursue is one characterized by harmonious coexistence between man and nature. In addition to creating more material and cultural wealth to meet people's ever-increasing desire for a better life, we need also to provide more quality ecological goods to meet people's ever-growing demands for a beautiful environment. We should, acting on the principles of prioritizing resource conservation and environmental protection and letting nature restore itself, develop spatial layouts, industrial structures, and ways of work and life that help conserve resources and protect the environment. With this, we can restore the serenity, harmony, and beauty of nature.

1. Promoting green development

We will step up efforts to establish a legal and policy framework that promotes green production and consumption, and promote a sound economic structure that facilitates green, low-carbon, and circular development. We will create a market-based system for green technology innovation, develop green finance, and spur the development of energy-saving and environmental protection industries as well as clean production and clean energy industries. We will promote a revolution in energy production and consumption, and build an energy sector that is clean, low-carbon, safe, and efficient.

We will encourage conservation across the board and promote

recycling, take action to get everyone conserving water, cut consumption of energy and materials, and establish linkages between the circular use of resources and materials in industrial production and in everyday life. We encourage simple, moderate, green, and low-carbon ways of life, and oppose extravagance and excessive consumption. We will launch initiatives to make Party and government offices do better when it comes to conservation, and develop eco-friendly families, schools, communities, and transport services.

2. Solving prominent environmental problems

We will get everyone involved in improving the environment and address environmental issues at the root. We will continue our campaign to prevent and control air pollution to make our skies blue again. We will speed up prevention and control of water pollution, and take comprehensive measures to improve river basins and offshore areas. We will strengthen the control of soil pollution and the restoration of polluted soil, intensify the prevention and control of agricultural pollution from non-point sources, and take measures to improve rural living environments. We will improve the treatment of solid waste and garbage.

We will enforce stricter pollutants discharge standards and see to it that polluters are held accountable. We will improve our systems for assessing the honesty and accuracy of claims about performance in environmental protection, for mandatory release of environmental information, and for imposing rigorous sanctions in cases of environmental violation. We will establish an environmental governance system in which government takes the lead, enterprises assume the main responsibility, and social organizations and the public also participate. We will get actively involved in global environmental governance and fulfill our commitments on emissions reduction.

3. Intensifying the protection of ecosystems

We will carry out major projects to protect and restore key ecosystems, improve the system of shields for ecological security, and develop ecological corridors and biodiversity protection networks, so as to strengthen the quality and stability of our ecosystems. We will complete work on drawing red lines for protecting the ecosystems, designating permanent basic cropland, and delineating boundaries for urban development.

We will promote afforestation, take comprehensive steps to control desertification, stony deserts, and soil erosion, strengthen wetland conservation and restoration, and better prevent and control geological disasters. We will improve the system for protecting natural forests, and turn more marginal farmland into forests and grasslands. We will rigorously protect farmland and expand trials in crop rotation and keeping land fallow. We will improve systems for regeneration of croplands, grasslands, forests, rivers, and lakes, and set up diverse market-based mechanisms for ecological compensation.

4. Reforming the environmental regulation system

We will strengthen overall planning, organization, and leadership for building an eco-civilization. We will establish regulatory agencies to manage state-owned natural resource assets and monitor natural ecosystems, and improve environmental management systems. These agencies will, in a unified way, perform the duties of the owner of public-owned natural resource assets, the duties of regulating the use of all territorial space and protecting and restoring ecosystems, and the duties of monitoring the discharge of all pollutants in urban and rural areas and conducting administrative law enforcement.

We will establish systems for developing and protecting territorial space, improve supporting policies on functional zones, and develop a nature reserves system composed mainly of national parks. We will take tough steps to stop and punish all activities that damage the environment.

Comrades,

What we are doing today to build an eco-civilization will benefit generations to come. We should have a strong commitment to socialist eco-civilization and work to develop a new model of modernization with humans developing in harmony with nature. We must do our generation's share to protect the environment.

X. Staying Committed to the Chinese Path of Building Strong Armed Forces and Fully Advancing the Modernization of National Defense and the Military

We have reached a new historical starting point in strengthening national defense and the armed forces. Confronted with profound changes in our national security environment and responding to the demands of the day for a strong country with a strong military, we must fully implement the Party's thinking on strengthening the military for the new era and the military strategy for new conditions, build a powerful and modernized army, navy, air force, rocket force, and strategic support force, develop strong and efficient joint operations commanding institutions for theater commands, and create a modern combat system with distinctive Chinese characteristics. Our armed forces must be up to shouldering the missions and tasks of the new era entrusted to them by the Party and the people.

We will adapt to the trend of a new global military revolution and to national security needs; we will upgrade our military capabilities, and see that, by the year 2020, mechanization is basically achieved, IT application has made significant progress, and strategic capabilities have seen a big improvement. In step with our country's modernization process, we will modernize our military across the board in terms of theory, organizational structure, service personnel, and weaponry. We will make it our mission to see that by 2035, the modernization of our national defense and armed forces is basically completed; and that by the mid-21st century our people's armed forces have been fully transformed into world-class forces.

We will strengthen the Party in the military. We will launch activities under the theme of "passing on the traditions of revolution; stepping up to the task of making the military strong". We will move forward with the development of the military honors system. We will train the revolutionary officers and soldiers of a new era with faith, ability, courage, and integrity, and see that our forces forever preserve their nature, purpose, and character as the forces of the people.

We will continue to deepen national defense and military reform. We will further the reform of major policy systems, including the career officers system, the system for posting civilian personnel in the military, and the military service system. We will push ahead with transformation of military management, and improve and develop our distinctive Chinese socialist military institutions. We must keep it firm in our minds that technology is the core combat capability, encourage innovations in major technologies, and conduct innovations independently. We will strengthen the system for training military personnel, and make our people's forces more innovative. We will govern the military with strict discipline in every respect, push for a fundamental transformation in the way our military is run, and strengthen the role of rule of law in enhancing national defense and military capabilities.

A military is built to fight. Our military must regard combat capability as the criterion to meet in all its work and focus on how to win when it is called on. We will take solid steps to ensure military preparedness for all strategic directions, and make progress in combat readiness in both traditional and new security fields. We will develop new combat forces and support forces, conduct military training under combat conditions, boost the application of military strength, speed up development of intelligent military, and improve combat capabilities for joint operations based on the network information system and the ability to fight under multidimensional conditions. This will enable us to effectively shape our military posture, manage crises, and deter and win wars.

We should ensure that efforts to make our country prosperous and efforts to make our military strong go hand in hand. We will strengthen unified leadership, top-level design, reform, and innovation. We will speed up implementation of major projects, deepen reform of defense-related science, technology, and industry, achieve greater civil-military integration, and build integrated national strategies and strategic capabilities. We will improve our national defense mobilization system, and build strong, well-structured, and modern border, coastal, and air defenses. We will establish an administration for veterans; we will protect the legitimate rights and interests of military personnel and their families; and we will make military service an occupation that enjoys public respect. We will carry out further reforms to build a modernized armed police force.

Comrades,

Our military is the people's military, and our national defense is the responsibility of every one of us. We must raise public awareness about the importance of national defense and strengthen unity between the government and the military and between the people and the military. Let us work together to create a mighty force for realizing the Chinese Dream and the dream of building a powerful military.

XI. Upholding "One Country, Two Systems" and Moving Towards National Reunification

Since Hong Kong and Macao's return to the motherland, the practice of "one country, two systems" in both regions has been a resounding success. The policy of "one country, two systems" has proved to be the best solution to the questions of Hong Kong and Macao, left by history, and the best institutional guarantee for the long-term prosperity and stability of Hong Kong and Macao after their return.

To maintain long-term prosperity and stability in Hong Kong and Macao, it is imperative to fully and faithfully implement the policies of "one country, two systems", "the people of Hong Kong governing Hong Kong", "the people of Macao governing Macao", and a high degree of autonomy for both regions. It is imperative, too, to act in strict compliance with China's Constitution and the basic laws of the two special administrative regions, and to improve the systems and mechanisms for enforcing the basic laws.

We will continue to support the governments and chief executives of both regions in pursuing the following endeavors: exercising law-based governance, uniting and leading the people of all sectors in an active and concerted effort to promote development and harmony, ensuring and improving people's wellbeing, taking well-ordered steps to advance democracy, maintaining law and order, and fulfilling the constitutional responsibility of safeguarding China's sovereignty, security, and development interests.

The development of Hong Kong and Macao is closely tied up with that of the mainland. We will continue to support Hong Kong and Macao in integrating their own development into the overall development of the country. We will give priority to the development of the Guangdong-Hong Kong-Macao Greater Bay Area, cooperation between Guangdong, Hong Kong, and Macao, and regional cooperation in the pan-Pearl River Delta, thus fully advancing mutually beneficial cooperation between the mainland and the two regions. We will formulate and improve policies and measures to make it more convenient for people from Hong Kong and Macao to develop careers on the mainland.

We will remain committed to the policy for the Hong Kong people to govern Hong Kong and the Macao people to govern Macao, with patriots playing the principal role. We will develop and strengthen the ranks of patriots who love both our country and their regions, and foster greater patriotism and a stronger sense of national identity among the people in Hong Kong and Macao. With this, our compatriots in Hong Kong and Macao will share both the historic responsibility of national rejuvenation and the pride of a strong and prosperous China.

Resolving the Taiwan question to realize China's complete reunification is the shared aspiration of all Chinese people, and is in the fundamental interests of the Chinese nation. We must uphold the principles of "peaceful reunification" and "one country, two systems", work for the peaceful development of cross-Straits relations, and advance the process towards the peaceful reunification of China.

The one-China principle is the political foundation of cross-Straits relations. The 1992 Consensus embodies the one-China principle and defines the fundamental nature of cross-Straits relations; it thus holds the key to the peaceful development of relations between the two sides of the Taiwan Straits. Recognize the historical fact of the 1992

Consensus and that the two sides both belong to one China, and then our two sides can conduct dialogue to address through discussion the concerns of the people of both sides, and no political party or group in Taiwan will have any difficulty conducting exchanges with the mainland.

Blood is thicker than water. People on both sides of the Taiwan Straits are brothers and sisters; we share the bond of kinship. Guided by the conviction that we are all of the same family, we respect the current social system and way of life in Taiwan and are ready to share the development opportunities on the mainland with our Taiwan compatriots first. We will expand cross-Straits economic and cultural exchanges and cooperation for mutual benefits.

We will ensure that over time, people from Taiwan will enjoy the same treatment as local people when they pursue their studies, start businesses, seek jobs, or live on the mainland, thus improving the wellbeing of Taiwan compatriots. We will encourage people from both sides to work together to promote Chinese culture and forge closer bonds between them.

We stand firm in safeguarding China's sovereignty and territorial integrity, and will never allow the historical tragedy of national division to repeat itself. Any separatist activity is certain to meet with the resolute opposition of the Chinese people. We have the resolve, the confidence, and the ability to defeat separatist attempts for "Taiwan independence" in any form. We will never allow anyone, any organization, or any political party, at any time or in any form, to separate any part of Chinese territory from China.

Comrades,

Realizing the rejuvenation of the Chinese nation is a dream shared by all of us as Chinese. We remain firm in our conviction that, as long as all the sons and daughters of the Chinese nation, including our compatriots in Hong Kong, Macao, and Taiwan, follow the tide of history, work together for the greater national interests, and keep our nation's destiny firmly in our own hands, we will, without doubt, be able to achieve the great rejuvenation of the Chinese nation.

XII. Following a Path of Peaceful Development and Working to Build a Global Community of Shared Future

The Communist Party of China strives for both the wellbeing of the Chinese people and human progress. To make new and greater contributions for humanity is our Party's abiding mission.

China will continue to hold high the banner of peace, development, cooperation, and mutual benefit and uphold its fundamental foreign policy goal of preserving world peace and promoting common development. China remains firm in its commitment to strengthening friendship and cooperation with other countries on the basis of the Five Principles of Peaceful Coexistence[17], and to forging a new form of international relations featuring mutual respect, fairness, justice, and win-win cooperation.

The world is undergoing major developments, transformation, and adjustment, but peace and development remain the call of our day. The trends of global multi-polarity, economic globalization, IT application, and cultural diversity are surging forward; changes in the global governance system and the international order are speeding up; countries are becoming increasingly interconnected and interdependent; relative international forces are becoming more balanced; and peace and development remain irreversible trends.

And yet, as a world we face growing uncertainties and destabilizing factors. Global economic growth lacks energy; the gap between rich and poor continues to widen; flashpoints arise often in some regions; and unconventional security threats like terrorism, cyber-insecurity, major infectious diseases, and climate change continue to spread. As human beings we have many common challenges to face.

Our world is full of both hope and challenges. We should not give up on our dreams because the reality around us is too complicated; we should not stop pursuing our ideals because they seem out of our reach. No country can address alone the many challenges facing humanity; no country can afford to retreat into self-isolation.

We call on the people of all countries to work together to build a global community of shared future, to build an open, inclusive, clean, and beautiful world that enjoys lasting peace, universal security, and common prosperity. We should respect each other, discuss issues as equals, resolutely reject the Cold War mentality and power politics, and take a new approach to developing state-to-state relations with communication, not confrontation, and with partnership, not alliance. We should commit to settling disputes through dialogue and resolving differences through discussion, coordinate responses to traditional and non-traditional threats, and oppose terrorism in all its forms.

We should stick together through thick and thin, facilitate free trade and investment, and make economic globalization more open, inclusive, and balanced so that its benefits are shared by all. We should respect the diversity of civilizations. In handling relations among civilizations, let us replace estrangement with exchange, clashes with mutual learning, and superiority with coexistence. We should be good friends to the environment, cooperate to tackle climate change, and protect our planet for the sake of human survival.

China remains firm in pursuing an independent foreign policy of peace. We respect the right of the people of all countries to choose their own development path. We endeavor to uphold international fairness and justice, and oppose acts that impose one's will on others or interfere in the internal affairs of others as well as the practice of the strong bullying the weak.

China will never pursue development at the expense of others' interests, but nor will China ever give up its legitimate rights and interests. No one should expect us to tolerate anything that undermines our interests. China pursues a national defense policy that is in nature defensive. China's development does not pose a threat to any other country. No matter what stage of development it reaches, China will never seek hegemony or engage in expansion.

China has actively developed global partnerships and expanded the convergence of interests with other countries. China will promote coordination and cooperation with other major countries and work to build a framework for major-country relations featuring overall stability and balanced development. China will deepen relations with its neighbors in accordance with the principle of amity, sincerity, mutual benefit, and inclusiveness and the policy of forging friendship and partnership with our neighbors. Guided by the principle of upholding justice while pursuing shared interests and the principle of sincerity, real results, affinity, and good faith, China will work to strengthen solidarity and cooperation with other developing countries. We will strengthen exchanges and cooperation with the political parties and organizations of other countries, and encourage people's congresses, CPPCC committees, the military, local governments, and people's organizations to engage in exchanges with other countries.

China adheres to the fundamental national policy of opening up and pursues development with its doors open wide. China will actively promote international cooperation through the Belt and Road Initiative. In doing so, we hope to achieve policy, infrastructure, trade, financial, and people-to-people connectivity and thus build a new platform for international cooperation to create new drivers of shared development.

China will increase assistance to other developing countries, especially the least developed countries, and do its part to reduce the North-South development gap. China will support multilateral trade regimes and work to facilitate the establishment of free trade areas and build an open world economy.

China follows the principle of achieving shared growth through discussion and collaboration in engaging in global governance. China stands for democracy in international relations and the equality of all countries, big or small, strong or weak, rich or poor. China supports the United Nations in playing an active role in international affairs, and supports the efforts of other developing countries to increase their representation and strengthen their voice in international affairs. China will continue to play its part as a major and responsible country, take an active part in reforming and developing the global governance system, and keep contributing Chinese wisdom and strength to global governance.

Comrades,

The future of the world rests in the hands of the people of all countries; the future of humanity hinges on the choices they make. We, the Chinese, are ready to work with the people of all other countries to build a global community of shared future and create a bright tomorrow for all of us.

XIII. Exercising Strict Governance over the Party and Improving the Party's Ability to Govern and Lead

As socialism with Chinese characteristics has entered a new era, our Party must get a new look and make new accomplishments. As the saying goes, it takes a good blacksmith to forge good tools. For the Party to unite the people and lead them in carrying out our great struggle, advancing our great cause, and realizing our great dream, we must unwaveringly uphold and improve Party leadership and make the Party still stronger.

Ensuring that Party self-governance is exercised fully and strictly is a journey to which there is no end. The future of a political party or a government is determined by whether it enjoys public support. We must guard against and correct with resolve the practices the people oppose and resent. The whole Party must be soberly aware that the governance environment our Party faces is complex, and that so too are the factors undermining the Party's advanced nature and integrity; prominent problems of unwholesome thinking, organization, and conduct in the Party have not been solved root and branch.

We must fully recognize the long-term and complex nature of the tests confronting the Party as they relate to governance, reform and opening up, the market economy, and the external environment. We must also fully recognize the intensity and severity of the dangers of a lack of drive, incompetence, disengagement from the people, inaction, and corruption. So we must focus on solving problems, maintain strategic resolve, and ensure strict Party self-governance.

The general requirements for strengthening the Party for the new era are:

– Uphold and strengthen overall Party leadership and ensure that the Party exercises effective self-supervision and practices strict self-governance in every respect;

– Take strengthening the Party's long-term governance capacity and its advanced nature and integrity as the main thrust; take reinforcing the Party's political foundations as the overarching principle; take holding dear the Party's ideals, convictions, and purpose as the underpinning; and take harnessing the whole Party's enthusiasm, initiative, and creativity as the focus of efforts;

– Make all-round efforts to reinforce the Party's political foundations, buttress ideological commitment, consolidate the organization, improve conduct, and enforce discipline, while always focusing on opportunities to create stronger institutions;

– Step up efforts to combat corruption and continue to improve the efficacy of strengthening the Party;

– Build the Party into a vibrant Marxist governing party that is always at the forefront of the times, enjoys the wholehearted support of the people, has the courage to reform itself, and is able to withstand all tests.

1. Putting the Party's political foundations first

Taking a clear political stance is the fundamental requirement our Party must meet as a Marxist party. Reinforcing the Party's political foundations is of fundamental importance, as it determines the direction and efficacy of the effort to strengthen the Party.

The primary task of reinforcing our Party's political foundations is to ensure that the whole Party obeys the Central Committee and upholds its authority and centralized, unified leadership. All Party members must closely follow the Party's political line, strictly observe its political discipline and rules, and closely align themselves with the Central Committee in terms of political stance, direction, principle, and path.

Every member of the Party must hold the Party Constitution in great reverence, act in strict accordance with the code of conduct for intra-Party political life under new circumstances, and make intra-

Party activities more politically oriented, up-to-date, principled, and effective. We must guard against the rules of business dealings eroding intra-Party conduct, and foster a healthy political ecosystem within the Party.

We must improve and implement the systems of democratic centralism, and practice both democracy-based centralism and centralism-guided democracy. This means we should both give full play to democracy and practice centralism on this basis.

We must foster values like loyalty, honesty, impartiality, adherence to fact, and integrity; guard against and oppose self-centered behavior, decentralism, behavior in disregard of the rules, a silo mentality, unprincipled nice-guyism, and sectarianism, factionalism, and patronage. We must resolutely oppose double-dealing and duplicity.

All Party members, especially high-ranking officials, must strengthen their Party consciousness, political awareness, and political ability. We must regard it as our fundamental political responsibility to be loyal to the Party, share the Party's concerns, fulfill our obligations to the Party, and work for the people's wellbeing, and forever preserve the political character of Communists.

2. Arming the whole Party with the Thought on Socialism with Chinese Characteristics for a New Era

Theory is fundamental to strengthening the Party. Our revolutionary ideals soar beyond the skies. The noble ideal of communism and the shared ideal of socialism with Chinese characteristics are our source of strength and political soul as Chinese Communists; they also form the theoretical foundation of Party solidarity and unity.

Our top priority in strengthening the Party through theory is to stay true to our ideals and convictions. We should make all Party members keep firmly in mind the Party's purpose, have unwavering convictions as Communists, resolve the fundamental issue of the worldview, outlook on life, and values we should embrace, and maintain deep belief in and faithfully practice communism and socialism with Chinese characteristics.

We will foster a Marxist style of learning, and make it a regular practice and an institutionalized requirement for all Party members to gain a good command of the Party Constitution, Party regulations, and related major policy addresses and to meet Party standards. We will launch a campaign under the theme of "staying true to our aspiration and founding mission" to enable all Party members, especially officials at and above the county and director level, to arm themselves with the Party's new theories and become more purposeful in working tirelessly to accomplish the Party's historic mission in the new era.

3. Training a contingent of competent and professional officials

Party officials are a central pillar of strength for the cause of our Party and country. We must adhere to the principle of the Party supervising officials; select officials on the basis of both integrity and ability, with priority given to integrity, and on the basis of merit regardless of background; and ensure that those who are dedicated, impartial, and upright should be appointed. We must implement in earnest the criteria for evaluating good officials.

In selecting and appointing officials, we must adopt the right approach, with emphasis on political performance. We will promote and put in important positions those Party officials who do well according to the following criteria: They maintain their political commitment, think in terms of the general picture, follow the core leadership of the CPC Central Committee, and act in accordance with its requirements; they have full confidence in the path, theory, system and culture of socialism with Chinese characteristics; they uphold the authority of the Central Committee and faithfully follow the Party's theories, lines, principles, and policies; and they are loyal to the Party, have moral integrity, and demonstrate a keen sense of responsibility. We will strengthen leadership teams at all levels by appointing competent officials.

We will take seriously the development of specialized expertise and professionalism, and enhance Party officials' ability to meet the requirements of developing socialism with Chinese characteristics in the new era. We will work harder to identify promising young officials and get them well prepared for future jobs. We will focus on their practical training in local communities, in work on the front line, and in areas where conditions are harsh, and work to produce a constant stream of outstanding young officials who have passed the test of practice. We will ensure coordinated training and selection of female officials, officials from ethnic minorities, and non-Party officials. We will ensure that retired officials receive proper care.

We will be both strict and caring, and place equal emphasis on providing incentives and imposing constraints. We will improve the performance assessment and evaluation system for officials, institute incentive mechanisms and mechanisms to allow for and address errors, and take a clear stand in supporting officials who are willing to assume responsibility, who take a down-to-earth approach in their work, and who do not seek personal gain. Party organizations at every level should care about officials working at the primary level, and help solve the problems and difficulties they encounter.

People with talent are a strategic resource for China as it endeavors to achieve national rejuvenation and stay ahead in international competition. We must follow the principle of the Party exercising leadership over personnel, assemble the best minds across the land and draw fully on their expertise, and step up efforts to make China a talent-strong country.

We will pursue a more proactive, open, and effective policy on training competent professionals. We should value people with talent, be adept at identifying talent, have the foresight to employ them, be earnest in keeping them, and welcome them into our ranks. This will better enable us to attract bright people from both within and outside the Party and both in China and abroad to join us in pursuing the great endeavor of the Party and the people. We will encourage and guide people with talent to work in remote poor areas, border areas with mainly ethnic minority populations, and old revolutionary base areas, as well as in communities and on the front lines. We will work to foster a positive environment in which everyone wants, strives, and is able to excel themselves, and can do full justice to their talent. With this, we aim to see that in every field the creativity of talent is given great expression and their ingenuity and expertise flow freely.

4. Strengthening primary-level Party organizations

Primary-level Party organizations do the groundwork to ensure the Party's lines, principles, policies, decisions, and plans are implemented.

We will work to ensure that primary-level Party organizations in enterprises, villages, Party and government institutions, schools, research institutes, sub-districts, communities, and social organizations play a key role in communicating the Party's propositions, carrying out the Party's decisions, overseeing community-level social governance, uniting and mobilizing the people, and promoting reform and development. In doing so, we will focus on improving the organizational capability of primary-level Party organizations and give priority to enhancing their political functions.

Party branches should fulfill their responsibilities for directly guiding, managing, and overseeing their members and for organizing, communicating with, uniting, and serving the people. They should encourage their members to play an exemplary role.

We must practice the system of holding Party branch general meetings, meetings of Party branch committees, Party group meetings, and Party lectures. We will develop new ways for setting up primary-level Party organizations and for them to carry out their activities, strengthen the training of their heads, and expand their reach. We must work harder to address the problems that some primary-level Party organizations are weak, ineffective, and marginalized. We will expand intra-Party democracy at the primary level, make Party affairs more transparent, and ensure channels are open for Party members to participate in Party affairs, oversee Party organizations and officials, and submit opinions and suggestions to the Party organization at the next level up.

We will do more to recruit new Party members from among industrial workers, young people working in agriculture, well-educated groups, and people working in non-public economic entities and social organizations. We will give more incentives, solicitude, and assistance to Party members. We will make our guidance and management of Party members better targeted and more effective, and handle Party members who do not meet the mark in a prudent and orderly way.

5. Working ceaselessly to improve Party conduct and enforce Party discipline

Our Party comes from the people, has its roots among the people, and is dedicated to serving the people. Once the Party becomes disengaged from the people, it will lose its vitality. In improving Party conduct, we must focus on maintaining the Party's close bond with the people, keep them firmly in mind, develop a closer affinity with them, and keep working to foster stronger public support for the Party's governance. We must earnestly address all issues the people are strongly concerned about, and resolutely correct any behavior that undermines the people's interests.

Our Party officials should lead by example in consolidating and building on the advances made in implementing the central Party leadership's Eight Rules on improving Party and government conduct. We should continue to address the practice of favoring form over substance, bureaucratism, hedonism, and extravagance, and oppose mindsets and acts of privilege seeking. We will focus on strengthening the enforcement of political and organizational discipline, and use this to prompt stricter observance of discipline on upholding integrity, on interacting with the people, and regarding work and life.

We will continue to carry out criticism and self-criticism in keeping with the principle of learning from mistakes to prevent recurrence and treating the illness to save the patient. We will conduct four forms of oversight over discipline compliance[18], identify problems early and correct them while they are nascent. Party organizations with the power to supervise officials will be given corresponding power to take disciplinary action as called for, and accountability for overseeing compliance will be tightened. We will raise Party members' awareness of discipline and strengthen discipline enforcement, and demand that Party members and officials hold discipline in awe and respect, do not cross the line, and become used to working and living under oversight and constraints.

6. Securing a sweeping victory in the fight against corruption

The people resent corruption most; and corruption is the greatest threat our Party faces. We must have the resolve and tenacity to persevere in the never-ending fight against corruption. Only by intensifying efforts to address both the symptoms and root causes of corruption – by making sure that officials are honest, government is clean, and political affairs are handled with integrity – can we avoid history's cycle of rise and fall[19] and ensure the long-term stability of the Party and the country.

Currently, the fight against corruption remains grave and complex; we must remain as firm as a rock in our resolve to build on the overwhelming momentum and secure a sweeping victory. We will continue to see that there are no no-go zones, no ground is left unturned, and no tolerance is shown for corruption. We will impose tight constraints, maintain a tough stance and a long-term deterrence, punish both those who take bribes and those who offer them, and prevent interest groups from arising within the Party.

We will institute a system of disciplinary inspection for city and county level Party committees in an intensified effort to address corruption that occurs on the people's doorsteps. Wherever offenders may flee, they will be brought back and brought to justice. We will work for the adoption of national anti-corruption legislation and create a corruption reporting platform that covers both disciplinary inspection commissions and supervision agencies.

We will strengthen deterrence so officials do not dare to, strengthen the cage of institutions so they are unable to, and strengthen their vigilance so they have no desire to commit acts of corruption. Our political environment will, through tireless efforts, like seas fallen calm and rivers running clear, be clean and free of corruption.

7. Improving Party and state oversight systems

To improve the Party's ability to cleanse itself, it is essential that we strengthen Party self-supervision and subject ourselves to public oversight. We must strengthen checks on and oversight over the exercise of power, and ensure that power is exercised under public oversight, in broad daylight, and in an institutional cage. We will strengthen top-down organizational oversight, improve bottom-up democratic oversight, practice peer oversight, and tighten regular supervision over Party members in positions of leadership. We will intensify political inspection to identify problems and ensure that deterrence works; we will establish an oversight network that facilitates coordination in disciplinary inspections conducted at different levels.

We will deepen reform of the national supervision system, conduct trials throughout the country, and establish supervisory commissions at the national, provincial, city, and county levels, which will each keep their own identity while working together with the Party's disciplinary inspection commissions as one office. This will ensure that supervision covers everyone working in the public sector who exercises public power. A national supervision law will be formulated. Supervisory commissions will be given responsibilities, powers, and means of investigation in accordance with the law. The practice of *shuanggui*[20] will be replaced by detention.

We will reform the auditing management system and improve the statistics system. We will establish an authoritative, efficient oversight system with complete coverage under the Party's unified command; and integrate intra-Party oversight with oversight by state organs, democratic oversight, judicial oversight, public oversight, and oversight through public opinion. All this will create a powerful synergy for conducting oversight.

8. Strengthening every dimension of our ability for governance

To lead a large socialist country of more than 1.3 billion people, our Party must be both politically strong and highly competent.

We should be good at learning. We will foster a strong atmosphere of learning and practicing in the Party, and build our Party into a Marxist learning party. We will nurture a love of learning in our people.

We should be good at exercising political leadership. We should adopt a strategic perspective, and develop creative thinking and a dialectical approach to thinking; we should think in terms of the rule of law, and think about worst-case scenarios. We should formulate sound Party lines, principles, and policies and resolutely implement them, ensuring that the Party exercises overall leadership and coordinates work in all areas.

We should be good reformers and pioneers. We should be enterprising, work creatively in light of actual conditions, and adeptly apply information technology, including the internet, in our work.

We should be good at promoting sound development. We should effectively put into practice the new development philosophy, and continue to break new ground in development.

We should be good at exercising law-based governance. We will act more quickly to put in place a system of Party rules and regulations that covers all aspects of Party leadership and Party development, and strengthen and improve Party leadership over bodies of state power.

We should be good at engaging with the people. We will develop new systems, mechanisms, ways, and means for this work. We will urge trade unions, Chinese Communist Youth League organizations, women's federations, and other people's organizations to strengthen their political consciousness, become more advanced, and better represent the people; to play their role as bridges linking the Party with the people; and to organize and motivate the people to follow the Party.

We should be good at implementing policy. We should be open and frank, take effective measures to address real issues, and seek good outcomes. We should be ready both to act resolutely and swiftly and to make sustained efforts to tackle tough issues head-on. We should have the perseverance to hammer away until a task is done, and make concrete, meticulous, and effective efforts in all our work.

We should be good at managing risks. We will improve risk prevention and control mechanisms in all areas, skillfully handle various complex issues, overcome all difficulties and obstacles that we meet on our way, and keep a firm hold on the initiative in our work.

Comrades,

A great cause calls for leadership of a strong party. As long as our Party keeps itself competent and strong, always remains true to the people's aspiration and works in concert with the people, we can and will navigate the great ship bearing the great dream of the Chinese people to conquer the waves and reach our destination.

Comrades,

The Chinese nation is a great nation; it has been through hardships and adversity but remains indomitable. The Chinese people are a great people; they are industrious and brave; and they never pause in the pursuit of progress. The Communist Party of China is a great party; it has the courage to fight and the mettle to win.

The wheels of history roll on; the tides of the times are vast and mighty. History looks kindly on those with resolve, with drive and ambition, and with plenty of guts; it does not wait for the hesitant, the apathetic, or those shy of a challenge.

All of us in the Party must work hard and live simply, guard against arrogance and impetuosity; and lose no time in progressing along the long march of the new era.

We must consciously safeguard the solidarity and unity of the Party, maintain the Party's deep bond with the people, and strengthen the great unity of the Chinese people of all ethnic groups and the great unity of all the sons and daughters of the Chinese nation at home and abroad. We must unite all the forces that can be united and work as one to progress towards the brilliant future of national rejuvenation.

A nation will prosper only when its young people thrive; a country will be full of hope and have a great tomorrow only when its younger generations have ideals, ability, and a strong sense of responsibility. The Chinese Dream is a dream about the past, the present, and the future. It is a dream of our generation, but even more so, a dream of the younger generations. The Chinese Dream of national rejuvenation will be realized ultimately through the endeavors of young people, generation by generation.

All of us in the Party should care about young people and set the stage for them to excel. To all our young people, you should have firm ideals and convictions, aim high, and have your feet firmly on the ground. You should ride the waves of your day; and in the course of realizing the Chinese Dream, fulfill your youthful dreams, and write a vivid chapter in your tireless endeavors to serve the interests of the people.

A just cause should be pursued for the common good. Rooted in a land of more than 9.6 million square kilometers, nourished by a culture of more than 5,000 years, and blessed with the strength of more than 1.3 billion people, we have an infinitely vast stage of our era, a heritage of unmatched depth, and incomparable resolve that enable us to forge ahead on the road of socialism with Chinese characteristics.

We, the entire Party and the Chinese people of all ethnic groups, should rally closely around the Party Central Committee, and uphold socialism with Chinese characteristics. We should keep on working with great determination to accomplish the three historic tasks of advancing modernization, realizing China's reunification, and preserving world peace and promoting common development; we should secure a decisive victory in finishing the building of a moderately prosperous society in all respects, strive for the great success of socialism with Chinese characteristics for a new era, realize the Chinese Dream of national rejuvenation, and see that our people realize their aspirations for a better life.

Notes

[1] This refers to China's overall plan for building socialism with Chinese characteristics, that is, to promote coordinated progress in the economic, political, cultural, social and eco-environmental fields.

[2] This refers to China's strategic plan for building socialism with Chinese characteristics, that is, to make comprehensive moves to complete a moderately prosperous society in all respects, to further reform, to advance the rule of law, and to strengthen Party self-governance.

³ This refers to the initiative of building the Silk Road Economic Belt and the 21st Century Maritime Silk Road. It was first proposed by Xi Jinping in September and October 2013 during his visits to Central and Southeast Asia. – *Tr.*

⁴ The united front under the leadership of the CPC is the broadest revolutionary, socialist and patriotic united front formed by all ethnic groups, all political parties, all social strata and people of all circles in China during the New Democratic Revolution (1919-1949), socialist construction and reform, to achieve national independence, democracy and prosperity and the rejuvenation of the Chinese nation. – *Tr.*

⁵ The core socialist values: Prosperity, democracy, civility and harmony are values that underpin our nation; freedom, equality, justice and the rule of law are values that buttress our society; patriotism, dedication, good faith and amity are values that underlie individual conduct.

⁶ This refers to an oral agreement reached at a November 1992 meeting between the Association for Relations Across the Taiwan Straits representing the mainland and the Straits Exchange Foundation based in Taiwan. The meeting discussed how to express the one-China principle in negotiations on general affairs, and agreed that "both sides of the Straits belong to China and both sides will work together for the realization of reunification of the country".

⁷ It is a cherished tradition that enables the CPC to maintain its vitality and combat capability. The CPC has always been and will always be obligated to do everything in the interests of the people and rely on their strength, and carry out the principle of "from the people, to the people", translating its policies into the people's conscientious action and implementing the mass line in all its activities. – *Tr.*

⁸ The Three Guidelines for Ethical Behavior and Three Basic Rules of Conduct require all officials to be strict with themselves in self-cultivation, in the exercise of power, and in self-discipline, and act in good faith when performing official duties, undertaking initiatives, and interacting with others.

⁹ The Eight Rules were set by the Political Bureau of the 18th CPC Central Committee to urge all officials to improve their ways of doing things and maintain close ties with the people. They are summarized as follows: improving investigation and fact-finding trips, streamlining meetings and other activities, reducing documents and briefings, standardizing arrangements for visits abroad, improving security procedures, improving news reports, imposing restrictions on publishing writings, and practicing diligence and frugality.

¹⁰ This refers to keeping to the socialist road and upholding the people's democratic dictatorship, the leadership of the CPC, and Marxism-Leninism and Mao Zedong Thought.

¹¹ Mao Zedong Thought has always been the fundamental guiding thought of the CPC. It is a series of theoretical summarizations and conclusions that Chinese Communists represented by Mao Zedong drew from their unique experience in

China's revolution and development in accordance with the basic tenets of Marxism. It includes correct theories, principles and systems of scientific thinking on China's revolution and development which have been attested by facts. It is the crystallization of the collective wisdom of the CPC, and the principal proponent is Mao Zedong. – Tr.

[12] Deng Xiaoping Theory is an important component of the system of theories of Chinese socialism, and a guiding thought of the CPC. For the first time, Deng Xiaoping Theory systematically answered a series of basic questions concerning the building of socialism in economically and culturally backward China, and the consolidation and development of socialism there. The principal proponent is Deng Xiaoping. – Tr.

[13] The Theory of Three Represents is a major component of the system of theories of Chinese socialism, and a guiding thought of the CPC. This theory emphasizes that the CPC must always represent the requirements for developing China's advanced productive forces, the orientation of China's advanced culture, and the fundamental interests of the overwhelming majority of the Chinese people. The principal proponent is Jiang Zemin. – Tr.

[14] The Scientific Outlook on Development is an important component of the system of theories of Chinese socialism, and a guiding thought of the CPC. It gives top priority to development, puts people first and seeks all-round, balanced and sustainable development with a holistic approach. The principal proponent is Hu Jintao. – Tr.

[15] The Two Centenary Goals were put forth by the CPC at its 18th National Congress in November 2012 for building socialism with Chinese characteristics. The two goals are to complete a moderately prosperous society in all respects by the centenary of the CPC (founded in 1921) and to build China into a modern socialist country that is prosperous, strong, democratic, culturally advanced, and harmonious by the centenary of the PRC (founded in 1949). The CPC drew up a development plan for the new era at its 19th National Congress. In the first stage from 2020 to 2035, we will build on the foundation of the moderately prosperous society with a further 15 years of hard work to see that socialist modernization is basically realized. In the second stage from 2035 to the middle of the 21st century, having achieved basic modernization, we will work hard for a further 15 years and develop China into a great modern socialist country that is prosperous, strong, democratic, culturally advanced, harmonious, and beautiful.

[16] The three-step strategic plan for modernization refers to China's development strategy for realizing initial modernization in three steps. The 13th CPC National Congress in October 1987 put forth doubling the 1980 GNP by the end of the 1980s and ensuring that the people would have adequate food and clothing as the first step; doubling the 1990 GNP by the end of the 20th century and ensuring

the people a moderately prosperous life as the second step; and increasing the per capita GNP level to that of moderately developed countries, ensuring the people a relatively affluent life, and realizing basic modernization by the middle of the 21st century as the third step.

[17] The Five Principles of Peaceful Coexistence are the principles of mutual respect for each other's territorial integrity and sovereignty, mutual non-aggression, mutual non-interference in each other's internal affairs, equality and cooperation for mutual benefit, and peaceful coexistence. From December 1953 to April 1954 delegates of the Chinese government and the Indian government held negotiations on China-India relations concerning the Tibet region of China. On December 31, 1953, the first day of the negotiations, Chinese Premier Zhou Enlai met with the delegation from India, and first put forward the Five Principles of Peaceful Coexistence. Later, the five principles were officially written into the preamble to the Agreement on Trade and Intercourse Between the Tibet Region of China and India. During his visit to India and Burma (Myanmar) in June 1954, Zhou Enlai issued joint declarations with Indian Prime Minister Jawaharlal Nehru and Burmese Prime Minister U Nu successively, advocating the establishment of the Five Principles of Peaceful Coexistence as the basic norm governing relations between states. – Tr.

[18] The four forms are: (1) criticism and self-criticism meetings and oral and written inquiries which are to be conducted regularly, to ensure that those who have committed minor misconduct are made to "flush and sweat", be embarrassed and ashamed of themselves; (2) light penalties and minor organizational adjustments to official positions, which are to be applied in the majority of cases; (3) heavy penalties and major adjustments to official positions, which are to be applied in a small number of cases; and (4) investigation and prosecution, which are to be undertaken in a very small number of cases involving serious violations of discipline and suspected criminal activity.

[19] In a conversation with Mao Zedong during a visit to Yan'an in July 1945, Huang Yanpei, a prominent non-Party individual, expressed the hope that the government to be established by the CPC would bring an end to the cycle of rise and fall characteristic of governments in Chinese history. Mao Zedong replied that the CPC had found a new path to break this cycle, and that the new path was democracy. Only under public scrutiny, will a government be clean and efficient; only when everyone takes responsibility, will good governance prevail.

[20] A form of intra-Party disciplinary action that requires a Party member under investigation to cooperate with questioning at a designated place and a designated time. – Tr.

Thought on Socialism with Chinese Characteristics for a New Era

New Requirements for Chinese Socialism in the New Era*

October 25, 2017

We should fully understand the new requirements of socialism with Chinese characteristics in the new era, and constantly strengthen all undertakings of the Party and the state. This new era will have an important historic bearing on China's future. Since the 18th CPC National Congress in 2012, based on the great achievements made after the founding of the PRC in 1949, and especially after the launch of the reform and opening-up policy in 1978, China has reached a new historic starting point, and Chinese socialism has entered a new stage. This demonstrates that we are moving on from the first to the second of the Two Centenary Goals. Prospects are looking bright for our tasks of achieving moderate prosperity in all respects, accelerating the drive for socialist modernization, and realizing national rejuvenation, and they are also placing a demand on us for more efforts.

On this new journey, all our Party members must keep abreast with the new requirements of the new era, improve our capacity for strategic, innovative and dialectical thinking, bear in mind the rule of law and our principles, take a holistic, forward-looking and innovative approach to work, and better understand the changing domestic and international situation. We must put into practice the Party's theories, guidelines, principles and policies – especially the guidelines, development strategies and policy measures established at the 19th CPC National Congress, promote the great cause of Chinese socialism and

---

* Part of the speech at the First Plenary Session of the 19th CPC Central Committee.

the great project of strengthening the Party, and unite all the Chinese people and lead them to strive for a moderately prosperous society and a modern socialist country in all respects.

Fully Implement the Thought on Socialism with Chinese Characteristics for a New Era*

October 25, 2017

We must ensure that the Thought on Socialism with Chinese Characteristics for a New Era and its basic principles are fully implemented, so as to raise the level of understanding of Marxism within the whole Party. The thought and its basic principles have come neither from thin air nor subjective assumptions. They are the results of the rigorous theoretical quest of the Party and the Chinese people since the 18th CPC National Congress in 2012, based on our Party's innovation in theory and practice since the founding of the PRC in 1949 and particularly since the launch of reform and opening up in 1978. They therefore represent a crystallization of the creative wisdom of our Party and the people. As the saying goes, "Forever green is the tree of life." A theory can only find its inspiration in the richness and vibrancy of real life and in the practical need to resolve social problems. On our journey in the new era, all Party members should combine theory with practice, that is, linking theoretical study closely with the historic changes in the undertakings of the Party and the state, with the new realities of Chinese socialism in the new era, with the great changes in the principal problems confronting our society, and with the work required to fulfill the Two Centenary Goals. To achieve this, we must consciously guide practice with theory and ensure that all aspects of our work better conform to the demands of objective and scientific laws. In this way, we will constantly enhance our capacity to uphold and develop Chinese

---

* Part of the speech at the First Plenary Session of the 19th CPC Central Committee.

socialism in the new era, and turn our Party's theories into a powerful force for us to realize the Two Centenary Goals and the Chinese Dream of national rejuvenation.

New Era, New Initiatives, New Achievements*

October 25, 2017

The First Plenary Session of the 19th CPC Central Committee has just elected a new central leadership. I was re-elected general secretary of the Central Committee. I see this as approval of my work, and a spur to further endeavors.

Now, I wish to present to you the other six Standing Committee members elected at the session: Li Keqiang, Li Zhanshu, Wang Yang, Wang Huning, Zhao Leji and Han Zheng. Among them, Li Keqiang was a member of the Political Bureau Standing Committee of the 18th CPC Central Committee, and the other five colleagues were members of the Political Bureau of the 18th CPC Central Committee. You can learn more about them from the media. So I have no need to elaborate.

Here on behalf of the newly-elected central leadership, I wish to extend our heartfelt thanks to all the members of the Party for the great trust they have placed in us. We will work diligently to carry out our duties, fulfill our mission and merit their trust.

Over the past five years, we have set out a broad agenda. Some tasks have been completed while others need further work. This Party congress has set new goals and new tasks; we must make coordinated efforts to see them through.

Following decades of hard work, socialism with Chinese characteristics has entered a new era. In this new context, we must undertake new initiatives, and more importantly, achieve greater success. The coming five years between the 19th and the 20th CPC national

---

* Part of the speech at the press conference by members of the Standing Committee of the Political Bureau of the 19th CPC Central Committee.

congresses are a period in which the timeframes of the Two Centenary Goals will converge. We must deliver the First Centenary Goal; we must also embark on the journey towards the Second Centenary Goal. As I look ahead to the next five years, I see several important junctures.

In 2018 we will mark the 40th anniversary of the launch of reform and opening up. Reform and opening up is a crucial move that is shaping China's future. Forty years of reform and opening up has made it possible for our people to lead decent, comfortable lives. Reviewing our experience and building on a strong momentum, we will continue to modernize the state governance system and capacity, achieve deeper all-round reform, and open China still wider to the world. We will see that reform and opening up complement and reinforce each other. It is my conviction that the rejuvenation of the Chinese nation will become a reality in the course of reform and opening up.

In 2019, we will celebrate the 70th anniversary of the founding of the PRC. We will act on the new development philosophy, and strive for sustained and healthy economic growth that benefits people in China and all around the world. We will continue our efforts to accomplish all the tasks laid down in the 13th Five-year Plan, develop a new blueprint for China's future, and see all our endeavors bear fruit. These efforts will contribute towards a more prosperous and stronger People's Republic.

In 2020, we will achieve moderate prosperity in all respects throughout the country. This is a society to be enjoyed by each and every one of us. On the march towards common prosperity, no one will be left behind. We will mobilize the whole Party and the whole country in the resolute push to deliver on our pledge – eradicating poverty in China. The aspiration of the people to live a better life must always be the focus of our efforts. We must remain committed to the people-centered philosophy of development, strive to guarantee and improve living standards, make steady progress towards enhancing our people's sense of gain, happiness and security, and realize common prosperity for all our people. I have no doubt that our people's lives will further improve year after year.

In 2021, we will mark the centenary of the CPC. For the Party that champions the cause of lasting prosperity of the Chinese nation, this centenary sees us in the prime of life. As the world's largest political party, the CPC must behave in a way commensurate with its status. History makes it abundantly clear that our Party is equally capable of leading the people to spearhead a great social revolution and engaging in significant self-reform. We, as its members, must always be youthful in spirit, and forever be the servant of the people, the vanguard of the times, and the backbone of our nation. Exercising full and rigorous governance over the Party is a journey to which there is no end. We should never entertain the idea of slowing our pace or halting our step for a break; rather, we must continue to rid ourselves of any contaminant that erodes the Party's fabric, make great efforts to foster a healthy political environment of integrity, and generate waves of positive energy throughout our Party, which build to a mighty nationwide force driving China's development and progress.

The CPC and the Chinese people have gone through trials and tribulations. These experiences have taught us that peace is precious and development must be valued. With confidence and pride, the Chinese people will be steadfast in upholding our country's sovereignty, security and development interests. We will also work with other nations to build a global community of shared future, and make a new and greater contribution to the noble cause of peace and development for all humanity.

The people are the creators of history. It is to them that we owe all our achievements. As long as we keep close ties with the people and rely on them, we can and will have boundless strength to forge ahead whatever the circumstances.

As a Chinese saying goes, it is better to see once than to hear a hundred times. We encourage members of the media to visit and see more of China. We hope that after this congress, you will continue to follow China's development and changes, and acquaint yourselves with and report on more dimensions of China. We do not need lavish praise from others. But we do welcome objective reporting and constructive suggestions, for this is our motto, "Not bent on praise for its bright colors, but on leaving its fragrance to all."[1]

Notes

[1] Wang Mian: "Ink Plum" (Mo Mei). Wang Mian (1310-1359) was a painter and poet of the Yuan Dynasty. The allusion in the poem is to appreciate things for their qualities rather than their looks, and President Xi was indicating that while China seeks no flattery, it expects honest and balanced reporting. – Tr.

Continue the Great Historic Struggle*

January 5, 2018

CPC Central Committee members and principal officials at the provincial and ministerial level are critical to the sound development of our Party and good governance of the country. We officials must raise our political awareness, adopt a historic perspective, reinforce theoretical reflection, think in terms of the broader picture, enrich our knowledge and intellectual attainments, and keep to a problem-oriented approach, so as to see and understand major theoretical and practical issues from a broader perspective that takes into consideration both history and the present, the international and domestic situation, and theory and practice. By doing so, we will be able to consistently uphold and develop socialism with Chinese characteristics, advance the great new project of strengthening our Party, stay alert against peril, and guard against risks and challenges. Time waits for no one. We will race against time to unite the whole Party and the whole people on the guiding principles of the 19th CPC National Congress, and pool all our strength to achieve the goals and tasks set at this congress, striving to break new ground for socialism with Chinese characteristics in the new era.

Socialism with Chinese characteristics in the new era is both a result and the continuation of the great social revolutions of the Chinese people led by the CPC. We must carry it forward. Both history and reality have shown to us that any social revolution requires

---

* Main points of the speech at the opening ceremony of a study session on Xi Jinping Thought on Socialism with Chinese Characteristics for a New Era and the guiding principles of the 19th CPC National Congress. Members and alternate members of the newly elected CPC Central Committee and principal officials at the provincial and ministerial level attended the session.

a long process to achieve the final victory. We can grasp the essence of many problems only by looking back over the path we have taken, comparing it with other paths, looking to the road ahead, and by understanding where we came from and where we are going.

Chinese socialism did not drop from the sky, but has stemmed from 40 years of reform and opening up and nearly 70 years of exploration since the founding of the PRC in 1949. It is the result of the Chinese people's experiences during 97 years of great social revolutions under the leadership of the CPC founded in 1921. It is the result of more than 170 years of historical progress since 1840 during which the Chinese nation has evolved from decline to prosperity. It is the bequest and development of the Chinese civilization in the past 5,000 years or more. It is a valuable result of the painstaking efforts made by our Party and the people at great cost. It is a hard-won achievement.

The success of scientific socialism in China is of great significance for Marxism, scientific socialism, and socialism across the world. The 19th CPC National Congress reached a major political conclusion that socialism with Chinese characteristics has entered a new era. We must realize that this era is one for socialism with Chinese characteristics, not for some other models. It is fundamental that the Party uphold Chinese socialism so as to realize its historic mission in the new era.

To remain true to our original aspiration and founding mission, we must never forget that we are Communists and revolutionaries and we must never lose our revolutionary spirit. The successes of yesterday do not guarantee future successes, and the glories of the past do not guarantee glories in the future. We are like examinees sitting the tests posed by this era, and the people will review our results. To achieve prosperity, enduring peace and stability of the Party and the country, all Party members should keep their revolutionary spirit and maintain the courage to carry forward the 97-year social revolution. We should neither get lost in the pride of victory, nor rest on achievements, nor retreat from difficulties. We should strive to make socialism with Chinese characteristics demonstrate more powerful and convincing truth.

Our Party must have the courage to carry out self-reform and become stronger in order to uphold and develop Chinese socialism in the new era. To have the courage to carry out self-reform and conduct strict self-governance is the most distinctive characteristic of our Party, and strict governance of the Party is a permanent feature. The great new project of strengthening our Party in the new era will play a decisive role in realizing our country's great cause and dream. In the new era, our Party must promote the social revolution it leads, and build itself into a vibrant Marxist ruling party that is always at the forefront of the times, enjoys the wholehearted support of the people, has the courage to reform itself, and is able to withstand all tests. This is not only an objective requirement for our Party to lead the people in advancing this social revolution, but also an innate need of our Party, which is a Marxist party, to strengthen and develop itself.

We must see that the arduous task of securing a decisive victory in building a moderately prosperous society in all respects and the historic mission of realizing the Chinese Dream of national rejuvenation have placed unprecedented challenges and new demands on our Party. The various factors that weaken the Party's progressive nature and integrity are very dangerous and destructive. This drives the need to push forward the great new project of strengthening the Party in the new era. Our Party should consolidate its foundations, innovate in a pioneering spirit, grasp key issues, and judge from the overall situation, especially in a spirit of thorough self-reform.

One can draw lessons from history by studying failures and successes of the past. In times of success, it is not easy to guard against potential dangers and maintain the hard-working and motivated spirit our Party had in the early days of the PRC, or to remain modest and frugal and stay true to our original aspiration after coming into power. Neither is it easy to exercise strict discipline on officials and prevent and fight corruption in times of peace, nor to follow the tide of the times and respond to the wishes of the people at junctures of significant change. To remain as the vanguard and the backbone of the nation, and a Marxist ruling party, our Party must always hold itself to the highest standards.

To strengthen the Party, we must focus on key senior officials.

CPC Central Committee members and principal officials at the provincial and ministerial level must be true believers of the ideals of communism and socialism with Chinese characteristics. At the same time, they should also be faithful practitioners of these ideals.

They must be politically upright and embrace the Four Consciousnesses[1]. These require that they must adhere to correct political stance, direction, path, and principles; they must uphold the authority of the Party's central leadership, follow its political guideline, and strictly observe its political discipline and rules.

They must develop a stronger sense of responsibility, adopt a correct view of their achievements, seek truth, and be down to earth. They should work tenaciously to be truly responsible to history and the people.

They must be highly competent, continue to acquire new knowledge, understand new fields, open up new horizons, and improve capabilities in leadership and governance in all respects.

They must be strictly disciplined in conduct, bear the people in mind, and make fact-finding trips and profound analysis. In this way they will enhance their political caliber and work competence while serving the people wholeheartedly; they must expand their vision, enrich their work experience, and better combine theory with practice while learning sincerely from the people; they should conduct self-questioning, self-criticism, and self-education while listening to the voice of the people and accepting public scrutiny. That is to say, they should improve themselves while serving the people, and continuously oppose the practice of favoring form over substance, bureaucratism, hedonism, and extravagance.

Officials must practice the Three Guidelines for Ethical Behavior and Three Basic Rules of Conduct at work, as well as in their daily life. Furthermore, they should turn the practice into a habit. They should enhance morality and self-cultivation, take the lead in promoting the core socialist values, discern between right and wrong and between good and evil, develop healthy pursuits, and keep up with the high standards of clean governance and self-discipline, so that they are prudent in mind and deed and observe rules and principles. All officials should first preserve moral integrity, being self-disciplined on small matters and resolutely opposing ideas and actions born of privilege, so that they will develop a habit of working and living under supervision and restraint, and become strictly disciplined in their conduct.

"Prepare in advance against the unexpected, which is a basic principle of governing a country."[2] At present, China is in a period of promising historic opportunities. The overall prospects for development are good, but the road ahead will not be smooth. The more our country achieves, the more prudent and prepared we should be, as though walking on thin ice, in order to avoid making strategic or fatal mistakes. In the face of a confusing and changing international landscape, a complex and sensitive neighboring environment, and the formidable tasks of reform, development and maintaining stability at home, we must take the precaution of guarding against risks, while adopting effective measures to address and resolve them when they arise. We must be fully prepared and make proactive strategic moves to convert danger into safety and adversity into opportunity. We will continue the great historic struggle with many new features, prepare to overcome all difficulties and obstacles, and march forward towards the great goals set by our Party.

Notes

[1] This refers to maintaining political commitment, thinking in terms of the general picture, following the core leadership of the CPC Central Committee, and acting in accordance with its requirements.

[2] Wu Jing: *Governance of the Zhenguan Period* (*Zhen Guan Zheng Yao*). Wu Jing (670-749) was a historian and official of the Tang Dynasty.

Broader Dimensions for Marxism in Contemporary China and the 21st Century*

May 4, 2018

The CPC is a political party armed with Marxism; Marxism is the soul of the ideals and convictions of Chinese Communists. In 1938, Mao Zedong noted that "our Party's fighting capacity will be much greater ... if we have one or two hundred comrades with a grasp of Marxism-Leninism which is systematic and not fragmentary, genuine and not hollow."[1]

The history of our Party shows that there is a reason for its ability to grow stronger despite all difficulties – it has always provided strong philosophical and theoretical training for its members and officials, so as to have a shared faith, a strong will, coordinated action, and great strength.

At present, the formidable tasks of reform, development and stability, the quantity and degree of problems, risks, and challenges, and the tests for governance of the country are all unprecedented. To win the competitive edge, seize the initiative, and secure our future, we must keep improving our ability to apply Marxism to analyze and resolve practical problems and our ability to utilize scientific theories to guide us in addressing major challenges, withstanding major risks, overcoming major obstacles, and resolving major problems. In this way, we can reflect on and deal with a range of major issues facing China's future development from a broader and longer-term perspective, and strengthen belief in Marxism and the ideals of communism.

It has been 170 years since the publication of *Manifesto of the*

---

* Part of the speech at the ceremony commemorating the bicentenary of the birth of Karl Marx.

Communist Party, during which time earthshaking changes have occurred in human society. However, on the whole, the general principles which Marxism sets forth are still entirely valid. We need to uphold and apply the worldviews and methodologies of dialectical and historical materialism. We need to uphold and apply the Marxist stance, viewpoint and methodology. We need to uphold and apply Marxist views on the materiality of the world and the law governing its development, the natural and historic significance of social development and related laws, human emancipation, the full and free development of every individual, and the essence of knowledge and its development. In this light, we need to uphold and apply Marxist views on practice, the people, class, development, and contradictions, and truly master and apply well these key skills.

All our Party members, especially officials at all levels, must study harder Marxism-Leninism, Mao Zedong Thought, Deng Xiaoping Theory, the Theory of Three Represents, the Scientific Outlook on Development, and the Thought on Socialism with Chinese Characteristics for a New Era. We must study these in a thorough, painstaking, and assiduous way, and apply them to problems and reality, so as to better transform such ideas and theories into a material force for understanding and changing the world. We Communists must take reading Marxist classics and understanding Marxist principles as a way of life and an intellectual pursuit, and apply the classics to foster our integrity, temper our way of thinking, broaden our horizon, and guide our practice.

A rational approach is needed to study theories. Engels once pointed out, "Marx's whole way of thinking [Auffassungsweise] is not so much a doctrine as a method. It provides, not so much ready-made dogmas, as aids to further investigation and the method *for* such investigation."[2] He also noted that theories are "a historical product, which at different times assumes very different forms and, therewith, very different contents."[3] The basic principles of scientific socialism cannot be discarded; once discarded it would cease to be socialism. Likewise, scientific socialism is not a fixed dogma. I once said that the sweeping social changes that China is undergoing are not simply the extension of China's historical and cultural experiences, the repetition of socialist practices of other countries, or the duplication of modernization endeavors elsewhere, nor can they be readily slotted into the template devised by earlier writers of Marxist classics. There is no orthodox, fixed version of socialism. A blueprint will become a bright reality only when we combine the basic principles of scientific socialism with China's realities, historical and cultural traditions, and contemporary needs, and constantly analyze and summarize the lessons gained from our practice.

The lifeline of a theory lies in innovation, and it is a sacred duty of Chinese Communists to develop Marxism. We need to use Marxism to observe and decipher the world today and lead us through it, and develop it in dynamic and abundant practice in contemporary China. We should learn from all the achievements of human civilization with an extensive view. To outdo ourselves we need to protect our foundations while innovating, and learn widely from the strengths of others to improve ourselves. Finally, we need to have a deeper understanding of governance by a communist party, the development of socialism, and the evolution of human society, and open up new prospects for the development of Marxism in contemporary China and the 21st century.

Notes

[1] Mao Zedong: "The Role of the Chinese Communist Party in the National War", *Selected Works of Mao Zedong*, Vol. II, Eng. ed., Foreign Languages Press, Beijing, 1965, p. 209.

[2] Frederick Engels: "To Werner Sombart", *Karl Marx & Frederick Engels: Collected Works*, Vol. 50, Eng. ed., Progress Publishers, Moscow, 1979, p. 461.

[3] Frederick Engels: "Dialectics of Nature", *Karl Marx & Frederick Engels: Collected Works*, Vol. 25, Eng. ed., Progress Publishers, Moscow, 1979, p. 338.

Focus on Our Tasks – Bear in Mind the National Goal and Changing Conditions*

May 21, 2019

I have often said that leading officials should have two factors in mind: One is the strategic goal of achieving national rejuvenation, the other is the world experiencing a level of change unseen in a century. This is the prerequisite to planning our work.

China is still in an important period of strategic opportunities, but the international situation is becoming increasingly complex. We must be clearly aware of the long-term and complicated factors both at home and abroad that will hinder our development, and thus be well prepared for various difficulties. Properly completing our own tasks is the most important thing. We should conduct in-depth research and prepare coordinated plans before pressing forward with reform, development and social stability in a balanced manner, and be fully prepared and more proactive to accomplish our tasks.

---

* Part of the speech at the Seminar on Promoting the Rise of Central China.

Speech at the Celebration of the 70th Anniversary of the Founding of the PRC

October 1, 2019

Compatriots,

Comrades and friends,

We are gathered here today for a grand rally to celebrate the 70th anniversary of the founding of the People's Republic of China. For the Chinese people of all ethnic groups and Chinese sons and daughters at home and abroad, this is a joyful moment. We take pride in and give our best wishes to our great motherland.

Here on behalf of the CPC Central Committee, the National People's Congress (NPC), the State Council, the Chinese People's Political Consultative Conference (CPPCC) and the Central Military Commission, I pay the highest tribute to all revolutionary forefathers and martyrs for their feats in pursuing national independence and liberation of the people, and in creating a prosperous and strong country, and a better life for the people. I extend warm congratulations to the Chinese people of all ethnic groups and all fellow Chinese at home and abroad, and express heartfelt gratitude to friends around the world for their support to China.

Seventy years ago on this day, Mao Zedong solemnly declared here to the world that the People's Republic of China was founded and the Chinese people had stood up. This great event put an end to China's misery born of poverty, weakness, oppression and humiliation over more than 100 years since the advent of modern times. The Chinese nation has since embarked on the path of realizing its great rejuvenation.

Over the past seven decades, through concerted efforts and

arduous struggle, the Chinese people's great achievements have amazed the world. Today, a socialist China is standing firm in the East. No force can ever undermine our great motherland's status, or stop the Chinese people and the Chinese nation from marching forward.

Comrades and friends,

On our journey forward, we must uphold the CPC's leadership, ensure that the people are the masters of the country, stay on the path of socialism with Chinese characteristics, and fully implement the Party's underlying theories, basic guidelines, and fundamental principles. We must strive to constantly meet the people's desire for a better life and reach new and historic heights.

On our journey forward, we must uphold the principles of peaceful reunification and "one country, two systems", maintain lasting prosperity and stability in Hong Kong and Macao, promote the peaceful development of cross-Straits relations, unite all Chinese sons and daughters, and continue to strive for complete reunification of the motherland.

On our journey forward, we will stay on the path of peaceful development and pursue a mutually beneficial strategy of opening up. We will continue to work with people from all countries to jointly build a global community of shared future.

The Chinese People's Liberation Army and the People's Armed Police Force should forever preserve their nature, purpose and character as the forces of the people, resolutely safeguard the country's sovereignty, security and development interests, and firmly uphold world peace.

Comrades and friends,

China's past made its mark on human history; China's present is being created by the hands of hundreds of millions of Chinese people; China's future will be even brighter. All members of the Party, the armed forces and the people of all ethnic groups should unite closer, stay true to our original aspiration and founding mission, and continue to consolidate and develop our People's

Republic. We should continue to enhance our efforts to achieve the Two Centenary Goals and to realize the Chinese Dream of national rejuvenation.

Long live the great People's Republic of China!
Long live the great Communist Party of China!
Long live the great Chinese people!

Overall CPC Leadership

Strengthen Commitment to the Four Consciousnesses, the Four-Sphere Confidence, and the Two Upholds*

October 25, 2017-May 31, 2019

I

Political leadership is crucial to the CPC Central Committee's authority and its centralized, unified leadership. When we assess the caliber and capabilities of Party members and officials, especially those in high positions, we will judge in the first place whether they are politically resolute and reliable. A purposeful and trustworthy official must have the Four Consciousnesses, keep in line with the Central Committee in thinking, action and political orientation, uphold the authority of the Central Committee and its centralized, unified leadership, resolutely implement the Central Committee's decisions and plans in all their work, and not engage in political maneuverings.

Every member of the Central Committee must take a clear political stance. They must apply strict requirements to themselves as a Marxist statesman, adopt an appropriate political perspective, enhance political awareness, and undertake political responsibilities. They need to improve their political abilities, particularly the ability to set the direction, to grasp the general trend, to manage the overall situation, to maintain their political resolve, to cope with political issues, and to prevent political risks.

---

* Excerpts from speeches made between October 25, 2017 and May 31, 2019.

When planning future developments, formulating policies and measures, training officials, or implementing plans, we must aim to strengthen our Party's status as the ruling party in order to further the cause of the Party and the people. We must abide by political discipline and rules, fully observe the regulations on intra-Party political activities, ensure the implementation of the Central Committee's policies and decisions, make sure local interests submit to overall interests, and guarantee the right political orientation in all our work.

(from the speech at the First Plenary Session of the 19th CPC Central Committee, October 25, 2017)

II

Upholding the CPC Central Committee's authority and its centralized, unified leadership is the prerequisite for bolstering overall Party leadership. Full and strict implementation of the Central Committee's decisions within the Party is crucial to the future of our Party and the country, and to the fundamental interests of all the people of China. Members of the Political Bureau must be clearly aware of this.

The report to the 19th CPC National Congress incorporates a focus on reinforcing the Party's political foundations into the general requirements for strengthening our Party for the new era, and makes it our primary task in promoting political progress to ensure that the whole Party defers to the Central Committee and upholds its authority and centralized, unified leadership. This stems from the wealth of experience we have accumulated through the process of revolution, economic development and reform, and is one of the founding principles of a mature Marxist ruling party. Members of the Political Bureau must take this principle as an essential political norm and a fundamental political requirement, endorse it in our thinking, safeguard it in our political philosophy, comply with it in organizational arrangements, and follow it in our actions. We must remain highly consistent with the Central Committee in political stance, orientation, principles and path, and uphold its authority. This is a test of our Party spirit; it is our Party's most fundamental political discipline and rule.

(from the speech at a meeting of criticism and self-criticism among members of the Political Bureau of the 19th CPC Central Committee, December 25-26, 2017)

III

It is a primary requirement to uphold CPC leadership. We must be clear and steadfast in this stance, rather than being hesitant, vague, evasive, or diffident. To uphold Party leadership, the most fundamental thing is to safeguard the authority of the CPC Central Committee and its centralized, unified leadership. In the Four Principles of Deference[1] provided in the Party Constitution, what is most essential is that all organizations and members of the Party defer to the National Congress and the Central Committee. Among the Four Consciousnesses underlined by the Central Committee, upholding the authority of the Central Committee and its centralized, unified leadership is pivotal. None of these are empty slogans.

Our officials should not simply express their compliance verbally, but must put it into action. The Central Committee requires that officials at all levels, high-ranking ones in particular, take a clear-cut political stance and stay loyal to the Party. This means they must conscientiously consider and plan their work in accordance with the Central Committee's overall plans, respond promptly to its calls, fully implement its decisions, and put a stop to anything it prohibits. The implementation of the Central Committee's decisions and plans should be unconditional. There should be no unauthorized alterations or any attempt to "negotiate the terms".

(from the speech at the Second Plenary Session of the 19th CPC Central Commission for Discipline Inspection, January 11, 2018)

IV

The Party exercises overall leadership over all endeavors across the country. The primary requirement in adhering to Party leadership is to uphold the CPC Central Committee's authority and centralized, unified leadership. This is the paramount principle in maintaining Party leadership, and we must never equivocate or waver at any time and in any situation. We require the whole Party to hold in the highest regard the Party Constitution, and improve the Four Consciousnesses. We must improve the institutions and mechanisms for upholding Party leadership, and strengthen the Party's ability and resolve to chart the course, craft overall plans, design policies, and promote reform. Resolute efforts should be made to prevent any weakening of CPC leadership and any failure to strengthen the Party in any locality or local authority, and ensure that the whole Party maintains a high degree of unity with the Central Committee in thinking, action and political orientation.

(from the speech at the CPC's National Conference on Organizational Work, July 3, 2018)

V

Our Party was established in line with the Marxist principle of creating a political party, with a complete setup consisting of the central, local and grassroots units. This gives us a great strength that no other political party in the world possesses. The Central Committee, like the brain and main part of a body, must be the sole authority that makes the final decisions, so that it can control the subordinate parts just as "the body employs the arms and the arms employ the fingers without any difficulty, then the country runs as a whole"[2].

The fundamental task of local Party organizations is to ensure the full and strict implementation of the Central Committee's decisions and plans, and to act or cease to act as ordered by the Party. CPC leadership groups have a special position in the Party's structure. They must carry out the decisions and plans of the Central Committee and higher Party organizations, and do everything required in setting the direction, managing the overall situation, and guaranteeing implementation.

All Party members, especially those in official positions, must strengthen their Party identity and their commitment to the Party. They must keep in line with the Party in thinking, follow its political orientation, defer to its orders in their work, and uphold the Party from the heart.

(from the speech at the CPC's National Conference on Organizational Work, July 3, 2018)

VI

The Four Consciousnesses, the Four-sphere Confidence[3], and the Two Upholds[4] are not abstract but concrete requirements. Officials, particularly high-ranking ones, should examine, make demands of, and review themselves, checking if their deeds accord with their thoughts. They must firmly and fully implement the decisions and plans of the Central Committee. They must strictly observe political discipline, and have a clear-cut and staunch stance on major matters of principle. They should be selfless and properly maintain the Central Committee's authority. They must say no to misconduct such as interference for personal gain by central leaders' family members, relatives, immediate staff, and close associates, and reject importuning by any person who claims a special relationship with central leaders.

(from the speech at the Third Plenary Session of the 19th CPC Central Commission for Discipline Inspection, January 11, 2019)

VII

We should quicken our pace in making our Party more of a learning-oriented Marxist party, and nurturing a love of learning in our people, with studying and putting into practice the Thought on Socialism with Chinese Characteristics for a New Era as the top priority. In this process, we should combine theory with reality, comprehend the fundamentals, seek truth, and understand the reasons and logic behind things. Strengthening their commitment to the Four Consciousnesses, the Four-sphere Confidence, and the Two Upholds, all Party members and officials should improve themselves against the standards of being loyal, upright and responsible, foster a pioneering spirit, and increase their abilities, so that in terms of thinking, ability and action they can keep abreast of the times, our cause, and the requirements of the Central Committee.

(from the preface to the reading materials for the fifth group of trainee officials, written on February 27, 2019)

VIII

This education campaign calls for strengthening our Party with sound political philosophy and theories, integrating our learning, thinking and practice, and seeking unity between what we know, what we believe in, and how we behave. Party members and officials are encouraged to study in a systematic way, to reflect on what they have learned, and to connect knowledge with reality. It is crucial for them to enhance the Four Consciousnesses, reinforce the Four-sphere Confidence, and ensure the Two Upholds. We should also try to guide them to strengthen their beliefs, reinforce the marrow of their faith, and maintain the correct way of thinking.

(from the speech at the Conference on the Aspiration and Mission Education Campaign, May 31, 2019)

Notes

[1] This means that individual Party members defer to Party organizations, the minority defers to the majority, lower-level Party organizations defer to higher-level

Party organizations, and all organizations and members of the Party defer to the National Congress and the Central Committee of the Party.

² Lü Zhong: *Records of Major Events of the Dynasty* (*Lei Bian Huang Chao Da Shi Ji Jiang Yi*). Lü Zhong (dates unknown) was a scholar of the Southern Song Dynasty (1127-1279).

³ This refers to confidence in the path, theory, system and culture of socialism with Chinese characteristics.

⁴ This refers to upholding General Secretary Xi Jinping's core position on the CPC Central Committee and in the Party as a whole, and upholding the Central Committee's authority and its centralized, unified leadership.

Maximize the Institutional Strength of CPC Leadership*

February 26, 2018

Strengthening overall leadership by the Party is an important principle that we must adhere to when furthering reform of Party and state institutions. Leadership by the Party is the defining feature of socialism with Chinese characteristics. It represents the common will and fundamental interests of the entire Party and all the Chinese people, and is the fundamental guarantee for a decisive victory in building a moderately prosperous society in all respects and the great success of socialism with Chinese characteristics for a new era. Governing a large country with more than 1.3 billion people, the Party must improve its leadership systems and mechanisms, give full play to the great strength of leadership by the Party, and shoulder the major responsibilities of carrying out our great struggle, developing our great project, advancing our great cause, and realizing our great dream. Only in this way can we ensure national reunification, uniform laws and policies and consistent market management, achieve economic development, clean political administration, cultural prosperity, social justice and healthy ecosystems, and smoothly advance the causes of Chinese socialism in the new era.

In China's political arena, the CPC exercises leadership. Strengthening the centralized, unified leadership of the Party operates in tandem with supporting a range of bodies in performing their functions and playing their roles: the people's congresses, governments,

---

* Part of the "Note to the Draft Decision and Draft Program on Further Reform of Party and State Institutions" delivered at the Third Plenary Session of the 19th CPC Central Committee.

the Chinese People's Political Consultative Conference (CPPCC), supervisory departments, courts, prosecuting agencies, people's organizations, enterprises, public institutions and social organizations. The draft decision focuses on adapting to the requirements for developing Chinese socialism in the new era and establishing a functional system of Party and state institutions that upholds Party leadership in all respects and reflects the fundamental interests of the people. It aims to bring into full play the great strength of Party leadership at the institutional level, adopt a comprehensive approach to the setup of Party and government institutions, coordinate and give play to the functions and roles of various institutions, improve the systems and mechanisms for sound leadership, decision-making, and effective management and enforcement, and ensure the long-term governance of the Party and the lasting stability of the country.

Strengthening leadership by the Party in all respects is entirely consistent with our people-centered philosophy. The purpose of further reform of Party and state institutions is to better develop the causes of the Party and the state, meet the expectation of the people for a better life, and promote the well-rounded personal development, comprehensive social progress, and common prosperity of the people. We must ensure the principal status of the people, and adhere to the Party's commitment to serving the public good and exercising power in the interests of the people. We must implement the Party's principle of the mass line, improve the system through which the people are the masters of the country, and improve the systems and mechanisms for bringing benefits to the people, serving them, addressing their concerns, protecting their rights and interests, and accepting their supervision, so as to provide a stronger guarantee for the people to manage both state affairs and social, economic and cultural affairs.

Initiative and Resolve in Reinforcing the Party's Political Foundations*

June 29, 2018

Today we gather here for the sixth group study session of the Political Bureau of the 19th CPC Central Committee. The subject of this session is reinforcing our Party's political foundations. This critical issue was raised at the 19th National Congress in 2017, which underlined that the issue is of fundamental importance to our Party, deserves top priority, and should be the overarching principle for strengthening the Party. The goal of our study at today's session is to further understand this subject and consequently adopt a more purposeful and resolute approach.

There is profound thinking behind raising the issue of reinforcing the Party's political foundations at our 19th National Congress. Every political party has its political nature, mission, and goals. A Marxist party has lofty political ideals, and pursues noble goals. Its political character is wholesome, and its discipline is strict. If it is no longer politically wholesome, there is no way it can retain its progressive nature and integrity. This is why reinforcing its political foundations is of fundamental importance to our Party.

With more than 89 million members and 4.5 million grassroots organizations, it is not easy for our Party to preserve and develop its nature as a Marxist political party. A broad-brush approach or a few targeted campaigns are not the solution. Reinforcing our Party's political foundations is a mission without end that must never in any way be neglected. At the Gutian Meeting[1] in 1929 Mao Zedong put forward

---

* Speech at the sixth group study session of the Political Bureau of the 19th CPC Central Committee.

the principle of strengthening the Party and army with a sound political philosophy. The Seventh CPC National Congress in 1945 declared its intention to focus on strengthening the Party's ideological commitment and reinforcing its political foundations while strengthening its organization. After the People's Republic of China was founded in 1949, Mao Zedong observed that "political work is the lifeline of all economic endeavors"[2]. After reform and opening up started in 1978, Deng Xiaoping emphasized, "We have to lay great stress on politics at all times."[3] All this served to indicate that reinforcing the Party's political foundations is an important guarantee that our Party will go from strength to strength and from victory to victory.

In the course of strengthening our Party's self-governance since the 18th CPC National Congress in 2012, we have clearly realized that many of our problems are related to political issues and attributable to a slack political approach. "If the root cause of a problem is addressed, there will be immediate change for the better; if only trivial matters are addressed, the problem will stay forever."[4] If we do not perceive and deal with a problem from the political perspective, we will put ourselves in the position of juggling with stopgap measures, and fail to produce a fundamental solution. This is why I have reiterated that strict governance over the Party must start with political effort, and that political issues need political solutions.

Giving prominence to reinforcing our Party's political foundations, we have achieved significant results in the following respects: reinforcing our political belief, strengthening the Four Consciousnesses, upholding the authority of the Central Committee and its centralized, unified leadership, enforcing strict political discipline and rules, enhancing and regulating intra-Party political activities in the new era, cleaning up the political environment within our Party, improving Party conduct, fighting corruption, and punishing wrongdoing. Experience has taught us that reinforcing the Party's political foundations determines the direction and effect of strengthening the Party. If we neglect them or stray from that direction, it will be hard to achieve the anticipated results in other areas.

We must be aware that despite our achievements since the 18th CPC National Congress, the political issues existing within the Party have not been fully solved. It remains a conspicuous problem that some colleagues overlook or downplay political matters. Some are weak in the Four Consciousnesses. Some pay only lip service to upholding Party leadership. Some show no political acuity and discernment, or lack the will to respond to erroneous words and deeds. Some are a law unto themselves and ignore our Party's political discipline and rules, and others run things according to unspoken rules or act as if doing business deals in the Party. Reinforcing the Party's political foundations is a long and arduous task that demands our perseverance.

To this end, the 19th CPC National Congress set out specific requirements, and I have elaborated on them several times. We must implement them to the full. Here, I would like to emphasize the following points:

First, adhering to the correct political direction. Political direction is an issue of paramount importance to our Party's existence and development, and determines its future and the prospects of its cause. When the Red Army was crossing the marshes during the Long March, the very first question that concerned the cook in the morning was not whether there was rice to cook. Instead, he would ask whether the army was heading south or north. This shows that even a cook understood that where to go was more important than what to eat. Straying from the right path will cause fatal mistakes. We must have a clear understanding on this matter.

The political direction we must follow is the noble ideal of communism, our ideal of socialism with Chinese characteristics, the Two Centenary Goals, and the Party's underlying theories, basic guidelines, and fundamental principles. For the Party to make political progress, we need to do three things:

One, we need to make political commitment the compass for our work, guide all Party members to hold to our Party's ideals and convictions, and have full confidence in the path, theory, system and culture of Chinese socialism, clarify any confusion and ambiguity, remove all obstacles, and concentrate the wisdom and strength of the whole Party on the task of upholding and developing Chinese socialism in the new era.

Two, we must urge the whole Party to follow the correct political direction in devising major strategies, formulating major policies, advancing major plans, and implementing major tasks. We must conduct regular self-examination against our goals and standards in order to make prompt adjustments and improvements, and rectify practices that deviate from or run counter to our Party's political direction. We can thereby ensure that all undertakings of the Party and the state will always proceed in the correct political direction.

Three, we must build Party organizations at all levels in such a way so as to firmly safeguard the correct political direction, and guide all Party members and officials accordingly. Those who err on this issue must be reprimanded, and those guilty of serious misconduct must be punished in accordance with Party discipline.

Second, upholding the Party's political leadership. The leadership of the CPC is the defining feature of Chinese socialism and the greatest strength of this system. Our Party is the highest force for political leadership. Without our Party's leadership, national rejuvenation would be unattainable. Having been put into this position by historical developments and our people, our Party must shoulder its political responsibilities by exercising effective political leadership.

Through the painstaking efforts we have made since the 18th CPC National Congress, an awareness of upholding overall Party leadership has clearly grown among all Party members. Nevertheless, we still face the fact that some localities and entities fail to translate this awareness into actions in their work. We need to establish sound organizational frameworks, systems, and mechanisms for strengthening overall Party leadership in all realms and respects, including reform, development, social stability, domestic affairs, foreign relations, national defense, and governance of the Party, the state, and the military.

Upholding the authority of the Central Committee and its

centralized, unified leadership is of utmost importance to the Party's political leadership, and is the primary task in reinforcing the Party's political foundations. We need to guide all Party members to enhance the Four Consciousnesses, maintain a high degree of unity with the Central Committee in their thinking, actions and political stance, and ensure that the Central Committee is the sole authority and has the final say. High-ranking officials, especially members of the Political Bureau, should lead by example – acting in line with the overall interests of the Party and country when performing their duties.

Third, consolidating the political foundation. The support of the people is the unfailing source of our Party's strength. In the past, "Workers and peasants are wakened in their millions to fight as one man"[5], creating an indomitable force that enabled us to win the revolution by relying on the people. Today, our Party makes its goal the people's desire for a better life, creating a mighty force that will enable us to realize the Chinese Dream.

"The people are the foundation of a country, and are also what the rule of a country is for."[6] To reinforce the Party's political foundations, we must make the support of the people our top priority, and focus on winning the people's hearts and pooling their wisdom and strength. We must stand on the people's side, implement our Party's principle of the mass line, concern ourselves with the people's needs, and work together with them. Moreover, we must resolutely oppose the Four Malfeasances of favoring form over substance, bureaucratism, hedonism, and extravagance – particularly the first two – and always maintain our Party's deep bond with the people. Public support, approval and satisfaction depend not only on what we say but on what we do. Only hard work can make our country prosperous and strong and our people better off. Complacency, laxity, muddling through in one's work, considering self-interests first in the face of difficulties, and making half-hearted efforts are all incompatible with the needs of the people and the demands of the new era.

We need to train and motivate all Party members and officials to press ahead with great determination, work hard, maintain stable growth, advance reform, adjust the economic structure, improve living standards, guard against risks, address intractable problems, overcome formidable obstacles, and solve the most pressing, most immediate issues that concern the people the most. We must give encouragement and support to officials who perform their duties, do solid work, and are bold in shouldering responsibilities. We must reprimand and hold accountable those who are negligent in their work, never follow words with deeds, or cavil at, undermine, and even frame false charges against those who get things done. This is how we will foster an atmosphere in the Party of taking pride in performing one's duties and feeling ashamed of inaction and lack of drive.

Fourth, fostering a healthy political environment. With a sound political atmosphere, a political party will be imbued with a sense of integrity; without it, it will be infested with noxious influences. For a certain period prior to the 18th CPC National Congress, the political atmosphere in some localities and entities deteriorated seriously. As a result, their cohesion was undermined, public ethics were poisoned, and the people's faith in our Party was severely eroded. Since the 18th CPC National Congress the political atmosphere within the Party has seen a marked improvement, which we can feel personally. But we must be aware that there are problems yet to be eradicated. Sometimes intra-Party political activities are conducted in a perfunctory, superficial, ineffective, or inappropriate way. This deserves our full attention.

Fostering a healthy political environment is a long-term task that must be made a basic and regular activity in reinforcing our Party's political foundations. Like tending the natural environment by clearing up the sources of waterways and cultivating forests, we need to make long, tenacious efforts to foster political integrity and build a strong foundation. The selection and appointment of officials is the weathervane of the political environment, and has direct bearing on it. In selecting and appointing officials, we must adopt the right approach, with emphasis on political performance.

Party members and officials must act in accordance with the Regulations for Political Activities Within the Party in the New Era, and have regular political "health checks" through intra-Party activities. We can thereby "sweep off the dust", keep our souls wholesome, and boost our immune system in the political realm. Intra-Party political culture exerts an imperceptible influence on our Party's political atmosphere. We need to intensify our efforts to cultivate a healthy political culture within the Party, and foster the ideals, convictions, values, and fine traditions of the Party in the hearts and minds of all Party members and officials. We also should promote the core socialist values, and advocate and practice values such as loyalty, honesty, impartiality, pragmatism, and integrity. By virtue of a healthy political culture, we will maintain a wholesome political atmosphere.

Fifth, guarding against political risks. "Be alert to danger in times of peace, and be wary of unrest in times of stability."[7] Our Party was born amid domestic turmoil and foreign aggression, grew up through hardships and setbacks, and has become stronger in the course of overcoming risks and challenges. It therefore has an acute sense of dangers and risks. Since the 18th CPC National Congress I have emphasized on many occasions that we must make preparations for worst-case scenarios. My purpose is to warn all Party members that we must always bear in mind the ancient adage, "One should be mindful of possible danger in times of peace, downfall in times of survival, and chaos in times of stability."[8] China is currently facing a complex and volatile environment, and is exposed to a growing number of threats, both foreseeable and unforeseeable, which could evolve into political threats if not managed promptly and effectively. All Party members, especially those in official positions at all levels, must be highly sensitive to these and improve their ability to guard against them.

We need to train and guide officials to enhance their political acuity and discernment, have a keen eye for sensitive matters and tendencies that may trigger off political issues – especially serious emergencies – whenever they emerge, and take preemptive and swift action to remove all potential political dangers. Close attention should be paid and prompt action taken to intercept transmission of risks between different sectors. The goal is to ward off "cross-infection" – preventing non-public risks from growing into public ones and non-political risks from escalating into political ones. We need to build up our fighting spirit, take an unequivocal stance, and resolutely prevent and overcome political lethargy, which will render us unable to detect hostile moves, distinguish right from wrong, or see the correct direction.

Sixth, maintaining the political integrity of Communists. A significant number of the corruption cases investigated recently took place after the 18th and even the 19th national congresses of the Party. In spite of the repeated orders of the Central Committee, certain officials could not restrain themselves from wrongdoing. Instead they continued to commit offenses, tempting fate. This shows that the fight against corruption remains grave and complex. We must remain firm in our resolve to build on our overwhelming momentum and secure a sweeping victory in this fight. In reinforcing our Party's political foundations, we must have the determination and tenacity to persevere in the never-ending fight against corruption, so that our Party will never change its nature or betray its colors.

We must maintain a tough stance on corruption. Showing zero tolerance, the fight covers all those holding public office without exception. We will impose tight constraints, maintain a tough stance and a long-term deterrence, and punish both those who take bribes and those who offer them. We will prevent interest groups from arising within the Party, and guard against such groups preying on or perverting officials. All officials, especially those in senior positions, are expected to have political, public and private virtues, setting a good example in upholding integrity and self-discipline, exercising public power for clean government, and creating a culture of integrity in their families. We will establish a tight-knit scrutiny network, reinforce relevant institutions, and let discipline inspection cut like a blade through corruption and misconduct. As strict governance over the Party extends to the grassroots, we will ensure that upright officials, a clean government, and political integrity are visible and accessible to the people.

Seventh, improving our political ability. In strengthening the ranks of officials as part of our political foundations, we need to improve the ability of officials, especially those in senior positions, to stay on the right course, keep in line with the general trend, and bear the broader picture in mind. We should enhance our ability to distinguish between right and wrong on political issues, maintain our political resolve, navigate political currents, and forestall political risks. A key aspect of this is to hone the ability to analyze and resolve problems from a political perspective. Only by doing so can we comprehend the true nature of an issue and get to its root cause. Officials, especially those in senior positions, should have good political judgment. We should let no fleeting phenomena cloud our vision, and shoulder the political responsibilities entrusted to us by the Party and the people.

Notes

[1] This refers to the Ninth Party Congress of the Fourth Army of the Red Army, held in Gutian Village of Shanghang County, Fujian Province in December 1929. It was at this meeting that the principle of employing the CPC's political philosophy to cultivate the army was established.

[2] Mao Zedong: "Editorial Notes from *Socialist Upsurge in China's Countryside*", *Collected Works of Mao Zedong*, Vol. VI, Chin. ed., People's Publishing House, Beijing, 1999, p. 449.

[3] Deng Xiaoping: "Remarks During an Inspection Tour of Tianjin", *Selected Works of Deng Xiaoping*, Vol. III, Eng. ed., Foreign Languages Press, Beijing, 1994, p. 169.

[4] Su Shi: "Reasons for Vagrants in the Guanlong Area Counterfeiting Coins and Grain Transport Troops in Areas Between Yangtze and Huaihe Rivers Committing Robbery" (Guan Long You Min Si Zhu Qian Yu Jiang Huai Cao Zu Wei Dao Zhi You). Su Shi (1036-1101), also known as Su Dongpo, was a man of letters, painter and calligrapher of the Northern Song Dynasty.

[5] Mao Zedong: "Against the First 'Encirclement' Campaign", *Mao Zedong Poems*, Chin./Eng. ed., Foreign Languages Press, Beijing, 1999, p. 21.

[6] Zhu Xi: *Commentaries on the Four Books* (*Si Shu Zhang Ju Ji Zhu*). Zhu Xi (1130-1200) was a neo-Confucian philosopher of the Southern Song Dynasty.

[7] Wei Yuan: *Essays by Wei Yuan* (*Mo Gu*). Wei Yuan (1794-1857) was a thinker and writer of the Qing Dynasty.

[8] *Book of Changes* (*Yi Jing*).

Ensure the Two Upholds in Central Party and Government Departments*

July 9, 2019

The primary task of strengthening our Party in central Party and government departments is to lead by example in ensuring the Two Upholds. One of the important goals of the Aspiration and Mission education campaign is to cultivate the loyal, upright and responsible political character of Party members and officials, especially those in leadership positions, and to ensure that the whole Party is united in thought and concerted in action.

Central Party and government departments must be conscious of their role as political organs. Every institution performs different functions, but each of them has political responsibilities. Central Party and government departments are at the forefront of ensuring the Two Upholds. The slightest deviation from the theories, guidelines, principles and policies of our Party will lead to huge mistakes at the grassroots level. If the first baton of implementation is dropped, the race will be lost from the very beginning.

In doing their work, Party members and officials, especially officials and heads of central Party and government departments, should take the lead in upholding the Party's underlying theories, basic guidelines, and fundamental principles and the Central Committee's decisions and plans. They must adopt an appropriate political perspective, maintain the correct political orientation, strengthen their political stance, clarify their political values, and observe political discipline. They should regularly correct deviations, so as to respond with resolution

---

* Part of the speech at the National Conference on Strengthening the Party in Central Party and Government Departments.

to the calls of the Central Committee, fully implement its decisions, and refrain from doing what it prohibits. They must never go astray in their political direction.

The meaning of the Two Upholds is specific and consistent. The whole Party must act consistently with the Central Committee, and must not compromise democratic centralism within a specific institution in the name of upholding the authority of the Central Committee. Party members and officials, no matter what kind of work they do and how high their rank, are first and foremost Party members. They must bear in mind that their primary duty is to work for the Party, and they must align their major statements with those of the Central Committee. All important issues and progress relating to important initiatives must be promptly reported to the Central Committee for instruction in accordance with relevant provisions.

Political awareness is not abstract. The Two Upholds should be embodied in the implementation of the Central Committee's decisions and plans, in the performance of our duties, in the effectiveness of our work, and in our daily words and deeds. During the war times, the Central Committee and Chairman Mao commanded the whole Party and the entire army by radio transmission. The signals conveyed their instructions, which were carried out unconditionally in the Party and the army. If anyone had failed to listen to or properly execute the command, the Central Committee's authority and its centralized, unified leadership would have lost all meaning.

To take the lead in ensuring the Two Upholds is, in essence, to be loyal to the Party. This loyalty is to the beliefs, organizations, theories, guidelines, principles and policies of our Party. This loyalty must start with the most basic work. If we do not do our own job well, shirking our responsibilities, sitting idle all day, and neglecting the duties assigned by Party organizations, then ensuring the Two Upholds will be nothing but empty talk.

In the new era, we must strengthen education on loyalty to our Party, give full play to the strengths of central Party and government departments imbued with our Party's heritage, and reread our written applications for joining the Party and the Party admission oath, so as to foster an intra-Party political culture with characteristics unique to the central Party and government departments. We should encourage the emulation of model Party members as an important starting point for furthering the education campaign, which should be combined with the establishment of model Party and government departments, to encourage Party members and officials to look up to the role models and make progress. Those in leadership positions should incorporate loyalty to the Party into family culture and family value education, and encourage their family and relatives to follow the Party's leadership.

To take the lead in ensuring the Two Upholds, we should identify with the principle on both a rational and emotional level, and have both the ability and resolve to do this well. We must rely on study and practice to strengthen our political resolve and competence. I have always emphasized that the rejuvenation of the Chinese nation will be no easy task. It will not be achieved by simply beating drums and gongs. We cannot overcome all the risks and challenges we face on the way forward without a true fighting spirit. Chairman Mao summarized the key to our victory in resisting US aggression and aiding Korea: The enemies have more steel than morale, while we have less steel but higher morale. We Party members and officials of central Party and government departments should stay true to our principles, be prepared for adversity, maintain our fighting spirit, and be adept at foreseeing developing trends and detecting potential risks and challenges. In avoiding and resolving risks, we must have the courage to take on responsibility and fulfill our duties to the letter.

State System and National Governance

Improve the Functions of Party and State Institutions[*]

July 5, 2019

Further reform of Party and state institutions is a systematic and overall restructuring in terms of organization and management. We have promoted this overhaul at all levels and restructured and improved the systems of Party leadership, the government, the military, and people's organizations, systematically enhancing the leadership of our Party, the government's capacity to deliver, the combat effectiveness of armed forces, and the vitality of people's organizations. The main functional framework of Party and state institutions for the new era is by and large in place. It provides a strong organizational guarantee for developing and improving the socialist system with Chinese characteristics and for modernizing China's system and capacity for governance. We need to summarize the major achievements and valuable experience gained from reform, consolidate these achievements, continue to improve the functions of our Party and state institutions, and further modernize China's system and capacity for governance.

Further reform of Party and state institutions is an important means of implementing the decisions and plans of the 19th CPC National Congress in 2017. It is a major move to continue reform in all respects and a centralized action to modernize China's system and capacity for governance. After the Third Plenary Session of the 19th CPC Central Committee in 2018, all provincial authorities and central departments implemented the decisions and plans of the

---

[*] Main points of the speech at the meeting reviewing further reform of Party and state institutions.

Central Committee. They looked for ways to strengthen coordination, define reform rules and measures, handle personnel affairs well, and enforce strict discipline. In just over a year, the tasks defined at the Third Plenary Session were generally completed, and a series of important theoretical, institutional and practical results were achieved. We strengthened the Party's overall leadership and improved the institutions' functions in upholding the Party's centralized and unified leadership. Party and state institutions are performing their duties more smoothly and efficiently, and the composition and functions of all kinds of institutions are better adapted to implementing the Five-sphere Integrated Plan and the Four-pronged Comprehensive Strategy. The setup and functions of major departments at provincial, city, and county levels are basically consistent with those of the central authorities, enabling a dynamic work system that ensures smooth operations right down through every level. We have carried out reform tasks covering both military and civilian services. We have also simultaneously promoted reform in relevant institutions of all types to enhance the overall impact.

In furthering reform of Party and state institutions, we have explored and accumulated valuable experience. The approach is to uphold the Party's overall leadership over reform, establish new institutions before dissolving the old, optimize the functions of the institutions and improve their coordination and efficiency, carry out institutional reform both at the central and local levels under an overall plan, coordinate reform and the rule of law, and carry out education on political guidelines throughout the process. Practice has proven that the strategic decision of the Party Central Committee on further reform of Party and state institutions is completely correct, and the implementation of the reform has been effective. This fully demonstrates the high degree of political awareness in both thinking and action of the whole Party, the positive impact of strict enforcement of Party discipline since the 18th CPC National Congress in 2012, and the political strengths of the centralized and unified leadership of our Party and the socialist system of our country.

Organizational and functional restructuring has solved only "hardware" problems; there remains much to be done for components of the functional framework to achieve synergy. Upholding and strengthening overall Party leadership should be the guideline of the reform, with the focus on optimizing the functions of Party and state institutions and making them more coordinated and efficient. We need to combine the tasks of adjusting and optimizing the functions of these institutions with improving systems and mechanisms, and combine enhancing our Party's long-term governance capacity with improving our state governance capacity. We should continue to consolidate what we have achieved in this round of reform. We should improve the Party's leadership over major undertakings. Decision-making, deliberative and coordinating institutions should focus on planning, discussing, and oversight of major tasks. Party institutions should take the lead in upholding and strengthening Party leadership in all respects, better play their functions, and enforce strict political discipline and rules. We should work to better coordinate Party and state institutions in performing their functions and give full play to the functions of unified, centralized, and coordinated management of Party departments, especially management of major tasks under their respective jurisdiction. We should improve the capability of institutions in fulfilling their duties and responsibilities. All central departments should perform their duties and responsibilities in accordance with the plans that define their duties, internal bodies and staffing, focus on their main responsibilities, highlight the key tasks, think and act consciously in consideration of the overall situation, and perform their duties to meet the growing expectation of the people for a better life. We need to fully leverage the initiative of Party and state institutions at both central and local levels, and ensure the centralized and unified leadership of the Central Committee and the consistency of state systems and government policies. Central Party and government departments should guide and supervise their own systems and fields of responsibility. While implementing the decisions and plans of the Central Committee, local institutions should carry out their work with more initiative and more creativity in the light of local realities. We need to advance reform in related sectors. We should extend reform of public institutions in accordance with the principle of relieving them of government functions, keeping them away from business activities, and letting them run their own day-to-day operations while remaining under supervision. We should also build a strong contingent of coordinated law enforcement personnel, enhance social management and public services at the grassroots level, and improve supporting policies for reform of these institutions. We need to codify the staffing of institutions, manage all kinds of organizations and institutions in accordance with the law, and continue to strictly control their personnel expansion. We should enhance our capability to perform our duties, break new ground, and shoulder responsibilities, and understand the new requirements brought about by new institutions and functions. In line with the ongoing Aspiration and Mission education campaign, we need to educate and guide Party members and officials to keep in alignment with the Central Committee in terms of our thinking, political orientation, and actions, stand on the side of the people, and temper the political character of being loyal, clean and responsible. With a strong sense of urgency and a hardworking spirit, we must have the perseverance to hammer away until a task is done.

Further reform of Party and state institutions is planned and advanced on the sand table of comprehensive reform as one of its strategic campaigns. We should make good use of the favorable conditions created in the reform of Party and state institutions to promote comprehensive and in-depth reform. The results we have achieved from this round of reform will help break new ground in our further reform on all fronts. It is a demanding task for us to complete the comprehensive reform measures put forward at the Third Plenary Session of the 18th CPC Central Committee in 2013. Now there is only a little more than a year to go before 2020, when we have scheduled decisive results in the reform of important areas. We must maintain our momentum, keep fighting with all of our strength, take on tough issues, and concentrate our efforts on making breakthroughs in important areas.

While promoting further reform of Party and state institutions, we also need to improve the systems and mechanisms for Party leadership over reform, as well as decision-making and implementation mechanisms. We will strengthen the links between central and local authorities, between leading and participating departments, between main reform and supporting programs, between reform measures and legal guarantees, between pilots and rollouts, and between the implementation of reform tasks and the adjustment of institutional functions to forge a synergy. We should remain confident in our reform strategies and promote reform to better serve economic and social development. We should work out ideas on reform and development, solve outstanding problems, guard against risks and challenges, and stimulate the vitality of innovation. We need to correctly handle the relationship between reform, development, and social stability, and combine Party leadership with respect for the pioneering spirit of the people. We should make reform systematic, holistic and coordinated, and coordinate the progress of reform in various fields to achieve overall effect. We need to give greater substance to reform to ensure the quality of plans and the effectiveness of their implementation. Our situation, tasks, and work requirements are all changing, which requires us to accurately understand, effectively respond to, and take the initiative in seeking changes. We need to solve practical problems and take this as the starting point for making reform plans, and give priority to the implementation of reforms that have a bearing on overall economic and social development, involve major institutional innovation, and enhance people's sense of gain. We should facilitate the systematic integration of reform achievements, review and apply the results in a coordinated manner, and make various systems more mature and well-defined as a whole.

Note to the Decision of the CPC Central Committee on Upholding and Improving Chinese Socialist System and Modernizing State Governance*

October 28, 2019

On behalf of the Political Bureau of the CPC Central Committee, I will now explain to the plenary session the drafting process of the "Decision of the Central Committee of the Communist Party of China on Upholding and Improving the Socialist System with Chinese Characteristics and Modernizing the State System and Capacity for Governance".

I. Background and Considerations

We have just celebrated the 70th anniversary of the founding of the People's Republic of China. Our extraordinary achievements of the past seven decades have fully proved that socialism with Chinese characteristics is the fundamental guarantee for progress and development in contemporary China. From a long-term and overall perspective on the causes of the Party and the country, the Political Bureau has decided that this plenary session will focus on the topic of upholding and improving Chinese socialism and modernizing our system and capacity for governance. This is based on the following considerations:

First, upholding and improving Chinese socialism and modernizing our system and capacity for governance is key to achieving the Two Centenary Goals. Building a modern socialist country and realizing

---

* Speech at the Fourth Plenary Session of the 19th CPC Central Committee.

national rejuvenation are two great goals our Party has always pursued. Since its founding, our Party has led the people and made unremitting efforts towards these goals. As we drive reform and opening up to deeper levels, we have developed a better understanding of our systems.

In 1980, Deng Xiaoping summarized the lessons from the Cultural Revolution and pointed out that "the problems in the leadership and organizational systems are more fundamental, widespread and long-lasting, and that they have a greater effect on the overall interests of our country." "If these systems are sound, they can place restraints on the actions of bad people; if they are unsound, they may hamper the efforts of good people or indeed, in certain cases, may push them in the wrong direction."[1] In 1992, he said on a field trip to south China, "It will probably take another thirty years for us to develop a more mature and well-defined system in every field."[2] The report to the 14th CPC National Congress in 1992 envisaged: "In the 1990s we must establish a preliminary new economic system and attain the objective of the second stage of development – a relatively comfortable level of life for all our people. In another 20 years, when we mark the 100th anniversary of the founding of the Party, a whole set of more mature and better-defined systems will have taken shape in every field of work." The reports to the 15th, 16th and 17th national congresses of the Party all set out clear requirements for improving our systems.

Since its 18th National Congress in 2012, our Party has laid extra emphasis on improving our state systems, stating, "To build a moderately prosperous society in all respects, we must, with greater political courage and vision, lose no time in furthering reform in key sectors, and resolutely discard all notions and mechanisms that hinder efforts to pursue balanced and sustainable development. We should set up a well-developed, well-conceived, procedure-based and effective framework of systems, and ensure that all our systems are more mature and better-defined." The Third Plenary Session of the 18th CPC Central Committee in 2013 put forward the idea of "modernizing the state governance system and capacity", and defined the goals of comprehensive reform as "to improve and develop socialism with Chinese characteristics and to modernize the state governance system and capacity". The Fifth Plenary Session of the 18th CPC Central Committee in 2015 further stressed that, during the 13th Five-year Plan period (2016-2020), "systems in all areas are to become more mature and better-defined, and key progress is to be made in modernizing the state governance system and capacity, with basic systems established in all fields."

The 19th CPC National Congress in 2017 determined our primary goal by the middle of this century – to develop China into a great modern socialist country that is prosperous, strong, democratic, culturally advanced, harmonious, and beautiful, and the goals for enhancing our governance system and capacity – our systems in all fields are further improved and modernization of the state governance system and capacity is basically achieved by 2035, and modernization of our state governance system and capacity is fully realized by the middle of the 21st century. The second and third plenary sessions of the 19th CPC Central Committee in 2018 made plans for constitutional amendments and further reform of Party and government institutions, marking a major step forward in improving our governance system and capacity. The Third Plenary Session of the 19th CPC Central Committee pointed out: "To better lead the people in advancing the great struggle, the great project, and the great cause to realize our great dream, our Party must accelerate the modernization of the state governance system and capacity, and develop a more mature and better-defined system of socialism with Chinese characteristics. This is a key task of our Party." It is now imperative for us to summarize past experience on improving Chinese socialism and modernizing the state governance system and capacity, and set the direction and requirements for future development.

Second, upholding and improving Chinese socialism and modernizing the state governance system and capacity is fundamental to further reform and opening up in the new era. Forty years ago, the

Third Plenary Session of the 11th CPC Central Committee in 1978 was a landmark event that introduced the policy of reform and opening up and ushered in a new period of socialist modernization. The Third Plenary Session of the 18th CPC Central Committee was another milestone, initiating a new era in which reform has been extended through a systematic and holistic plan. The session rolled out 336 reform measures. With our efforts over the five years since then, reform in key areas has delivered striking results, and basic systems in major fields have taken shape, laying a solid foundation for modernizing our state governance system and capacity. However, we must also understand that some reform measures are yet to be completed, and some demand perseverance in the long run. Although many formidable obstacles have been surmounted, there are more to overcome. We must never pause or slacken our efforts. At the gathering to celebrate the 40th anniversary of reform and opening up last year, I emphasized, "We must advance reform and opening up in the right direction, on the right course, and with consistent force, so as to steadily promote reform and opening up in the new era." This requires us to make plans for further comprehensive reform, based on the overall needs in building a modern socialist country.

Reform and opening up in the new era has new content and new features, one of which is that reform attaches greater importance to the improvement of systems. Compared with the past, reform now aims to solve deep-seated problems of our systems and mechanisms, and this sets higher requirements for top-level design. It becomes more imperative to pursue reform in a systematic, holistic, and coordinated way, and to establish frameworks of systems and institutions. When we plan to further reform in the new era, we must focus on upholding and improving Chinese socialism and modernizing the state governance system and capacity, with a deep understanding of the requirements for further development and the trends of the times. To achieve this, we will continue to reform systems and mechanisms in all sectors and areas, and ensure that our systems become more mature and better-defined.

Third, upholding and improving Chinese socialism and modernizing the state governance system and capacity will guarantee that we can seize the initiative in addressing risks and challenges. "If a dynasty cannot continue to rise, it will fall; if a country cannot improve its governance, the state of order will deteriorate."[3] The world today is undergoing a scale of change unseen in a century, and the international situation is becoming increasingly variable and complex. We are confronted with formidable tasks in reform, development, social stability, domestic and foreign affairs, national defense, and the governance of the Party, the country and the military. We are facing greater risks and challenges than ever before. Some risks and challenges are domestic, some are external; some relate to the economy and society, some come from Mother Nature. In order to resolve them, we must uphold and improve Chinese socialism and modernize our state governance system and capacity, and give full play to the strengths of our systems.

Based on the above considerations, the Standing Committee of the Political Bureau and the Political Bureau convened meetings on February 28 and March 29 this year, and decided the topic of this plenary session – upholding and improving Chinese socialism and modernizing the state governance system and capacity, and the establishment of a drafting group working under the leadership of the Standing Committee.

II. Drafting Process

The drafting group started work after its first meeting on April 3. The Central Committee issued a notice to all provincial authorities and central departments on April 7 to solicit opinions and suggestions on the topic. The 109 responses received provided many valuable opinions and suggestions, mainly covering the following areas:
- our achievements and experience in upholding and improving Chinese socialism and modernizing the state governance system and capacity;

- the principles and the fundamental, basic and important systems we must hold to; and
- the main problems and tasks facing us, and key measures we must take.

All agreed that the Central Committee's broad vision and strong sense of responsibility were reflected in its choice of the topic for its Fourth Plenary Session, and that the topic bore far-reaching significance for achieving moderate prosperity in all respects throughout the country, building a modern socialist country, and ensuring the Party's leadership and the long-term stability of the Party and the country.

During the six months after it was established, the drafting group conducted an intense study of relevant literature, summarized the evolution and innovation of systems in the process of revolution, economic development and reform in our country – in particular the achievements in theoretical research, practice and systems made since the 18th CPC National Congress. Based on the opinions and suggestions from all sectors, the drafting group studied specialized subjects, and discussed and revised the draft decision many times.

Following the order of a Political Bureau meeting, in early September the draft was circulated among a certain number of Party members and retired senior Party officials for suggestions. After careful review and discussion, provincial authorities and central departments submitted 118 responses. On September 25, I presided over a forum attended by leaders from the central committees of other political parties, head of the All-China Federation of Industry and Commerce, and personages without party affiliation. I heard their opinions and received the texts of 10 speeches from them.

The drafting group collated all opinions and suggestions. In total the group received 1,948 revision suggestions, and 1,755 remained after removing duplicates. These included 380 general opinions and 1,375 detailed suggestions.

The feedback showed full approval of the draft decision. All consulted groups and individuals had reached the consensus that the decision has a correct understanding of the evolution of China's national system and state governance system. It prioritizes upholding and improving Party leadership, which is key to state governance. It emphasizes that we must maintain the correct political direction and break new ground, and manifest our confidence in Chinese socialism. It highlights efficiency, integration and coordination among different systems, with a focus on solving problems and achieving practical results.

The decision answers major political questions: What should we uphold and consolidate? What should we improve and promote? It defines the major systems and principles we must support, and introduces the tasks and measures for improving our systems. It underscores coordination between the fundamental, basic and important systems, between top-level design and its implementation at different levels, and between reform and operation of systems. As both a summary of experience and a vision for the future, it maintains the stability of our systems while introducing reform and innovation, and remains committed to our goals while aiming to solve problems. The decision will certainly have a profound impact on the systems of our country, making them more mature and better-defined, and turning their strengths into efficient state governance.

Many constructive suggestions were collected, mainly including:

First, to list comprehensive reform and law-based governance as strengths of our national system and state governance system;

Second, to highlight the role of science and technology systems in boosting innovation;

Third, to attach greater importance to the systems that guarantee food security, rural revitalization, and the prioritized development of agriculture and rural areas;

Fourth, to make more use of IT technologies, such as AI, the internet and big data, to modernize our governance capacity;

Fifth, to fully apply the principle of the Party supervising the performance of officials, and set targets on improving the management of officials, motivating officials to take on responsibilities and ensure effective implementation, and encouraging them to work harder and be more enterprising and competent;

Sixth, to promote theoretical research in our national system and state governance system, and public education on the subject; and

Seventh, to implement the guidelines set at this session along with the reform tasks laid out by the Central Committee since the 18th CPC National Congress, and formulate an overall plan and mechanism for this purpose.

The Central Committee instructed the drafting group to carefully study the opinions and suggestions from all sides. The group analyzed them item by item, took them all into consideration, and absorbed all pertinent suggestions. Through thorough deliberations, 283 changes were made to the draft decision, reflecting 436 opinions and suggestions.

The Standing Committee of the Political Bureau held three meetings and the Political Bureau two meetings to review the draft versions, and finally produced this final draft for submission.

III. Framework of the Draft

Focusing on the topic of this plenary session, the draft decision is based on the goals and tasks set at the 19th CPC National Congress. It aims to uphold and consolidate Chinese socialism and ensure the Party's long-term governance and the country's long-term peace and stability, to improve Chinese socialism and build a modern socialist country in all respects, and to give full play to the strengths of Chinese socialism and modernize the state governance system and capacity. It summarizes the achievements, experience and principles that our people have gained in improving the state system and governance under the leadership of the Party, elaborates on upholding and improving the fundamental, basic and important systems that underpin Chinese socialism, makes plans for major systems and mechanisms, and defines the essential tasks to be performed on our way forward.

The draft decision is divided into three parts with 15 sections.

The first part, namely, the first section, presents the general principles, setting forth the monumental achievements we have made in developing Chinese socialism and state governance, and their strengths. It also explains why it is important for us to uphold and improve Chinese socialism and modernize the state governance system and capacity, and sets out the overall requirements.

Detailed expositions on our fundamental, basic, and important systems that underpin Chinese socialism are given in the 13 sections of the second part. This part defines the fundamentals we must hold to and the direction for our systems to improve, and makes plans for future work.

The 15th section and the conclusion constitute the third part, which sets requirements for the Party's leadership over the endeavor.

To fulfill the purpose of this session, we hope that all colleagues fully digest the guidelines laid out by the Central Committee, focus our discussions on what we should uphold and consolidate and what we should improve and promote, and share constructive opinions and suggestions for revising the draft decision.

Notes

[1] Deng Xiaoping: "On the Reform of the System of Party and State Leadership", *Selected Works of Deng Xiaoping*, Vol. II, Eng. ed., Foreign Languages Press, Beijing, 1995, pp. 331-332.

[2] Deng Xiaoping: "Excerpts from Talks Given in Wuchang, Shenzhen, Zhuhai and Shanghai", *Selected Works of Deng Xiaoping*, Vol. III, Eng. ed., Foreign Languages Press, Beijing, 1994, p. 360.

[3] Lü Zuqian: *Essays on* Zuo's Commentary on the Spring and Autumn Annals (*Dong Lai Bo Yi*). Lü Zuqian (1137-1181) was a writer and neo-Confucian philosopher of the Southern Song Dynasty.

Uphold and Improve the Chinese Socialist System and Modernize State Governance*

October 31, 2019

The plenary session has listened to the Political Bureau's work report, analyzed the current situation and tasks, and deliberated and adopted the "Decision of the Central Committee of the Communist Party of China on Upholding and Improving the Socialist System with Chinese Characteristics and Modernizing the State System and Capacity for Governance". All items on the agenda have been completed.

Upholding and improving the socialist system with Chinese characteristics and modernizing the state governance system and capacity is a major issue that impacts on the full development of the undertakings of our Party and state, the long-term stability of the country, and the happiness and wellbeing of the people. The CPC Central Committee decided to focus on these issues at this plenary session from a political, national and strategic perspective, and based on the prevailing situation in China and a vision for the future. The decision passed at the plenary session provides a comprehensive answer to these questions concerning state and governance systems: What should we uphold and consolidate? What should we improve and promote? The report adopted at the plenary session is a Marxist guiding document and a political proclamation. All Party members must align themselves with the decision of the plenary session in both thought and deed, and make its full implementation a key political commitment.

Now, on behalf of the Political Bureau, I will make a few points

---

* Part of the speech at the second full assembly of the Fourth Plenary Session of the 19th CPC Central Committee.

on how we should understand and implement the decision of the plenary session.

I. Have Full Confidence in the Chinese Socialist System

Our ancestors said, "A state system must be established when founding a country."[1] A well-founded system is the biggest strength a country has, and competition in terms of systems is the most essential rivalry between countries. A country cannot remain stable without a sound system. The fundamental reason that the Chinese nation has stood up, become better off and grown in strength over the seven decades since the founding of the People's Republic in 1949 is that the CPC has led the people in establishing and improving the Chinese socialist system, in forming and developing systems for Party leadership, the economy, politics, culture, society, eco-civilization, the military, and foreign affairs, and in enhancing state governance.

The state and governance systems that a country adopts are determined by its history and culture, the nature of its society, and the stage of economic development it has reached. The Chinese socialist system and state governance system did not fall out of the sky, but emerged from Chinese soil through a long process of revolution, economic development, and reform. They are the results of a combination of the tenets of Marxism with China's conditions and the outcome of a range of innovations in theory, practice and system. They crystalize the wisdom of the Party and the people and are in alignment with its history, theory and practice.

First, China's socialist system and state governance system have a profound historical background. Over several thousand years of history, the Chinese nation has created a splendid civilization, and developed a wealth of ideas on state systems and governance, including:
- the ideal of great harmony believing that "When the Great Way rules, the land under Heaven belongs to the people";
- the same tradition across the country so that all areas follow similar customs and all people are of the same family;

- the idea of prioritizing ethics over sanctions in governance and guiding people with virtue;
- the people-centered philosophy holding that the people have primacy over the ruler and the aim of governance is to ensure and improve the people's wellbeing;
- the idea of equality among all people in terms of social status and wealth, and taking the wealth of the rich to help the poor;
- the idea of justice and impartiality of the law;
- moral standards advocating filial piety, fraternity, loyalty to the country, good faith, propriety, justice, integrity, and conscience;
- standards for the appointment of officials based on virtue and competence;
- the reformist spirit as exemplified by such adages as: "Although Zhou is an ancient state, its destiny hinges on reform"[2];
- the principle of good neighborliness and harmony in relations with all other countries; and
- the belief in the primacy of peace and opposition to bellicosity.

These ideas constitute a major part of traditional Chinese culture and the ethos of the Chinese nation. Since the introduction of Marxism to China, scientific socialism has become widely accepted by the Chinese people. It has gone on to take root in this country and delivered impressive results. This is clearly not accidental. It is consistent with the culture and values that our people have taken up and passed on for several thousand years. Karl Marx made a shrewd observation on the slogans of ancient Chinese peasant uprisings that had some socialist content. He said, "Now Chinese socialism may admittedly be the same in relation to European socialism as Chinese philosophy in relation to Hegelian philosophy."[3]

Over a long period of history China led the world in development. It forged a complete set of state and governance systems covering the court, administration of prefectures and counties, land, taxation, civil service examination, supervision and the military, many of which were absorbed by neighboring nations. With the advent of modern times, China was reduced to a semi-feudal and semi-colonial society due to the decadence and impotence of the feudal government and the invasion and occupation of imperialist powers. The autocratic monarchical system that had ruled China for several millennia was confronted by a grave crisis. Facing increasing political and national challenges, countless progressives struggled in search of ways to create a better future for the nation. They pioneered new state and governance systems, and experimented with various solutions such as constitutional monarchy, parliamentary systems, multiparty politics, and presidential government. But all these efforts ended in failure.

Only after the founding of the CPC in 1921 did China find the path to national independence and prosperity and the people's liberation and happiness. During the New Democratic Revolution (1919-1949), our Party rallied and led the people in establishing the people's government in the revolutionary base areas, and exploring new democratic economic, political and cultural systems, which generated valuable experience for founding a country where the people are the masters. After assuming state power, our Party led the people in enacting the Common Program[4] in 1949 and the Constitution in 1954, by which the systems and structures of our state and government were established. On this basis, the Party led the people in conducting socialist transformation, establishing socialism as our basic system, and completing the broadest and most profound social change in China's history. It created the fundamental political conditions and national systems for achieving all the progress in China today. Since the launch of reform and opening up in 1978, the Party has led the people in developing socialism with Chinese characteristics and improving China's state governance, so that contemporary China is full of new vigor.

In summary, guided by Marxism, the Chinese socialist system and state governance system have developed from the real conditions and culture of China, and they enjoy the full support of the people. They represent the most fundamental achievement of the Party and the people through lengthy struggle and strenuous effort. We must treasure them, uphold them with determination, and keep them up to date.

Second, the Chinese socialist system and state governance system have great strengths in many respects. The plenary session has summarized these strengths in a systematic way, with the goal of bringing them to the fore and increasing public confidence in our systems. We should keep up our efforts to maintain and grow these strengths in a bid to enhance our socialist system and modernize our state governance system and capability in the new era.

The merits of a system should be assessed from a political and an overall perspective. In his speech titled "On the Reform of the System of Party and State Leadership", Deng Xiaoping said, "In the drive for socialist modernization, our objectives are: economically, to catch up with the developed capitalist countries; and politically, to create a higher level of democracy with more substance than that of capitalist countries. We also aim to produce more and better-trained professionals than they do.... The merits of our Party and state institutions should be judged on the basis of whether or not they help us advance towards our objectives."[5] At the conference marking the 60th anniversary of the National People's Congress in 2014, I said, "The best way to evaluate whether a country's political system is democratic and efficient is to observe whether the succession of its leaders is orderly and in line with the law, whether all people can manage state affairs and social, economic and cultural affairs in conformity with legal provisions, whether the public can express their requirements without hindrance, whether all sectors can efficiently participate in the country's political affairs, whether national decisions can be made in a rational, democratic way, whether people of high-caliber in all fields can be part of the team of the national leadership and administrative systems through fair competition, whether the ruling party can serve as a leader in state affairs in accordance with the Constitution and the law, and whether the exercise of power can be kept under effective restraint and supervision."

One of the factors crucial to the strengths of our state and governance systems is that our Party, over many years, has combined Marxism with China's actual conditions, and integrated its efforts to open up the right path, develop sound theories and establish effective systems. The CPC has guided the development of the state and governance systems with dynamic Marxism adapted to the Chinese context. The Party works to improve its understanding of the inner rules behind its governance, the development of socialism, and the evolution of human society. The results of our success in practice are institutionalized in a timely manner. All these efforts enable our state and governance systems to embody the basic principles of scientific socialism and manifest distinct features of our nation and our times.

The essential attribute of our state and governance systems is that they always represent the fundamental interests of the people, safeguard the people's status as masters of the country, reflect the people's common will, and protect the people's legitimate rights and interests. This is precisely why the operation of the systems in our country is so effective and dynamic. They are always directed to realize, protect and develop the fundamental interests of the greatest possible majority of the people, guarantee and improve their wellbeing, and share the fruits of reform among all our people in a fair way. This means they can deter conflicts among political parties, guard against the partiality of interest groups, and prevent a small "elite" from manipulating politics. In this sense, they are more advanced than any other system.

We are always open to useful governance experience from other countries, digesting its essence and employing it for our own use on the basis of our own systems. For example, we learned a lot from the valuable experience of the Soviet Union during the initial period of the PRC in building socialism. Since the launch of reform and opening up, we have opened wider to the outside world and combined our socialist system with a market economy, allowing the market to play the decisive role in resource allocation and the government to better fulfill its functions. This has significantly helped unleash and develop the productive forces, and boost vitality throughout society.

What distinguishes scientific socialism from utopian socialism is that the former, which is not a set of fixed dogmas, sees socialism as a constantly-improving process. After the Cultural Revolution, Deng

Xiaoping pointed out, "Our Party and people established a socialist system after long years of bloody struggle. After all, although our socialist system is still imperfect and has suffered disruption, it is much better than the capitalist system based on the law of the jungle and the principle of 'getting ahead' at the expense of others. Our system will improve more and more with the passage of time. By absorbing the progressive elements of other countries, it will become the best in the world. Capitalism can never achieve this."[6]

Reform and opening up over the past 40 years has greatly improved our socialist system and state governance system by remedying the shortcomings of our systems and mechanisms. After the 18th CPC National Congress in 2012, we extended our comprehensive reform. This fully demonstrates the capacity for self-improvement of our state and governance systems. It is foreseeable that as we drive reform to deeper levels, these systems will show greater vitality and give us a cutting edge in international competition.

Third, the Chinese socialist system and state governance system have generated substantial results. "Approach tells more than words, and conduct reveals more than approach."[7] Practice is the best touchstone of the efficacy of our systems. Over the seven decades since the founding of the PRC, our Party has led the people in creating two miracles.

The first is rapid economic growth. In only a few decades we have achieved a degree of industrialization that took developed countries several centuries. China is now the world's second largest economy. Our overall national strength, capacity in science and technology, national defense capabilities, cultural influence, and international status have increased remarkably, and our people's lives have greatly improved. The Chinese nation now stands tall and steadfast in the East.

The second is lasting social stability. Our country has maintained social harmony and stability for a long period of time, and the people live happy and stable lives. China is recognized as one of the countries whose people enjoy a strong sense of security.

It is fair to say that no other state and governance system in human history could have achieved these two miracles in such a short time.

We must uphold and consolidate our tried and tested systems, and improve and develop them, so as to transform their strengths into efficient state governance.

I have often said that only the wearer of the shoes knows if they fit or not. The Chinese people know best whether the Chinese socialist system suits the country or not. We must be definite and determined on this critical political issue, and must never lose our bearings or become confused. All Party members, especially leading officials, must take a clear political stance on this issue, and maintain confidence in the Chinese socialist path, theory, system and culture at all times and in all circumstances. We must be as tenacious as bamboo, as described by Zheng Xie: "In the face of all blows, not bending low, it still stands fast. Whether from east, west, south or north the wind doth blast."[8]

II. Fully Implement the Decision of the Plenary Session

The plenary session has defined a comprehensive plan and set clear requirements for upholding and improving the Chinese socialist system and modernizing the state governance system and capacity. We must make sound plans for both short-term and long-term goals, and ensure well-organized and coordinated implementation of all the tasks set out at the plenary session. To this end, we need to focus on three points. The first is about upholding and consolidating; the second is about improving and developing; and the third is about implementing and following up.

First, we must resolutely uphold and consolidate socialism with Chinese characteristics. It is well-knit and complete, and supported by fundamental, basic and important systems, with the system for CPC leadership in the dominant position. CPC leadership is the fundamental element of our country's leadership system. Since the 18th CPC National Congress we have stated that the defining feature of Chinese socialism is CPC leadership, that the greatest strength of the Chinese socialist system is CPC leadership, and that the CPC is the highest force for political leadership. This plenary session also emphasizes: "We must ensure the Party exercises overall leadership over all areas of endeavor in every part of the country, and resolutely safeguard the Central Committee's authority. We must improve the leadership system in which the Party exercises overall leadership and coordinates the efforts of all, and implement the Party's leadership in all aspects of state governance." This is the most valuable experience the Party has drawn from leading the people in revolution, economic development, and reform. We must uphold Party leadership in developing our systems, push forward all our undertakings, and improve our work in all areas. We must conscientiously implement the fundamental requirement that the Party exercises overall leadership and coordinates the efforts of all.

This plenary session has summed up the experience we have gained through practice, and redefined some concepts on the basis of our fundamental, basic and important systems. For instance, it has confirmed that the basic socialist economic system contains the following elements:
- public ownership playing the dominant role while developing together with other forms of ownership,
- multiple modes of distribution with "to each according to their work" as the principal form, and
- a socialist market economy.

The plenary session has also highlighted the fundamental system which ensures that Marxism guides all our ideological work. It has further expounded on a set of systems:
- the rule of law under Chinese socialism,
- the administrative system under Chinese socialism,
- the system for promoting the advanced socialist culture,
- the system ensuring the wellbeing of urban and rural residents,
- social governance based on collaboration and broad participation with the goal of benefiting all,
- the system for promoting eco-civilization,

- the CPC's absolute leadership over the people's armed forces,
- the framework of "one country, two systems", and
- CPC and state supervision.

The fundamental, basic and important systems of Chinese socialism are the institutional frameworks for various undertakings of the Party and the state. We must strictly follow these systems when drawing up development plans, promoting the rule of law, formulating policies and measures, and making concrete plans for our tasks. They must be followed to the letter. We always say that leading officials, especially those of high rank, must have a keen political sense, clear political insight, and strong political capacity. One of the key requirements is to unswervingly uphold these systems, and conduct conscious self-examination against them when we contemplate problems, make decisions and ensure implementation. When encountering problems concerning our fundamental goal, we must take these systems as the guidelines in solving such problems. We must take an unequivocal stance on the cardinal issues of principle. In judging whether Party committees and Party leadership groups at all levels have played their role in leadership and supervision in their respective areas, the key lies in whether they have faithfully followed and implemented these systems. If they are put in place with precision, we will not make any fatal or political mistake.

Second, we must improve and develop the Chinese socialist system and state governance system to keep up with the changing times. An ancient Chinese scholar observed, "Plants with strong roots grow well, and efforts with the right focus ensure success."[9] As Chinese socialism has entered a new era, our country now finds itself at a new development stage. The principal challenge facing Chinese society is the gap between unbalanced and inadequate development and the people's growing expectation for a better life. This sets many new tasks and requirements for state governance. This, naturally, requires us to further improve and develop our socialist system and state governance system.

Making our state system more mature and better-defined constitutes a dynamic process. Modernizing state governance capacity is also a dynamic process. We cannot get there in one step, neither can we falter in our efforts. The goals we set in this regard must also be updated appropriately to suit the changing circumstances. We should never idealize our goals or rush for quick results; nor should we become complacent and satisfied with the old ways.

In his article "Proposals on Governance", Su Shi of the Song Dynasty (960-1279) said, "Only by solving the hardest problems can one achieve the loftiest goals." Most of the targets and tasks set out at this plenary session are designed to fill in blanks and remedy weaknesses in our state and governance systems. They are oriented to solve problems. In practice, we must place the emphasis on upholding and improving the fundamental, basic and important systems that underpin Chinese socialism, and devote all our efforts to consolidating our foundations, leveraging our strengths, and addressing our weaknesses, so as to establish a well-developed, procedure-based and effective framework of systems.

To implement the decision of this plenary session, we must combine them with the existing reform tasks, and establish an effective mechanism that ensures all tasks are carried out. We need to review the status of previous reform tasks, consolidate what we have achieved and carry on with the tasks yet to be completed. At the same time, we need to integrate the new tasks into our existing agenda and ensure tangible results.

Party committees and Party leadership groups at all levels, under the unified leadership of the Central Committee, should improve our systems and governance capacity in the local context, study and implement the systems that are urgently needed for improving state governance as specified by the Central Committee, and the systems that are essential for satisfying the people's expectation for a better life. We need to encourage bold innovation and experimentation at the grassroots level, and act quickly to document and analyze governance concepts, approaches and measures that prove to be effective at the grassroots, thereby creating a constant flow of improvements to the systems. Being proactive in this regard, all local authorities, departments and entities must also follow the overall plan of the Central Committee and abide by laws and regulations. It is forbidden to breach rules, reject the overall plan, or rush to action. The key is to fulfill the tasks and goals set out at this plenary session.

Third, we must strictly follow and implement our systems. The vitality of a system lies in its implementation. Some people today still lack reverence for our systems. They do not act in accordance with them and even bend them to their will. Some make every effort to exploit loopholes and circumvent them. Some fear or are reluctant to obey them, and try by every means to evade the restrictions and supervision they impose. Therefore, we need to strengthen enforcement and supervision to put our systems into better practice.

Party committees and governments at all levels and their leading officials must have a stronger awareness of our systems, lead by example in safeguarding their authority and execution, and ensure the implementation of major decisions and plans of the Party and the state in line with our systems. Different areas are not allowed to work on their own without synergy, to apply different standards, or to enforce systems to different degrees. We should give full play to the role of our systems in guiding direction, regulating conduct, increasing efficiency, maintaining social stability, and preventing and diffusing risks. We need to establish a full-coverage mechanism to enforce and supervise them – from regional governance, governance in different sectors and industries, and community-level governance to governance of a work unit. Selective or compromised enforcement is forbidden. Those who fail to implement the decisions and prohibitions by the Central Committee, or feign compliance, should be investigated and punished, so that the authority of our systems is effective at all times and in all places. In order to strengthen the caliber of officials in the new era, we should focus on improving their governance capacity, and enhancing their ability to advance undertakings, fulfill duties, exercise power and work strictly within the framework of our systems.

Party organizations at all levels, especially public communication departments, should conduct communication with the public on the Chinese socialist system. They should guide all Party members and all of society to understand the defining features and strengths of Chinese socialism, and understand that we must cherish our state and governance systems, as they have been created through hard efforts and have withstood the test of time. To improve and develop them, we must proceed from our national conditions. We must take into consideration both our traditions and the path, experience and principles the Party and the people have created. We should not blindly copy the systems of other countries. We must build deep-rooted confidence in our own among our youth through public education. We must create new and better ways of communication with our people and the international community, to make our discourse on China's state and governance systems more persuasive and appealing.

Party committees and Party leadership groups at all levels must carry out the plans of the Central Committee, and communicate the decision of the plenary session to the public in a well-organized manner. We need to take targeted approaches for different audience groups, so as to ensure that the plenary session has a real impact on the people. We will strengthen our supervision of the implementation of these decisions. Relevant departments of the Party should provide timely updates to the Central Committee on the progress of the respective tasks in local areas and sectors. It is necessary to summarize their best practices in executing the decisions. The Central Commission for Further Reform is responsible for coordinating the execution of the reform tasks decided at the plenary session.

Dear colleagues, to uphold and improve the Chinese socialist system and modernize the state governance system and capacity has long-term strategic significance. It also represents a practical issue for today. Holding a strong sense of political duty and historic responsibility, and maintaining firm confidence and resolve, we must apply an innovative spirit to accomplishing the tasks put forward at the plenary session, and guarantee the realization of the Two Centenary Goals and the Chinese Dream of national rejuvenation.

Notes

¹ *Book of Lord Shang (Shang Jun Shu)*. This book is a representative work by Shang Yang and his followers. It is also an important basis for research into the legal philosophy of the Shang Yang school.

² *Book of Songs*. This quote highlights the importance of reform. In the late Shang Dynasty (1600-1046 BC) the vassal state of Zhou, led by Ji Chang, became powerful by undertaking a number of reforms. Ultimately the vassal state, led by Ji's son, overthrew the Shang and founded the Zhou Dynasty (1046-256 BC). – Tr.

³ Karl Marx and Frederick Engels: "Review [January-February 1850]", *Karl Marx & Frederick Engels: Collected Works*, Vol. 10, Eng. ed., Progress Publishers, Moscow, 1979, p. 267.

⁴ The Common Program, adopted in 1949 at the First Plenary Session of the Chinese People's Political Consultative Conference which exercised the functions and powers of the later National People's Congress, served as the provisional Constitution. – Tr.

⁵ Deng Xiaoping: "On the Reform of the System of Party and State Leadership", *Selected Works of Deng Xiaoping*, Vol. II, Eng. ed., Foreign Languages Press, Beijing, 1995, pp. 321-322.

⁶ *Ibid.*, p. 335.

⁷ Fu Xuan: *Fu Zi*. Fu Xuan (217-278) was a writer, philosopher and politician who lived during the Three Kingdoms Period and the Western Jin Dynasty.

⁸ Zheng Xie: "Bamboos amid Rocks" (Zhu Shi). Zheng Xie (1693-1765), also known as Zheng Banqiao, was a painter and writer of the Qing Dynasty.

⁹ Liu Xiang: *Garden of Stories (Shuo Yuan)*. Liu Xiang (77-6 BC) was a writer and bibliographer of the Western Han Dynasty.

People-Centered Development

A Better Life for All Our People*

November 30, 2017

China's development path is the path of socialism with Chinese characteristics. It is a choice of the times and of the people. After the founding of the PRC in 1949, and especially since reform and opening up started about 40 years ago, China has witnessed unprecedented changes. China is now the world's second largest economy, and the standard of living of our 1.3 billion people continues to improve. More than 700 million people have escaped from poverty. Practice is the sole criterion for testing truth. All our historic achievements have strengthened our confidence in the path, theory, system and culture of Chinese socialism. As I pointed out in 2017 in the report to the 19th CPC National Congress, after several decades, Chinese socialism has entered a new era. The principal challenge facing Chinese society is the gap between unbalanced and inadequate development and the ever-growing expectation of the people for a better life. In the past, we worked to provide for people's basic needs; now we are striving to improve their quality of life. We must focus on improving the quality and efficiency of development to better meet the growing expectation of our people in all areas, and further promote well-rounded personal development and common prosperity for all. By 2050, we will build China into a great modern socialist country that is prosperous, strong, democratic, culturally advanced, harmonious and beautiful.

The 19th CPC National Congress made comprehensive plans to promote economic, political, cultural, social and eco-environmental progress in China. We will continue people-centered development and

---

* Main points of the speech during a meeting with members of the World Leadership Alliance attending the 2017 Imperial Springs International Forum.

further implement the vision of innovative, coordinated, green, open, and shared development. By introducing in-depth reform in all areas, we hope to inspire creativity throughout society and unleash new impetus for development. We will raise opening up to higher levels and cover all areas. China will not close its door to the world; we will only open it wider. We have a grand yet simple goal – a better life for all our people. And we have full confidence in achieving this goal.

The People Are Our Greatest Strength in Governance*

March 1, 2018-December 27, 2019

I

The people are the creators of history, the fundamental force determining the future of the Party and the country. Our Party comes from the people, has its roots in the people, and serves the people. We will lose this vital force if we are detached from the people. We should learn from Comrade Zhou Enlai, and adhere to the Party's commitment to building itself for the public good and exercising power for the people. We must champion the Party's principle of serving the people wholeheartedly, implement the mass line in every aspect of national governance, and strive to help the people fulfill their desire for a better life. We must always rely on the people to create history.

(from the speech at a seminar commemorating the 120th birthday of Zhou Enlai, March 1, 2018)

II

We must address the most pressing issues that are essential to people's immediate interests. Their concerns, be they big or small, should be handled with the greatest care and attention. We must start by addressing issues of public concern, delivering the outcomes that satisfy public needs. We will strengthen extensive employment services,

---

* Excerpts from speeches made between March 1, 2018 and December 27, 2019.

make it a priority to help and support people in straitened circumstances, and move faster to complete a multitiered social security system. We will strengthen the system for community governance, continue with targeted poverty alleviation and elimination, and promote more targeted and meticulous measures to ensure public wellbeing.

(from the speech during a visit to Hubei Province,
April 24-28, 2018)

III

We must always uphold our fundamental stance of siding with the people, and striving for the wellbeing of the people as our ultimate mission. We must remain committed to the principle of serving the people wholeheartedly, and carry out the mass line. We must respect the people's principal position and pioneering spirit, always maintain close ties with them, channel their strength into an invincible force, and unite and lead them to create historic achievements. This is a natural choice we have made in keeping with the trend of this era, and a responsibility we undertake as Communists in staying true to our original aspiration.

(from the speech at the ceremony commemorating the bicentenary of
the birth of Karl Marx, May 4, 2018)

IV

Our Party serves the people wholeheartedly in pursuit of their wellbeing. On the long way ahead, we bear heavy responsibility and must not stop or slacken our efforts. Only with determination and perseverance can we carry on to fulfill our mission, do justice to these great times, and live up to the people's expectations.

(from the speech at a seminar on pressing problems related to the
Two Assurances and Three Guarantees during a visit to
Chongqing Municipality, April 15-17, 2019)

V

The people are our Party's greatest strength in governance. They are the solid base of our republic, and the foundation of a well-built Party and a prosperous nation. Our Party is from the people, for the people, and successful because of the people. It must always be close to the people, and work vigorously by their side through thick and thin.

Every Party member must bear these in mind: The Party works for the people's interests and has no interests of its own. All it does is to realize, safeguard and develop the fundamental interests of the people. The people are the creators of history; the people are the true heroes. We must trust and rely on them. We are always ordinary members of the working people, and must maintain close ties with the people.

(from the speech at the Conference on the Aspiration and Mission Education Campaign, May 31, 2019)

VI

The people are our Party's foundation and greatest strength in governance. It is in this sense that we say people's support is of paramount importance. It is the people who will judge whether our Party members and officials still remember and honor our mission. Their commitment will be tested in practice. To improve the people's wellbeing in all respects, officials at all levels must always bear in mind our purpose of serving the people wholeheartedly, always work to ensure the people live and work in peace and contentment, and always be mindful of their difficulties and needs.

(from instructions on the Aspiration and Mission education campaign during a visit to Inner Mongolia Autonomous Region, July 15-16, 2019)

VII

Staying true to our founding mission is, in essence, a matter of whom we serve and whose support sustains us. Our Party was founded for the people and has always been of one heart with the people. Bound to the people by an inseverable tie, the Party will always be in the service of the people to fulfill its mission. All our work and decision-making must proceed from the people's interests. We must solicit the people's opinions, understand their needs, and welcome their criticisms and suggestions. We must make solid efforts to address their concerns, alleviate their grievances, and warm their hearts, so that they will always have a strong sense of gain, happiness, and security.

(from the speech at a meeting of criticism and self-criticism on the Aspiration and Mission education campaign of the Political Bureau of the 19th CPC Central Committee, December 26-27, 2019)

Always Put the People First*

March 20, 2018

I was elected at this session to continue to serve as the president of the People's Republic of China. I would like to express my heartfelt gratitude for the trust placed in me by all the deputies and Chinese people of all ethnic groups.

It is a glorious mission and a weighty responsibility to take on this great position of the president of the People's Republic of China. I will, as always, faithfully fulfill the responsibilities prescribed by the Constitution, be loyal to the country and the people, perform my duties scrupulously, do my best, be diligent at work, and remain devoted and dedicated. I will continue to act as a servant of the people and accept scrutiny by the people, and will never in any way betray their great trust.

Any member of any state organ, no matter how high a position one holds, should keep firmly in mind that our republic is the People's Republic of China, and that we must always put the people first, always serve the people wholeheartedly, and always work hard for the people's interests and happiness.

The people are the creators of history. The people are the true heroes. The magnificent history of the Chinese nation has been written by the Chinese people. The extensive and profound Chinese civilization has been created by the Chinese people. The spirit of the Chinese nation, kept fresh and alive throughout history, has been cultivated by the Chinese people. The endeavor of the Chinese people has led to a tremendous transformation of the Chinese nation: It has stood up, become better off and grown in strength.

---

* Part of the speech at the First Session of the 13th National People's Congress.

The character and endowment of the Chinese people have fostered the Chinese civilization over thousands of years. They have also exerted a far-reaching influence on the development of China and on the ethos of today's Chinese. The great national spirit, fostered, passed down, and developed by the Chinese people during their long struggle, has provided a strong impetus for the betterment of China and humanity.

– The Chinese people are highly creative. Throughout thousands of years of history, they have always been ready to labor, to innovate, and to create with diligence.

Our country has been the birthplace of world-renowned thinkers such as Lao Zi, Confucius, Zhuang Zi, Mencius, Mo Zi, Sun Zi and Han Fei Zi.[1] The Chinese people's great scientific achievements such as papermaking, gunpowder, printing, and the compass have profoundly influenced the progress of human civilization. We created such great literary works as the *Book of Songs*, *Songs of Chu*, *fu* poetry of the Han Dynasty (206 BC-AD 220), poetry of the Tang (618-907) and Song (960-1279) dynasties, operas of the Yuan Dynasty (1206-1368) and the novels of the Ming (1368-1644) and Qing (1616-1911) dynasties. We have passed down the powerful epics – *King Gesar*, *Manas* and *Jangar*.[2] We have built mighty projects – the Great Wall, the Dujiangyan flood control and irrigation system, the Grand Canal, the Forbidden City, and the Potala Palace.

Today, the creativity of the Chinese people is being unleashed to an extent never seen before, which is enabling our country to develop rapidly and stride forward at the forefront of the world. I am confident that as long as 1.3 billion Chinese people continue to demonstrate such great creativity, we will continue to create more miracles.

– The Chinese people are people with a great spirit of endeavor. Over thousands of years, they have been able to discard the outdated and bring in the new. Our pursuit of progress has never paused. We have developed and built an immense and beautiful country, and explored vast expanses of territorial seas. We have opened up extensive and productive farmland, harnessed numerous turbulent rivers, and overcome countless natural disasters. We have built towns and villages dotted all over the country and developed a complete range of industries. Our lives are varied and colorful.

The Chinese people have been well aware since ancient times that we cannot sit idle and enjoy the fruits of others' work, and that happiness can only be achieved through great endeavor. What the Chinese people have achieved stems from ingenuity and expertise, hard work, and enormous sacrifice. I believe, as long as all the Chinese people uphold this mighty spirit of endeavor, we will fulfill the great goal of creating a better life.

– The Chinese people are people with a great spirit of unity. Over thousands of years, they have remained united and stuck together through thick and thin. We have built a united multiethnic country, and developed harmonious relationships between 56 diverse but closely interwoven ethnic groups; we have formed one great Chinese family where all care for and help each other. Especially in modern times, confronted by aggressive and pitiless foreign occupation, all ethnic groups have joined to create a magnificent epic of defending the Chinese nation against external aggression. They have stood shoulder to shoulder and fought heroically and relentlessly, defeating every malicious invader and safeguarding national independence and freedom.

China today, with all ethnic groups striving with one heart, has achieved extraordinary successes. The Chinese people have learned from our own experiences that only when we are united can we be strong and march forward. A divided country will not prosper. I believe as long as all the Chinese people uphold the spirit of unity, we will forge an unstoppable and invincible force.

– The Chinese people are people with a great spirit of dreams. Over a history of thousands of years, they have held fast to their dreams and persevered in pursuing their goals. We have formed the ideal of living in prosperity, but also aspiring for the common good.

Ancient Chinese mythologies, such as Pangu creating the world, Nüwa patching up the sky, Fuxi drawing the eight diagrams, Shennong testing herbs, Kuafu chasing the sun, Jingwei filling up the sea, and

Yugong removing mountains, reflect our determination in dauntlessly pursuing and realizing dreams. It is our firm belief that no matter how high a mountain is, if we keep climbing, we will reach the top; no matter how long a road is, if we keep walking, we will reach the destination.

Since the modern era began, to realize the Chinese Dream of national rejuvenation has become the greatest dream of the Chinese nation. Chinese people never yield to reverses, and they stand firm and indomitable. With the spirit of fighting the enemy to the end, the resolve of recovering the lost on the basis of self-reliance, and the ability to stand firm among the community of nations, the Chinese people have made continuous efforts for more than 170 years to fulfill their great dreams.

Today, more than ever before, we are closer to, more confident of, and more capable of making the goal of national rejuvenation a reality. I believe that as long as all the Chinese people keep carrying forward this spirit of dreams, we can and will realize the rejuvenation of the Chinese nation.

Comrades, such a great people, a great nation and great national spirit give us the pride and the strength to remain confident in the path, theory, system and culture of socialism with Chinese characteristics, and the force to go forward in spite of all difficulties.

China is a socialist country of people's democratic dictatorship under the leadership of the working class based on an alliance of workers and farmers. It is a country where all power of the state belongs to the people. We must base our efforts on the interests of the people, ensure the principal status of the people, humbly learn from the people, listen to their voices, and draw on their wisdom. We must ensure that the basic criterion of our work is whether we have the people's support, acceptance, satisfaction and approval. We must focus our efforts on addressing the most pressing, immediate issues that concern the people the most. We must also ensure that all Chinese people share the happiness and pride stemming from the historic course of national rejuvenation.

Notes

[1] Lao Zi (dates unknown), also known as Lao Dan or Li Er, was a philosopher and the founder of Taoism in the Spring and Autumn Period (770-476 BC).

Confucius (551-479 BC), also known as Kong Qiu or Zhongni, was a philosopher, educator, and statesman in the Spring and Autumn Period. He was the founder of Confucianism.

Zhuang Zi (369-286 BC), also known as Zhuang Zhou, was a Taoist philosopher in the Warring States Period.

Mencius (c. 372-289 BC), also known as Meng Ke or Ziyu, was a philosopher, thinker and educator in the Warring States Period.

Mo Zi (c. 468-376 BC), also known as Mo Di, was a philosopher, thinker and statesman in the Warring States Period. He was the founder of the Mohist school.

Sun Zi (dates unknown), also known as Sun Wu or Changqing, was a military strategist in the late Spring and Autumn Period.

Han Fei Zi (c. 280-233 BC) was a leading exponent of the Legalist school in the Warring States Period.

[2] *King Gesar* is an epic of the Tibetan people. *Manas* is an epic of the Kirgiz people. *Jangar* is an epic of the Mongols.

Never Fail the People*

March 22, 2019

Running such a huge country is a grave responsibility, and it brings arduous work. I will fully commit to the people and never fail them. I am ready to put aside my own interests and devote my all to China's development.

A weightlifter can lift only a 50-kg barbell at the beginning. But through proper training he may achieve as much as 250 kg. I believe that through my work, through the concerted effort of more than 1.3 billion Chinese, we can definitely take on this weighty responsibility and build our country well. In this I am fully confident; the Chinese people are fully confident.

---

* Main points of the talk with Roberto Fico, president of the Italian Chamber of Deputies.

Making a report to the 19th CPC National Congress, October 18, 2017.

Rereading the oath of admission to the Party in Shanghai, October 31, 2017, along with other members of the Standing Committee of the Political Bureau of the 19th CPC Central Committee – Li Keqiang (3rd right), Li Zhanshu (3rd left), Wang Yang (2nd right), Wang Huning (2nd left), Zhao Leji (1st right), and Han Zheng (1st left) – at the site where the First CPC National Congress was held in 1921.

With officers and soldiers from a company noted for its former scouting hero Yang Zirong, while inspecting an army division in the Central Theater Command of the PLA, January 3, 2018.

Chatting with village representatives and resident working team members on targeted measures to eradicate poverty around the fire pit in a villager's home in Sanhe Village, Liangshan Yi Autonomous Prefecture, Sichuan Province, February 11, 2018. The following day Xi presided over the Seminar on Targeted Poverty Elimination in the provincial capital Chengdu.

Taking a public oath of allegiance to the Constitution. Xi was elected president of the PRC and chairman of the Central Military Commission of the PRC at the First Session of the 13th National People's Congress, March 17, 2018.

Inspecting the Chenglingji Hydrological Station in Yueyang, Hunan Province, April 25, 2018. Xi chaired a forum on further development of the Yangtze River Economic Belt in Wuhan, Hubei Province the following day.

Chatting with workers at Qixing Farm in Jiansanjiang, an important grain production base in Heilongjiang Province, September 25, 2018. During his inspection tour to the provinces of Heilongjiang, Jilin and Liaoning from September 25 to 28, Xi chaired a meeting on the revitalization of northeast China.

Announcing the opening of the Hong Kong-Zhuhai-Macao Bridge in Zhuhai, Guangdong Province, October 23, 2018.

At the conference celebrating the 40th anniversary of China's launch of reform and opening up in the Great Hall of the People, Beijing, December 18, 2018, along with Li Keqiang (4th right), Li Zhanshu (3rd left), Wang Yang (3rd right), Wang Huning (2nd left), Zhao Leji (2nd right), Han Zheng (1st left), and Wang Qishan (1st right).

Delivering a speech in the Great Hall of the People in Beijing, at the meeting marking the 40th anniversary of the release of the Message to Compatriots in Taiwan, January 2, 2019.

With teachers and students at the State Key Laboratory of Elemento-organic Chemistry in Nankai University, Tianjin, January 17, 2019.

Offering good wishes to couriers in Shitou Alley in central Beijing, during a visit to extend New Year greetings to local residents in the lead-up to the Chinese Spring Festival, February 1, 2019.

At a primary school in Zhongyi Township of Shizhu Tujia Autonomous County, April 15, 2019. During an inspection tour to Chongqing from April 15 to 17, Xi presided over a seminar on pressing problems related to the Two Assurances and Three Guarantees.

Paying tribute at a monument marking the departure of the Long March of the Central Red Army in Yudu County, Jiangxi Province, May 20, 2019, prior to the launch of the Aspiration and Mission education campaign by the CPC Central Committee.

Presiding over the Seminar on Promoting the Rise of Central China in Nanchang, during his inspection tour of Jiangxi Province, May 21, 2019. Xi listened to work reports from officials of local authorities and central departments and made a speech.

Inspecting the Babusha Forest Farm in Wuwei City, Gansu Province, August 21, 2019. Xi heard reports about the city's initiatives to prevent sand encroachment and control desertification, and was told of the afforestation work started by six local residents and continued over three generations.

Visiting a Yellow River management point to learn about protection and flood control projects on the river in Lanzhou, Gansu Province, August 21, 2019.

Visiting the exhibition "Laying the Foundation for the People's Republic of China" at a revolutionary memorial site in the Fragrant Hills in suburban Beijing, September 12, 2019.

Greeting members of staff from the teams responsible for building and running Beijing Daxing International Airport, September 25, 2019. Xi announced the official opening of the airport at its launch ceremony, and inspected the terminals.

Accompanying awardees to the presentation ceremony for national medals and honorary titles of the People's Republic of China in the Great Hall of the People, September 29, 2019.

Reviewing the armed forces during the celebrations to mark the 70th anniversary of the founding of the People's Republic of China on Tian'anmen Square in Beijing, October 1, 2019.

Meeting with Lam Cheng Yuet-ngor, chief executive of the Hong Kong Special Administrative Region, on her visit to Beijing to deliver her annual work report at Zhongnanhai, December 16, 2019.

Reviewing the guard of honor on China's first home-built aircraft carrier, the Shandong, *after its commissioning ceremony in Sanya, Hainan Province, December 17, 2019.*

Presiding over the swearing-in ceremony of Ho Iat Seng as the fifth-term chief executive of the Macao Special Administrative Region, December 20, 2019. Xi delivered a speech at the gathering in the Macao East Asian Games Dome to celebrate the 20th anniversary of Macao's return to the motherland and the inauguration of its fifth-term government.

Poverty Elimination and a Moderately Prosperous Society

Complete the Work of Building a Moderately Prosperous Society in All Respects*

October 25, 2017

We must do everything possible to succeed in building a moderately prosperous society in all respects, and continue to raise the level of China's socialist modernization. Now and for the near future, the highest priority of our Party and country is to bring our journey towards moderate prosperity to a satisfactory conclusion. The 19th CPC National Congress in 2017 further reaffirmed our commitment to achieving this goal on schedule. In terms of timing, the three years remaining to us will pass in the blink of an eye, so we must act with urgency – for time waits for no one. In terms of requirements, moderate prosperity must be genuine and not adulterated or exaggerated in any way if it is to earn the people's approval and stand the test of time. In terms of tasks, there are many difficulties we have yet to overcome in focusing on priorities, addressing inadequacies, and shoring up points of weakness. In particular, we must be resolute in forestalling and defusing major risks, making targeted efforts against poverty, and preventing and controlling pollution. Completing such an extraordinary mission requires exceptional drive and outstanding deeds. The victory ahead calls us all to join the charge. On our journey in the new era, all Party members must act in accordance with plans made at the 19th CPC National Congress regarding economic, political, cultural, social, and eco-environmental development, and bring all relevant tasks to full completion. This will guarantee that we achieve moderate prosperity

---

* Part of the speech at the First Plenary Session of the 19th CPC Central Committee.

throughout the country on schedule, an achievement which will serve as a stepping stone for us to start a new journey towards a modern socialist country.

A New Chapter in the Fight Against Poverty*

February 12, 2018

At its 18th National Congress in 2012, the CPC vowed to achieve moderate prosperity in all respects throughout the country. Accordingly, the CPC Central Committee has included development-driven poverty alleviation in the Five-sphere Integrated Plan and the Four-pronged Comprehensive Strategy, and made it one of the key tasks for realizing the First Centenary Goal. We have produced a raft of major strategies for the fight against poverty on all fronts. This is a fight of unprecedented intensity, scale and influence. But we have made decisive progress, significantly improving the working and living conditions of poor areas and poor people, and in so doing we have written a new chapter in the history of the fight against poverty.

First, we have set records in the history of poverty reduction in China. The rural poor population living under the current poverty line fell from 98.99 million at the end of 2012 to 30.46 million at the end of 2017, a decrease of 68.53 million and about 70 percent. The incidence of poverty fell from 10.2 percent at the end of 2012 to 3.1 percent at the end of 2017, a decrease of 7.1 percentage points. The average annual decrease was 13.7 million in the five years, which is more than double the annual decrease of 6.39 million during the Seven-year Priority Poverty Reduction Program (1994-2000)[1] period, and double the annual decrease of 6.73 million during the 2001-2010 period when the first Outline for Development-driven Poverty Reduction in Rural Areas was implemented. This is a departure from the old pattern that the population escaping poverty would decrease after new standards were adopted. The number of impoverished counties has

---

* Part of the speech at the Seminar on Targeted Poverty Elimination.

dropped for the first time, with 28 emerging from poverty in 2016, and it is estimated that 2017 will see around 100 more such cases when the final evaluation is complete. This shows our solid progress in addressing regional poverty.

Second, we have promoted faster development in poor areas. We have strengthened poverty alleviation by developing industries and businesses that leverage local strengths, including new models of poverty alleviation such as tourism, photovoltaic technology, and e-commerce programs. This approach has strengthened poor areas' endogenous vitality and motivation for development.

By promoting eco-environmental protection, relocating the impoverished population from inhospitable areas to places with better economic prospects, and returning farmland back to forest, poor areas have seen significant improvements in the environment and good results achieved in poverty alleviation through environmental protection.

The development of infrastructure and public services has greatly improved basic conditions in poor and especially rural areas, breathing new life into them.

By identifying those living under the poverty line, helping them escape poverty, and carrying out poverty alleviation projects, grassroots governance and management in poor areas have seen significant improvement, and rural grassroots Party organizations have strengthened their cohesion and vitality.

By dispatching first Party secretaries and resident working teams to impoverished villages, we have trained government officials and produced competent people working in the countryside. To date, we have dispatched a total of 435,000 officials to work as first Party secretaries and 2,778,000 working team members resident in poor villages. Right now the corresponding figures are 195,000 first Party secretaries and 775,000 working team members. Shouldering heavy responsibilities, these officials fight side by side with their local peers in leading villagers to emerge from poverty. These officials work hard to bring happier lives to the poor, and some have even given their lives to this cause, demonstrating their strong sense of responsibility and deep love for the people.

Third, we have formed a strong synergy by pooling all social forces to fight poverty. Government investment is the major input and plays a guiding role. We have strengthened collaboration between the eastern and western regions. We have reinforced the efforts of Party and government institutions directed towards designated regions, buttressed the role of the military and armed police forces, and extended the participation of social forces.

The state budget allocated to poverty alleviation grew at an average annual rate of 22.7 percent, and provincial funds for poverty alleviation at 26.9 percent. Impoverished counties have integrated agricultural development funds totaling RMB529.6 billion for poverty alleviation. Government financial departments have arranged loans of RMB350 billion for relocation of the poor, and granted small loans of more than RMB430 billion and re-lending loans of more than RMB160 billion for poverty alleviation. Local governments of poor areas brought in more than RMB46 billion by transferring surplus land quotas for urban construction.

In cooperation between the eastern and western regions, 342 more-developed counties in the east paired up with 570 impoverished counties in the west, contributing to poverty alleviation in western China and promoting coordinated development between regions. By providing poverty alleviation assistance to designated targets, Party and government institutions, particularly central Party and government departments, are able to gain a better understanding of rural and impoverished areas, and improve their working practices and train their officials in the process.

All sectors of society have participated widely in poverty alleviation. State-owned enterprises directly under the central government have provided targeted assistance to more than 10,000 impoverished villages in around 100 counties in former revolutionary base areas. Private enterprises have participated in the pairing-up program to help more than 10,000 poor villages. By the end of 2017, 46,200 private enterprises had provided assistance to 51,200 villages, investing RMB52.7 billion in poverty alleviation projects through support for local businesses and donating RMB10.9 billion to programs for public benefit. These endeavors have benefited more than 6.2 million registered poor. The China Glory Society organized more than 500 well-known entrepreneurs to participate in targeted poverty alleviation activities in Liangshan Prefecture, Sichuan Province. Cooperation agreements were reached on 149 projects with a contract value totaling RMB203.7 billion, and more than RMB40 million was donated for public welfare in the prefecture. These activities have not only helped impoverished villages and people to escape from poverty, but also promoted the great Chinese tradition of helping the poor and assisting those in difficulty.

Not long ago, I received a letter from 20 young Party members of the China Railway Tunnel Group who were working on the Chengdu-Kunming Railway expansion project. They said that more than 50 years before, the fathers or grandfathers of many of them had been involved in constructing the Shamulada Tunnel, the most difficult section of the Chengdu-Kunming Railway. Builders of the previous generations feared neither danger nor death, and dared to break through natural barriers; with this heroic spirit they turned natural chasms into thoroughfares, and their achievements are unsurpassed in the history of railway construction anywhere in the world. Now these young people have taken on the mantle from previous generations, and accepted the mission of building the Xiaoxiangling Tunnel, the longest and most difficult run on the new Chengdu-Kunming Railway. Determined to match their predecessors and remain true to their mission, they are working hard to complete the expansion project as quickly as possible. Once complete, the railway will become an "accelerator", helping people along its route to escape poverty. Reading the letter, I am very pleased to see that the younger generations take responsibility for and are loyal to the country and the people.

Fourth, we have established an institutional framework with Chinese characteristics for the fight against poverty. While strengthening CPC

leadership, we have included in the framework the following systems:
- a responsibility system where every party fulfills their own duties and functions;
- a working system where targets of assistance are accurately identified and targeted efforts are made to help them out of poverty;
- a policy system where policies at all levels are coordinated;
- an investment system to guarantee financial support and provide human resources;
- an assistance system where targeted measures are implemented for different regions, villages, households, and individuals;
- a social mobilization system to elicit extensive participation and build synergy;
- a multi-channel and omni-dimensional oversight system; and
- a stringent evaluation system.

This framework provides a strong institutional guarantee to back up the fight against poverty. The most fundamental element of this framework is a working mechanism whereby the central leadership makes overall plans, provincial authorities take overall responsibility, and city and county authorities take charge of implementation – authorities at all levels sign written pledges so that clear goals are set, accountability is ensured, and implementation measures are adopted. With these achievements, we have contributed China's vision and approaches to the global cause of poverty reduction.

We have gained valuable experience in the following respects from the practice of fighting poverty.

Firstly, we uphold CPC leadership to provide a strong organizational guarantee. Strong leadership is vital to the fight against poverty. We have given play to the role of Party committees at all levels in exercising overall leadership and coordinating the efforts of all. In addition, we have put in place a system whereby top leaders of the Party and government at the provincial, city, county, township and village levels take full responsibility for this work. This provides a firm political guarantee for poverty alleviation.

Secondly, we uphold the strategy of targeted poverty alleviation to improve effectiveness. Targeted efforts are essential to the fight against poverty. We must take targeted measures to reduce and eradicate poverty, including:
- identify the poor accurately,
- arrange targeted programs,
- utilize capital efficiently,
- take household-based measures,
- dispatch first Party secretaries based on village conditions, and
- achieve the set goals.

We identify the targets of poverty alleviation, determine who will carry out the work and how they should do it, and make clear how to apply an exit mechanism for those who have emerged from poverty. We do not spray preferential policies indiscriminately or "kill fleas with a hand-grenade". Instead, we adopt targeted measures for different villages, households and individuals according to their specific conditions, so that we can address the root causes of poverty.

Thirdly, we increase investment and strengthen financial support. Funding is a key guarantee for the fight against poverty. We have ensured multi-channel funding and diversified investment: government funding is the main source and plays a guiding role; input from financial institutions is increasing; the capital market's role in supporting poverty alleviation is tapped; and private funds are going into poverty alleviation on an extensive basis.

Fourthly, we mobilize people from all quarters. To fight poverty, all parties should combine in a joint effort. Both the government and society play their roles to the full, with government-sponsored projects, sector-specific programs, and corporate and societal assistance supplementing each other. We have mobilized all sectors and coordinated the market and society, so a poverty alleviation framework with extensive social participation is now in place.

Fifthly, we have strict requirements to encourage hard work and concrete results. This is essential to the fight against poverty. We must exercise full and rigorous Party self-governance throughout the process, and implement regular inspections and stringent evaluation, so as to ensure that concrete efforts are made in poverty eradication, and that the results are genuine, can prove their worth in practice, and will also withstand the test of time.

Sixthly, we ensure the principal role of the people in poverty elimination and arouse their enthusiasm in fighting poverty. Impoverished people's self-motivation is the foundation of the fight against poverty. We must rely on the people. We stimulate the enthusiasm, initiative, and creativity of the poor, help them access education and build aspirations. We must balance the relationship between external assistance and the poor's own efforts. To this end, we foster among the poor an awareness of escaping poverty through self-reliance, conduct training programs to improve their skills and abilities in work and business, and organize, guide and support them in their efforts to escape poverty through their hard work. Through these endeavors, our fight against poverty gains traction from the motivation of the people.

All of this valuable experience should be carried forward and developed further.

Notes

[1] The State Council launched the Seven-year Priority Poverty Reduction Program in April 1994. The program set forth the goal, to be achieved within the seven years up to 2000, of concentrating human, material, and financial resources and mobilizing all sectors of society to help 80 million impoverished rural residents meet their basic needs of life.

Win the Battle Against Poverty*

February 12, 2018

The 19th CPC National Congress in 2017 has made overall plans for the final stage of the battle against poverty, and relevant measures have been set out at the Central Conference on Economic Work, the Central Conference on Rural Work, and the National Conference on Development-driven Poverty Alleviation. To implement these plans and measures, we should prioritize the results of poverty alleviation, focus on severely impoverished areas, and make solid progress on all fronts.

First, we should strengthen organization and leadership. We must win the tough battle against poverty, as our Party has made a solemn promise to the people. We must be true to our promise. Since the 18th CPC National Congress in 2012, poverty eradication is the only issue on which Party and government heads at the provincial level have signed written pledges. All Party and government officials, especially top leaders at every level, must enhance their political awareness and sense of responsibility, and lead efforts to fulfill this mission.

Here I would like to emphasize that Party committees and governments of impoverished counties assume the main responsibility in poverty elimination, and their top leaders are the first persons responsible. During the final stage of the fight against poverty, officials should remain steadfast in their posts and focus on this task. Those incapable of the task should be replaced, and those involved in fraud and falsification must be held accountable. The central departments concerned should research and formulate an action plan on poverty elimination, and set a timetable and roadmap for ending

---

* Part of the speech at the Seminar on Targeted Poverty Elimination.

extreme poverty in three years.

Second, we should adhere to our goals and standards. Our goals are: Firstly, we will help all rural population defined as poor by current standards to emerge from poverty, thus eradicating extreme poverty; secondly, we will help all impoverished counties out of poverty, thus eliminating regional poverty.

The poverty standards are an important gauge for deciding targets and measures, and also for evaluating the results of poverty elimination. The CPC Central Committee has reiterated on many occasions that in the final stage of the fight against poverty, the standards are set to deliver the Two Assurances and Three Guarantees[1], and bring key indicators of basic public services in poor areas close to the national average. We must stick to these standards from beginning to end and ensure sustainable results, neither lowering the bar nor setting expectations too high.

Third, we should enhance relevant systems and mechanisms. We will continue the working mechanism whereby the central leadership makes overall plans, provincial authorities take overall responsibility, and city and county authorities take charge of implementation. The central leadership produces the top-level design in two respects: establishing policies and providing funds for local poverty eradication on the one hand, and tightening oversight over the evaluation of results on the other. Provincial authorities make action plans in accordance with central policies, and guide and supervise implementation. City and county authorities take specific measures based on local conditions to ensure that all poverty alleviation policies and plans will deliver.

We will improve the mechanism for evaluating poverty alleviation results as our work progresses, so that provincial authorities take the lead not only in setting requirements and taking on responsibilities, but also in performance evaluation. Third-party evaluation will be improved to narrow down the scope and simplify procedures, with the focus on assessing whether the Two Assurances and Three Guarantees have been fully delivered. The provincial authorities should evaluate and review whether a county has emerged from poverty.

Supervision and inspection teams sent by central authorities conduct spot checks to ensure the authenticity of evaluation results. The process of summoning provincial-level officials for inquiries into problems in their poverty alleviation work will be improved. We plan to hold another round this year, and will make this a regular practice and talk to officials whenever problems arise.

Fourth, we should take targeted measures. To win the fight against poverty, the key lies in targeted measures. To support macro decision-making and guidance, we should improve the system for registering the poor, with a focus on strengthening data sharing and analysis. We should advance targeted policy implementation. We should take into consideration local conditions, and apply different measures for different villages, households, and individuals. Solid work should be done to help the poor population by developing businesses, relocating them from inhospitable areas, creating more job opportunities, renovating dilapidated houses, improving education and health care, and developing the eco-economy.

Here I would like to emphasize poverty alleviation through business development and relocation. These are the main solutions to increasing income and eliminating poverty in the long run. Now that food and clothing are secured for the poor, we should plan for the future and aim for sustainable development of agriculture, and we must not be shortsighted in pursuit of quick successes and instant benefits. The state has invested very heavily in relocation projects for the poor. We cannot relocate people indiscriminately, for example moving households that need not move and leaving poor households where they are. In the next three years all registered poor in need of relocation will be relocated first, and other residents in the same villages who are eligible for relocation will also be catered for. Poor people who cannot be relocated for the time being should be guaranteed basic food and clothing and proper access to compulsory education, medical care, and safe housing. Future poverty alleviation can be combined with the rural revitalization strategy to relocate the poor step by step, for the purpose of protecting the eco-environment and making steady progress in poverty elimination and towards prosperity.

Fifth, we should improve fund management. Often substantial in value and covering many areas and locations, poverty alleviation funds are managed over a long course, making their supervision difficult and thus attracting wide attention. We should strengthen supervision to ensure that the use of funds is transparent and clean. We should increase financial input to ensure it matches the goals of poverty elimination. We should integrate funds for poverty alleviation and improve the management of agricultural funds, to ensure that they support the targeted programs while increasing efficiency and benefits.

We will establish databases of county-level poverty alleviation programs, strengthen evaluation, and expand the reserve of potential programs, preventing funds from lying idle or being wasted. We should improve the public information system, in which the allocation and utilization of poverty alleviation funds at the provincial, city and county levels will all be made public; programs and their use of funds at the township and village levels will be open to public scrutiny. Those committing corruption in poverty alleviation, once identified, must be investigated and held accountable.

Sixth, we should improve our conduct. The CPC Central Committee has designated 2018 a year of improving Party conduct in fighting poverty. We should focus on identifying and resolving problems, particularly weaknesses in the Four Consciousnesses, unfulfilled responsibilities, untargeted measures, poor management and use of funds, improper working practices, and lax performance evaluation. A long-term mechanism should be put in place to ensure that prominent problems in poverty alleviation, once reported, are thoroughly investigated. Confirmed cases of misconduct must be made public, and those responsible held accountable. We must draw lessons from those cases, improve our policies and measures, and strengthen regulatory systems to close the gap between the bars of the institutional cage.

Seventh, we should enhance the training of officials. The key to fighting poverty lies in their way of thinking, capabilities and drive. Competent personnel are what poor areas most need. In recent years we have selected and dispatched large numbers of officials and professionals to work in poor areas. In the long run, however, the number of people we can send is always limited. Poor areas must rely on their own officials and professionals to develop. This year we will focus on training for poverty alleviation officials at all levels. Central authorities will organize training for leading officials at the provincial level. Provincial, city and county authorities should strengthen training for officials at their own levels, with different priorities and focuses.

For officials at the county level and above, the focus of training should be improving their political awareness, forming a sound attitude towards performance, mastering approaches to targeted poverty elimination, and developing the ability to analyze and resolve problems. For officials working at the grassroots, the focus is improving their ability to tackle practical problems, so there should be more case studies and on-the-spot training. To enhance their ability in targeted poverty alleviation and eradication, we should cultivate officials to be well-versed in poverty reduction policies, capable of solving problems, and disciplined in their conduct.

We should attract a broad range of professionals to join poverty elimination and rural development, encouraging college graduates, former servicepeople, and people working or doing business elsewhere to return to their home villages or take leadership positions or start businesses. We should take better care of grassroots officials fighting poverty and encourage them to work harder during the toughest stage towards final success, by making sure that the capable are in the right positions, the hard-working are duly rewarded, and those who sacrifice themselves for the cause are remembered by all.

Eighth, we should motivate the poor. Impoverished people are both recipients and implementers of poverty alleviation. We should help them access education and build aspirations. We should boost their enthusiasm and initiative, and motivate and guide them to improve their lives through their own efforts, so as to make the poverty eradication process an internally sustainable force.

We should improve our approach to the fight against poverty

by providing jobs instead of giving grants, and by rewarding and subsidizing productive activities, so that the poor get more involved in poverty alleviation programs. We cannot do their work for them or simply dole out money and supplies. Instead we must encourage more pay for more work. By strengthening guidance through regular communication sessions and material rewards, we will encourage the poor to learn from and catch up with each other, and motivate them to rise out of poverty as soon as possible.

The role of village rules and established practices should be brought into play. We can establish poverty alleviation councils, ethics panels, and wedding and funeral councils to guide the poor in abandoning outdated customs and cultivating healthy practices through different channels. This will also ease people's financial burdens. Role models should be leading protagonists. Their stories should be spread so that the poor are motivated and feel proud of freeing themselves from poverty, and earn a better living through hard work.

In three years' time, when we have defeated poverty in this generation, we will have brought to an end, once and for all, the extreme poverty that has shackled the Chinese nation for millennia. This will be a source of great pride. Let us work together to achieve this goal, one of great significance to the Chinese nation and to the whole of humanity. It is my belief that as long as the whole Party and the people pull together and work hard, we are sure to win this battle.

Notes

[1] This refers to assurances of adequate food and clothing, and guarantees of access to compulsory education, basic medical services and safe housing for impoverished rural residents.

Deliver the Two Assurances and Three Guarantees*

April 16, 2019

It is a basic requirement and core indicator in our poverty eradication effort that by 2020 we will succeed in delivering the Two Assurances and Three Guarantees for impoverished rural residents. This is key to the success of the final stage of our fight against poverty. Generally speaking, the Two Assurances have been delivered, but there are still some weak aspects relating to the Three Guarantees.

In compulsory education, over 600,000 school-age children have dropped out of school nationwide. Rural boarding schools do not have adequate infrastructure to meet the needs of all children who remain in rural areas while their parents leave to work in cities. In medical services, some impoverished people are not covered by basic medical insurance, and some cannot receive timely treatment for common and chronic diseases. Impoverished counties, townships, and villages lack adequate medical facilities, and some villages do not even have clinics or qualified doctors. In housing safety, roughly 1.6 million households fall into the four categories[1] that are given priority in renovation of dilapidated houses, including about 800,000 impoverished households that have been registered. In some rural areas, safe home assessment is inaccurate or not conducted at all. Drinking water quality is still an issue; about 1.04 million impoverished people do not have access to safe drinking water, and the infrastructure for over 60 million rural people needs to be improved. All these prob-

---

* Part of the speech at a seminar on pressing problems related to the Two Assurances and Three Guarantees.

lems, if not properly solved by 2020, will chip away at the success of our poverty elimination effort.

All provincial authorities and central departments must give priority to these problems, build consensus and solve them effectively. To address these pressing problems, we should adopt a working mechanism whereby the central leadership makes overall plans, provincial authorities take overall responsibility, and city and county authorities take charge of implementation. The State Council Leading Group of Poverty Alleviation and Development should strengthen coordination and supervision to adjust the overall work in a timely manner. The Ministry of Education, Ministry of Housing and Urban-Rural Development, Ministry of Water Resources, National Health Commission, and National Healthcare Security Administration, as both members of the Leading Group of Poverty Alleviation and Development and authorities responsible for addressing the Three Guarantees, should make sure that the leading officials take charge of the overall effort and other officials are responsible for specific work to ensure the implementation of policies. They should define their criteria and supporting policies in line with respective departmental functions to guide all regions to identify and solve problems. Relevant provinces, autonomous regions and municipalities directly under the central government (hereinafter "provinces and equivalent administrative units") should organize grassroots agencies to examine the situation, and form a clear picture before working out targeted plans and measures by coordinating all organizational resources. Cities and counties should implement these plans and measures, and closely track the progress to make sure the Three Guarantees are provided to all households.

I have emphasized repeatedly that we should maintain the current poverty eradication standard, neither raising nor lowering it. Guaranteeing access to compulsory education means ensuring that children from poor families do not drop out of school during the compulsory education period. Guaranteeing access to medical care means covering all impoverished people with medical insurance which will make treatment of common and chronic diseases accessible and affordable for them, and allow them to maintain their normal life should they suffer from a serious illness. Guaranteeing access to safe housing means moving impoverished people out of dilapidated houses. Ensuring drinking water safety means giving all rural people access to safe drinking water through a coordinated approach. This is a basic national requirement, but the situation varies from place to place. For example, in terms of housing safety, attention should be given to ventilation in south China while keeping warm is essentially important in north China; in terms of drinking water safety, northwest China should focus on accessibility of water while southwest China needs to solve the problems of water supply, storage and quality. All regions should be flexible and take their own realities into consideration rather than imposing a uniform requirement. Various measures have been explored in solving pressing problems concerning the Three Guarantees, but some regions have raised the standard either consciously or unconsciously. The regions that have raised the threshold far beyond the national standard should scale it down, and those that have kept the bar by and large unchanged should continue to maintain the stability and consistency of policies.

The effort to deliver the Two Assurances and Three Guarantees should be based on a clear knowledge of the actual situation and any pressing problems. But in some localities, things remain vague. This is not acceptable. The relevant authorities should help all localities to identify the problems so as to take targeted measures. They should also coordinate efforts to make statistics accurate and consistent. The authorities in charge of specific sectors should take the lead in working out plans, and all provinces and equivalent administrative units should formulate specific measures, timetables, and schemes to ensure that tasks are completed as scheduled. We have adequate policies and enough funds for addressing the Three Guarantees, but the key is to get things done. We should work harder and direct more attention to the most prominent problems, identifying gaps and improving weaknesses one by one and from household to household.

We should fully publicize our policies and standards, to ensure an accurate understanding among all sectors of society and unify our thinking.

Notes

[1] This refers to registered impoverished households, households entitled to subsistence allowances, severely impoverished rural residents cared for at their homes with government support, and impoverished families of individuals with disabilities.

Further Reform

Follow the Guidance of the Third Plenary Session of the 19th CPC Central Committee*

February 28, 2018

Here, I'd like to make a few points on how we should implement the decision of the plenary session from the perspective of the guiding philosophy, overall plans, objectives and tasks it has set out.

First, we must be clear on the fundamental issue of upholding the authority and the centralized, unified leadership of the CPC Central Committee. Upholding and strengthening overall Party leadership is an intrinsic requirement and an important element of further reform of Party and state institutions. It is a political theme that underpins the entire process of reform. It was clearly stated at the Party's 19th National Congress last year that the primary task in reinforcing the Party's political foundations is to ensure that the whole Party obeys the Central Committee and upholds its authority and centralized, unified leadership. The power of making principles and guidelines of the Party and the state rests with the Central Committee, and the whole Party must safeguard the final and sole authority of the Central Committee through concrete action. Any organization and member of the Party, whatever their level or field and wherever they are, must obey the centralized, unified leadership of the Central Committee. All the work under the charge of central departments and local authorities must be planned and implemented in a context of resolutely implementing the decisions and plans of the Central Committee, so that all the orders from the top are carried out.

"Governing a country is like planting a tree. If the roots are firm,

---

* Part of the speech at the second full assembly of the Third Plenary Session of the 19th CPC Central Committee.

the branches and leaves flourish."[1] The roots of our governance are the leadership of the Party and the Chinese socialist system. We must pronounce it confidently and unequivocally. Party leadership must be comprehensive, systematic and holistic, and it must be followed in all respects – economic, political, cultural, social and eco-environmental progress, national defense and armed forces, national reunification, foreign affairs and strengthening the Party. If it were absent or weakened in any field, respect or stage, the Party's strength and the causes of our Party and country would be undermined.

Our emphasis on upholding the authority and the centralized, unified leadership of the Central Committee does not mean that democratic centralism and intra-Party democracy can be ignored. It is wrong to regard the two as mutually contradictory. Promoting intra-Party democracy and exercising centralized, unified leadership are consistent rather than contradictory. Democratic centralism is the Party's fundamental organizational principle, and intra-Party democracy its lifeline. Our democratic centralism is a system in which we have both centralism and democracy, both discipline and freedom, both unity of will and personal ease of mind. It is a system that integrates democracy and centralism.

Since the 18th CPC National Congress, the Central Committee has attached great importance to developing intra-Party democracy and drawing on collective wisdom. Before issuing important materials – reports to the Party's congresses, documents of the plenary sessions of the Central Committee, important documents and major decisions of the Party, reports on the work of the government, key measures for reform and development, and important documents on the work of central departments – we always solicit opinions from a certain number of Party members. In some cases we solicit several rounds of opinions. Sometimes, the range of solicitation covers all the provinces and equivalent administrative units, or dozens of departments of the Central Committee and the central government. When reviewing major decisions, the Central Committee requires that the opinions collected are reported, whether they are favorable or not.

The Central Committee strictly follows these institutionalized and standardized procedures. Of course, after collecting opinions and advice from all parties involved, it is the Central Committee that makes the final decision. During the process of deliberation and discussion, we give broad rein to democracy and let everyone speak up their mind freely. Once a decision is made by the Central Committee, however, it must be implemented without fail. During the course of implementation, complaints and problems may be reported in accordance with the relevant intra-Party procedures to higher-level authorities and even to the Central Committee.

With such a huge Party in a vast country like ours, if the final and sole authority of the Central Committee were undermined, the decisions of the Central Committee were ignored, and everyone followed their own way of thinking and worked their own way, nothing would be achieved. We adopt centralism on the basis of giving broad rein to democracy and upholding the authority and centralized, unified leadership of the Central Committee, so that we can pool the wisdom of the entire Party and reflect the will of all Party members. This is one of our Party's great innovations – it is a major strength of Party leadership and the socialist system. It is conducive to rational, democratic and law-based decision-making and avoiding major – or even worse, fatal – mistakes; it can also help us overcome segmentation and a silo mentality and avoid a situation where there is only deliberation but no decision or where decisions are made but not implemented. It can help form a powerful synergy propelling the development of the Party and the country.

The relationship between the Party and the government is not only a major theoretical issue; it is also an important practical one. After the beginning of reform and opening up in 1978 we discussed the separation of the Party and the government with the goal of solving the problems of low efficiency, excessive and overstaffed departments and a dilatory approach to work. Admittedly, at that time we lacked both theoretical understanding and practical experience, and our efforts to solve our problems of governance and governing capability were tentative. Since the beginning of reform and opening up, whatever adjustments have been made to the relationship between the Party and the government, there has been one unchanging principle, which was stated by Deng Xiaoping, "We must uphold leadership by the Party and never abandon it, but the Party should exercise its leadership effectively."[2] On this subject of leadership, Deng quoted Vladimir Lenin, "The dictatorship of the proletariat means a persistent struggle – bloody and bloodless, violent and peaceful, military and economic, educational and administrative – against the forces and traditions of the old society.... Without a party of iron that has been tempered in the struggle, a party enjoying the confidence of all honest people in the class in question, a party capable of watching and influencing the mood of the masses, such a struggle cannot be waged successfully."[3] Deng emphasized that this truth expressed by Lenin still holds.

When it comes to properly handling the relationship between the Party and the government, the first and foremost principle is to uphold the leadership of the Party. This is a precondition for the division of functions. Furthermore, no matter how functions are divided, the prime purpose is to uphold and improve the leadership of the Party. As the CPC is the ruling Party in our country, its leadership position and ruling status are closely linked. The Party's power to exercise centralized, unified leadership cannot be divided. We cannot talk about the separation of the Party and the government or the integration of the two in a simplistic way. Rather, we should constantly improve the way the Party exercises leadership and governance according to specific features and basic conditions in different fields.

In this round of reform of Party and state institutions, we have reflected deeply on strengthening the overall leadership of the Party, taking a holistic approach to the setup of Party and government institutions, and improving the efficiency of the Party and the government in the new era. The focus of our efforts is to design and organize institutions to ensure stronger leadership by the Party over all areas. We will adjust those Party and government institutions whose jurisdiction is too narrow and whose functions overlap, and place the offices of some CPC Central Committee's bodies for decision-making, deliberation and coordination in government departments, in an effort to remove the demarcation between the Party and the government and have one matter dealt with in a joint manner. Our purpose is to strengthen the leadership of the Party, improve the government's capacity to deliver, smooth out the relationship between the Party and the government, and establish and improve the decision-making and coordination mechanisms of the Central Committee for important work. This is a major decision made by the Central Committee based on positive and negative past experiences.

For local Party committees at various levels, strengthening leadership over important work means improving their capacity for organization and coordination so as to ensure the effective implementation of major decisions and plans of the Central Committee. They can set up specific institutions in light of local conditions. Other than those Party and government institutions and functions that fall under the centralized, unified leadership of the Central Committee and those concerning consistency of the legal regime, administrative orders and policies, and market management, other institutions and functions at local levels do not have to correspond to national ones. In addition, local authorities should identify priorities and address themselves to tasks with a decisive bearing on reform and development in their localities, and refrain from trying to attend to major and minor issues at one and the same time.

Second, we must understand the goal of further reform of Party and state institutions. It was determined at this plenary session that the objective of further reform of Party and state institutions is to establish a functional system of these institutions that is complete, well-conceived, standard and efficient; a Party leadership system that ensures the Party's core role in exercising overall leadership and coordinating the efforts of all; a law-based administrative governance system with clear functions and responsibilities; world-class armed forces with Chinese characteristics; and a sound system of people's organizations for bridging and serving the general populace. With these systems in place, we will be able to promote coordinated actions and form synergy among the people's congresses, governments, political advisory bodies, and supervisory, judicial and prosecuting organs, people's organizations, enterprises, public institutions, and social groups under the unified leadership of the CPC, so as to comprehensively raise the national governance capacity.

As an important part of socialist system with Chinese characteristics, the functional system of Party and state institutions encompasses the administrative activities of the Party and state at various stages and levels and in various fields, the interactive relationship between them, and the intrinsic connections within them. By reforming and improving the systems of Party leadership, government administration, the armed forces, and people's organizations, we need to promote the integration of various institutions and functions, improve coordination and efficiency in the handling of Party and state affairs, and establish a basic framework of Party and state institutional setup and functional allocation that adapts to the requirements of the new tasks in the new era. The Party leadership system that ensures the Party exercises overall leadership and coordinates the efforts of all is of primary importance, covering all areas and elements. Under the leadership of the Party, people's congresses, governments, political advisory bodies, and supervisory, judicial and prosecuting organs, people's organizations, enterprises, public institutions, social groups, and armed forces fulfill their respective duties and responsibilities and coordinate with one another in an orderly manner. This ensures that the central and local authorities have consistent policies that are implemented smoothly, effectively and with vitality.

Looking to realize the Two Centenary Goals and implementing both the Five-sphere Integrated Plan and the Four-pronged Comprehensive Strategy in a coordinated way, we have defined farsighted institutional strategies in this round of further reform of Party and state institutions, with the goal of establishing the basic framework of the setup and functions of Party and state institutions and achieving optimization, coordination and efficiency. Optimization means that the setup and functions must be well-conceived and rational, and power must be matched with responsibilities. Coordination means the need to balance central leadership and the delegation of power, and the need to address priority areas. Efficiency means good performance and smooth procedures. To meet these requirements, we should properly handle the following bilateral relationships.

The relationship between centralized leadership and delegation of power. In further reform of Party and state institutions, the two are inherently coherent. With proper centralization we can ensure that departments function methodically and avoid acting in disunity, thus improving the overall efficiency of the system. Through proper delegation of power, we can stimulate the enthusiasm, initiative and creativity of every unit and every sub-system. In this round of further reform, we will establish and improve the systems and mechanisms by which the Party exercises leadership over major tasks, and optimize the Central Committee's bodies for decision-making, deliberation and coordination, which are responsible for top-level design, overall planning, coordination and promotion of major work. We will also strengthen and optimize the Party's leadership over tasks regarding further reform, law-based governance, the economy, agriculture and rural areas, discipline inspection and supervision, organization, communication and culture, national security, the judiciary and law enforcement, the united front, ethnic and religious affairs, education, science and technology, cybersecurity and information technology, foreign affairs, and auditing. These arrangements are intended to enable the Party to exercise more effective leadership and coordination over major initiatives that have an overall bearing on the undertakings of the Party and the state, exert stronger centralized leadership at a higher level, better wield its power, and fulfill its responsibilities, so as to improve efficiency and ensure that all of its decisions are implemented. It is important to note that the Party exercises overall leadership over major issues rather than attending to all matters big and small.

The relationship between the part and the whole and between the present and the future. Further reform of Party and state institutions has an overall bearing on the undertakings of the Party and the state and involves all areas and aspects of economic and social development. In this round of further reform, some departments need to be strengthened, some will be merged, some are to be dissolved, some will be placed under new or other superior bodies, and so forth. If one takes a local perspective and sees from the existing organizational makeup and authorization, they may well come up with a lot of reasons for maintaining the status quo. However, faced with new circumstances and tasks and the need for long-term development, if we follow the old mentality and believe that it is fine to remain the same and there is no need to reform, we will be unable to solve the outstanding problems and may even create problems. In this round of further reform, we plan to establish the Ministry of Natural Resources, Ministry of Ecology and Environment, Ministry of Veterans Affairs, Ministry of Emergency Management, National Healthcare Security Administration, China International Development Cooperation Agency, National Immigration Administration and other institutions. To set up these agencies, we have taken into consideration both the need to solve the most prominent problems of the present stage and the need to adapt to developing trends in future. As plans made for the overall progress of the undertakings of the Party and the state, they are meant to address both pressing current problems and also preset measures for some strategic goals, so as to meet the long-term needs of the Party and the state.

The relationship between large and small departments. An important goal of this round of further reform is to solve the problem of overlapping and fragmented departmental functions, and to set up institutions in a coordinated and integrated manner so as to better tap into their efficiency and strengths. To achieve this goal, we have taken substantial steps towards establishing larger government departments, and this should be carried out steadily. Not all departments need to be large, since some are specialized and some are comprehensive. Even for comprehensive ones, large size does not fit all, nor is it essential to put all related functions in a single department. The key is to group functions in a rational manner in line with reality that facilitates work and improves efficiency. Large or small, it all depends on needs.

The relationship between optimization and coordination. This round of further reform involves Party, government, military and people's organizations and is related to economic, political, cultural, social, and eco-environmental systems and the development of the Party. The transfer of functions and adjustments of institutional setup are closely linked, and the internal correlation and interaction between various reforms is strong. Each reform will have an impact on other reforms and need their support. This requires us to place greater importance on advancing different reforms in a coordinated and mutually reinforcing manner while optimizing institutional setup and functional assignment, so that institutional efficiency is improved across the board.

Third, we must understand the direction and requirement of the reform of the socialist market economy and see to it that the market plays the decisive role in resource allocation and that the government plays its role more effectively. All rounds of institutional reform since the beginning of reform and opening up in 1978 have focused on reform of our economic system featuring the separation of government functions from the management of enterprises, state assets, public institutions, and social groups. They have promoted reform and opening up and socialist modernization. Currently, there are still many institutional obstacles holding up our high-quality development, and the potential of economic reform needs to be further tapped. We need to accelerate reform under the precondition of keeping overall economic and social stability, and work hard to develop an economy with more effective market mechanisms, dynamic micro-entities, and sound macro-regulation, so as to provide institutional support for high-quality development.

In this round of further reform, we have made substantial adjustments to institutions and their functions in the fields of macro-management and market regulation. This is meant to give full play to the strengths of the market and the government so that they complement and coordinate with each other for better quality, more efficient, fairer and more sustainable development. The reform emphasizes the need to reduce micro-management and the number of items subject to government approval, and minimize the government's direct allocation of market resources and direct intervention in economic activities. The aim is to realize effective incentives generated from property rights and ensure free flows of factors, flexible prices, fair and orderly competition, and business survival based on competition, so that market players have more room to develop the economy and create wealth with vigor and vitality and to maximize the effectiveness and efficiency of resource allocation.

Ensuring that the market plays the decisive role in resource allocation does not mean the government has no role to play. It should do what is needed and never go beyond its purview. Since our country applies a system of socialist market economy, we should do full justice to the strengths of its socialist system by allowing the Party and the government to play an active role in matters beyond the market's capability.

To achieve innovation and improvement in macro-control, we have taken big steps to reduce micro-management and the number of items subject to approval. Responsible departments should shift their main focus to macro-management of the economy. They should improve the system for macro-control, employ national development plans for strategic guidance, improve coordination between economic policies in the fields of finance, monetary management, industry, and regional development, and make macro-control more forward-looking, targeted and coordinated.

To strengthen market regulation, we have created a top-level design geared to dealing with pressing current problems and the need for future development. Therefore, we have decided to set up the State Administration for Market Regulation, which will integrate the main functions of the departments for industry and commerce, quality supervision, and food and drug administration. We have devised clear requirements for comprehensive law enforcement in market regulation and maintained unified anti-monopoly law enforcement and IPR protection in a centralized manner. These measures will reduce government-imposed transaction costs for businesses and give more powerful impetus to economic and social development.

Fourth, we must understand the people-centered philosophy of development and address the most pressing and immediate problems that concern the people the most. To ensure that the people enjoy a happy life is the ultimate goal of all our work and is an important manifestation of our Party's fundamental purpose of serving the people wholeheartedly. For this reason, we must follow the people-centered philosophy of development in furthering institutional reform and fulfill the people's expectation for a better life.

This round of further reform focuses on improving people's wellbeing in key areas, aiming to make the social security system and access to public services fairer and more sustainable. We will redouble our efforts to reorganize and optimize the setup of the institutions and establish a number of new agencies in areas of public concern such as education, culture, public health, medical insurance, veteran affairs, immigration service, eco-environmental protection, and emergency management. These measures are meant to reinforce government functions in public services and social management, ensure and improve public wellbeing, and safeguard public security in a better way. Relevant departments should have a strong sense of purpose, mission and responsibility. They should see improving people's lives as their greatest achievement, treat people's concerns and worries as their own, and serve to meet people's urgent needs. They should quicken their pace to straighten out their functions and activities, so as to form synergy as soon as possible and do a good and solid job for the benefit of the people.

Law enforcement is an important way for administrative organs to fulfill their governmental functions. To resolve serious problems of failure to enforce the law in a procedure-based, strict, transparent and non-abusive manner as well as nonfeasance and malfeasance in law enforcement, we must step up our pace in establishing a law-based administrative system that matches power with responsibility and is authoritative and efficient. Reform in law enforcement is a special task in this round of further reform. Law enforcement teams are to be established in market regulation, eco-environmental protection, the cultural industry, transport, and agriculture on the basis of integrating relevant functions. We will make a substantial reduction in the categories of law enforcement teams, and allocate law enforcement forces on a rational basis, address the problem of laws being enforced by multiple departments at different levels, and work to ensure strict, procedure-based, impartial, and non-abusive law enforcement. All provincial authorities and central departments should improve the system for listing their powers and obligations, speed up the codification of institutional setup, functions, purviews, procedures and responsibilities, strengthen checks on and oversight over administrative power, and see to it that power is designated, disciplined, restricted and supervised in accordance with the law.

Fifth, we must understand the importance of keeping both central and local authorities motivated. The relationship between central and local authorities is always critical in our political life. In April 1956, Mao Zedong pointed out in the important report titled "On the Ten Major Relationships": "... our attention should now be focused on how to enlarge the powers of the local authorities to some extent, give them greater independence and let them do more, all on the basis that the unified leadership of the central authorities is to be strengthened. This will be advantageous to our task of building a powerful socialist country. Our territory is so vast, our population is so large and the conditions are so complex that it is far better to have the initiative come from both the central and the local authorities than from one source alone." Giving full play to the initiative of both central and local authorities has always been a fundamental principle.

We must uphold the authority and centralized, unified leadership of the Central Committee when carrying out institutional reform at local levels. This is essential for ensuring the smooth implementation of policies and orders from the central authorities across the country. As a unitary state, local Party committees and governments must first of all ensure effective implementation of the decisions and plans of the Central Committee. The nature of our state and the duties of local authorities determine that the setup of key institutions at the provincial, city and county levels must basically correspond with that of the central authorities and should not be multifarious. Other than this, local authorities should be allowed to set up institutions in certain fields in accordance with local conditions, so as to adapt to the needs of social management and public services and bring into full play the initiative of the localities. In recent years, some central departments have interfered with the setup of local institutions, some exerting control through projects and finance, others through assessments and inspections, and still others through speaking directly to provincial Party secretaries and governors. Although the intention of these departments is to maintain the coherence of the vertical institutional setup, and to make their own systems operate well, they should not ignore the overall situation and harm the initiatives of local authorities. Here I declare that other than as authorized by the Central Committee, no department shall intervene in any way in the setup of local institutions.

Quotas on the number of institutions represent the main binding limit on institutional setup at the provincial, city and county levels, and an issue of common concern to localities. Reform must follow strict and standard management and give sufficient consideration to local realities. The number of Party institutions and government agencies should be counted together and must not exceed the total quota, and Party and government institutions at sub-department, sub-division and sub-section levels under provincial, city and county governments as well as public institutions with administrative functions are to be included in quota management. The current quotas should be adjusted accordingly. All local authorities must meet their quota by dissolving departments established without proper procedures, ending the malpractice of "cloning" organizations[4], and doing away with "public institutions" set up without authorization.

In this round of reform, based on the experience of pilot reform projects in some localities, we have set a new requirement of establishing community-level administrative systems that are simple and highly efficient. Our main idea is to integrate community-level institutions for approvals, services and law enforcement, use institutional staffing resources in a coordinated manner, and establish comprehensive institutions by integrating relevant functions. We should try our best to let community-level institutions have access to resources, provide services and be vested with management responsibilities. We must ensure that community affairs are run by communities themselves, that community-level powers are delegated to communities, and that there are people responsible for community affairs. We should make life convenient for the public by ensuring that they can get problems solved at one single department and with one-stop service. It is made clear in this round of reform that higher-level institutions need to improve their leadership over community-level institutions. Both the "one to many" model in which one community-level institution undertakes assignments from multiple superior institutions and the "many to one" model in which different community-level institutions request instructions from and report to the same higher-level institution can coexist.

Notes

[1] Wu Jing: *Governance of the Zhenguan Period (Zhen Guan Zheng Yao)*.

[2] Deng Xiaoping: "On Reform of the Political Structure", *Selected Works of Deng Xiaoping*, Vol. III, Eng. ed., Foreign Languages Press, Beijing, 1994, p. 181.

[3] V. I. Lenin: "'Left-Wing' Communism – an Infantile Disorder", *V. I. Lenin: Collected Works*, Vol. 31, Eng. ed., Progress Publishers, Moscow, 1966, pp. 44-45.

[4] Some Party or government institutions have a principal title and one or more subsidiary names, which might be used for non-core activities. "Cloning" occurs when a subsidiary name is converted into a real organization and provided with staff and other resources, for the purpose of expanding areas of jurisdiction and power. – *Tr.*

Deeper Reform Requires Greater Resolve*

July 6, 2018-November 26, 2019

I

Since the 19th CPC National Congress in 2017, on the basis of the achievements of reform after the 18th National Congress in 2012, the CPC Central Committee has lost no time in advancing reform measures of overall importance, making major progress in furthering reform in all respects. To move ahead, we should focus our strength on major difficulties and tough battles, stimulate the vitality of our systems, take advantage of all experience gained at the grassroots, and encourage officials to work hard and be achievers, thereby effectively furthering reform in all respects.

(from the speech at the third meeting of the Central Commission for Further Reform, July 6, 2018)

II

Implementation is the key to successful reform, and it is also a difficult task. As we enjoy ever more favorable conditions for pursuing and implementing reform, and the theoretical, practical and institutional foundations of reform grow stronger, along with public support, we should concentrate more energy and make greater efforts to ensure effective implementation, improve leadership and

---

* Excerpts from speeches made between July 6, 2018 and November 26, 2019.

coordination, and focus our reform on practical problems.

(from the speech at the fourth meeting of the Central Commission for Further Reform, September 20, 2018)

III

Starting a new historical period of reform and opening up and socialist modernization, the Third Plenary Session of the 11th CPC Central Committee in 1978 was a landmark event. The Third Plenary Session of the 18th CPC Central Committee in 2013 was also a milestone because it started a new era for further reform on all fronts and for planning and advancing reform in a systematic and holistic way. It broke new ground in our drive for reform and opening up. Aiming for decisive achievements in important areas and key aspects of reform by 2020, we should continue to fight tough battles, crack hard nuts, and ensure we succeed in every single reform that we initiate, so as to lay a firm foundation for completing the reform tasks set at the 2013 session.

(from the speech at the sixth meeting of the Central Commission for Further Reform, January 23, 2019)

IV

At present, the reform and development in our country is undergoing profound changes. As uncertain and unstable external factors increase, our reform and development are faced with new circumstances and issues. In this context, we must maintain strategic resolve, focus on solving problems, guide reform in the light of circumstances, make coordinated plans, implement targeted policies, and adopt effective and powerful measures to forestall and resolve major problems, so as to ensure that reform can better serve the overall development of our economy and society.

(from the speech at the eighth meeting of the Central Commission for Further Reform, May 29, 2019)

V

Further reform in all respects is an important manifestation of our Party's commitment to its original aspiration and founding mission. The deeper the reform, the more resolute we should be in shouldering responsibilities, taking actions, making rapid and steady progress, and forging ahead with courage. We must never pause or slacken our efforts. Through our Aspiration and Mission education campaign, we need to take a more proactive approach to reform in thinking, action, and political principles. We must brave problems and difficulties, concentrate on addressing inadequacies, shore up points of weakness, stimulate vitality, and ensure implementation. We must have the determination to break impediments of vested interests and remove all institutional barriers to development.

(from the speech at the ninth meeting of the Central Commission for Further Reform, July 24, 2019)

VI

In implementing the reform tasks set by the CPC Central Committee since the Third Plenary Session of the 18th CPC Central Committee, the key in the early stage is to build a solid foundation and a strong framework, and the focus in the middle phase is to advance reform in all respects and build up momentum. Our task now is to boost integration, collaboration and efficiency, consolidate and entrench the achievements we have made in recent years in removing institutional barriers and fostering innovation in policy, and develop a more mature and well-defined system in every field.

(from the speech at the 10th meeting of the Central Commission for Further Reform, September 9, 2019)

VII

The Fourth Plenary Session of the 19th CPC Central Committee in 2019 and the Third Plenary Session of the 18th CPC Central Committee in 2013 follow the same themes, support each other theoretically, and reinforce each other in actual practice. They share the same goals and have drawn up important plans that are consistent and progressive. The former systematically integrates the theoretical, institutional and practical gains on furthering comprehensive reform since the Third Plenary Session of the 18th CPC Central Committee, and maps out a clearer top-level design for the new era. We must focus on upholding and improving socialism with Chinese characteristics and modernizing our state governance system and capacity. With that in mind, we should be more proactive in improving state systems and governance through reform, and extend reform in all respects with a focus on improving the systems. We should examine the progress of all reform tasks against our goals, and log on our agenda the key measures decided at the Fourth Plenary Session in a timely manner. We must analyze and define measures to address badly-needed systems for state governance as defined by the CPC Central Committee and systems that are essential for meeting the people's expectation for a better life, and ensure that reform measures are well coordinated, fully integrated, and truly effective.

(from the speech at the 11th meeting of the Central Commission for Further Reform, November 26, 2019)

Valuable Experience from 40 Years of Reform and Opening Up*

December 18, 2018

To keep up with the times, our best recourse is to comply with the trends of history, and to seek and proactively respond to change. As an ancient Chinese scholar said, "Practice improves understanding and a deeper understanding guides further practice."[1] The valuable experience we have gained from 40 years of reform and opening up is the intellectual wealth of the CPC and the Chinese people. The experience provides significant guidance for upholding and developing socialism with Chinese characteristics for a new era. That is why we must value it, uphold it, and continue to enrich and develop it through further practice.

First, we must ensure Party leadership over each and every aspect of our work, and continue to strengthen and develop that leadership. Forty years of reform and opening up have taught us that Party leadership is the defining feature of socialism with Chinese characteristics and the greatest strength of China's socialist system.

The Party exercises overall leadership across all areas of endeavor in every part of the country. Relying on this, we have been able to achieve a historic transformation, usher in a new era of reform and opening up, and embark on a new journey towards the great rejuvenation of the Chinese nation. We have been able to address major risks and challenges and overcome repeated hardships and setbacks. We have been able to cope with changes, quell political turbulence, battle against such threats as floods, SARS, and earthquakes, and

---

* Part of the speech at the conference celebrating the 40th anniversary of reform and opening up.

deal with various crises. Finally, we have been able to adhere to the path of socialism with Chinese characteristics rather than following the old path of a rigid closed-door policy, or an erroneous path by abandoning socialism. To uphold Party leadership, we must keep improving it and adapting to the demands of practice, the current era and the people. Upholding Party leadership is an essential principle that defines the future of the Party and the Chinese nation, and all Party members and the Chinese people must keep alignment with the Central Committee in their way of thinking, in political principles, and in actions without wavering.

On the path ahead, we must enhance our sense of the Four Consciousnesses, the Four-sphere Confidence, and the Two Upholds. Party leadership should be exercised and manifested in all areas, including reform, development, stability, domestic affairs, foreign policy and national defense, and in governance of the Party, the country and the armed forces. Every step in reform and opening up is difficult, and we will certainly face risks and challenges of all kinds, even raging waves and storms. Our Party must exercise overall leadership and coordinate work in all areas. Its governance must be scientific, democratic and law-based. We must improve the way the Party exercises leadership and governance, improve the Party's ability to lead and govern, and strengthen the Party's ability and resolve to chart our course, craft overall plans, design policy and promote reform. All these efforts must be directed to ensuring that reform and opening up is on the right course.

Second, we must pursue people-centered development and fulfill their desire for a better life. Forty years of reform and opening up have taught us that it is Chinese Communists' original aspiration and founding mission to seek happiness for the Chinese people and rejuvenate the Chinese nation. It is also why we started reform and opening up.

Our Party comes from the people, has its roots among the people, and works for the benefit of the people. Serving the people wholeheartedly is the fundamental purpose of the Party. Therefore, meeting the fundamental interests of all our people is the starting point and ultimate goal of all our work. Our policy-making should be based on what the people support, approve of and are content with. We should comply with the people's aspirations, respect the people's opinions, be attentive to public sentiment, and be dedicated to improving people's wellbeing. We need to formulate and implement the right theories, guidelines, principles and policies to lead the people forward, and at the same time draw impetus from people's creativity and demands for development. We must ensure the people share the benefits of reform and opening up, and be motivated to engage in further reform and opening up and socialist modernization.

On the path ahead, we must always have as our goal the people's desire for a better life. We must fulfill the Party's fundamental purpose of serving the people wholeheartedly, put into practice the mass line, and ensure the people's principal status. We must respect the expectations the people have expressed, the experience they have created, the rights and interests they enjoy, and the role they have played, so as to fully release their immense creativity. We need to improve our democratic systems, expand democratic channels, diversify forms of democracy, and enhance legal guarantees for democracy, so as to ensure the people enjoy democratic rights that are extensive and full, real and concrete, and effective and applicable in accordance with the law. We should address people's needs, concerns and expectations, ensure that they share the achievements of economic, political, cultural, social and eco-environmental development, give them a stronger sense of having direct and substantial benefits, happiness and security, and continue to promote well-rounded human development and common prosperity for everyone.

Third, we must maintain the guiding role of Marxism and encourage theoretical development based on practice. Forty years of experience has taught us that innovation is the lifeline of reform and opening up.

Development has no final destination; free minds know no bounds. Frederick Engels said, "the final causes of all social changes and political revolutions are to be sought, not in men's brains, not in men's better insights into eternal truth and justice, but in changes in the modes of production and exchange."[2] We need to combine theory and practice, answer the questions posed by the times and the people, and dispel the mist clouding our practices and judgment, in an effort to adapt Marxism to China's conditions, keep it up-to-date, enhance its popular appeal, and break new ground.

On the path ahead we must free our minds while seeking truth from facts, and be guided by Marxism-Leninism, Mao Zedong Thought, Deng Xiaoping Theory, the Theory of Three Represents, the Scientific Outlook on Development, and the Thought on Socialism with Chinese Characteristics for a New Era. Developing Marxism in the 21st century and China today is a mandatory responsibility of contemporary Chinese Communists. To achieve this, we need to be more conscious about resolving problems, keeping up with the times, and developing a strategic mindset. We need a keen historical insight and a broad global vision to identify the nature of things and the intrinsic connections between them. We need to follow closely the creative activities of all peoples, learn from the outstanding achievements of all civilizations, and respond to the new and significant challenges constantly posed by our times and our practice. In this way, we will increase the appeal of Marxism in the contemporary Chinese context.

Fourth, we must adhere to the path of socialism with Chinese characteristics and continue to develop Chinese socialism. Forty years of reform and opening up have taught us that the direction in which we advance decides our future; the path we have chosen decides our destiny.

To ensure our future rests in our own hands, we must be firmly committed to our ideal and path. Over the past 40 years of reform and opening up, our Party has focused its theory and practice on upholding and developing socialism with Chinese characteristics. China is a vast country with over 5,000 years of history and a huge population. There is no manual to which we can refer in promoting reform and development, neither do we have any need for condescending instructors to lecture our people. Lu Xun[3] said, "What is a road? It comes of trampling places where no road was before, of opening up wasteland where only brambles grew."[4] The path of socialism with Chinese characteristics will allow China to catch up with the times in great strides and play a leading role.

On the path ahead, we must act under the guidance of the Thought on Socialism with Chinese Characteristics for a New Era and the guiding principles of the Party's 19th National Congress held in 2017. We must have full confidence in our path, theory, system and culture, and keep reform and opening up in the right direction. What to reform and how to reform must be assessed against the overall goal of improving and developing socialism with Chinese characteristics and modernizing our system and capacity for governance. We must reform what should be reformed and can be reformed; we must not reform what should not be reformed and cannot be reformed. We must remain committed to the Party's basic line, fulfilling the central task of economic development while upholding the Four Cardinal Principles and furthering reform and opening up, in the great practice of socialism with Chinese characteristics. This is a long-term principle which we shall never abandon.

Fifth, we must improve and develop the system of socialism with Chinese characteristics, and continuously build on our institutional strengths. Forty years of reform and opening up have taught us that systems are of fundamental significance to the overall, stable and long-term development of the Party and the country.

Improving and developing the Chinese socialist system is key to China's progress. It provides a strong guarantee for unlocking and developing productivity, for releasing and enhancing social vitality, for maintaining the vigor of the Party and the country, for overall social stability, for the people to live and work in contentment, and for national security. It facilitates the establishment of dynamic systems and mechanisms that allow all elements such as labor, knowledge, technology, management and capital to fully function, and to bring forth all surging sources of social wealth.

On the path ahead we must, without hesitation, consolidate and develop the public sector, and at the same time, encourage, support and guide the development of the non-public sector. We must give full play to the decisive role of the market in resource allocation, give better play to the role of government, and invigorate all market entities.

We must ensure that the Party's leadership, the people's position as masters of the country, and law-based governance form an indivisible whole. We must uphold and improve the system of people's congresses, the system of CPC-led multiparty cooperation and political consultation, the system of regional ethnic autonomy, and the system of grassroots self-governance. We must advance law-based governance, consolidate and develop the broadest possible patriotic united front, develop socialist consultative democracy, and provide institutional guarantees to ensure that the people are the masters of the country.

We need to strengthen cultural systems. We must uphold socialism, rally public support, foster a new generation with sound values and ethics, develop Chinese culture, and build a positive image of China. We need to foster and observe the core socialist values, promote the creative evolution of fine traditional culture, keep alive our revolutionary culture, and develop advanced culture, so that the Chinese culture will be shaped into one that shines in the current era and in the world.

We need to reinforce our systems of social governance. We should continue to promote social equity and justice, and maintain social order and security.

We need to reinforce eco-environmental protection, and put in place the strictest possible systems.

We must eliminate all institutional obstacles and vested interests impeding our country's development, speed up the establishment of systems and mechanisms that are comprehensive, procedure-based and effective, and make the socialist system more mature and better-defined.

Sixth, we must pursue development as a top priority and increase our overall national strength. Forty years of reform and opening up have taught us that the essential requirement and fundamental task of socialism is to unleash and develop productive forces and increase the overall strength of our socialist country.

Economic development is the absolute principle, and what we pursue is sound and high-quality development. We must focus on the central goal of economic development and promote sustained and sound social and economic development. This is our best recourse if we are to increase China's economic power, technological base, defense capabilities, and overall strength, and to lay a solid material foundation for upholding and developing Chinese socialism and rejuvenating the Chinese nation.

On the path ahead, we must resolve the principal challenge facing our society – the gap between unbalanced and inadequate development and the growing expectation of the people for a better life. We must pursue with resolve the concept of innovative, coordinated, green, open and shared development. We must implement the Five-sphere Integrated Plan and the Four-pronged Comprehensive Strategy to promote high-quality development. We must see to it that new industrialization, IT application, urbanization, and agricultural modernization go forward hand in hand. We must quicken our pace in developing a modernized economy, and strive to achieve better quality, more efficient, fairer, and more sustainable development.

We should pursue supply-side structural reform as our main task, transform the growth model, improve the economic structure, and foster new drivers of growth. We should expand domestic demand and implement the coordinated regional development strategy and the rural revitalization strategy. We must take tough steps to forestall and defuse major risks, carry out targeted poverty eradication, and prevent and control pollution.

We should pursue the philosophy that innovation is the primary impetus and talent is the resource of first importance. We should implement the innovation-driven development strategy, improve the national innovation system, and speed up innovation in key and core technologies, to create new engines for social and economic development.

We should strengthen our commitment to eco-civilization. Lucid waters and lush mountains are invaluable assets. Acting on this understanding, we should develop eco-friendly growth models and ways of life, so that our country will be more beautiful and our people will enjoy a more pleasant environment.

Seventh, we must open the country wider to the outside world and join other countries in building a global community of shared future. Forty years of reform and opening up have taught us that openness brings progress, while isolation leads to backwardness.

China cannot develop in isolation from the rest of the world; and the world needs China for global prosperity. We need to give overall consideration to domestic development and the international situation, adhere to the fundamental national policy of opening up, and adopt a proactive opening-up policy. In this way we will establish a multidimensional, multitiered and wide-ranging framework for opening up which creates a favorable international environment for China to enjoy a broad space for development.

On the path ahead, we must champion the cause of peace, development, cooperation and mutual benefit, uphold the fundamental foreign policy goals of preserving world peace and promoting common development, and forge a new approach to international relations featuring mutual respect, equity and justice, and win-win cooperation. We respect the right of the peoples of all countries to choose their own development path. We endeavor to uphold international equity and justice, stand for democracy in international relations, and oppose acts that impose one's will on others or interfere in the internal affairs of others. The strong must not be allowed to bully the weak.

China will continue to play its part as a major and responsible country. It will support the development of the vast number of developing countries, take an active part in reforming and developing the global governance system, and join the global endeavor to build an open, inclusive, clean and beautiful world that enjoys lasting peace, universal security, and common prosperity.

We support multilateral trade regimes that are open, transparent, inclusive and nondiscriminatory – regimes that liberalize and facilitate trade and investment, and make economic globalization more open, inclusive and balanced so that its benefits are shared by all.

We will focus on promoting the Belt and Road Initiative, and work with other countries to build a new platform for international cooperation and create new drivers for common development. China will never pursue development at the expense of others' interests, nor will China ever give up its own legitimate rights and interests.

China pursues a national defense policy that is in nature defensive. China does not pose a threat to any other country. No matter what stage of development it reaches, China will never seek hegemony.

Eighth, we must exercise full and rigorous governance over the Party, and improve its ability to innovate, power to unite, and energy to fight. Forty years of reform and opening up have taught us that it takes a good blacksmith to forge good tools.

China's success hinges on our Party, so we must ensure that the Party exercises effective self-supervision and practices strict self-governance in every respect. In leading social reform, such as reform and opening up and socialist modernization, the Party must have the courage to reform itself and rid itself of any virus that erodes its health. In order to forever maintain its close ties with the people, the Party must keep cleansing, improving and reforming itself, and strengthen its ability to lead politically, to guide through theory, to organize the people, and to rally public support.

On the path ahead, we must act in accordance with the general requirements for strengthening the Party for the new era, and with reinforcing the Party's political foundations as the overarching principle, continue to enhance the Party's solidarity, creativity and capacity for governance, to make it stronger and more capable. We need to scrutinize ourselves according to the requirements of the times, remind ourselves to guard against potential dangers, elevate ourselves in the spirit of reform and innovation, improve ourselves by addressing risks and challenges, cleanse ourselves by resolving striking problems within the Party, and keep improving our ability in governing the Party.

We should select officials on the basis of both integrity and ability, with priority given to integrity, and on the basis of merit. We need to train a large number of high-caliber officials and professionals who are loyal to the Party, have moral integrity, and demonstrate a keen sense of responsibility.

We must have the resolve and tenacity to persevere in the never-ending fight against corruption, intensifying our efforts to address both the symptoms and root causes in order to clean out all corrupt officials. We must ensure that officials are honest, government is clean, and political affairs are handled with integrity, striving to build a corruption-free political environment for further reform and opening up.

Ninth, we must uphold dialectical and historical materialism to balance reform, development and stability. Forty years of reform and opening up have taught us that China as a large country cannot afford any fatal mistake on issues of fundamental importance.

To ensure sustained and steady progress of reform and opening up, we need to uphold Party leadership while respecting the people's creativity; we need to explore experiences, like crossing a river by feeling for stones, while enhancing top-level design; we need to adopt a problem-solving approach while sticking to our goal; we need to launch pilot programs while advancing reform on all fronts; we need to encourage bold experiment while being realistic and pragmatic.

On the path ahead, we should adopt a strategic perspective, develop creative thinking and a dialectical approach; we should think in terms of the rule of law, and prepare for the worst-case scenarios. We need to enhance macro thinking and top-level design, remain problem-oriented, and focus on prominent problems facing our country. We need to carry out in-depth research, and encourage experiments in grassroots reform. We need to make decision-making on reform consistent with decision-making on legislation, and make the former more rational.

In the spirit of "leaving a mark in the iron tools we clutch and footprints in the stones we tread", we should resolve problems with force and tenacity as a hammer drives a nail, and ensure that all major reform measures are implemented to the letter. We should have the courage to break new ground and try out new experiments, and at the same time, make active yet prudent efforts to advance reform swiftly and steadily. In so doing, we will strike a balance between promoting reform, pursuing development, and maintaining stability. We must advance reform and opening up in the right direction, on the right course, and with consistent force, so as to steadily promote reform and opening up in the new era.

Notes

[1] Zhang Shi: *Understanding* The Analects of Confucius (*Lun Yu Jie*). Zhang Shi (1133-1180) was a neo-Confucian philosopher and educator of the Southern Song Dynasty.

[2] Frederick Engels: "Anti-Dühring", *Karl Marx & Frederick Engels: Collected Works*, Vol. 25, Eng. ed., Progress Publishers, Moscow, 1979, p. 254.

[3] Lu Xun (1881-1936) was a man of letters, thinker and revolutionary, and one of the founders of modern Chinese literature.

[4] Lu Xun: "Random Thoughts (66) – The Road of Life", *Lu Xun: Selected Works*, Vol. 2, Eng. ed., Foreign Languages Press, Beijing, 1980, p. 54.

All-Round Opening Up

China Will Open Even Wider*

April 10, 2018

Held last October, the 19th CPC National Congress ushered socialism with Chinese characteristics into a new era and drew a blueprint for turning China into a great modern socialist country in all respects. This new era of Chinese socialism marks a new chapter in China's efforts to achieve national rejuvenation and share prosperity with the rest of the world.

All ages and generations have their own challenges and missions. China has come a long way, but it has to overcome new challenges on its way ahead. In this new era, the Chinese nation will continue to progress through reform. We will stay committed to advancing reform in all respects, and prevail over whatever challenges may lie ahead. We will tackle longstanding problems with courage and resolve, and break the impediments of vested interests to carry reform through. The Chinese people will continue to take bold steps in breaking new ground to boost development. Following the people-centered development philosophy and the new development vision, we will modernize our economic system, deepen supply-side structural reform, and accelerate implementation of the strategies of innovation-driven development, rural revitalization, and coordinated regional development. We will continue to work on targeted poverty alleviation and promote social equity and justice, so that our people will have a greater sense of fulfillment, happiness, and security. The Chinese people will continue to open up further and expand cooperation. We will stay committed to the strategy of opening up for win-win results. We will

---

* Part of the keynote speech at the opening ceremony of the Boao Forum for Asia Annual Conference 2018.

pay equal attention to "bringing in" and "going global", and break new ground in opening China further through links running eastward and westward, across land and over sea. We will adopt policies to effectively liberate and facilitate trade and investment, and explore the opening of free trade ports adapted to Chinese conditions. The Chinese people will continue to work together with the rest of the world and make a greater contribution to humanity. China will stick to the path of peaceful development, actively pursue global partnerships, firmly support multilateralism, and take an active part in reforming the global governance system. By doing so, we will promote a new type of international relations and a global community of shared future.

No matter how much progress China has made, it will not threaten anyone, attempt to overturn the existing international system, or seek spheres of influence. China will stay as determined as ever to build world peace, contribute to global prosperity, and uphold the international order.

A comprehensive study of world development trajectories shows that economic globalization is an irreversible trend of our times. In line with this conclusion, I emphasized in my report to the 19th CPC National Congress that China will maintain its fundamental state policy of opening up and pursue development with its door wide open. I wish to make it clear to all that China's door will not be closed and will only open even wider.

Past events prove that opening up has been key to China's economic growth over the past 40 years and in the same vein, China can only achieve high-quality economic development in the future with greater openness. Opening up is a strategic decision made by China based on its need for development as well as a concrete action taken by China to move economic globalization forward in a way that benefits people across the world.

China will adopt the following major measures to pursue further opening up:

First, we will significantly broaden market access. A number of landmark measures are to be launched this year. On services, and on financial services in particular, an important announcement was made at the end of last year on measures to raise foreign equity caps in the banking, securities and insurance industries. We will ensure that these measures materialize and at the same time make more moves towards further opening, including accelerating the opening up of the insurance industry, easing restrictions on the establishment of foreign financial institutions in China and expanding their business scope, and opening up more areas of cooperation between Chinese and foreign financial markets. On manufacturing, we have largely opened up this sector, except for a very small number of industries, such as automobiles, ships and aircraft. Now these industries are also in a position to open up. Going forward, we will ease foreign equity restrictions in these industries as soon as possible, automobiles in particular.

Second, we will create a more attractive investment environment. The investment environment is like air, and only fresh air attracts more foreign capital. China used to rely mainly on providing favorable policies for foreign investors, but now we will have to rely more on improving the investment environment. We will enhance alignment with international economic and trade rules, increase transparency, strengthen property rights protection, uphold law-based governance, encourage competition, and oppose monopoly. We established a host of new agencies this past March, such as the State Administration for Market Regulation, as part of a major readjustment of government institutions. The purpose is to remove the systemic and institutional obstacles that prevent the market from playing the decisive role in resource allocation and enable the government to better play its role. In the first six months of this year, we will finish the revision of the negative list on foreign investment and implement across the board a management system based on pre-establishment national treatment and a negative list.

Third, we will strengthen protection of intellectual property rights (IPR). This is the centerpiece of the system for improving property rights protection, and it will provide the biggest boost to the competitiveness of the Chinese economy. Stronger IPR protection is requested by foreign enterprises, and even more so by Chinese enterprises. This year, we are re-instituting the National Intellectual Property Administration to strengthen the ranks of its officials, step up law enforcement, significantly raise the cost for offenders, and fully unlock the deterrent effect of relevant laws. We encourage legitimate technological exchanges and cooperation between Chinese and foreign enterprises, and protect the lawful IPR of foreign enterprises in China. At the same time, we hope foreign governments will also improve protection of Chinese IPR.

Fourth, we will take the initiative to expand imports. Domestic demand is the fundamental driving force for China's economic development, and it is an essential requirement for us to meet the people's growing expectation for a better life. China does not seek a trade surplus; we have a genuine desire to increase imports and achieve a better balance of international payments under the current account. This year, we will significantly lower the import tariffs for automobiles and some other products. We will import more products that are competitive and needed by our people. We will seek faster progress towards joining the WTO Government Procurement Agreement. We hope developed countries will stop imposing restrictions on normal and reasonable trade in high-tech products and relax export controls on such trade with China. This November, we will hold the First China International Import Expo in Shanghai. It is not just another expo in an ordinary sense, but a major policy initiative and commitment, taken of our own accord, to open up the Chinese market. Friends from around the world are welcome to participate.

I wish to emphasize that with regard to all those major opening-up initiatives I have just announced, we have every intention to translate them into reality, sooner rather than later. We want the outcomes of our opening-up efforts to deliver benefits as soon as possible to all enterprises and people in China and around the world. I am confident that with these efforts, China's financial sector will be much more competitive, our capital market will continue to enjoy healthy development, the building of a system of modern industries will accelerate, our market environment will greatly improve, and intellectual property rights will be effectively protected. In short, China will enter a new phase of opening up.

Five years ago, I put forward the Belt and Road Initiative (BRI). Since then, more than 80 countries and international organizations have signed cooperation agreements with China. The BRI may be China's idea, but its opportunities and outcomes are going to benefit the world. China has no geopolitical motives, seeks no exclusionary blocs, and imposes no business deals on others. It must be pointed out that as the BRI is a new initiative, it is perfectly natural to have different views. As long as the parties involved embrace the principle of extensive consultation, joint contribution and shared benefits, we can surely enhance cooperation and resolve differences. This way, we can make the BRI the broadest platform for international cooperation in keeping with the trend of economic globalization and to the greater benefit of all peoples.

Roll Out Free Trade Ports*

April 13, 2018

Economic globalization is a requirement for the development of productive forces and an outcome of scientific and technological progress. It provides strong impetus for world economic growth, and promotes the flow of goods. It encourages commodity and capital flow, scientific, technological and cultural progress, and exchanges between peoples, which correspond with the common interests of all countries. At present, the world economy is still confronted by complex challenges. There is a lack of momentum for growth and a widening gap in growth. We cannot attribute these troublesome problems simply to economic globalization. Any resort to protectionism in trade and investment goes against the historic trend, and will drag us back into the old era of isolation. The only sensible option is to make full use of every opportunity to deal with all challenges through cooperation.

I have made it clear in the report to the 19th CPC National Congress in 2017 that China will not close its door to the world; we will only open it wider. This is a solemn commitment. China adheres to the basic national policy of opening up and pursues a mutually beneficial strategy of opening up. We abide by and maintain the world trade system and rules to make economic globalization more open, inclusive, and balanced, so that it works to the benefit of all. We will make the process of economic globalization more vigorous, more inclusive and more sustainable to ensure that different countries, people from different social strata, and different groups of

---

* Part of the speech at a gathering celebrating the 30th anniversary of the founding of the Hainan Province and the Hainan Special Economic Zone.

people may all share the benefits.

Here I solemnly announce that the CPC Central Committee has consented to the building of a pilot free trade zone across Hainan Island, and providing support for Hainan to explore and phase in free trade port policies and the necessary institutional framework. This is a major policy made by the CPC Central Committee after in-depth research, full consideration, and rational planning, while taking into account the needs of both domestic and international economic growth. It is also an important measure to demonstrate our commitment to opening wider to the world and promoting economic globalization.

In building this zone, we should focus on institutional innovation, giving Hainan more autonomy to reform, and encouraging it to be bold in experiments and make breakthroughs in reform to build a business-friendly environment that is governed by law and up to international standards, along with a fair, open, integrated and efficient market. We need to make greater efforts to transform government functions, further streamline administration, and delegate powers, striking the right balance and optimizing services to improve our governance capacity in all sectors. We should adopt well-conceived policies to facilitate free trade and investment, and establish a management system of pre-establishment national treatment and a negative list for foreign companies. We will open the sectors of modern agriculture, new and high-tech industries, and modern services wider to the world, accelerate the development of trade in services, protect the legitimate rights and interests of foreign investors, and gradually open up the shipping industry. The focus will be put on sectors such as seeds, medicine, education, sports, telecommunications, the internet, culture, maintenance, finance, and shipping.

A free trade port represents the highest-level of opening up. The Hainan Free Trade Port should display distinctive Chinese features, conform to conditions in China, and be in accord with Hainan's economic orientation. It should learn from its international peers and draw on their advanced operation models and managerial experience.

We will invite investors worldwide to invest in Hainan, participate in building the free trade port, and share China's development opportunities and reform outcomes.

For a Global Economy – Open, Innovative and Inclusive*

November 5, 2018

Your Excellencies Heads of State and Government,
Your Royal Highness,
Your Excellencies Heads of International Organizations,
Your Excellencies Heads of Delegations,
Distinguished guests,
Ladies and gentlemen,
Friends,

In May 2017, I announced China's decision to hold the China International Import Expo (CIIE) starting from 2018. Today, after more than one year of preparations and with strong support from various parties, the first CIIE is officially opened.

At the outset, on behalf of the Chinese government and people and also in my own name, I wish to express a warm welcome, sincere greetings and best wishes to you all.

The CIIE is the world's first import expo held at the national level, an innovative move in the history of global trade. China has made an important decision to pursue a new round of high-level opening up, a major new initiative to further widen market access to the rest of the world. It demonstrates China's consistent position of supporting the multilateral trading system and promoting free trade. It is a concrete action by China to advance an open world economy and support economic globalization.

---

* Keynote speech at the opening ceremony of the First China International Import Expo.

Under the theme of "New Era, Shared Future", the CIIE will help friends from around the world to seize opportunities presented by China's development in the new era and offer a platform for us to expand international business cooperation for shared prosperity and progress. More than 3,600 companies from 172 countries, regions and international organizations are attending the event with over 400,000 Chinese and foreign buyers exploring business deals. The expo is utilizing a total area of 300,000 square meters.

I wish all friends participating in this expo a most pleasant and rewarding experience.

Ladies and gentlemen,

Friends,

The world is going through a new round of major development, transformation and adjustment. The economic and social wellbeing of all countries is increasingly interconnected. Reform of the global governance system and the international order is picking up speed. On the other hand, the world economy is going through profound adjustment, and protectionism and unilateralism are resurgent. Economic globalization faces headwinds, and multilateralism and the system of free trade are under threat. Uncertainties and instabilities still abound, and risks and challenges are growing. Living in such a complex world, we need to understand underlying trends, bolster confidence in our future through opening up and cooperation, and work together to cope with risks and challenges.

All around the world people of vision would agree that economic globalization, as an irreversible trend of history, has greatly boosted global growth. This is an overarching trend, something that is independent of people's will. What humanity can do is to understand and adapt to such historic trends, rather than try to prevent them from happening. The wheel of history, indeed, will keep rolling forward no matter what.

History tells us that openness and cooperation are major driving forces behind dynamic international economy and trade. The current situation calls for openness and cooperation to foster steady global recovery. Looking ahead, openness and cooperation will remain essential for continued human progress.

A great vision, simple and pure, requires credible actions. Given the profound shifts in the international economic landscape, the vision for a better world for all creates a call for countries to act with greater courage and actively champion openness and cooperation in order to secure shared development.

– It is important for all countries to open wider and expand the space for mutually beneficial cooperation. Openness brings progress while isolation leads to backwardness. Global trade and investment are driven by the needs of countries for mutual exchange and complementarity. The history of economic cooperation and international trade testifies to the fact that "economies make progress through exchange and interconnectivity and fall behind because of isolation and seclusion". Efforts to reduce tariff barriers and open wider will lead to interconnectivity in economic cooperation and global trade, while engaging in beggar-thy-neighbor practices, isolation and seclusion will only result in trade stagnation and an unhealthy world economy. Countries need to pursue an open policy, explicitly oppose protectionism and unilateralism, and strive to raise the level of opening up at both bilateral and multilateral levels, so that we can connect our economies and build an open world economy. We need to improve macroeconomic coordination and reduce the negative spillover of national policies to jointly promote global economic growth. We need to establish a set of global economic and trade rules that is fair, reasonable and transparent, and promote and facilitate free trade and investment to make the global economy more open through increased exchanges and integration.

– It is important for all countries to pursue innovative growth and speed up the transformation of growth drivers. Innovation is the premier engine for development. Only with bold innovation and reform can we break through the bottleneck in global growth. The world economy has just moved out of the shadow of the international financial crisis, but the recovery is still unstable. There is an urgent need for a concerted international effort to promote innovation in science and technology and foster new growth drivers. The wellbeing of humanity is the biggest driving force for this. In our interconnected global village, to share the fruits of innovation is the common aspiration and natural choice of the global community. We need to seize the opportunities presented by the new round of technological and industrial revolution, strengthen cooperation in frontier sectors such as the digital economy, artificial intelligence and nanotechnology, and work together to foster new technologies, new industries, and new forms and models of business.

– It is important for all countries to pursue inclusive development for the benefit of all. As a Chinese saying goes, "All flowers in full blossom make a beautiful spring." To lead a happy life is the common aspiration of people all over the world. The progress of human society requires a continued effort from all countries to further opening up, cooperation and win-win development, and reject isolation, confrontation and monopoly. In a world of deeper economic globalization, the pursuit of "the law of the jungle" and "winner-takes-all" leads nowhere. Inclusive growth for all is surely the right way forward. Countries need to rise above differences and leverage their respective strengths to pursue inclusive growth in the face of common risks and challenges. We need to implement the 2030 Agenda for Sustainable Development of the United Nations, reduce imbalances in global development, and make economic globalization more open, inclusive, balanced and beneficial for all. This way, people of all countries will be able to share the benefits of economic globalization and global growth.

Ladies and gentlemen,

Friends,

The last four decades of reform and opening up in China have been an epic journey for the Chinese people. With determination and through self-reliance and hard work, we have forged ahead on the road to national development and progress. China has pursued development with its door open and succeeded in transforming a closed and semi-closed economy into a fully open economy. Openness has become a trademark of China. China has grown by embracing the world, and the world has also benefited from China's opening up.

As I explained at the Boao Forum for Asia in April, China's economic growth over the past 40 years has been achieved with a commitment to opening up. In the same vein, a future of high-quality economic development in China can only be guaranteed by greater openness. I have made it clear again and again that China's door will never be closed. It will only open even wider. China will never waver in its effort to pursue higher-quality opening up. China will never falter in its effort to pursue an open world economy. And China will never relent in its effort to pursue a global community of shared future.

China will remain resolute in following a win-win strategy of opening up, adopting policies to promote and facilitate free trade and investment, and breaking new ground in opening up further through links running eastward and westward, across land and over sea. China will remain a strong advocate of openness at the global level, and will continue to act as a stable engine of global growth, a huge market with enormous opportunities, and an active supporter of reform in global governance.

To broaden its opening up, China will step up efforts in the following areas:

First, we will tap the potential for increased imports. China's initiative to expand imports is not a choice of expediency. It is a future-oriented step to embrace the world and to promote common development. To adjust to the upgrading trend in our domestic consumption, we will take more proactive measures to increase people's incomes and purchasing power, foster new growth areas of medium and high-end consumption, continue to unleash the potential of the domestic market, and expand the scope for imports. We will take further steps to lower tariffs, facilitate customs clearance, reduce institutional costs for imports, and step up cross-border e-commerce and other new forms and models of business. China has a market of more than 1.3 billion people, and it is our sincere promise to open the

Chinese market to all countries. The CIIE will be held on an annual basis, and will continue to improve with better performance and more results.

Second, we will continue to relax market access. The relaxation measures I announced in April are generally in place. China has shortened the negative list on foreign investment to reduce restrictions and facilitate investment. We are steadily increasing the openness of the financial sector, continuing to open up the service sector, and working towards greater openness in the agricultural, mining and manufacturing sectors. We are accelerating opening up in areas such as telecommunications, education, medical services and culture. In particular, the foreign equity limits are going to be eased in the education and medical service sectors, where there is both strong interest among foreign investors and a notable shortage in domestic supply. China's imports of goods and services are expected to exceed US$30 trillion and US$10 trillion respectively in the coming 15 years.

Third, we will foster a world-class business environment. China will accelerate the formulation of foreign investment laws and regulations, and make its foreign-related legal system more open and transparent. We will implement, across the board, a management system based on pre-establishment national treatment and a negative list. We respect international business rules and practices, and provide equal treatment to all types of businesses registered in China. We protect the lawful rights and interests of foreign companies, and are resolute in punishing those in violation of the lawful rights and interests of foreign investors, particularly intellectual property (IP) rights infringements. We will enhance the credibility and efficiency of IP examination, and put in place a punitive compensation system to significantly raise the cost for offenders. Improving the business environment is an ongoing process, and there is always room for a country to do better in this regard by addressing its own problems. No country should point fingers at others to gloss over its own problems, nor should any country target the flashlight at the weakness of others only, while ignoring its own.

Fourth, we will explore new heights of opening up. China will support deeper reform and innovation in its pilot free trade zones, continue to experiment with new differentiated policies and practices in these zones, and step up stress tests, so as to give full play to their role as a testing ground for reform and opening up. China will waste no time in putting in place policies and institutions for building the Hainan Free Trade Port in a phased and progressive manner, so as to speed up the development of free trade ports in accordance with conditions in China. This is a significant move by China to open wider to the world. It will set a new model and open up new prospects for reform and opening up at a higher level.

Fifth, we will promote international cooperation at multilateral and bilateral levels. China firmly upholds the rules of the World Trade Organization (WTO), supports its necessary reform, and defends the multilateral trading system. China will strive for the early conclusion of the Regional Comprehensive Economic Partnership (RCEP), and speed up negotiations on the China-EU investment agreement and the China-Japan-Republic of Korea free trade area. China will earnestly implement the eight major initiatives[1] announced at this year's Beijing Summit of the Forum on China-Africa Cooperation. China supports a greater role for mechanisms such as the G20, APEC, the Shanghai Cooperation Organization, and the BRICS in building a fairer and more equitable global economic governance system. China will continue to advance the Belt and Road Initiative through international cooperation in the spirit of consultation and collaboration for shared benefits. We will work with participating countries on major projects, set up more trade promotion platforms, and encourage more well-established and strong Chinese companies with good reputation to invest in countries along the Belt and Road and enhance cooperation in eco-environmental protection, science and technology, culture, and in improving people's lives. In so doing, we hope to set up for the whole world a platform for open cooperation.

Ladies and gentlemen,
Friends,

The Chinese economy is on the whole stable and making further progress. During the first three quarters of this year, China's GDP grew by 6.7 percent, including 6.5-percent growth registered for the third quarter, meeting our growth target. Grain output for the whole year is projected to surpass 1.2 trillion *jin* (600 million tons). Some 11.07 million new jobs have been created, hitting our annual goal ahead of schedule. Judged against the main economic indicators, from GDP growth, job creation, consumer prices and international balance of payment to companies' profit margins, government fiscal revenue and productivity, China's economy is performing reasonably well. This has given us a solid foundation for delivering the development goals for the whole year. And compared with other major economies, China still ranks among the leaders in terms of GDP growth.

So, when you talk about the future of the Chinese economy, you have every reason to be confident. The fundamentals for sound and stable growth remain unchanged. The necessary production factors for quality development remain unchanged. And the overall momentum of long-term stability and progress remains unchanged. As efforts to advance reform across the board unleash new drivers of growth, China's capacity for macroeconomic regulation is growing. With substantive progress made in advancing the Belt and Road Initiative, two-way investment and trade between China and partner countries continue to gather pace. All in all, favorable conditions are in place for the long-term, healthy and steady growth of the Chinese economy.

Of course, everything has two sides. The current economic situation both at home and abroad has created more uncertainties, more difficulties and more risks for the Chinese economy. In general, we believe these are typical problems that tend to occur in the course of development. However, the measures we have adopted either have manifested, or are manifesting, positive effects.

China is the world's second largest economy. We have a market of more than 1.3 billion consumers who live on a land of over 9.6 million square kilometers. To use a metaphor, China's economy is not a pond, but an ocean. The ocean certainly has its calm days, but also times of gales and storms. Without them, the ocean would not be an ocean. Gales and storms may ravage a pond, but never an ocean. Whatever the gales and storms, the ocean is still there. It is the same for China. After 5,000 years of trials and tribulations, China is still here. Looking ahead, China will always be here.

I am convinced that as long as we have confidence in our strategies, advance reform and opening up in all respects, intensify supply-side structural reform, and make greater efforts to solve outstanding problems, the Chinese economy will surely make a rapid transition to quality development; the Chinese people will surely overcome all difficulties on the way forward; and the country will surely embrace a brighter future.

Ladies and gentlemen,

Friends,

Every city has its character. Located at the juncture where the Yangtze River flows into the Pacific Ocean, Shanghai has been a pioneer of opening up in China. The city's development has been made possible by its open-mindedness, its competitive edge, and its bold opening-up actions. Since I once worked here, I know personally just how important it is for Shanghai to be open and for China to keep the city open. Indeed, openness, innovation and inclusiveness have become the hallmarks of Shanghai. They are also a vivid reflection of China's development and progress in the new era.

To capitalize on the important role of Shanghai and other areas in China's opening up, we have made the following decisions: First, we will expand the area of the China (Shanghai) Pilot Free Trade Zone with an additional section, and will encourage and support the city in experimenting with bolder and more creative policies of promoting and facilitating free trade and investment, so that more of its successful practices may be replicated in other parts of China. Second, we will launch a science and technology innovation board at the Shanghai Stock Exchange and experiment with a registration system for listed companies. We will also support Shanghai in cementing its position as an international financial center and a hub of science and technology innovation, and in steadily improving the fundamental institutions of its capital market. Third, we will support integrated development of the Yangtze River Delta region. We will make this a national strategy and implement our new development philosophy in earnest. We will build a modern economic system, and adopt higher standards for reform and opening up. The region will develop in tandem with the Belt and Road Initiative, the Beijing-Tianjin-Hebei Region, the Yangtze River Economic Belt, and the Guangdong-Hong Kong-Macao Greater Bay Area. Together, these will improve the overall framework of China's reform and opening up.

Ladies and gentlemen,

Friends,

The CIIE is an event hosted by China with the support of the WTO and other international organizations, as well as a large number of participating countries. It is not a solo performance by China, but rather a chorus by countries from all over the world. I hope that at the Hongqiao International Economic and Trade Forum, you will brainstorm ideas for reforming the global economic governance system, for jointly safeguarding free trade and the multilateral trading system, and for working together to foster an open global economy that is innovative and inclusive. Together, let us contribute to our common determined efforts to build a global community of shared future and usher in an even better tomorrow for humanity.

Thank you.

Notes

[1] This refers to industrial promotion, infrastructure connectivity, trade facilitation, green development, capacity building, health care, people-to-people exchanges, and peace and security.

Open Up and Cooperate Towards a Shared Future[*]

November 5, 2019

Your Excellency President Emmanuel Macron,
Your Excellencies Prime Minister Andrew Holness, Prime Minister Kyriakos Mitsotakis, and Prime Minister Ana Brnabić,
Your Excellencies Speakers of Parliament,
Your Excellencies Heads of International Organizations,
Your Excellencies Heads of Delegations,
Distinguished guests,
Ladies and gentlemen,
Friends,

In this colorful season of deep autumn, it gives me great pleasure to meet with you by the Huangpu River. I now declare the Second China International Import Expo open.

On behalf of the Chinese government and people, and in my own name, I extend a hearty welcome to all of you, friends old and new, from across the world.

A year ago here, the inaugural China International Import Expo was successfully held. Today, even more friends are attending the second expo with the theme of "New Era, Shared Future". I do hope that you will all find this event a worthwhile and rewarding experience.

At last year's Expo, I announced five new initiatives to open China further and outlined three steps for Shanghai to open itself wider to the world. One year later, these initiatives and steps are generally in place. We have launched Lingang Special Area, an expansion of China (Shanghai) Pilot Free Trade Zone, and six other new pilot free trade

---

[*] Keynote speech at the opening ceremony of the Second China International Import Expo.

zones across the country. The sci-tech innovation board of the Shanghai Stock Exchange has also been inaugurated, with a registration system being piloted for company listing. In the Yangtze River Delta region, a plan for promoting integrated development of the region has been adopted as a national strategy. At the national level, the Foreign Investment Law will enter into force on January 1 next year. A management system consisting of both pre-establishment national treatment and a negative list is fully operational. Major headway has been made in increasing imports to boost consumption and in bringing down tariff levels. During my meetings with foreign leaders at last year's expo, we agreed to launch 98 initiatives. Of these, 23 have been completed, 47 are making good progress, and 28 are under implementation.

Economic globalization represents the trend of history. It is just like the world's great rivers, the Yangtze, the Nile, the Amazon and the Danube: They all surge forward in great torrents, and nothing can stop their mighty flow, not the current of undertows or hidden shoals or rocks beneath the water.

None of the problems confronting the world economy can be resolved by one country alone. We must all put the common good of humanity first. No country should place its own interests above the common interests of all. We must be more open-minded and take more effective measures, and work together to make the global market bigger. We need to strengthen the mechanisms for sharing benefits with all, and explore new forms of international cooperation. The goal is to create more impetus for economic globalization and remove as many impediments as we can.

For this to happen, it is imperative that we take the following steps:

First, we need to work together to build an open global economy through cooperation. As global value and supply chains continue to develop, countries are becoming more interconnected. With shrinking distances between countries and growing interactions among them, differences and frictions are inevitable. The right solution to any problem lies in consultation and cooperation. All problems can be settled in the spirit of equality, mutual understanding and accommodation. We need to promote development through opening up, and enhance exchanges and cooperation. We need to stick together rather than drifting apart. We need to tear down walls rather than erecting them. We need to stand firm against protectionism and unilateralism. We need to continually bring down trade barriers, upgrade global value and supply chains, and jointly create market demand.

Second, we need to build an open, innovation-driven world economy. Innovation-driven development is essential to sustaining global growth. At present, a new round of scientific and technological revolution and industrial transformation has reached a historic juncture, and major breakthroughs are within reach. Countries need to step up cooperation in innovation. We need to embed science and technology in growth, and share more innovation outcomes. We need to remove barriers that hamper the flow of knowledge, technology, talent and other factors of innovation, and support our businesses in carrying out technical exchanges and cooperation. This will fully unleash the potential for innovation. To enable humanity to benefit from knowledge and innovation, we need to tighten the protection of intellectual property, rather than stifling the flow of knowledge, or creating or even widening the technology divide.

Third, we need to build an open global economy for mutual benefit. We need to pursue inclusive and mutually beneficial development. We need to work together to safeguard the international order with the purposes and principles of the UN Charter at its core, uphold the fundamental values and basic principles of the multilateral trading system, facilitate free trade and investment, and make economic globalization more open, inclusive, balanced and beneficial to all. We should strive to implement the UN 2030 Agenda for Sustainable Development and increase support for the least developed countries so that the benefits of development will reach more countries and peoples.

China, which has reached a new historic starting point, will open its door wider to the world. The Communist Party of China has just concluded the Fourth Plenary Session of the 19th Central Committee. A decision has been made to uphold and improve the socialist system with Chinese characteristics and modernize the country's system and capacity for governance. Many significant measures have been announced to extend reform and opening up. China will stay true to its fundamental state policy of opening up and carry out reform, development and innovation through opening up. This will raise opening up to an even higher level.

First, China will continue to open up its market. China has a population of close to 1.4 billion, with its middle-income population being the biggest in the world. The huge Chinese market has unlimited potential. There is a popular saying among us Chinese: "The world is a big place, and I want to see more of it." And this is what I want to say to you today: The Chinese market is so big that you should all come and see what it has to offer. China will better leverage the fundamental role of domestic consumption in fueling economic development and foster a more robust domestic market to boost growth at home and create more impetus for global growth. China will increase its imports. We will continue to lower tariffs and government-imposed transaction costs, develop demonstration zones to promote imports by innovative means, and import more high-quality goods and services from other countries. We will take steps to promote balanced growth of imports and exports, of trade in goods and services, of two-way trade and investment, and of trade and industry. By these means we will ensure a free yet orderly flow of both international and domestic factors of production, improve efficient allocation of resources, and boost market integration.

Second, China will continue to upgrade its opening up. China's opening up is pursued in multi-sectors. A new framework of all-round opening up is being put in place in our country. China will continue to encourage bold trials and experiments in pilot free trade zones and speed up the development of the Hainan Free Trade Port as the pacesetters of opening up in China. China will continue to promote the coordinated development of the Beijing-Tianjin-Hebei Region, and the development of the Yangtze River Economic Belt, the Yangtze River Delta region, and the Guangdong-Hong Kong-Macao Greater Bay Area. We will draw up a new national strategy for environmental protection and high-quality development in the Yellow River Basin. All these steps will boost opening up among different parts of the country.

Third, China will continue to improve its business environment. A sound business environment provides the necessary conditions for enterprises to survive and thrive. On October 24, the World Bank released its Doing Business Report 2020, which ranks China 31st, up 15 places from last year's ranking of 46th. Last month, China issued a set of regulations on improving its business environment. Going forward, China will continue to resolve major problems hindering economic development, speed up targeted reforms in key respects and fields, and modernize its system and capacity for governance to provide institutional support for pursuing high-standard opening up and high-quality development. China will continue to foster an enabling business environment that is based on market principles, governed by law, and aligned with international standards. We will give foreign investors greater market access, further cut the negative list, and improve institutions for promoting and protecting investments and for reporting information. With regard to IP protection, we will cultivate an environment that appreciates the value of knowledge, improve the legal framework, step up law enforcement, and enhance protection through both civil and criminal justice systems.

Fourth, China will continue to enhance multilateral and bilateral cooperation. China remains committed to international cooperation and multilateralism. China supports necessary reform of the WTO so as to enable it to play a bigger role in promoting openness and development and make the multilateral trade regime more authoritative and effective. Later this afternoon, China will host an Informal WTO Ministerial Meeting. We look forward to candid exchanges that will lead to joint actions to improve global economic governance. I am happy to note that yesterday, 15 countries taking part in the Regional Comprehensive Economic Partnership concluded negotiations on the text, and I hope the agreement will be signed and enter into force at an early date. China is ready to conclude high-standard free trade agreements with more countries. We will speed up negotiations on a China-EU investment agreement, China-Japan-ROK FTA, and China-Gulf Cooperation Council FTA. We will stay actively engaged in cooperation within the United Nations, the G20, APEC, and BRICS to advance economic globalization.

Fifth, China will continue to pursue Belt and Road cooperation. China has now signed 197 documents on Belt and Road cooperation with 137 countries and 30 international organizations. China will follow the principles of extensive consultation, joint contribution and shared benefits, pursue open, green and clean cooperation, and ensure high-quality Belt and Road cooperation that is high-standard, people-centered and sustainable.

Ladies and gentlemen,

Friends,

Looking forward, China will pursue a new development philosophy and the strategy of innovation-driven development. We will redouble efforts to foster new growth drivers and create new growth momentum by shifting the growth model and improving the economic structure. We believe such efforts will bring high-quality development opportunities not only to China but to the whole of the global economy.

I have every confidence in the prospects of China's economic development. China's development, viewed through the lens of history, is an integral part of the lofty cause of human progress. China will reach out to other countries with open arms and offer them more opportunities in markets, investment and growth. Together, we can surely achieve development for all.

The Chinese civilization has always valued universal peace and harmony among nations. Let us join hands to build an open global economy and a global community of shared future.

Thank you.

Risk Management

Ensure Absolute Party Leadership over National Security*

April 17, 2018

In terms of national security work in the new era, we should strengthen the Party's centralized and unified leadership, take cognizance of the current situation, adopt a holistic approach to national security, and strive for further progress. In so doing, we will provide a strong guarantee for the Two Centenary Goals and the Chinese Dream of national rejuvenation.

Since it was established four years ago, the National Security Commission has upheld overall leadership by the Party. In line with the requirements of a holistic approach to national security, the commission has put in place a general framework of the national security system, developed the theory, improved the strategy, and established a coordination mechanism. Many long-standing and complex problems have been solved, and many long-sought objectives accomplished. We have strengthened our work in all respects and have secured favorable conditions for safeguarding our national security.

The road ahead will not be plain sailing. The brighter the prospects, the more we should enhance our awareness of potential dangers, raise our vigilance, and fully understand and effectively address major risks and challenges. We must direct our attention to key issues and areas, and prevent internal and external risks and challenges from interacting, combining and accumulating, so as to constantly improve our national security.

---

* Main points of the speech at the first meeting of the National Security Commission under the 19th CPC Central Committee.

In order to implement a holistic approach to national security, we must:

– Coordinate development and security. We should make best use of our development achievements to consolidate the foundation for national security and cultivate a secure environment conducive to economic and social development.

– Consider the people's security, political security, and the supremacy of our national interests as three essential elements of an indivisible whole. The people's security is the purpose of maintaining national security, political security the foundation, and the supremacy of national interests the guideline. We must ensure that the people live in peace and contentment, the Party remains in power and the country enjoys lasting stability.

– Focus on prevention, and act effectively whenever risks arise.

– Safeguard and shape national security. To shape national security is to safeguard it at a higher level and with greater foresight. China will act as a responsible major country, and work with others to build a global community of shared future.

– Make coordinated plans. We must always approach national security in the context of overall development of socialism with Chinese characteristics, and fully mobilize all parties' initiative to form a joint force.

National security work should meet the requirements of the new era. While keeping one eye on the present, we must keep the other on the future. We need to safeguard political security, improve the national security system, refine the strategies and policies, strengthen our capacity, prevent and control major risks, strengthen the legal system, and raise the security awareness of the general public.

We must uphold the Party's absolute leadership over national security work and implement more effective command and coordination. The National Security Commission should play well its role of coordination, making sure that the national security principles and policies are implemented, improving the working mechanism, making great effort to improve its strategic capacity for understanding the overall situation and for planning future development. The commission must also continue to enhance its capability of managing risks and meeting challenges. We must also strengthen the Party and its work among national security departments, and guide the officials at all levels to enhance the Four Consciousnesses and the Four-sphere Confidence, and to resolutely uphold the authority of the Central Committee and its centralized, unified leadership so that we can build a loyal and reliable national security force.

Be Alert to Risks*

January 21, 2019

We should follow the Thought on Socialism with Chinese Characteristics for a New Era and fully implement the decisions of the 19th CPC National Congress and the second and third plenary sessions of the 19th CPC Central Committee. This requires a full and accurate understanding of the profound changes in the external environment as well as the new circumstances, problems, and challenges facing China in reform, development and stability. It is imperative to stay alert to potential risks and enhance our capacity for risk prevention and control. We must focus on preventing and resolving major risks to ensure sustained and sound economic development and social stability, so as to secure success in building a moderately prosperous society in all respects, advancing socialism with Chinese characteristics for a new era, and achieving the Chinese Dream of national rejuvenation.

At present China is generally in good shape. We have seen that the leadership of the CPC Central Committee is strong and effective. We have seen an enhanced awareness among Party members of the Four Consciousnesses, the Four-sphere Confidence and the Two Upholds. The political landscape is healthy and positive. Our economy is making steady progress. All our people are united and in high spirit. And social stability prevails throughout the country.

In the face of a confusing and changing international landscape, a complex and sensitive neighboring environment, and the formidable tasks of reform, development and maintaining stability at home, we

---

* Main points of the speech at the opening ceremony of a study session on worst-case scenario thinking to prevent and resolve major risks, which was attended by principal officials at the provincial and ministerial level.

should stay keenly alert to "black swan" and "gray rhino" events, and seize the initiative to prevent risks from arising, while adopting effective measures to address and resolve those that do arise. We must be fully prepared and make proactive strategic moves to convert danger into safety and adversity into opportunity.

Party committees and governments at all levels must pursue a holistic approach to national security and work to meet the requirements set out by the CPC Central Committee for political security in our country. We should continue to consolidate and strengthen the preponderance of mainstream opinions, and intensify guidance on public opinion. At the same time we need to accelerate the establishment of a system for integrated internet management to promote a law-based cyberspace. Priority should be given to improving the system of political education for young people with updated content and forms, helping them foster a sound outlook on the world, life and values, and building up their confidence in the path, theory, system and culture of Chinese socialism so as to ensure that new generations are well prepared to carry forward the socialist cause.

China's economy is doing well on the whole, while facing profound and complicated changes in the international and domestic environment. It is inevitable that we will encounter challenges in pushing ahead with supply-side structural reform. Despite some new and worrisome developments amid steady economic growth, it is essential for us to maintain confidence in our strategies and advance the economy in the right direction, while remaining alert and ready to identify and address potential major economic risks with appropriate measures. All provincial authorities and central departments should strike a balance between maintaining steady growth and defusing risks, and in doing so we must keep a proper pace and intensity. It is necessary to implement a long-term mechanism for promoting the steady and sound development of the real estate market. We should strengthen market psychological analysis, improve evaluations of the impact of new policies on the financial market, and better guide public expectations. Market monitoring and regulatory coordination should be enhanced to eliminate risks promptly. We should take concrete measures to make financing easier and more affordable for medium-sized, small and micro businesses, intensify our efforts to help enterprises in stabilizing employment, and put into practice the policy of giving high priority to employment. Greater efforts are needed to speed up the disposal of zombie enterprises and facilitate the redeployment of their employees, so as to unleash untapped resources and move faster towards a balanced market. All provincial authorities and central departments should take effective steps to stabilize employment, financial markets, foreign trade, foreign investment, domestic investment, and public expectations, and keep economic growth within a reasonable range.

Security in the field of science and technology constitutes a critical component of national security. We need to enhance our systems and capacity in this area. In order to achieve higher overall efficiency, the national innovation system should be improved to avoid duplicated resource allocation, to integrate dispersed research efforts, to clearly define the functions of innovative participants, and to solve other major problems. We should reinforce the systems and mechanisms for innovation by overcoming weaknesses. It is imperative to improve strategic analysis and adopt forward-looking plans for innovation in key areas. We should accelerate the configuration of national laboratories, restructure the system of key national laboratories, set up major innovation bases and platforms, and integrate the efforts of enterprises, universities and research institutes. We need to strengthen our overall planning for key scientific and technological programs concerning national security and overall economic and social development, and reinforce our national strategic strength in science and technology. We should accelerate the establishment of an early warning and monitoring system to ensure the security of our science and technology. We should advance legislation on artificial intelligence, gene editing, medical diagnosis, automated driving, drones, and service robots.

To maintain social stability, we should ensure the implementation of various measures for security and stability, and resolve the immediate concerns of the people. Efforts should be made in areas including employment, education, social security, medicine and health care, food safety, workplace safety, public security, and regulation of the housing market, to enhance the people's sense of gain, happiness and security. Strong and swift action should be taken to both protect the people's rights and strike hard at illegal and criminal activities. We must coordinate actions to prevent and combat crime with measures to resolve risks and maintain stability when dealing with economic cases involving large numbers of victims. We should take timely action to seize stolen property, control offenders, return the property to its owners, and provide necessary education and counseling to prevent criminal offenses. It is imperative to continue the fight against organized crime and local tyrants and keep a close watch on their sources of finance, support networks and protectors. We should focus on combining prevention and punishment and addressing both symptoms and root causes. We need to upgrade the multidimensional crime prevention and control system with the aid of information technology to maintain a strong deterrence against criminal acts and enhance the people's sense of security. Further efforts should be made to modernize social governance, carry on and develop the Fengqiao model[1] in maintaining public security, and improve the social coordination mechanism for a safe and secure society, thus fundamentally enhancing our capacity to better maintain social stability.

The world is undergoing profound changes at an accelerating pace, generating more sources of instability and risk. In the face of an increasingly complex and challenging international landscape, we must give consideration to both the domestic and the international situation, and balance development and security. We need to exercise overall coordination with a focus on major issues and take effective precautions against interconnected risks. It is imperative to reinforce the protection of our country's overseas interests and ensure the safety of major projects, personnel and institutions overseas. We should improve the guarantee system for the Belt and Road Initiative to safeguard our sovereignty, security and development interests, and create a sound external environment for China's reform, development and stability.

Since the 18th CPC National Congress in 2012, we have made marked progress in strengthening Party discipline in a spirit of self-reform and removing serious hidden threats to our Party. However, this does not mean we can rest on our laurels. Our Party is still confronted with long-term and complex tests of its capacity to exercise governance, carry out reform and opening up, develop the market economy, and respond to external volatility. At the same time, our Party is also facing intense and severe threats, such as lack of drive, incompetence, disengagement from the people, inaction, and corruption. This conclusion is drawn from the analysis of actual conditions. All Party members must continue to strengthen their commitment to the Four Consciousnesses, the Four-sphere Confidence, and the Two Upholds. It is essential to closely follow the Central Committee in terms of thinking, political orientation, and actions, conscientiously safeguard Party solidarity and unity, strictly abide by the Party's political discipline and rules, and always maintain close ties with the people.

As the country is at a crucial stage in its efforts to achieve national rejuvenation and remove major barriers to further reform and development, it is in need of officials who forge ahead with determination and tenacity and have the courage and ability to stand firm at critical moments. We have secured a sweeping victory in the fight against corruption since the 18th CPC National Congress, but the fight has not ended and we still face grave and complex challenges. We must remain firm in our zero-tolerance attitude to corruption, never slacken our efforts, and take resolute and sustained action to win this prolonged battle.

Preventing and resolving major risks is the political responsibility of Party committees, governments and officials at all levels. We must fulfill all our responsibilities in this regard through concrete, meticulous and effective efforts. We should sharpen our awareness of risks, remain mindful and thoughtful of the broader picture, remain sensitive to development trends, and plan ahead against potential risks. To enhance our ability to resolve risks, we should be able to perceive the nature of complex phenomena, identify the key problems and their causes, make prompt decisions, and effectively solve problems by guiding and organizing the people, and by integrating all forces. Officials should strengthen theoretical cultivation by conducting in-depth studies of the tenets of Marxism, fully understanding the Thought on Socialism with Chinese Characteristics for a New Era and their underlying dialectical materialist worldview and methodology. We should have strategic and historical perspectives, develop creative and worst-case scenario thinking, adopt a dialectical approach and think in terms of the rule of law, so as to discover the laws behind problems, and accumulate our experience and improve our capability. It is imperative to enhance risk prevention and control mechanisms, establish mechanisms for risk analysis and assessment, risk assessment in the decision-making process, and collaboration and division of responsibility in risk prevention and control. We should take the initiative to reinforce coordination and cooperation, so that each level of leadership exercises strict supervision on the work of the next lower level to ensure implementation.

Preventing and resolving major risks requires our energetic and persevering commitment. Officials should have the courage to take on responsibilities and confront problems while retaining determination and improving their capability to solve problems. Young officials should be field-trained through participation in major programs. Leadership teams and leading officials should become more experienced and capable through practice, maintain a strong will to overcome all challenges, properly deal with every major risk, and thoroughly promote reform, development and stability.

Notes

[1] In the early 1960s, the officials and citizenry of Fengqiao Town in Zhejiang

Province created the Fengqiao practice, which emphasized solving problems in situ rather than passing them up to higher authorities. The practice has developed over the intervening decades, and is now a model for promoting community-level governance and social harmony. Relying on the people, the Party committee and government devote their efforts to preventing disputes and solving problems, so as to maintain social stability and promote development.

Meet Challenges Head-On*

September 3, 2019

Officials, especially younger officials, must undergo strict theoretical and political studies and be tempered by practice. You should enhance your capability and meet challenges head-on, and work tenaciously towards the Two Centenary Goals and the Chinese Dream of national rejuvenation.

The emergence and development of Marxism and socialist countries are stories of hardship and struggle. The Communist Party of China, the People's Republic of China, the reform and opening-up policy, and socialism with Chinese characteristics for a new era all came into being, developed and grew in strength in the course of this struggle.

Today's world is in the midst of great changes that have not been seen in a century. The great struggle, the great project, the great cause, and the great dream are flourishing under the Party's leadership. The tasks of advancing reform, promoting development, and maintaining stability are arduous. We are facing a historic opportunity and also a series of major risks and tests. To achieve the goals and targets set by the Party, we must enhance our capability and meet challenges head-on.

Achieving national rejuvenation is no easy task. It will take more than drum beating and gong clanging to get there. Realizing this great dream demands a great struggle. The tests we face on the way forward will only become more complex as we press on, and we must be prepared to crest unimaginable waves.

---

* Main points of the speech at the opening ceremony of a training program for younger officials at the Central Party School (National Academy of Governance) during its 2019 fall semester.

The struggle on all fronts is not short-term but long-term, extending across the whole process of realizing the Second Centenary Goal. We must enhance the Four Consciousnesses, reinforce the Four-sphere Confidence, and ensure the Two Upholds. Furthermore, we need to strengthen our will to confront the grim challenges that lie in front of us; we must steel ourselves, take proactive action, and dare to fight and win.

We Communists have a clear direction, stance and principle in our struggle – the general direction is to uphold CPC leadership and the socialist system. We must fight resolutely and successfully against any risks and challenges that endanger Party leadership, the socialist system, the sovereignty, security and development interests of our country, our core national interests and principles, the fundamental interests of our people, the realization of the Two Centenary Goals, and the rejuvenation of the Chinese nation. We should be clear-headed, take a firm stance, and stay on the right course in major struggles. In the face of any major test, we should be "unperturbed by the cloud that obscures our vision"[1], and remain steadfast while "riotous clouds sweep past"[2].

Communists have always been ready for the struggle to resolve problems, threats and challenges. China has entered a period when threats and challenges will accumulate and may surface en masse. Major issues will therefore arise in no small number in the fields of the economy, politics, culture, society, the eco-environment, national defense and the military, Hong Kong, Macao and Taiwan affairs, foreign affairs, and the work to strengthen the Party. They will become increasingly complex, and leading officials should be sharp and quick in foreseeing and identifying potential threats, perceiving their locations, forms and likely trends, and resolving them as necessary.

Struggle is an art, and we must be adroit practitioners. In major endeavors, we should strengthen our awareness of potential dangers while maintaining strategic confidence, make sound strategic judgments and tactical decisions, and focus on both process and result. Leading officials should fulfill their due responsibilities, be ready and able to fight, and prevail at all times and in all circumstances.

We should pay close attention to strategies and methods and master the art of struggle. We should focus on major problems and key aspects of these problems, and always fight for just reasons, to our advantage, and with restraint. We should choose the right methods for addressing problems, take measured approaches, stick to our principles, and be flexible on strategies. We should adjust these as the situation demands, and apply them in a timely manner, to the proper extent, and for the best results. Moreover, we should unite all forces available, mobilize all favorable factors, and strive for unity, cooperation and mutual benefit in our endeavors.

Fighting spirit and capacity are not innate. Leading officials must undergo strict theoretical and political studies and put them into practice. We must brave storms, broaden our horizons, and strengthen our muscles and bones to withstand complex and severe challenges. We must grasp and apply new theories of the Party, master the Marxist stance, viewpoint and methodology, and thereby prepare our minds for courageous and successful struggle. Only when we are cognizant of the theories, can we be politically firm and have the courage and strength to fight. We must hone ourselves in major efforts of struggle. The more serious and complicated the situation is, and the more difficulties and problems there are, the better we can exercise our courage, sharpen our will, and develop our capacity. Leading officials should actively engage themselves in the struggle, take an unequivocal stance in major matters of principle, tackle problems and conflicts head-on, step up in the face of crisis, and resolutely fight against misconducts.

Society progresses in the movement of opposites, and where there are opposites, there will be conflicts. No matter what posts they hold, leading officials should have the courage to shoulder responsibilities and overcome difficulties, and have the ability to be both commanders and fighters, cultivating and maintaining a strong fighting spirit and greater capacity to fight and win. The problems we encounter in our work are diverse, covering reform, development, social stability, national defense, domestic and foreign affairs, and governance of the Party, the country and the military. We must be brave and able to confront such problems on all fronts, including strengthening Party self-governance, upholding the guiding position of Marxism in the ideological field, furthering reform in an all-round way, pushing forward supply-side structural reform, promoting high-quality development, eliminating hidden dangers in the financial sector, ensuring and improving people's wellbeing, eradicating poverty, protecting the eco-environment, dealing with serious natural disasters, advancing law-based governance, handling group incidents, combating organized crime and local tyrants, and safeguarding national security. All leading officials must become bold and capable fighters.

Notes

[1] Wang Anshi: "Mounting the Feilai Peak" (Deng Fei Lai Feng). Wang Anshi (1021-1086) was a thinker, writer and statesman of the Northern Song Dynasty.

[2] Mao Zedong: "The Fairy Cave: Inscription on a Picture Taken by Comrade Li Jin", *Mao Zedong Poems*, Chin./Eng. ed., Foreign Languages Press, Beijing, 1999, p. 79.

High-Quality Development

Enrich the Thought on the Socialist Economy in the New Era*

December 18, 2017

Historic achievements and transformations have been made in the work of the Party and the country since the 18th CPC National Congress in 2012. The same has also happened in the economic field, creating solid material conditions for reform and development in other sectors.

After the 18th CPC National Congress, China was confronted by a complex economic situation both at home and abroad, facing many challenges that had rarely been seen since the launch of reform and opening up in 1978. The underlying impact of the international financial crisis persisted, with the world economy suffering a sluggish recovery, world trade in the doldrums, and protectionism widespread. With mounting downward pressure on the domestic economy, excess production capacity was becoming a salient issue, industrial product prices were in steady decline, and potential financial risks were increasing. All of these required us to think about the direction of our economic development, and solutions to problems on which we found it hard to reach agreement.

At that time, our major challenge was to come to a sound judgment on the economic situation and make the right decisions on how to carry on with our economic work. In the past five years, the Standing Committee of the Political Bureau of the CPC Central Committee, the Political Bureau of the CPC Central Committee, the Leading Group for Further Reform under the CPC Central Committee, and the Leading Group for Financial and Economic Affairs under the

---

* Part of the speech at the Central Conference on Economic Work.

CPC Central Committee have held over one hundred meetings at which major decisions and judgments concerning overall national economic development have been made. This process – from practice to understanding and from practice to understanding all over again – is extraordinary, helping us to constantly sum up the underlying laws of the economy, enhance our understanding, unify our thinking, and make the right decisions. Practice is the sole criterion for testing truth. Practice has proven that the Central Committee's assessment of the economic situation, its decisions on economic work, and its adjustments on development ideas are sound, and this has guided us to achieve historic transformation and results in economic development.

First, our economic strength has reached a new level. In the past five years, our annual economic growth has averaged 7.1 percent, reaching over RMB80 trillion this year and making up 15 percent of the world total – 3.5 percentage points higher than five years ago. Our contribution to world growth was over 30 percent on a yearly basis, exceeding the US, Europe and Japan combined. Our country has become the major engine and anchor of world economic growth. Our market has expanded and attracted investors at an unprecedented rate.

Second, major changes have taken place in the economic structure. We have advanced supply-side structural reform, cutting overcapacity, reducing excess inventory, deleveraging, lowering costs, and strengthening areas of weakness. These measures were taken to reduce excess capacity, clear goods from the market, and promote balance between demand and supply. New technologies, new products, new industries and new business models have flourished, and innovation has played a more obvious role as the major driving force of the economy. The agricultural sector has witnessed stable growth and further structural adjustment. As a result of our concerted efforts, our economic growth now relies more on industry and services combined rather than industry alone, and more on consumption and investment combined rather than investment alone, and China has changed from a major exporter to both an importer and exporter. We have finally achieved long sought-after major structural changes.

Third, more vitality and resilience have become apparent in our economy. We have stated that we will let the market play the decisive role in allocating resources, let the government play its role better, and drive deeper reform in the economic system. On the whole we are making gradual and steady progress and have made breakthroughs in certain areas. The Leading Group for Further Reform under the CPC Central Committee reviewed and approved 105 major measures in structural economic reform. This reform was then rolled out across the board and major breakthroughs were made in key and fundamental fields, which served to emancipate the productive forces immensely.

Fourth, China has opened up further to the outside world. The Belt and Road Initiative, the Asian Infrastructure Investment Bank, and the Silk Road Fund that we have initiated and promoted, and the win-win cooperation philosophy we have advocated, have expanded our space for development. Foreign trade and foreign direct investment have seen stable growth. The Renminbi was included in the International Monetary Fund's special drawing rights (SDR) basket, a major step towards the internationalization of the Renminbi. Towards the goals of promoting free trade and investment, we have actively guided economic globalization onto the right path. Our influence on global economic growth and our voice in global economic governance have markedly increased.

Fifth, people's sense of gain and happiness has been heightened. Over the past five years, a total of over 65 million jobs have been created in urban areas. Income growth surpassed the overall rate of economic growth, and decisive progress was made in eliminating poverty, with over 66 million people helped out of poverty. The quality of education has improved. A social security network covering rural and urban residents is in place. Access to health and medical services has significantly improved, and basic public services have become equally accessible to more people. China now has the world's largest middle-income population.

Sixth, noticeable progress has been made in protecting the eco-environment. In the past five years, we have been firm in accelerating the pace of eco-civilization, leading to greater initiative and awareness of green development within the Party and the nation. Tangible results have been seen in the control and prevention of air, water and soil pollution. The average concentration of $PM_{2.5}$ declined by 30 percent in key areas, energy intensity fell by 20.7 percent, and forest acreage and stock volume increased by 10.87 million hectares and 1.9 billion cubic meters respectively. Regarding the eco-environment, our commitment, measures and achievements are unprecedented.

These historic economic achievements and transformations of the past five years have been made under the strong leadership of the Party Central Committee, and with the joint efforts of the Party and the whole country.

In the past five years, we have raised a series of new concepts, ideas, and strategies through observing general development trends, assessing the overall situation, and engaging in hard work, which can be summed up as follows:

First, we have strengthened the centralized and unified leadership of the Party over economic work. We have made it clear that the Central Committee must take overall responsibility and full leadership over economic work as it is the central task in state governance. The Central Committee is not a place for empty talk but a place for decision-making. All its decisions must be carried out to the letter. To steer our economy on the right course we have improved the Party institutions that lead economic work, enhanced the Central Committee's ability to analyze and assess the situation with regard to development, formulated major guidelines and strategies, made important decisions and work plans in a timely manner, and ensured they are implemented under the Party's leadership.

Second, we must always remain committed to a people-centered philosophy of development. We have made it explicit that the people's aspiration for a better life is our goal and their role as the dominant player in our country is a major driving force. We have taken measures to ensure their wellbeing and improve their lives, building a moderately prosperous society in all respects by focusing on their major concerns. The people-centered approach should be integrated into the Five-sphere Integrated Plan and the Four-pronged Comprehensive Strategy. We have put forward a strategy of targeted poverty alleviation and eradication, and made comprehensive plans and determined efforts to win the fight against poverty and ensure that impoverished people enjoy a decent life together with the rest of the country.

Third, we have adapted to and steered the new normal in economic development. We believe that we have now entered a stage in which we have to shift the gear to slow down the speed of economic development, to bear the pain resulting from the structural adjustment, and to accept and mitigate the impact of stimulus policies adopted in the early days of reform and opening up. In this new normal stage we should emphasize the need to embrace the new development philosophy and advance supply-side structural reform. When assessing the economic situation, we must take into consideration the broad view, have a good understanding of long-term economic trends and laws, and in particular, we should know how to correctly assess the performance of our leading officials. GDP must not be the sole criterion in assessing an official's performance, nor should we be swayed by the short-term fluctuations of economic indicators. These judgments have served to clarify our attitude towards our economic situation and our tasks in economic work. They have also helped the whole Party and all our people to better understand the economic situation, unify our thinking, and stabilize market expectations.

Fourth, we have ensured that the market will play the decisive role in resource allocation and that the government will exercise its functions better. We have underlined that reform is the major driving force of economic growth. Reform is not a mission accomplished, rather it is an ongoing process. We must have the courage to tackle tough issues, break through logjams and venture risky areas to remove institutional barriers to economic development. Correctly handling the relationship between the government and the market is the key to economic reform. We have also made efforts to improve the market mechanism, break down monopolies, bring into play the pricing mechanism, stimulate the vitality of market entities, and take full advantage of the government's role in macro-control, public services, market supervision, social management and environmental protection. In the meantime, the economic vitality, dominance, and influence of the state-owned sector have been enhanced, and the vigor and creativity of the private sector stimulated. A clean and cordial relationship between government and business has thus taken shape, fostering entrepreneurship and breathing new life into economic growth.

Fifth, we have adapted to changes of key problems in economic development and improved our macro-control. We have stated that macro-control must be based on the characteristics of the present development stage and changes in the economic situation – expanding demand and adjusting supply when necessary, which requires us to make discretionary choices and issue corresponding prescriptions. At present, the biggest challenge confronting our economy is in its structure and particularly in the supply side, which manifests itself in the inability of supply to adapt to changes in demand. In this case if we stimulate demand blindly, it will only end up creating more risks and overdrawing future growth potential. Fortunately, we have addressed the principal challenge, in particular the key factor of such a challenge, by adjusting our approach to macro-control and taking supply-side structural reform as the general goal; and we have made the right decisions for the sound and sustained development of our economy.

Sixth, we have taken a problem-oriented approach in developing new strategies for economic growth. It is our belief that we should focus on major issues and have a long-term vision to maintain economic momentum. We have implemented key strategies in sectors concerning our future overall development. For example, we have decided to adopt the strategy of coordinated development of the Beijing-Tianjin-Hebei Region with a view to relieving Beijing of functions not essential to its role as the capital of our country. We have put forward the development strategy of the Yangtze River Economic

Belt to strengthen environmental protection rather than seeking rapid growth at the cost of the environment, and we have put forward the Belt and Road Initiative to promote win-win cooperation. Other such strategies include:

- the development plan for the Guangdong-Hong Kong-Macao Greater Bay Area;
- a new urbanization strategy with a focus on quality urban development and well-rounded development of the people;
- an innovation-driven strategy that emphasizes stimulation;
- a new food security concept highlighting basic self-sufficiency in grain and absolute grain security;
- new thinking on water conservancy concerning coordinated management of water resources, water ecosystem, water environment and floods; and
- a new energy security strategy to boost consumption, supply, and technological development in energy, reform the energy system, and strengthen international energy cooperation.

These important strategies have exerted and will continue to exert a profound influence upon our economic growth and transformation.

Seventh, we have realized that in addition to good guiding philosophy and policies we should have sound tactics and approaches if we want to boost sound and sustainable economic development. We maintain stability while making progress in our work, and strike a balance between the two by being prudent in macro-control and making it more targeted and precise. We are steadfast and unremitting in implementing strategies, stay true to our principles, take into full consideration any difficulties and problems, and are always prepared to deal with the worst-case scenario. Like a hammer driving a nail, we need to move forward step by step, taking each small step as a big success, and in the process, we do everything we can to counter every possible risk and particularly systematic risk.

In conclusion, we have successfully steered the economy on the right course since the 18th CPC National Congress and developed the thought on the economy of socialism with Chinese characteristics in the new era with the new development philosophy as its core. As a valuable asset of our Party and the country, this thought crystallizes the experience of our economic development over the past five years and is a theoretical summary of our political economics guided by basic tenets of Marxism. We must uphold this thought for a long time to come, keep enriching it, and bring about a more profound, extensive and historic transformation in our economy.

China's Economy: From High-Speed Growth to High-Quality Development*

December 18, 2017

As socialism with Chinese characteristics has entered a new era, China's economic development has also embarked on a new phase, the basic feature of which is that our economy is now transitioning from rapid growth to high-quality development. I emphasized this in the report to the 19th CPC National Congress in 2017. It is a weighty conclusion, and its historical and current significance must be fully understood.

First, it is an essential requirement for our country to maintain sustained and sound economic development. China has reached a critical stage in transforming the growth model, and is faced with prominent problems such as rising labor costs, increased constraints imposed by resources and the environment, unsustainable models of extensive development, and impediments in the flows of the economy. At the same time, a new round of scientific and technological revolution and industrial transformation is gaining momentum, and multiple breakthroughs are being made all around the world. We must promote high-quality development if we are to adapt to new technological changes and new needs of the people, and we must form a high-quality, efficient and diversified supply system to provide more quality products and services. Only in this way can supply and demand achieve proper balance at a new level, and can our economy maintain sustained and sound development.

Second, it is an essential requirement for China to adapt to

---

* Part of the speech at the Central Conference on Economic Work.

the evolution of the principal challenge facing Chinese society, and achieve moderate prosperity and socialist modernization in all respects. This challenge involves low-quality development as represented by unbalanced and inadequate development. As it evolves, our economy is also entering a new historic stage. To address this challenge, we must promote high-quality development. We must not neglect quantitative development, but we must pay more attention to quality, so as to achieve effective growth in quantity through a substantial improvement in quality.

Third, it is an essential requirement for China to follow the well-established rules of economic development. The world hosts more than 100 middle-income economies. Since the 1960s, only a dozen of these have graduated to high-income economies. Following a phase of rapid economic growth, these successful countries all transformed from quantitative expansion to qualitative improvement. In contrast, those countries that have stagnated or even retrogressed are failing to grow because they have not achieved this fundamental transformation. Economic development is a process of spiral escalation, rather than linear. Once quantitative growth has accumulated to a certain degree, we must turn to qualitative improvement. China must follow this law in its economic development.

High-quality development can meet the people's ever-growing desire for a better life. It reflects the new development philosophy: In high-quality development innovation is the primary driving force; coordination is an endogenous feature; go-green is a prevailing mode; openness is the only path; and sharing is the fundamental goal.

In terms of supply, high-quality development requires a relatively complete industrial system, network-based and intelligent organization of production, and strength in innovation. It means understanding demand, exerting high brand influence, building strong core competitiveness, and delivering high-quality products and services.

In terms of demand, high-quality development should continuously meet the people's individual, diverse, and ever-growing expectations. These needs lead to changes in the supply system and structure, which in return generate new needs.

In terms of input and output, high-quality development should entail improving the efficiency of labor, capital, land, resources and the environment, raising the contribution level of scientific and technological progress to economic growth, and increasing total factor productivity.

In terms of distribution of the proceeds, high-quality development should ensure that investors obtain returns, enterprises make profits, employees earn incomes, and the government receives taxes, and that all such gains correspond to their respective contribution as evaluated by the market.

In terms of the macroeconomic cycle, high-quality development should ensure a smooth cycle of production, circulation, distribution and consumption, rational proportional relationships and configuration of major economic sectors, and stable economic development without excessive rises and falls. To be very specific, high-quality development means a change from seeking growth to seeking better growth.

To promote high-quality development, we need to develop a modern economic system, which is a strategic goal for China. To achieve this goal, we must take firm steps in the following areas:

- put quality first and give priority to efficiency in accordance with the requirements of high-quality development;
- advance supply-side structural reform;
- work hard for high quality, high efficiency and more robust drivers of economic growth through reform;
- build an industrial system that promotes coordinated development of the real economy, technological innovation, modern finance, and human resources; and
- develop an economic system with more effective market mechanisms, dynamic micro-entities, and sound macro-regulation.

Promoting high-quality development is the fundamental requirement behind our goals, our economic policies, and our macroeconomic regulation at present and in the period to come. We must put in place a framework for high-quality development that covers indicators, policies, standards, statistics, performance evaluation, and government appraisal of achievements. With this improved institutional environment, we will work to make constant new progress in high-quality economic development.

Accelerate Economic Modernization*

January 30, 2018

Developing a modernized economy is a major undertaking that demands in-depth discussions from the perspective of integrating theory with practice. It is a strategic goal for China's development, and an imperative for the transformation of the development model, the optimization of economic structure, and the fostering of new growth engines. The whole Party must have a good understanding of the importance and difficulty of developing a modernized economy and a good grasp of the goals and priorities of this task, and work together to bring out new vitality in economic development and elevate it to a new level.

Developing a modernized economy is an important strategy decided by the Central Committee in view of the overall requirements that our Party and our country meet the new calls of socialism with Chinese characteristics entering a new era, and realize the Two Centenary Goals. A strong country must have a strong economy. Only with a modernized economy can China better adapt to current international trends, seize the initiative in international competition, and provide support for modernization in other fields. We should develop a modernized economy quickly because this is an important part of building China into a great modern socialist country.

A modernized economy integrates all social and economic activities at every link and every level and in every area that are interconnected and internally related.

An industrial system should be built with innovation playing a

---

* Main points of the speech at the third group study session of the Political Bureau of the 19th CPC Central Committee.

leading role, featuring coordinated development of the real economy, science and technology innovation, modern finance and human resources, so that innovation will contribute more to the development of the real economy, modern finance will have a stronger capability of serving the real economy, and human resources will play an optimized role in supporting the real economy.

A modern market system will be put in place that is unified, open, competitive and well-ordered, to achieve smooth market access, an open and orderly market, full market competition, and sound market management, in which enterprises are responsible for their own operations and engage in fair competition, consumers are free to choose and consume, and goods and production factors flow freely and are exchanged on an equal basis.

An efficient and fair income distribution system is to be established, to achieve reasonable income distribution, social fairness and justice, and common prosperity for all, to promote equitable access to basic public services, and to gradually narrow the income distribution gap.

A system of coordinated urban-rural and regional development is to be built to help local regions develop their own strengths, to achieve benign regional interaction, integrated urban-rural development, and overall optimization of land and sea resources, to foster and leverage regional comparative strengths, to reinforce complementarity between regions, and to shape a new framework of coordinated regional development.

A green development system that conserves resources and is environmentally friendly is to be developed, to achieve green, circular and low-carbon development and harmonious coexistence between humanity and nature, to firmly establish and practice the concept that clear waters and green mountains are invaluable assets, and to bring into being a new model of modernization where humanity and nature develop in harmony.

A diverse, balanced, secure and efficient system for opening up on all fronts is to be promoted, to develop a higher-standard open economy and ensure that opening up helps to optimize structure, expand depth and improve efficiency.

An economic system that gives full play to market forces and the role of government is to be put in place, so that market mechanisms are effective, economic players active, and macro-regulation sound.

These systems make up an integral whole and should be developed and promoted together. In developing the modernized economy, we need to draw on the useful practices of developed countries, but this should be done in line with China's own national conditions and characteristics.

A modernized economy demands concrete and effective policies, measures and actions. We need to pay special attention to these fields.

First, develop the real economy to lay a solid foundation for the modernized economy. The real economy is the very foundation of an economy, the fundamental source of wealth creation, and an important pillar of national prosperity. China should extend its supply-side structural reform, develop advanced manufacturing industry, and integrate the real economy fully with the internet, big data and artificial intelligence technology. We should double our efforts to enhance the real economy, gathering resource elements and adopting preferential policies and measures for it. Our purpose is to create a development environment and social atmosphere that encourages practicality, diligence, entrepreneurship, and prosperity through developing the real economy.

Second, lose no time in implementing the innovation-driven strategy to strengthen the support for the modernized economy. China will build a stronger national innovation system, strengthen science and technologies of strategic importance, integrate innovation more deeply with economic and social development, and promote more leading-edge developments that are driven by innovation and first-mover advantages.

Third, actively promote coordinated development of urban and rural areas to optimize the spatial configuration of the modernized economy. It is necessary to better implement coordinated development strategies for the Beijing-Tianjin-Hebei Region, the Yangtze River Economic Belt, and the Guangdong-Hong Kong-Macao Greater Bay Area. Rural revitalization is a great plan, and we must work hard to execute it.

Fourth, develop an open economy to improve the international competitiveness of the modernized economy. China should better utilize global resources and markets and promote international cooperation within the framework of the Belt and Road Initiative.

Fifth, further reform our economic system to provide institutional guarantees for the modernized economy. China should improve the system of socialist market economy, resolutely break down institutional obstacles in all areas, and stimulate the vitality of the whole society in innovation and entrepreneurship.

Speed Up China's Maritime Development*

March 8, 2018-October 15, 2019

I

The ocean is a strategic area for high-quality development. We should redouble our efforts to build world-class ports, a sound modern marine industrial system, and a green and sustainable marine eco-environment, so as to turn China into a strong maritime nation.

(from the speech at the deliberation session of the Shandong delegation to the First Session of the 13th National People's Congress, March 8, 2018)

II

The marine economy has a boundless future. To build China into a strong maritime nation, we must take good care of, further understand, and manage the ocean, and facilitate innovation in marine science and technology.

(from the speech during a visit to Shandong Province, June 12-14, 2018)

III

We need to speed up innovation in marine science and technology, improve the ability to develop marine resources, and cultivate and strengthen strategic emerging industries in this sector. We will

---

* Excerpts from speeches made between March 8, 2018 and October 15, 2019.

promote maritime connectivity and cooperation in various fields, and develop "blue partnerships" with other countries. We should attach great importance to marine eco-environmental progress, strengthen the prevention and control of pollution, protect marine biodiversity, develop and utilize marine resources in an orderly manner, and leave turquoise seas and blue skies for our future generations.

(from the congratulatory letter to the 2019 China Marine Economy Expo, October 15, 2019)

Make China a Global Center for Science and Innovation*

May 28, 2018

With the advent of the 21st century, an unprecedented level of scientific and technological innovation has intensified around the globe. A new round of scientific and technological revolution and industrial transformation is redrawing the map of world innovation and reshaping the global economic structure. Breakthroughs are being made and put into application in the new-generation information technologies, including artificial intelligence, quantum information, mobile communication, the internet of things, and blockchain. A new revolution is in the making in life sciences represented by synthetic biology, gene editing, brain science and regenerative medicine. The advanced manufacturing technologies that integrate robots, digital manufacturing, and new materials are expediting the transformation of the manufacturing industry, which is becoming smarter, more service-oriented, and more eco-friendly. The rapid development of energy technologies that target cleanness, high efficiency, and sustainability is anticipated to trigger global energy reform. Space and marine technologies are expanding the living area of humanity. In short, the pioneering breakthroughs in information, life, manufacturing, energy, space and marine sciences have provided more sources of innovation in frontier and disruptive technologies. A trend of integration among different disciplines, between science and technology, among technologies, and between natural sciences and humanities and social sciences

---

* Part of the speech at the joint session of the 19th Meeting of the Members of the Chinese Academy of Sciences and the 14th Meeting of the Members of the Chinese Academy of Engineering.

is becoming increasingly obvious. Never before have we seen science and technology exercise such a profound influence on the future of our country and the lives of our people.

Currently, some prominent problems continue to interfere with China's scientific and technological development; they need to be addressed immediately. Our science and technology vision, framework, innovative capability, resource allocation, system and policies are not yet adapted to the new tasks and requirements set at the 19th CPC National Congress held in 2017. Our basic science research is still weak, remaining a prominent problem: Enterprises do not pay enough attention to basic research; we do not achieve enough results from original research; our capabilities in underlying technologies and fundamental techniques are weak; shortcomings in fields such as machine tools, high-end microchips, basic software and hardware, development platforms, basic algorithms, basic components, and basic materials hold back our development; and we still have to rely on other countries for core technologies in key fields. Our research and development (R&D) does not fully target our need for industrial development and our weaknesses. International scientific and technological cooperation with a global vision is insufficient, and our ability to transform research results into productive forces is weak. Our systems and mechanisms for cultivating talent and our incentive mechanism to inspire enthusiasm for innovation are incomplete, and we have a shortfall in top talent and research teams. Our scientific and technological management system has not been fully adapted to the need for building our country into a scientific and technological leader. There is a lack of synergy in the implementation of major policies on scientific and technological system reform. Policies on scientific and technological innovation are not yet fully aligned with economic and industrial policies. We need to improve the social environment and mechanisms required to encourage and accommodate innovation.

To achieve prosperity and rejuvenation, China must dedicate itself to advancing science and technology, and become a major world center for science and innovation. We are closer to the goal of rejuvenating the Chinese nation than at any time in history, so the need to build China into a world leader in science and technology is more urgent than ever.

The new round of scientific and technological revolution and industrial reform concurs with the transformation of China's development model. We are now in a historic period that brings us both rare opportunities and severe challenges. If we fail to overcome the challenges, we may fall even further behind developed countries. We must be fully aware that sometimes we can seize precious opportunities presented by the times and amplify our national strength, but sometimes we might miss them.

Facing the pressing situation, challenges and tasks, our scientists and engineers must closely follow current trends, take the initiative, confront problems head-on, and overcome difficulties. They should stay at the forefront of scientific and technological development and shape its direction, shoulder the great responsibilities they bear, and be the pioneers of scientific and technological innovation in the new era.

First, we should be fully aware that innovation is the primary force driving development and provides high-quality scientific and technological services to underpin a modern economic system. As the *Mohist Canon*[1] says, "Force is the reason that an object moves." We will focus on improving the quality and efficiency of development, take supply-side structural reform as our main task, and direct our efforts towards building a better-quality supply system. We will work hard through reform for better quality, higher efficiency, and more robust drivers of economic growth to make our economy stronger. Through strengthening weak areas, exploiting potential, and creating new strengths, we will facilitate the highly-efficient flow and optimized distribution of resources, revolutionize the industrial chain, upgrade the value chain, satisfy both effective and potential demand, achieve dynamic equilibrium between supply and demand, bolster market anticipation of growth, and boost confidence in the real economy.

We are in an era when the world economy is dominated by the information industry. We need to grasp the opportunity brought about by the integration of information, internet and smart technologies, and leverage information and smart technologies to grow new driving forces for the economy. Due to their leading and buttressing role, priority will be given to developing clusters of emerging industries of strategic importance, and setting up new industrial pillars. We will fully integrate the internet, big data and artificial intelligence with the real economy, and expand and strengthen the digital economy. We will steer the revolution, optimization and upgrade of industrial technology in the direction of intelligent manufacturing, and propel the fundamental transformation of business models and enterprise structures in the manufacturing sector. We will replace the old with the new, use new growth to boost existing capacity, and move Chinese industries up to the medium-high end of the global value chain.

Second, we should be committed to independent innovation and build up our confidence and our capability. Only with self-confidence can a nation move forward steadily on the road to the future. A high and exuberant tree grows from deep roots. It is self-reliance that has enabled China to stand firmly among nations of the world, and innovation is the only path to reach new heights in science and technology. Dr. Sun Yat-sen said, "If I believe I can do it, then I am able to complete any difficult task – even moving a mountain or filling up a sea; if I don't think I can do it, then I may not succeed in even the easiest tasks like flipping over my hands or breaking off a twig."[2] In innovation the odds of failure are much higher than those of success, but we should have the determination shown by patriotic poet Qu Yuan, "For the ideal that I hold dear to my heart, I will not regret a thousand deaths to die."[3] Our scientists and engineers should have great confidence and resolve in innovating, being neither self-abased nor conceited. They must strive to surmount all difficulties on the way to triumph, and gain an edge in scientific and technological competition and future development.

We have learned from our experience that China cannot ask for, buy, or beg for core technologies in key fields from other countries. Only by holding these technologies in our own hands can we ensure economic security, national security and security in other areas. Our scientists and engineers must have firm confidence in the path, theory, system and culture of Chinese socialism, and boldly explore uncharted courses in the research of core technologies, particularly key generic technologies, cutting-edge frontier technologies, modern engineering technologies, and disruptive technologies. In so doing we will realize the goal that core technologies are self-developed and controllable, and keep the initiative for innovation and development securely in our own hands.

A scientific and technological leader should have landmark achievements. We need to better guide the development of science and technology by devising strategies and setting specific goals, improve our innovation system and capacity, accelerate the process of creating first-mover advantage that can support leading-edge development, devote greater efforts to planning and studying scientific issues of fundamental and overall importance, focus prime resources, and make strategic plans to achieve rapid breakthroughs in key areas and on specific problems that have hindered us. We will strive to catch up with and eventually surpass advanced countries in overall science and technology, lead the pack in key areas, and become a pioneer in emerging frontier and interdisciplinary areas, to create more competitive strength. We should take the people's desire for a better life as the goal of scientific and technological innovation, and steer our innovations towards benefiting and enriching the people and improving their living standards.

Basic research is the bedrock of the whole scientific system. We should target frontier research, stay ahead of the curve, and lay good foundations for future development. Our scientists and engineers should be "planters of trees" and "diggers of wells", engaging in work that might bring no fame but can lay the groundwork for future research. We should make major breakthroughs in pioneering basic research and groundbreaking original innovations, so as to lay solid foundations for building China into a world leader in science and technology. We will strengthen basic research in applied sciences, focus on major scientific and technological projects, remove obstacles in the process, speed up the application of research results in industries, bolster the precise docking of the innovation chain and the industrial chain, expedite the transformation of research results from prototypes to commercial products, and fully apply scientific and technological advances to our modernization drive.

Engineering science and technology is a key engine driving human progress, and a powerful lever to promote industrial revolution, economic growth and social progress. Those working in this sector should show fine workmanship and team spirit. Focusing on the needs of national strategies, major technological issues that relate to economic development and national security, people's actual needs, and the demands of civil-military integration in the new era, we will accelerate the application of innovations, and take the initiative in pioneering and strategic fields.

Third, we should reform in depth the system of science and technology in all respects, improve innovation efficiency and inspire innovation vitality. Innovation determines the future, and reform is critical to the prospects of a nation. Science and technology are the fields where continuous reform is most needed. On June 9, 2014, I emphasized in my speech at the joint session of academicians of the Chinese Academy of Sciences and the Chinese Academy of Engineering that the most urgent priority for stimulating independent innovation is to remove institutional barriers and fully unleash the huge potential of science and technology as the primary productive forces. To complete these priority tasks, we have promoted institutional reform in science and technology for years. We have made an all-out effort in this reform and achieved breakthroughs on various fronts. The framework of reform has been established, and substantial results have been achieved in key areas.

In August 2015, the CPC Central Committee and the State Council issued the Implementation Plan for In-depth Institutional Reform in Science and Technology, which lists 143 reform tasks to be accomplished by 2020. We have to date completed more than 110. We have made substantive breakthroughs on a number of challenging issues which we had tried to tackle before but failed to solve. However, some outstanding problems still wait to be addressed, such as:

- low efficiency and capability in the national innovation system;
- scattered, duplicated, and ineffective allocation of scientific and technological resources;
- too many redundant projects, honorary title grants, and unnecessary institutions;
- poor returns from the input in science and technology;
- insufficient ability to convert research results into commercial applications and create business value;
- relatively slow progress in reforming research institutes, improving the mechanism that integrates science and technology with finance, and fostering innovative talent; and
- enthusiasm for original innovation yet to be fully aroused.

This year marks the 40th anniversary of reform and opening up. We must maintain firm resolve and courage to further reform in the new era. To reform science and technology, we should boldly address the most difficult problems, change our mindsets and remove all institutional barriers hindering scientific and technological innovation. As we have said, "Limits lead to changes; changes lead to solutions; solutions lead to development."[4]

Technological innovation should be accompanied by institutional innovation. Targeting existing problems and meeting actual needs, we will put more energy into improving institutional planning, policies, the general environment, and practices of innovation. We will devote a constant effort to fostering innovators, to enhancing the foundations and resources of innovation, and to creating a favorable environment, so as to increase our national strength in strategic science and technology and the overall efficiency and capability of the national innovation system. We will improve the top-level design for the technological innovation system, clarify the functions and positions of enterprises, universities and research institutes in the innovation chain, and arouse the enthusiasm and vitality of all parties. We will continue to transform the government's management of science and technology, and make full use of its organizational strength.

Enterprises play a leading role in innovation, and are the vital force for creation. Frederick Engels wrote in his letter to W. Borgius: "If society has a technical need, that helps science forward more than ten universities."[5] We should encourage enterprises to take the lead in decision-making on technological innovation, investment in R&D, and implementation of research and application of findings, and cultivate a group of leading innovative enterprises that boast strong capabilities in core technologies and integrated innovation. We will make the most of the market in guiding the direction of and approaches to technological research, the price of production factors, and the allocation of innovation factors, so that the market can play the decisive role in allocating innovation resources. To spur on the development of new technologies, products and business models, we will improve long-term mechanisms for policy support, input of production factors, guarantees with incentive measures, and administrative services and supervision. We will speed up the application of innovations, and remove any barriers that block smooth progress from technological breakthroughs, product manufacturing, to commercial application and the emergence of an industrial chain.

We will build national labs to the highest standards, and make optimal overall plans for mega science initiatives, projects and centers, and international innovation bases. We will set up a science and technology decision-making mechanism that enables scientific consultation to support administrative decision-making, and give full play to the role of think tanks and specialized research institutes. This will help us improve decision-making mechanisms and capacity in science and technology. We will accelerate civil-military integration, improve the organization, management, operation, and policies of this work, and break down the barriers that hinder the engagement of civilian contractors in the defense industry or the civilian use of military technologies. We will intensify law enforcement in the field of intellectual property (IP) protection and improve IP services.

In my speech on science and technology on May 30, 2016, I emphasized that we would reform and innovate the ways we use and manage R&D funds, and let money serve creative activities rather than vice versa; we would also reform the appraisal system and establish a classification model to appraise the quality, contribution and performance of scientific and technological innovations and make a correct assessment of their scientific, technological, economic, social and cultural value. We have promulgated several important reform plans since then, including Plan for Further Reforming the Management of Scientific and Technological Programs (Special Projects, Funds and Other Undertakings) Funded by the Central Government, Guidelines on Further Improving the Policies for Managing the Funding of Central Government-funded Research Programs, Guidelines on Adopting Policies Oriented to Rewarding Knowledge, Guidelines on Advancing the Reform of the Personnel Appraisal Mechanism by Category, and Reform Plan for the Scientific and Technological Reward System. All of these have been welcomed by those working in the fields of science and technology. Concurrently, we also received feedback that these reform measures still have room for improvement, and certain measures have not yet been carried out. Relevant departments should heed with an open mind the opinions offered and continue to press forward with reform, so as to release creative activities from the restraints of unreasonable administrative systems such as those regulating fund management and performance appraisal.

Fourth, we should be deeply engaged in global scientific and technological governance, contributing Chinese wisdom and helping to build a global community of shared future. Science and technology respond to the call of the times and have a global impact, so we should have a global vision in developing them. Rivers and seas are big because they never reject the small streams that flow in. Independent innovation should be pursued in an open environment, rather than behind closed doors. We should gather energy and strength from every part of the world. We will enhance scientific and technological exchange and cooperation with other countries, and promote innovation on this basis. We will take the initiative in planning and actively utilize international innovation resources, and establish a cooperative and mutually beneficial partnership with other countries to cope with the future challenges facing humanity – development, food and energy security, health, and climate change. We will bring benefits to more countries and their people while achieving our own development, and promote balanced development around the world.

We should always embrace a global vision when planning and promoting scientific and technological innovation. We should bolster international cooperation, integrate China into the global innovation network, further open up national science and technology programs, participate in and play a leading role in international mega science plans and projects, and encourage our scientists to initiate and organize international scientific and technological cooperation. The Belt and Road Initiative should become an initiative of innovation: We will cooperate with other participating countries to build scientific and technological innovation alliances and bases, and create more opportunities and platforms for common development. We will use to the maximum global innovation resources, raise China's status in the global innovation landscape across the board, and increase our influence and ability to participate in rule-making in global scientific and technological governance.

Fifth, we should make human resources the priority in our development, and bring together our best achievers to lay a solid foundation for innovation-driven development. Feats are accomplished by capable people; undertakings proceed because of capable people. People are our most precious resource. All innovations are created by people. Both hard and soft power are fundamentally based on strength in human resources. The whole history of science and technology proves that the country with the most capable people and scientists will gain strengths in scientific and technological innovation.

At present, China still lacks high-caliber innovative talent, especially talent that can spearhead scientific and technological development. Our talent appraisal system is flawed: It overemphasizes the number of theses scientists and engineers have published, their academic titles, and educational backgrounds; our scientists and engineers are deluged with appraisals and overburdened with the scramble for honorary titles; and our human resource management does not meet the needs of scientific and technological innovation or conform to the principles governing innovation. We will reform the appraisal mechanism, aiming to establish a system that highlights the innovative capability, innovation quality, and contribution of scientists and engineers, and create institutions that allow them to concentrate on their research and innovation. We should assess the performance of both individual researchers and their teams, respecting and recognizing the contribution of all members. We will improve the incentive system to ensure appropriate remuneration for outstanding scientists and engineers, so as to ignite the passion for innovation across society. Through reform, we will change the practice of permanently labeling talent by static appraisals, and of appraising talent with quantity of theses, patents or funds. Our scientists should not get mired in red tape or waste their precious time on redundant reports and applications.

Talented people are essential to innovation. We must expand the channels to build a large talent pool. We will create a favorable environment for innovation, and form effective training, hiring, incentive and competition mechanisms that can help talent to grow, to stand out and to give of their best, so that talented people will emerge in greater numbers from generation to generation. We should respect and develop talent, address structural problems in human resources, establish a multitiered human resource structure, and foster a large pool of world-class talent in strategic science and technology, leading scientists and engineers, young people of caliber, and innovation teams. We will increase investment in human resources, improve policies, create a favorable policy environment for innovation and start-ups, set up effective mechanisms to attract and employ talent, and finally bring about a situation where China attracts talented individuals from all over the world to work and compete in an innovative manner.

Notes

[1] *Mohist Canon* (*Mo Jing*) was one of the Mohist classics from the late Warring States Period (475-221 BC).

[2] Sun Yat-sen: "Plan for National Reconstruction", *Complete Works of Sun Yat-sen*, Vol. I, Chin. ed., People's Publishing House, Beijing, 2015, p. 15.

[3] Qu Yuan: "The Lament" (Li Sao). Qu Yuan (c. 339-278 BC) was a poet and statesman in the Warring States Period.

[4] *Book of Changes* (*Yi Jing*).

[5] Frederick Engels: "Engels to W. Borgius", *Karl Marx & Frederick Engels: Collected Works*, Vol. 50, Eng. ed., Progress Publishers, Moscow, 1979, p. 265.

Promote Rural Revitalization*

September 21, 2018

Rural revitalization is one of the major strategies put forward by the Party at its 19th National Congress in 2017. Focused on this topic, this group study session aims to further our understanding of the strategy so that we have a clear picture of the guidelines and improve our performance accordingly.

I. The Rural Revitalization Strategy – an Overarching, Historic Mission for Socialist Modernization

I have always emphasized that we will never have all-round modernization without the modernization of agriculture and rural areas. In the process of modernization, how we deal with the relationships between industry and agriculture and between urban and rural areas determines, to some extent, the success or failure of our modernization drive. The history of modernization tells us that in some countries failure to properly handle these relationships has resulted in underdeveloped agriculture and rural areas, short supply of agricultural products, and inability to effectively absorb rural labor. As large numbers of farmers without work flocked into urban slums, rural areas and the rural economy plunged into destitution, the progress of industrialization and urbanization halted, social order was disrupted, and the whole country eventually slipped into the "middle-income trap". The underlying problems lie in the systems of leadership and national governance. As a socialist country under

---

* Speech at the eighth group study session of the Political Bureau of the 19th CPC Central Committee.

the CPC's leadership, China should have the capacity and resources to properly handle the relationships between industry and agriculture and between urban and rural areas, and steadily steer socialist modernization.

China now has reached a historic stage at which we should properly handle the two relationships. After the founding of the PRC in 1949, faced with a seriously backward economy and a largely hostile international environment, we embarked on industrialization from scratch and, with the support of agriculture and rural areas, established a relatively complete industrial system and national economic system through our own efforts. Since reform and opening up was introduced in 1978, we have once again relied on rural labor, land, and capital input to give a powerful boost to industrialization and urbanization. Tremendous changes have taken place in China's cities and towns as a result. In this process, remarkable progress has also been witnessed in agriculture and rural areas, laying a solid foundation for China's reform, opening up and socialist modernization.

We have handled these two relationships appropriately and to good effect. With years of bumper harvests, farmers have increased their incomes, generally ensuring stability and harmony in rural areas. It is important to note that over a long period of time, hundreds of millions of migrant workers have traveled between rural and urban areas in an orderly manner and to good effect. They have not created social unrest but have provided essential support for our economic and social development.

However, we should also be aware that agricultural and rural development in China has lagged behind industrialization and urbanization. The imbalance in China's development is most visible between urban and rural areas, as rural areas suffered most from insufficient development. Since the 18th CPC National Congress in 2012, we have made up our mind to adjust the two relationships, and have taken a series of measures to support agriculture with industry, and rural areas with urban development. The Party put forward the strategy of rural revitalization at its 19th National Congress in order to handle the two relationships from an overall and strategic perspective.

It is an objective rule that in the process of modernization the share of urban development increases and that of rural development decreases. But we need to note that our country has a population of nearly 1.4 billion. No matter how far industrialization and urbanization go, agriculture always needs to develop, the countryside will never vanish, and urban and rural areas will continue to co-develop and coexist in China for a long time. This is also an objective rule. Even if China's urbanization rate reaches 70 percent, there will still be more than 400 million people living in rural areas. If these 400 million people are left behind in the process of modernization, there will be prosperous cities on the one side and destitute villages on the other, which is not in line with the mission of our Party or the essential requirements of socialism. We will not achieve real modernization in this way. Forty years ago we lifted the curtain of reform and opening up by introducing rural reform. Today, 40 years later, we should break new ground for integrated urban-rural development and modernization by revitalizing the countryside.

II. Implementation of the Rural Revitalization Strategy – Key to the Work on Agriculture, Rural Areas and Rural People in the New Era

In my report to the 19th CPC National Congress, I summarized the rural revitalization strategy, and proposed that we must prioritize the development of agriculture and rural areas, featuring thriving businesses, an eco-friendly environment, social etiquette and civility, effective governance, and prosperous rural population. We need to put in place sound systems, mechanisms, and policies for promoting integrated urban-rural development, and move faster to modernize agriculture and rural areas. Agricultural and rural modernization is the general goal of the strategy; prioritizing agriculture and rural areas is the general principle; thriving businesses, an eco-friendly environment, social etiquette and civility, effective governance, and prosperous rural population are the general requirements; and putting in place sound systems, mechanisms, and policies for integrated urban-rural development is the institutional guarantee.

The work on agriculture, rural areas and rural people in the new era must focus on the general goal of modernizing agriculture and rural areas. Over the decades, to make sure the people have enough to eat, we have expended a lot of energy on agricultural modernization and made considerable progress. At present, over 65 percent of the work on sowing, plowing and harvesting major crops has been mechanized, and technological advances in agriculture have accounted for more than 57 percent of the growth of agricultural output. Together with our per capita share of major agricultural products, they have all exceeded the world average. The supply of agricultural products is extremely rich.

However, compared to urban areas, rural areas lag far behind in infrastructure, public services and social governance. Rural modernization involves both material and people, and covers the rural governance system and governing capability. We need to design and implement agricultural modernization along with rural modernization, and transform China from a country with high agricultural output to one with a leading edge in agriculture.

The whole Party must address affairs related to agriculture, rural areas and rural people as a top priority. We have always emphasized that we should invest more in agriculture and rural areas, take less from farmers and reduce restrictions. But in reality, these commitments have not always been matched with action. We should no longer tolerate such negligence; we must take effective measures in terms of financial input, factor allocation, public services and assignment of officials, to bolster agricultural and rural development and narrow the gap between urban and rural areas. In so doing, we will make agriculture a promising industry, farming an attractive occupation, and the countryside an appealing place to live and work.

The general requirements of thriving businesses, eco-friendly environments, social etiquette and civility, effective governance and prosperous rural population reflect the inclusive nature of the rural revitalization strategy. At the beginning of this century, when China had just reached moderate prosperity in a general sense and was faced with the task of achieving moderate prosperity in all respects, the CPC put forth the general guidelines for building a new socialist countryside: more-developed production, better-off farmers, social etiquette and civility, a clean environment, and democratic administration. These were in line with the prevailing conditions of the time.

As socialism with Chinese characteristics has entered a new era, the principal challenges facing agriculture and society at large have undergone great changes. Higher expectations from farmers have set a higher bar for agriculture and rural development. Thriving businesses are the prerequisite for solving all rural problems. From "more-developed production" to "thriving businesses", the change reflects the new requirements for agriculture and the rural economy to adapt to changing market demand, speed up structural upgrading, and promote industrial integration. An eco-friendly living environment is an inherent requirement of rural revitalization. From a "clean environment" to an "eco-friendly environment", the change reflects farmers' desire for a beautiful environment and substantive progress towards an eco-civilization. Social etiquette and civility is an urgent need, and the emphasis is on carrying forward our core socialist values, protecting and continuing the best of traditional rural culture, strengthening public cultural services, helping rural people abandon outdated social mores and customs, and boosting their vitality as the countryside changes for the better. Effective governance is an important guarantee for rural revitalization. From "democratic administration" to "effective governance", the change reflects the need to modernize our rural governance for a vigorous, harmonious and orderly society. Prosperity is the main goal of rural revitalization. From "better-off farmers" to "prosperous farmers", the change reflects farmers' growing desire for a better life.

We can see that rural revitalization is a comprehensive drive that targets progress in businesses, the workforce, culture, eco-civilization and the organizational structure. It applies the principles of the Five-sphere Integrated Plan and the Four-pronged Comprehensive Strategy in our work on agriculture, rural areas and rural people. We need to make coordinated efforts to promote rural economic, political, cultural, social, and eco-environmental progress and strengthen Party organizations in rural areas, so as to upgrade agriculture, achieve overall growth for rural areas, and guarantee well-rounded development for the rural population.

III. Remaining Committed to Chinese Approach to Rural Revitalization

In order to implement the rural revitalization strategy, we must first of all establish rules based on practice. Rural revitalization has never been tried before in a country like China with a population of nearly 1.4 billion; it is a pioneering initiative that has no experience to follow but our own.

China has a large population and suffers from an acute shortage of arable land – the area of arable land per household is only 1/40 of that of the European Union and 1/400 of that of the United States. In many parts of the country, farmers work on small patches of land and individual households do not have enough land to till, which renders it impossible for China to develop large-scale and mechanized farming throughout the country as is practiced in Europe and the United States. Instead, we should, in most part of China, encourage small household farmers to engage in modern agriculture by improving agricultural service systems. Now and for the foreseeable future, we need to focus on farmers' cooperatives and family farms – two types of agricultural businesses that emerged in line with the two-tier system combining unified collective land management and individual household operations – to make agribusinesses more efficient.

China's long and rich agro-civilization is the root of traditional Chinese culture. Many villages go back hundreds or even thousands of years, and have been preserved well up to this day. Many customs and rules have deep cultural roots and still play an important role. We should give expression to morality and virtue while implementing law-based self-governance, so that our fine cultural and moral traditions support and enhance the rule of law, and vice versa. We need to continue to explore and spread good practices in this regard.

We must pursue integrated urban-rural development for the rural revitalization strategy to be successful. Our urbanization drive included rural towns when it was first initiated. The purpose was to promote integrated urban-rural development. We need to power the initiative with reforms and move faster to develop and improve institutions, mechanisms and policies for integrated urban-rural development. We need to enhance the multiple input guarantee mechanism, increase investment in agricultural and rural infrastructure, accelerate integration of urban and rural infrastructure, and promote the exchange of human resources, land, capital, and other factors between urban and rural areas. We should establish and improve institutions to extend basic public services to rural areas so that rural residents will enjoy equal access to these services with their urban counterparts. We need to further reform the household registration system, improve basic public services for farmers who have become permanent urban residents, and at the same time continue to protect their land contracting rights, their rights to use homestead, and their rights to share collective income of their villages.

Poverty elimination is the priority of rural revitalization. Poor villages and the counties and townships where they are located must focus on this priority and give it the utmost attention. We will have eliminated absolute poverty by the time we achieve moderate prosperity in all respects in 2020, but relative poverty will still exist for a long time. After 2020, the current measures aimed at eradicating absolute poverty will be gradually adjusted to regular support measures for helping the population in relative poverty, and integrated into the overall plans for rural revitalization. Early planning must be done to achieve this goal.

IV. Providing a Strong Political Guarantee for the Rural Revitalization Strategy

To implement the strategy of rural revitalization, Party committees and organizations at all levels must strengthen their leadership and bring together the strengths of the whole Party and all sectors of society. We must always follow the correct political direction, uphold the collective ownership of rural land, develop new types of collective economy, and take the road of common prosperity. We should give full play to the role of rural Party organizations, and strengthen these organizations with a strong leadership. Poor villages need strong Party branches to break new ground, and better-off villages also need capable Party branches to secure further progress. Human resources are the foundation of rural revitalization. We need to find innovative ways to improve the management of rural human resources, fully tap into the potential of the rural workforce, and attract more urban entrepreneurs and professionals of all kinds to rural areas.

In implementing the rural revitalization strategy, we should properly handle the following relationships:

First, the relationship between long-term and short-term goals. Rural revitalization is a long-term and arduous task. We must adopt a long-term perspective, and plan thoughtfully before taking action. We need to make rational plans, emphasize quality, and take our time to ensure efficacy. We need to focus on the tasks at hand, look for areas for breakthroughs, and set priorities. We will work away issue by issue, year in and year out, accumulating small successes and moving towards great achievements. We should have sufficient patience, and think ahead about problems that might emerge. We must not be overambitious or too impatient for success, and we must refrain from impulsive campaigns that might lead to missteps or about-turns.

Second, the relationship between top-level design and grassroots experimentation. With a clear top-level design for rural revitalization from the CPC Central Committee in place, all localities need to consider their own realities and make feasible local plans. Village plans should not be duplicates of urban plans, nor can all villages apply the same model. We should understand the differences between one village and another, and work out targeted plans and distinctive policies in line with local conditions, to make each a unique home. We should give full play to the principal role and initiative of hundreds of millions of rural people, mobilize their enthusiasm, creativity, and pioneering spirit, and summarize the creative experience at the grassroots level to constantly improve the top-level design.

Third, the relationship between the decisive role of the market and a better role of the government. We need to further free our minds and promote a new round of rural reform, beginning with the deep-seated problems in agriculture and rural development and focusing on the relationship between farmers and the land, between farmers and collectives, and between rural and urban residents. We need to define rural ownership more clearly, promote market-oriented allocation of rural resources, lend more effective support to agriculture, and modernize rural governance. We need to better organize ourselves and activate endogenous drivers of rural revitalization. We should extend supply-side structural reform and enhance the overall efficiency and competitiveness of our agriculture based on market demand. We should optimize the environment for creativity and entrepreneurship in rural areas, invigorate the rural economy with more flexible policies, and cultivate new drivers of rural growth. We need to give full play to the positive role of the government in planning and guidance, policy support, market supervision, and legal support. Rural reform cannot be completed overnight. We may have to endure temporary pain or make sacrifices, but we must not deviate from the correct course. I have always emphasized that no matter how rural reform evolves, we must never alter the collective ownership of rural land, reduce the size of arable land, weaken our grain production capacity, or harm the interests of farmers. We must stay true to these principles and never stray from this path.

Fourth, the relationship between enhancing the people's sense of gain and adapting to the current stage of development. We should focus on issues of the greatest concern to farmers and those affecting their most immediate interests, and improve areas of weakness in rural development and people's wellbeing, so that farmers will have a stronger sense of gain, happiness, and security. We need to rationally evaluate government revenues and expenditure, the strength of the collective economy, and public adaptability, determine the scale of investment, financing channels, and debt levels, and set goals, tasks and work priorities for different stages, so as to form a long-term mechanism for sustainable development. We must do the best we can. We should never extend our reach beyond our stage of development or set unrealistic goals, nor should we favor form over substance or indulge in showcase projects.

Boost the Private Sector*

November 1, 2018

The key to coping with all kinds of risks and challenges lies in staying focused, enhancing confidence, and pooling efforts to manage our own affairs well. Currently, our economy is growing steadily, while maintaining overall stability and keeping major indicators within a reasonable range. At the same time, it is faced with increasing uncertainties, mounting downward pressure, and growing difficulties with business operation. These are inevitable on our way forward.

We should be conscious of potential opportunities amidst the challenges we face, and have full confidence in our economic development.

First, our economy is solid and resilient. It has great potential and significant scope for adjustment, with a domestic market of more than 1.3 billion people. The country is boosting and synchronizing new industrialization, information technology applications, urbanization, and agricultural modernization. An expanding middle-income group is generating enormous demand as consumption moves up market. The imbalance between urban and rural areas and between regions present immense space for development.

Second, our country enjoys favorable conditions and has solid material foundations for development. It has the world's most complete industrial system and a growing capacity for innovation in science and technology, and its gross savings rate remains high.

Third, our country has abundant human resources. Among its workforce of more than 900 million, 170 million have received higher education or have vocational skills. Every year over 8 million students

---

* Part of the speech at a meeting on private enterprise.

graduate from universities. The comparative strength of its workforce remains obvious.

Fourth, our country has a vast territory rich in land resources and potential for intensive land use, providing enormous space for economic development.

Fifth, comprehensive analysis shows that the fundamentals of China's economy remain sound and stable, the factors of production supporting high-quality development remain unchanged, and growth built on stable economic performance remains on an upward trend. China's economic growth continues to rank among the highest compared with other major economies.

Sixth, our system has its unique strengths. The Party's strong leadership makes it viable in our country to pool all our resources to complete major missions. Further reform across the board provides an infinite driving force for development. The state's capacity for macroeconomic regulation and control continues to improve.

The world economy continues on its path to recovery. Peace and development remain the themes of our times. In the first three quarters of this year, our country's imports and exports maintained steady growth and the total trade volume with all major trade partners was on the increase. As the Belt and Road Initiative moves steadily forward, cooperation in trade and investment between China and the other countries involved has accelerated, providing greater opportunities for China's economy.

In short, as long as we maintain our strategic resolve, uphold the underlying principle of pursuing progress while ensuring stability, take supply-side structural reform as our main task, and further reform and opening up on all fronts, our country will be able to speed up its transition to high-quality development and embrace brighter growth prospects.

In the course of economic development, we should create a better environment for the private sector by addressing their difficulties and supporting their reform. We need to help the sector transform pressure into impetus, tap innovation as a lasting source of growth, and give full play to its creativity. Therefore, it is imperative to implement the following six policy measures:

First, taxes and fees on private enterprises should be reduced to effectively ease their burden. For this purpose, we should push forward supply-side structural reform, with a focus on lowering costs for private enterprises. To increase their sense of gain, it is necessary to extend tax reductions and make substantial cuts to the rates of VAT and other taxes through easily applicable measures. Universal tax exemptions can be provided for micro and small enterprises and technology startups.

The nominal rates for social insurance contributions should be lowered in accordance with the actual conditions of private enterprises. The methods of collecting social insurance premiums currently in operation will remain unchanged. Premium payments by private enterprises must be substantively reduced. While applying the most stringent standards to prevent tax evasion, we should remove inappropriate taxation that disrupts the normal operation of enterprises.

We need to further review and streamline administrative approval procedures concerning private investment management and fees charged to enterprises. Intermediate processes and intermediaries should be regulated to lessen the burden on enterprises, and efforts to eliminate government-levied fees on enterprises should be expedited, to lower their costs. We should move more rapidly to promote good local practices nationwide.

Second, measures should be taken to address the difficulties and high costs of finance for private enterprises. We should give priority to facilitating access to finance for private enterprises and in particular small and medium-sized enterprises (SMEs) while reducing financing costs step by step. To make financial institutions more willing to offer loans to private enterprises, we need to reform and improve the regulation, evaluation and internal incentive mechanisms for financial institutions, and evaluate the performance of banks by taking account of the support they provide to the private sector.

Access to the financial markets should be broadened to expand the fundraising channels of private enterprises and tap into channels such as private banks, small-loan companies, venture capital, stock shares, and bonds. Relevant authorities should design special measures to help private enterprises at risk of defaulting on their stock-based loans and changing ownership, and restore them to equilibrium. Local governments should be provided with guidance to grant the necessary financial aid to those private enterprises that contribute to the country's economic upgrading and have good prospects. On the condition that they take strict measures to prevent illegal fundraising and the loss of state assets, governments of provinces and equivalent administrative units and cities specially designated in the state plan can pool resources to establish policy-based funds and employ multiple means to assist local leading enterprises, major job providers, enterprises in strategic emerging industries, and other key private enterprises in difficulty. We should be keenly alert to debt chains, and rectify the misconduct of government departments and large enterprises that default on payments to private enterprises or abuse small enterprises by exploiting their position and strength.

Third, the playing field should be leveled. Hidden restrictions and hindrances for private enterprises should be eliminated. An environment of fair play should be created in market access, administrative approvals, business operations, tenders and bids, and civil-military integration to give them more space to expand their business. Private enterprises are encouraged to participate in the reform of state-owned enterprises. Differential and selective industrial policies should be replaced by inclusive and functional ones. Policies that run counter to fair, open and transparent market rules should be abolished. Law enforcement must be reinforced to combat monopolies and unfair competition.

Fourth, policy implementation should be improved. Any policy, no matter how well-intended, might have a potential downside, a discrepancy between expectations and practice, or a multiplying effect in combination with other policies. We need to take account of all these factors to better implement our policies. All provincial authorities and central departments should improve their methods and management skills, to better coordinate the implementation of policies and refine policy measures with quantitative indicators based on their actual conditions. Supportive steps should be taken to ensure that these policies can take root, become more specific, and produce substantive results, so that private enterprises can reap more tangible benefits.

In the process of cutting overcapacity and deleveraging, equal and uniform standards should be applied to all enterprises, whatever their forms of ownership, while indiscriminate reduction and cancelation of loans to private enterprises should be avoided. It is wrong to look at private enterprises through tinted glasses when applying policies. Government departments should improve their ability to perform their duties and follow the direction of macroeconomic regulation. In law enforcement involving workplace safety and environmental protection, authorities should see things as they are, do everything on the basis of reality, and avoid a one-size-fits-all approach. In implementing inspection reform to encourage the development of private enterprises, we should prioritize the special inspection of reform programs for protecting property rights, inspiring entrepreneurship, and undertaking fair competition review, as per the meetings of the Central Commission for Further Reform.

Fifth, a new type of cordial and clean relationship between government and business should be established. To this end, Party committees and governments at all levels should make solid efforts to support the development of private enterprises as a priority, and spend more time and energy genuinely attending to the needs of private enterprises and entrepreneurs rather than paying lip service. Officials must stick to principles and conduct themselves appropriately in their relations with entrepreneurs. This does not mean that officials can ignore their legitimate requests or refuse to protect their lawful rights and interests. On the contrary, officials should take proactive steps to provide the services they need. The departments concerned and principal leaders of local authorities should listen to their opinions and appeals and in particular take prompt action to help those in difficulty and solve their problems.

Supporting and guiding state-owned enterprises and private enterprises, especially SMEs, in overcoming difficulties and pursuing innovation-driven development should be an important part of officials' performance evaluation. People's organizations and federations of industry and commerce should reach out to private enterprises, find out the real situation, convey their difficulties in operations and management to the Party and government, and support their reform and resolve to break new ground. To better guide public opinion, major principles and policies of the Party and state should be explained correctly, and false assertions should be promptly cleared up.

Sixth, entrepreneurs' personal and property safety should be protected. Ensuring their security is the precondition for them to maintain an expectation for stability and put their entrepreneurship into full play. A more intense fight against corruption is essential for the Party to exercise effective self-supervision and strict self-governance. It aims to punish corrupt officials, foster a sound political environment, and oppose and rectify violations of Party discipline and state laws, such as abusing power for personal gain, trading power for money, embezzlement, bribery, creating obstacles to solicit bribes, and abusing the public. Success in this fight is conducive to the healthy development of the private sector.

When performing their duties and seeking entrepreneurs' cooperation in investigations, while endeavoring to solve individual cases, Party discipline inspection commissions and supervision departments should protect the legitimate personal and property rights of the entrepreneurs and ensure the lawful operation of their enterprises. We should look at the past irregularities of some private enterprises from a long-term perspective, and follow the principles of "no conviction or penalty without law" and "when in doubt, favor the accused", relieving entrepreneurs of their concerns and enabling them to move forward with full confidence. As I have emphasized on many occasions, unjust and misjudged cases involving infringement of the property rights of enterprises should be identified and corrected. Recent retrials of several such cases by the people's court have won a positive response from the public.

As I have said before, the healthy development of the non-public sector of the economy depends on those working in the sector. I hope that these people can dedicate themselves to self-study, self-development, and self-improvement. Entrepreneurs should cherish and maintain a positive social image, love the motherland, the people and the Party, practice the core socialist values, and promote entrepreneurship. They should set a good example of dedication to their work, abiding by the law in doing business, entrepreneurship and innovation, and making a contribution to society. Entrepreneurs should practice integrity and keep to the right path, focusing on growing their business, observing discipline and the law in business dealings, and strengthening corporate competitiveness in lawful operations. Abiding by the law is an overriding principle that all enterprises should uphold and the key to their long-term development. Entrepreneurs should enhance their approach to running their business by raising their operational and management capabilities, and improving their corporate governance structure. Private enterprises with the right conditions are encouraged to establish a modern corporate system. To make their enterprises stronger and better, the new generation of entrepreneurs should carry forward their predecessors' spirit of hard work, enterprise, professionalism, and focus more on their main business. Private enterprises should broaden their international horizons and improve their innovation capacity and core competitiveness, endeavoring to become world-class, globally competitive corporations.

Coordinated Quality Development Across Regions*

August 26, 2019

Circumstances have changed and new issues have arisen affecting China's regional economic development. It is imperative that we decide which existing policies to maintain and which to adjust in response to the changing domestic and international situation. We also need to prepare strategic plans for the Second Centenary Goal.

I. Regional Development in Its Current State

In contrast to most other countries, China has a vast territory and a large population, and its natural resources vary greatly from region to region. Coordinating development across different regions has always been a great challenge for us.

Since the founding of the People's Republic in 1949, there have been several major adjustments to the distribution of productive forces in the country. During the First Five-year Plan period (1953-1957), more than 70 percent of the 156 key projects supported by the Soviet Union were located in the north, and 54 were in the northeast. In his speech titled "On the Ten Major Relationships" in 1956, Mao Zedong proposed that the relationship between industry in the coastal regions and industry in the interior must be correctly handled. Development of the third-line[1] regions was initiated in the mid-1960s.

After reform and opening up started in 1978, China made a series of key moves such as establishing special economic zones and opening

---

* Part of the speech at the fifth meeting of the Commission for Finance and Economy under the CPC Central Committee.

up coastal cities. Since the mid- and late 1990s, while continuing to encourage the eastern region to take the lead in economic development, we have made a series of major strategic decisions, such as developing west China, revitalizing old industrial bases in the northeast and other parts of the country, and spurring the rise of the central region.

Since the 18th CPC National Congress in 2012, the Central Committee has put forward new regional development strategies, including the coordinated development of the Beijing-Tianjin-Hebei Region, the Yangtze River Economic Belt, the Belt and Road Initiative, the Guangdong-Hong Kong-Macao Greater Bay Area, and the integrated development of the Yangtze River Delta. Next, the Yellow River Basin will be put on agenda for ecological conservation and quality development in the region.

Despite sound regional development on the whole, we are confronted with new issues and circumstances that deserve our attention.

First, economic development varies greatly between regions. While the Yangtze River Delta, the Pearl River Delta and other regions have embarked on the track of quality development, some northern provinces have slowed down in growth. As a result, the national economy has further leaned towards the south. In 2018, the economic output of the north accounted for 38.5 percent of the national total, down 4.3 percentage points from 2012. Obvious imbalances also exist within some sectors and provinces.

Second, the driving forces for development are becoming increasingly polarized. There is a noticeable trend of the economy and population concentrating in big cities and city clusters, which enjoy growing advantages and good prospects for further growth. These include megacities such as Beijing, Shanghai, Guangzhou and Shenzhen, and large cities such as Hangzhou, Nanjing, Wuhan, Zhengzhou, Chengdu and Xi'an. They form regional growth poles for quality development.

Third, some regions are facing difficulties in their development. The northeast and northwest lag behind. From 2012 to 2018, the northeast's share of China's total economic output dropped from 8.7 to 6.2 percent, and the number of permanent residents decreased by 1.37 million, most of whom were young people and those working in high-tech industries. Some cities are ailing, especially resource-exhausted cities and those in traditional industrial and mining areas.

Generally speaking, our economic configuration is undergoing profound change, and leading cities and city clusters are becoming the main repositories of development resources. We must adapt to this new situation and develop new ideas for coordinated development across regions.

II. Guidelines for Coordinated Regional Development

The guidelines for promoting coordinated, quality development across regions are:
- adjust and improve regional policies in accordance with the objective laws of economics;
- give full play to the comparative strengths of different regions, and promote the rational flow and concentration of resources;
- stimulate innovation-driven development and enhance the dynamics for quality growth;
- increase the economic and population carrying capacity of regions with development edges, including leading cities and city clusters; and
- strengthen the capacity of other regions for food, eco-environmental and border security.

Our economy is transitioning from rapid growth to quality development, which has set new requirements for coordinated regional development. We cannot simply expect all regions to reach the same level of growth. Instead, each region should optimize its economic structure and growth model in light of local conditions. It is necessary to have a number of new growth drivers for quality development, such as the Beijing-Tianjin-Hebei Region, the Yangtze River Delta and the Pearl River Delta in particular, and some important city clusters.

Imbalances are common, and we should pursue a relative balance between regions – this is a dialectical approach to coordinated regional development. In order to achieve this goal, we must follow four principles:

First, we should respect the objective laws of economics. It is natural that industry and population gather in regions with comparative advantages, where city clusters emerge to serve as the main engines for growth and higher overall efficiency of the economy. We need to remove obstacles to the natural flow and concentration of resources, and enable the market to play the decisive role in resource allocation for higher efficiency. That said, Beijing, Shanghai and other megacities should keep the size of their population at a level based on their available resources and principal functions.

Second, we should give full play to the comparative strengths of different regions. Regions with conditions favorable for economic development should take on more industries and population and play a stronger role in creating economic value. Regions of eco-environmental importance should be effectively protected and their eco-functions reinforced. For the purpose of national security, border regions should enhance their capacity for development so that their population and economy can grow, laying the foundation for national unity and border stability.

Third, we should make the best use of our territorial space. We need to implement and improve the strategy of functional zoning, refine the configuration of functional zones, and formulate and implement targeted policies for key development zones, ecologically fragile zones, and zones with abundant energy resources. In so doing, we will form a rational process of territorial development strictly based on functional zoning.

Fourth, we should guarantee people's wellbeing. One basic requirement of coordinated regional development is to ensure equal access to essential public services and a balanced distribution of infrastructure. We should improve supporting policies involving land, household registration and transfer payments, enhance the carrying capacity of city clusters, and promote the stable settlement of the migrant population. To help rural people settle in urban areas, we should be results-oriented, do solid work, and ensure that people can move out and settle down easily. We need to ensure equal access to public services in regions which serve the strategic functions of security and eco-environmental protection.

III. Measures for Coordinated Regional Development

We need to improve the mechanism for coordinated regional development and push forward relevant policies and measures.

First, we should form a unified, open, competitive and orderly national market for products and resources. We should implement a unified negative list for market access in all regions, eliminate discriminatory and hidden barriers between regional markets, break administrative monopolies, and eliminate local protectionism. In addition to established policies and regulations from the central government, we need to comprehensively ease the conditions for granting permanent urban residency, improve supporting policies, break down barriers hindering the flow of labor, and promote the optimal allocation of human resources. We should improve market integration, reinforce regional cooperation, and strengthen inter-regional cooperation in infrastructure, environmental protection and industry.

Second, we should bring pension premiums under national unified management as soon as possible. This is of great importance to a nationwide unified market, fair competition between enterprises, and the free flow of labor. While ensuring the unified collection and allocation of provincial funds in 2020, we should accelerate the effort towards unified management of pension premiums nationwide to ensure consistent rules across the country and mutual assistance between regions.

Third, we should reform the land management system. We need to speed up reform in this area and prioritize leading cities and key city clusters in the use of land for construction. With land use planned and rural land rights certified, provincial governments are mainly responsible for managing and coordinating the land quotas for urban and rural construction. More land should be provided for the development of regions with comparative strengths.

Fourth, we should improve the system for dual control over the amount and intensity of energy consumption. This system has played a positive role in energy conservation and pollution prevention and control. However, more than 10 provinces have suggested that it is difficult for them to meet the targets of energy consumption control for the 13th Five-year Plan (2016-2020). This deserves careful study. We should give full consideration to the actual conditions of individual regions while striving to control energy consumption. For fast developing regions where the intensity of energy consumption meets the standard, the control over the total amount of energy consumed can be relaxed appropriately.

Fifth, we should establish a comprehensive system to provide recompense for eco-protection. We need to improve the inter-regional mechanism under which eco-protectors are properly recompensed by the beneficiaries. We need to improve the vertical subsidy mechanism and increase transfer payments to the protection of forests, grasslands, wetlands and key eco-environmental functional zones. We should also spread the Xin'anjiang experience gained in a pilot program for the protection of the river water environment, and encourage mutual recompense between the upper and lower reaches of a river through means such as financial, industrial and personnel support. We need to build a market-oriented, multidimensional mechanism to provide recompense for eco-protection, and introduce a pilot mechanism for realizing the value of eco-environmental undertakings in the Yangtze River Basin.

Sixth, we should enhance the government transfer payment system. We need to improve the fiscal system and define a reasonable proportion of central expenditure in the overall spending on eco-environmental protection. We should provide effective transfer payments to key eco-environmental functional zones, major agricultural production areas, and poor areas. Basic public services must be provided to residents where they live. To facilitate the flow of labor across the country, we need to use information technology to build an accessible and efficient public service platform.

IV. Comprehensive Revitalization of the Northeast

The northeast is an important industrial and agricultural base in our country. It has a strategic bearing on national defense, and on food, eco-environmental, energy and industrial security. Since the 18th CPC National Congress, I have made five field trips to the northeast and held two meetings there. In the next step, especially during the 14th Five-year Plan period (2021-2025), we will take new strategic measures to promote the comprehensive revitalization of the northeast.

The northeast has good foundations for a modern economy. Comprehensive revitalization does not mean giving undue support to declining industries and enterprises. Rather, it means effectively integrating resources and adjusting the economy, so as to form a new industrial structure that facilitates balanced development. Through improving its weak points and tapping its strengths, the northeast should carry out technological transformation in the traditional manufacturing industry, develop new technologies, new industries and new forms of business, and cultivate new growth areas such as care for the elderly, tourism and entertainment. The region should promote the transformation of resource-exhausted areas, speed up the cultivation of alternative industries, and extend the industrial chain. We will increase investment in innovation to provide new impetus for industrial diversification.

The state-owned sector accounts for a large proportion of the economy in the northeast. We should speed up reform of state-owned enterprises to give them a boost. We need to create a new frontier of opening up and attract more multinational companies to invest in the northeast. The central government can provide preferential policies to this end, but it is more important for the northeast to change its mindset and forge ahead boldly. The region should accelerate the transformation of government functions, substantially reduce direct resource allocation by the government, strengthen supervision and follow-up, and create conditions for market development. It should support the growth of both local businesses and businesses from elsewhere, and encourage entrepreneurship. A capable workforce is key to revitalization. We need to take measures to make Shenyang, Dalian, Changchun, Harbin and other important cities more attractive to investment and business. We should give incentives to good officials, take the right approach to appointing officials, and provide a platform for responsible and competent officials to do their job well and get rewarded.

Notes

[1] In the early 1960s, to prepare for the possibility of war, the CPC Central Committee under the leadership of Mao Zedong decided to classify the provinces and regions of the country into first, second and third lines in accordance with their strategic importance. The first line represented the strategic front, the third line the strategic rear and the second line the areas in between.

Socialist Democracy

Constitutional Safeguards for Chinese Socialism in the New Era*

January 19, 2018

Since the 18th CPC National Congress in 2012, I have emphasized on many occasions that comprehensively implementing the Constitution is the primary and basic task for governing the country in accordance with the law and building China into a socialist country under the rule of law. We place the implementation of the Constitution at a prominent position in comprehensive law-based governance, and have taken effective measures to strengthen oversight of the process of implementation to ensure that it complies with the terms of the Constitution, and to uphold the authority of the Constitution and the law. In 2014, to implement the decisions of the Fourth Plenary Session of the 18th CPC Central Committee, the NPC Standing Committee designated December 4 as China's Constitution Day. Since then we have celebrated four Constitution Days, which we have used to promote the Constitution throughout society.

In 2015, the NPC Standing Committee decided that all those elected or appointed to public office by people's congresses at all levels or by the standing committees of people's congresses at and above county level, and all those appointed to public office by people's governments, courts and procuratorates at all levels, must publicly pledge allegiance to the Constitution on assuming office. The goal is to inspire civil servants to observe, safeguard, and give their allegiance to the Constitution. That same year, in accordance with the Constitution, the NPC Standing Committee adopted the decision to

---

* Part of the speech at the second full assembly of the Second Plenary Session of the 19th CPC Central Committee.

grant pardons to certain categories of prisoner, for which I signed the order. This was the first such occasion in China since the beginning of reform and opening up in 1978, and was therefore of great political and legal significance. In 2016, the NPC Standing Committee, in accordance with the Constitution and relevant laws, took prompt and proper actions to deal with the election fraud in Liaoning Province, working resolutely to uphold the authority and sanctity of the system of people's congresses. Also in 2016, exercising the power granted by the Constitution and the Basic Law of the Hong Kong Special Administrative Region, the NPC Standing Committee issued a convincing interpretation of Article 104 of the Basic Law, making clear the resolution of the central authorities in implementing the principle of "one country, two systems" and their firm stance in opposing "Hong Kong independence".

In 2017, the NPC Standing Committee adopted the National Anthem Law of the People's Republic of China, which, together with the National Flag Law and the National Emblem Law, institutionalized these national symbols as stipulated by the Constitution. Recently, the NPC Standing Committee ratified an agreement on establishing a one-stop checkpoint at the West Kowloon terminus of the Guangzhou-Shenzhen-Hong Kong Express Rail Link between Hong Kong and the mainland, confirming that the arrangement complies with both the Constitution and the Basic Law of Hong Kong.

We are improving the system for documenting and reviewing regulations, rules, judicial interpretations, and other normative documents. We have established mechanisms for coordination between Party committees, people's congresses, governments, and the armed forces, and stepped up work on the process for documentation and review. We have ensured that all normative documents are filed for record and examined, and mistakes, if any, are rectified.

"Laws should be made based on the developments of the times, and rituals should be instituted to meet specific needs."[1] One of the important considerations of the CPC Central Committee in proposing revisions to the Constitution is the need to continue reform of the national supervision system as a major measure for the political reform launched and promoted by the Central Committee. It requires us to make significant adjustments and improvements to the top-level design of our state institutions, which in turn necessitates revisions to the Constitution.

After pilot reform programs had been proposed by the Central Committee, the NPC Standing Committee decided in 2016 that they would first be piloted in Beijing and the two provinces of Shanxi and Zhejiang, and it decided in 2017 that the reform would be extended to the rest of the country. Meanwhile, the NPC Standing Committee was actively preparing for and driving forward national legislation. Currently we are advancing legislation on revisions to the Constitution and national supervision, and the drafts will be submitted in accordance with statutory procedures to the 13th NPC for deliberation. Given the progress in reforming the supervision system, we have properly coordinated endeavors to continue reform and promote the rule of law, and met the requirement that all major reform measures must be law-based, thereby highlighting the Party's governing principle that it must act within the confines of the Constitution and the law.

The Constitution embodies the common will and aspiration of the CPC and the people and is the highest expression of state will. "The law is what the state relies on to gain popular trust."[2] The Constitution is what the state relies on to gain the greatest popular trust. To make laws, we must emphasize the spirit of scientific inquiry and fully understand and consciously apply this truth. In Karl Marx's words, "The legislator ... should regard himself as a naturalist. He does not make the laws, he does not invent them, he only formulates them, expressing in conscious, positive laws the inner laws of spiritual relations."[3] Formulating and revising the Constitution is the most important political and legislative activity in all countries, and it must be conducted in a serious and scientific manner. When presiding over the drafting of the first Constitution of the PRC in 1954, Mao Zedong stated, "Creating a constitution is a matter of science."[4] Elsewhere he observed, "The Constitution was drafted prudently, and every single article or term was worded with deliberation."[5] This should also apply to the current revisions to the Constitution.

The Central Committee's proposed revisions are based on thorough consideration and comprehensive analysis. They serve three goals, subject to the conditions of maintaining the continuity, consistency, and authority of the Constitution. The first is to better embody the will of the people. The second is to better reflect the strengths of socialism with Chinese characteristics. The third is to better extend the Party's capacity in long-term governance, in implementing comprehensive law-based governance, and in modernizing China's system and capacity for governance, so as to provide the constitutional guarantee for upholding and developing Chinese socialism in the new era.

Based on opinions solicited within the Party and beyond, we can see that there is a strong consensus on the revisions to the Constitution, and the proposal enjoys universal support among Party members. We believe that the general public will share this view. We can therefore conclude that the Central Committee's proposal to revise the Constitution is absolutely right and necessary. It is of great significance in ensuring that the Constitution is always aligned as closely as possible with our national conditions and the demands of the times.

Notes

[1] *Strategies of the States (Zhan Guo Ce)*.

[2] Wu Jing: *Governance of the Zhenguan Period (Zhen Guan Zheng Yao)*.

[3] Karl Marx: "The Divorce Bill", *Karl Marx & Frederick Engels: Collected Works*, Vol. 1, Eng. ed., Progress Publishers, Moscow, 1979, p. 308.

[4] Mao Zedong: "On the Draft Constitution of the People's Republic of China", *Collected Works of Mao Zedong*, Vol. VI, Chin. ed., People's Publishing House, Beijing, 1999, p. 330.

[5] An excerpt from the speech made by Mao Zedong when presiding over a meeting of the Central People's Government Council on September 14, 1954. See *Chronicle of Mao Zedong (1949-1976)*, Vol. II, Chin. ed., Central Party Literature Publishing House, Beijing, 2013, p. 281.

Advance the Rule of Law Under Chinese Socialism*

August 24, 2018

Since the 18th CPC National Congress in 2012, the Central Committee has made a series of major decisions and worked out a chain of major measures on law-based governance. To further the cause of our Party and state, we have strengthened legislation in key areas and improved our socialist legal system with distinctive Chinese features. Upholding Constitution-based governance, we have amended the Constitution as required by the times, designated the national Constitution Day, and established the institution of pledging allegiance to the Constitution. In addition, the oversight of the implementation of the Constitution has been strengthened. We have advanced law-based government, substantially reduced items for administrative approval, completely ruled out examination and approval for non-administrative licenses, and introduced a power list, a negative list and a responsibility list for governments at various levels, so as to regulate the exercise of executive power and see that law is enforced in a strict, procedure-based, impartial and non-abusive way. We are resolutely carrying forward reform in the domain of rule of law, promoting the adoption of judicial accountability, personnel quota systems and reform measures to establish a criminal litigation system centering on trials. We have abolished the system of reeducation through labor and rectified a batch of cases involving serious miscarriages of justice. Therefore our judicial performance, efficiency and credibility have improved remarkably. We regard our efforts to

---

* Part of the speech at the first meeting of the Commission for Law-based Governance under the CPC Central Committee.

carry out basic legal education among the people and to encourage them to abide by the law as fundamental tasks of law-based governance. We have carried out a responsibility program in which state law enforcement departments are responsible for strengthening public legal awareness. We have incorporated education on the rule of law into the national education system. As a result, public awareness of the rule of law has been noticeably enhanced. We are raising the competence of those responsible for implementing the rule of law. We are developing a workforce of legal service professionals and strengthening legal education and the training of legal personnel. We have kept our commitment to law-based governance, developing and improving Party rules and regulations, pushing forward the reform of the national supervision system, punishing corruption and crimes in accordance with the law, and exercising full and strict governance over our Party. As a result, remarkable results have been achieved in all those areas.

Since the 18th CPC National Congress in 2012, we have put forward new concepts, new thinking and new strategies on law-based governance and defined the guiding philosophy, development path, work plan and key tasks of law-based governance, which can be summarized in the following ten principles:

First, strengthen the CPC's leadership role in law-based governance. Leadership by the CPC is the most fundamental guarantee for socialist rule of law. In absolutely no way does the rule of law amount to weakening the leadership of the CPC. Instead, it is meant to strengthen and improve its leadership, constantly enhance its capacity and performance in law-based governance, and bolster its position as the governing party. We must ensure the Party's leadership over legislation, its guarantee of law enforcement, its support for judicial justice, and its exemplary role in abiding by the law. We must improve the institutions and mechanisms by which our Party plays its leadership role in law-based governance. We must turn the views of our Party into the will and laws of the state through legal procedures, ensure effective implementation of our Party's policies through the law and ensure that we are on the right track in exercising law-based governance.

Second, uphold the principle that the people enjoy the principal status in our society. We must develop the rule of law for the people and rely on them, and it must benefit and protect them. We must uphold social equity and justice, which is the goal of the rule of law, and make sure that the people can see that equity and justice are served in every law, every law enforcement action, and every judicial case. In the whole process of our law-based governance we must represent the people's interests, reflect their wishes, protect their rights and interests, and improve their wellbeing. We must ensure that the people, under the leadership of the CPC, are able to administer state affairs and manage economic, cultural and social affairs through various channels and in various ways as provided by law.

Third, uphold socialist rule of law with Chinese characteristics. In advancing law-based governance, we must take the right path. We need to bear in mind our own national context and realities and take a path of rule of law best suited to our own specific conditions. Under no circumstance should we imitate the models and practices of other countries or adopt the Western models of "constitutionalism", "separation of powers", and "judicial independence".

Fourth, develop a system of socialist rule of law with Chinese characteristics. Such a system is a legal manifestation of the Chinese socialist system. We must focus on our goal of building socialist rule of law with Chinese characteristics and work hard to establish a complete system of laws, a highly effective enforcement system, a stringent scrutiny system, effective supporting measures, and a sound system of Party regulations, thereby constantly breaking new ground in law-based governance.

Fifth, push forward coordinated progress in law-based governance, exercise of state power, and government administration, and promote the integrated development of the rule of law for the country, the government, and society. Comprehensive law-based governance is a great systematic endeavor. Therefore, we must take many factors into consideration, identify priorities, and formulate integrated plans. We must pursue it in a more systematic, holistic and coordinated way. Law-based governance, exercise of state power and government administration form an indivisible whole, the key to which is that the CPC must keep its commitment to law-based governance and that governments at all levels must administer in accordance with the law. A law-based country, government, and society each have their own areas of focus, allowing them to exert a mutually reinforcing effect on one another. A law-based country is the goal of developing the rule of law; a law-based government is the main force in building a law-based country; a law-based society is the foundation for building a law-based country. We must be adept at using institutions and laws to govern our country and improve our capacity for well-conceived, democratic and law-based governance.

Sixth, govern the country and exercise state power within the framework of the Constitution. In pursuing law-based governance, we must first uphold Constitution-based governance; in pursuing law-based exercise of state power, we must first uphold Constitution-based exercise of state power. The CPC leads the people in enacting and enforcing the Constitution and the law, and it must confine its activities to the areas prescribed by the Constitution and the law. All individuals, organizations and state organs must regard the Constitution and the law as their code of conduct, and exercise powers, enjoy rights, perform duties, and fulfill obligations accordingly. They will not be permitted to enjoy any special privilege that places them above the Constitution and the law, and all acts in violation of the Constitution or the law must be punished.

Seventh, ensure sound lawmaking, strict law enforcement, impartial administration of justice, and the observance of law by all. To solve the prominent conflicts and problems in devising, enforcing, applying and observing the law, we must resolutely advance reform in the domain of law-based governance. We must focus on the key areas of law-based governance and improve the legislative system and the quality of our legislation. We must promote strict law enforcement, establish an efficient system, improve administrative procedures, and fully implement administrative accountability. We must support the lawful and independent functioning of judicial organs and make better institutional arrangements for the exercise of judicial power in which the division of powers is both complementary and mutually restrictive. We must make greater efforts to raise public legal awareness and create an environment for the rule of law in which all of our people work in accordance with the law, look to the law when running into problems, and rely on the law to resolve problems and conflicts.

Eighth, properly handle the dialectical relationships concerning law-based governance. In implementing law-based governance, we must correctly deal with the relationships between leadership by the Party and the rule of law, between reform and the rule of law, between the rule of law and the rule of virtue, and between law-based governance and rule-based Party discipline. Socialist rule of law must uphold CPC leadership, while CPC leadership must rely on socialist rule of law. Reform and the rule of law are like the two wings of a bird or the two wheels of a cart. We must promote reform under the rule of law and improve the rule of law in the process of reform. We must integrate the rule of law with the rule of virtue so that they complement and reinforce each other. We must bring into play the complementary roles of law-based governance and rule-based Party discipline, and ensure that the CPC governs the country in accordance with the Constitution and the law, and govern and discipline itself strictly with Party rules and regulations.

Ninth, develop a contingent of high-caliber legal personnel with moral integrity and professional competence. To advance law-based governance, we must train legal professionals devoted to socialist rule of law and loyal to the Party, the country, the people and the law. We must strengthen education in our ideals and convictions, carry out in-depth education on the core socialist values and the socialist concept of law-based governance, and enable judicial personnel to be more consistent, specialized and professional in their conduct. We must stick to our goal of legal education to foster virtuous specialists who are morally and professionally strong. We must be innovative in training legal talent and cultivate a large number of legal professionals of high caliber and their successors.

Tenth, make sure that leading officials, though small in number, play a key role in implementing the rule of law. It is leading officials who exercise the ruling power of the Party and the legislative, administrative, supervisory and judicial powers of the state. Therefore, they are key to law-based governance. They must set a good example in upholding the law and treating it with respect, in understanding and having a good mastery of the law, in observing the law and defending the rule of law, and in applying the law and working in accordance with the law. They must strive to become more adept at using law-based thinking and approaches to carry out reform, promote development, resolve problems, and maintain stability. They must provide the example whereby the whole of society upholds, studies, observes and applies the law.

These new concepts, thinking and strategies are the latest achievements in adapting Marxism to the Chinese context. They provide fundamental principles for us in implementing law-based governance. Thus we must uphold them on a long-term basis and constantly enrich and develop them.

Protect and Promote Human Rights in the Chinese Context[*]

December 10, 2018

The Universal Declaration of Human Rights is a significant document in the history of humanity, which has profoundly impacted progress in human rights around the world. Together with the peoples of other countries, and based on the common values of humanity – peace, development, equity, justice, democracy and freedom – China is committed to safeguarding human dignity and rights, and promoting fairer, more equitable and inclusive global governance of human rights, so as to build a global community of shared future and strive for a better world.

The ultimate human right is that people can lead a happy life. Since the first day of its founding in 1921, the CPC has fully committed itself to the wellbeing of the Chinese people and human development. During the 70 years since the founding of the People's Republic in 1949, and in particular the 40 years since the launch of reform and opening up in 1978, the Chinese nation has achieved a tremendous transformation: It has stood up, become better off and grown in strength. This achievement can be summed up as improving the living standards of all Chinese people.

The times are moving forward, and human rights are making progress. Combining the principle of universal human rights with the reality of modern times, China remains committed to a path for human rights that accords with its prevailing conditions. Adhering to a people-centered vision, China takes the rights to subsistence and

---

[*] Main points of the congratulatory letter to a forum marking the 70th anniversary of the Universal Declaration of Human Rights.

development as the primary and basic human rights, works for coordinated progress in economic, political, social, cultural and environmental rights, defends social fairness and justice, and promotes the right to all-round development.

Chinese researchers on human rights need to advance with the times, maintain the right orientation, break new ground, and make a greater contribution to cultural diversity and the global cause of human rights.

Enhance Local Legislation and Supervision*

July 2019

Setting up a standing committee for each local people's congress at or above the county level represents a significant improvement to the people's congress system. Committed to the integration of the Party's leadership, the people's position as masters of the country, and law-based governance, local people's congresses and their standing committees have fulfilled their duties, shown enterprise, and made a great contribution to the reform, development and stability of their respective areas over the past four decades.

However, new tasks for the new era impose new and higher requirements upon the work of people's congresses. Local people's congresses and their standing committees need to fulfill their duties in line with the Party Central Committee's requirements for the work of people's congresses and the decisions and plans made by local Party committees for implementing the Central Committee's policies and strategies. These include taking an innovative approach to their work in legislation and supervision, in accordance with their respective local conditions, so as to facilitate economic and social development and the completion of reform tasks. They should conscientiously follow the leadership of local Party committees at their respective levels. They need to maintain close ties with the people and give better play to the role of deputies to the people's congresses, who should be familiar with the true situation of local people, solicit their opinions, garner their ideas, safeguard their rights and interests through the rule of law, and improve their wellbeing. The deputies also need to achieve

---

* Main points of the directive on the work of local people's congresses and their standing committees.

self-improvement, in order to increase their ability to fulfill their duties in accordance with the law, and improve the efficiency of their work.

Consolidate Socialist Consultative Democracy*

September 20, 2019

The Chinese People's Political Consultative Conference (CPPCC) is a great achievement of the CPC in combining the Marxist-Leninist theories of the united front, political parties, and democratic politics with the conditions in China. It is an innovative political system involving political parties, prominent individuals without any party affiliation, people's organizations, and people from all walks of life and all ethnic groups under the leadership of the CPC. For 70 years the CPPCC has been dedicated to the two major themes of unity and democracy. It has served as a support to the central tasks of the Party and the state, and played a significant role in founding the PRC and in each historical period of socialist revolution, development and reform.

The First Plenary Session of the CPPCC exercised the functions and powers of the later National People's Congress (NPC) and made comprehensive preparations for the founding of the PRC. The meeting adopted the Common Program of the CPPCC, which served as the provisional Constitution, the Organic Law of the CPPCC, and the Organic Law of the Central People's Government of the People's Republic of China. The meeting also issued resolutions on the capital, the national flag and anthem, and the system of chronology of the PRC, and elected the CPPCC National Committee and the Central People's Government Council. This marked the formal establishment of the CPPCC system. After the founding of the PRC, the CPPCC made a great contribution to restoring and developing the national

---

* Part of the speech at the Central Conference on the CPPCC's Work marking the 70th anniversary of the organization.

economy, consolidating the nascent people's political power, completing the socialist revolution, establishing the basic socialist system, and building socialism. After the NPC was inaugurated in 1954, the CPPCC continued to play an important role in the country's political and social affairs.

In 1978, the Third Plenary Session of the 11th CPC Central Committee was held, and the CPPCC entered a new stage in its development. The Central Committee further clarified the nature, tasks, themes, and functions of the CPPCC, had the nature and role of the CPPCC enshrined in the Constitution, and established multi-party cooperation and political consultation under the leadership of the CPC as China's basic political system. The CPPCC implemented the Party's theories, lines, principles and policies, and worked hard to mobilize all resources, unite all available forces, and make important contributions to reform, opening up and socialist modernization.

Socialism with Chinese characteristics has now entered a new era, and the CPC Central Committee has made a series of major plans for the CPPCC. The CPPCC implements the Thought on Socialism with Chinese Characteristics for a New Era, remains true to its nature and role, focuses on advancing the Five-sphere Integrated Plan and the Four-pronged Comprehensive Strategy, and works wholeheartedly to achieve our Two Centenary Goals and realize the Chinese Dream of national rejuvenation. It has rallied strength for the development of the Party and the country, and broken new ground for its own undertakings.

Since the 18th CPC National Congress, building on our experience, we have put forward a series of new requirements for the CPPCC, mainly as regards the following:

First, the Party's leadership over the CPPCC should be strengthened. The Party's leadership is supported by the Chinese people from all political parties, people's organizations, ethnic groups, social strata, and all walks of life. It is the founding principle of the CPPCC and the fundamental guarantee for its progress. The CPPCC should always follow the Party's leadership, and earnestly implement the requirements of the CPC Central Committee.

Second, the CPPCC should always be clear about its nature and role. As an organization for maintaining the united front, an institution for multiparty cooperation and political consultation, and a major form through which people's democracy is practiced, the CPPCC is an important channel and specialized body for socialist consultative democracy and an important part of the state governance system. It is an institution with Chinese characteristics. The CPPCC should remain true to its nature and role and unswervingly take the path of socialist political development with Chinese characteristics.

Third, the CPPCC should give full play to its role as a specialized consultative body. Consultative democracy is an important way for the Party to exercise its leadership. It is a unique form and a distinctive strength of China's socialist democracy. The CPPCC should uphold consultative democracy in performing its duties. It should integrate efforts to promote democracy and enhance unity while working to offer suggestions on state affairs and build consensus. It should also carry out democratic scrutiny over the implementation of important decisions and plans made by the Party and the state.

Fourth, the CPPCC should support and help improve China's political party system. The system of multiparty cooperation and political consultation under the leadership of the CPC is China's basic political system and a new model that has grown out of the soil of China. The CPPCC should create conditions for other political parties and prominent individuals without any party affiliation to play a better role in this regard.

Fifth, the CPPCC should gather extensive support and pool strength. It should perform its role as an organization for maintaining the united front, promote solidarity and unity, balance commonality and diversity, consolidate the common theoretical and political foundation, strengthen political guidance, and build consensus. It should strive to seek the greatest common ground, draw the widest possible inclusive circle, and create a powerful driving force for national rejuvenation.

Sixth, the CPPCC should focus on the central tasks of the Party and the state while fulfilling its responsibilities. It should direct its efforts towards achieving the first of the Two Centenary Goals before moving on towards the second, and give priority to addressing unbalanced and inadequate development. Mindful of the general picture, it should target key issues, weaknesses, and shortcomings, conduct in-depth consultations on state affairs, strengthen scrutiny, and promote implementation.

Seventh, the CPPCC should uphold the principle of serving the people. It should focus on fulfilling the people's desire for a better life and improving their living standards. It should listen to public appeals, reflect public aspirations, and tackle practical problems concerning people's daily lives, so as to assist the Party and the government in improving the wellbeing of the people.

Eighth, the CPPCC should improve its ability to perform its duties in the spirit of reform and innovation. It should become more capable of developing its political acumen, conducting research, maintaining contact with the people, and working collaboratively. The CPPCC should strengthen the ranks of its members and help them learn more about the organization, be more adept at conducting consultations and discussing state affairs, observe discipline, abide by the rules, and act with moral integrity.

Practice over the past 70 years has proved that the CPPCC system has many unique strengths. Marx and Engels said, "What is democracy? It must have a meaning, or it would not exist. It is all a matter, then, of finding the true meaning of democracy."[1] There are diverse ways to realize democracy, so we must not be confined to just one particular rigid model. Experience has shown that China's model of democracy is workable and effective in the country. In this new era, we must adhere to the CPPCC system, champion the cause of the CPPCC, carry out the work related to the united front with a strong sense of responsibility, and unite more people around the Party.

Today's world is undergoing a scale of change unseen in a century, and we are now in a critical phase of realizing the rejuvenation of the Chinese nation. The closer we get to the goal, the more complex the situation becomes, the more arduous the task is, and the more we should give play to the political strengths of the leadership of the CPC and the institutional strengths of socialism with Chinese characteristics. We must pool wisdom and strength to forge a strong synergy with which the Chinese people at home and abroad focus their thoughts and efforts towards the same goal.

In the current era, the overall requirements for strengthening and improving the work of the CPPCC are:

- enhance the Four Consciousnesses, bolster the Four-sphere Confidence, and remain committed to the Two Upholds under the guidance of the Thought on Socialism with Chinese Characteristics for a New Era;
- make upholding and developing socialism with Chinese characteristics the goal of consolidating the common theoretical and political foundation, make serving the Two Centenary Goals its main focus, and take strengthening theoretical and political guidance and building extensive consensus as the central task;
- champion the two major themes of unity and democracy and forge effective consensus by enhancing the CPPCC's capacity for political consultation, democratic scrutiny, and participation in the deliberation and administration of state affairs;
- shoulder the political responsibility of carrying out the CPC Central Committee's decisions as well as its requirements for the CPPCC, and bring together the wisdom and strength of the Chinese people at home and abroad; and
- contribute to the initiatives of securing a decisive victory in building a moderately prosperous society in all respects and of making all-round efforts to build a great modern socialist country.

In particular, the CPPCC should do the following well, now and in the future:

First, the CPPCC should make the most of its role as a specialized consultative body. I have said that under China's socialist system, whenever a problem crops up, we should turn to deliberation first. Matters involving many people are discussed by all those involved; to reach the greatest common ground on the wishes and needs of the whole of society is the essence of people's democracy. Consultative democracy is an important mechanism through which the Party can lead the people in effectively governing the country and ensure that the people are the masters of the country. It complements electoral democracy. In its consultations, the CPPCC promotes extensive unity, advances multiparty cooperation, and practices people's democracy, which is in line with our historical traditions and reflects the features of our time. This fully embodies the characteristics and strengths of our socialist democracy in settling differences, solving problems and reaching consensus through consultation.

Being open to different opinions, better still, taking criticism with courage and making improvements accordingly are signs of confidence and strength. We should develop socialist consultative democracy, make good use of democratic centralism, carry forward the fine tradition of "unity – criticism – unity", draw on collective wisdom, and promote full expression and in-depth exchange of different ideas and viewpoints. We should respect each other, consult on an equal footing, follow the rules, hold orderly discussions, be inclusive and tolerant, and negotiate in good faith. In this way, we can cultivate a good environment for consultation in which everyone can express their own views freely, rationally and in accordance with the law and rules. We must let them voice their opinions and criticism, as long as the Party's underlying theories, basic guidelines and fundamental principles are upheld. Even if their comments are harsh and sharp, we should be glad to hear them, so that we can correct our mistakes if we have made any and guard against them if we have not.

To ensure that the CPPCC plays its role as a specialized consultative body, we need to improve the relevant systems and mechanisms. We should stick to the system in which the Party committee works with the government and the CPPCC to formulate annual consultation plans and improve the mechanism to ensure consultation before and during decision-making. Only after due deliberation by the CPPCC can the matters defined as requiring consultation in the annual plan be submitted for decision-making and then acted on. The scope of participants for consultation, the principles of discussion, the basic procedures, and the mode of communication should be clearly prescribed.

Second, the CPPCC should strengthen theoretical and political guidance and build extensive consensus. Mao Zedong said that politics meant making more people support us and fewer people oppose us. This is the key to the Party's success in leading revolution, economic development, and reform. In the new era, to move forward, we must enhance the unity of people of all ethnic groups and mobilize all resources.

This requires theoretical guidance and consensus. The CPPCC should, by working effectively, become an important platform for upholding and strengthening the Party's leadership, for uniting and guiding representatives from all sectors of society and ethnic groups with the Party's innovative theories, and for resolving differences and conflicts and building consensus on the basis of shared political ideals. We should guide the political parties, organizations, and prominent figures participating in the CPPCC to thoroughly study the Party's theories, current affairs and policies, and the history of the CPC, the PRC, the united front, and the CPPCC, so that they will develop an accurate understanding of history and a broad vision.

To strengthen theoretical and political guidance, we must correctly handle the relationship between commonality and diversity. The former means a shared theoretical and political foundation, whereas the latter is indicative of diverse interests and ideas. We should achieve commonality while respecting diversity and avoid an overemphasis on uniformity. We should stay attuned to the current thinking and political trends within the united front, strengthen theoretical and political guidance on sensitive issues, issues that pose risks, and issues of broad concern, and combine this with regular theoretical and political work, so as to seek common ground while shelving and narrowing differences. We should promote common progress in political awareness among all political parties, organizations, and representatives of various ethnic groups and sectors of society. The CPPCC should maintain extensive contacts with the public and mobilize them to assist the Party and the government in coordinating relations, developing positive sentiments in society and defusing conflicts. It should encourage its members to be more community-focused in their work, stay close to the people they represent, reflect the people's views and convey their suggestions and opinions to relevant authorities in a timely fashion, and better inform them of the policies of the Party and the state.

We must extensively gather positive energy for the nation to unite and work together in order to realize the Chinese Dream of national rejuvenation. To this end, we should give full play to the role of the CPPCC as an important political and organizational platform in China's political party system, and make institutional arrangements for non-communist parties to express their views and put forward suggestions in the CPPCC. We should improve the communication and liaison mechanism with intellectuals who are not CPC members, prominent figures in the private sector of the economy, and those from the New Social Group[2]. We should fully implement the Party's ethnic and religious policies, promote exchanges, interaction and integration among all ethnic groups, and encourage religions to adapt to socialist society. We should comprehensively and accurately implement the principles of "one country, two systems", "Hong Kong people administering Hong Kong", "Macao people administering Macao", and a high degree of autonomy for both regions, guide CPPCC members from Hong Kong and Macao to support the governments and chief executives of the two special administrative regions (SARs) to perform their duties in accordance with the law, and strengthen the ranks of patriots who love both our country and the SARs. We must follow the one-China principle and the 1992 Consensus, expand exchanges with relevant political parties, organizations, and people from all walks of life in Taiwan, and promote integrated development across the Taiwan Straits. We resolutely oppose "Taiwan independence" activities in any form. We should extensively unite overseas Chinese and give their representatives access to CPPCC activities. We should carry out international exchanges to contribute to the building of a global community of shared future.

Third, the CPPCC should enhance the sense of responsibility among its members. As representatives of political parties, organizations, ethnic groups and different sectors of society selected through extensive consultations within their respective circles, CPPCC members participate in deliberation on state affairs and perform their duties on behalf of all the people. This membership is not only an honor, but also a responsibility. CPPCC members should perform their duties for the country and fulfill their responsibilities to the people. They should always bear the CPPCC's cause in mind and shoulder responsibilities in earnest.

CPPCC members come from various sectors, and their views and understanding of some issues are not necessarily the same, but their political stance cannot be nebulous nor their political principles weak. They must study and implement the Party's underlying theories, basic guidelines, and fundamental principles, and identify closely with the CPC and socialism with Chinese characteristics in thought and theory, in politics and in spirit. They should improve their knowledge of theory, their ability to reason, and their practical skills, acquire a wide range of knowledge, master ways and means of performing duties, conduct in-depth research and studies, be active in making suggestions, and enhance their performance in an all-round way. They should maintain close bonds with the people, provide help to those in need, and help resolve doubts, negative sentiments and conflicts. They should abide by the Constitution and the CPPCC Charter, practice the core socialist values, improve their moral conduct, remain clean, honest and self-disciplined, and demonstrate the qualities of CPPCC members in the new era through exemplary actions.

Notes

[1] Karl Marx and Frederick Engels: "Reviews from the Neue Rheinische Zeitung. Politisch-Ökonomische Revue No. 4, April 1850", *Karl Marx & Frederick Engels: Collected Works*, Vol. 10, Eng. ed., Progress Publishers, Moscow, 1979, p. 304.

[2] This refers to groups of people that have emerged with the socialist market economy, mainly management and technical personnel in private and foreign-funded enterprises, those working in intermediary agencies and social organizations, free lancers, and new media professionals. – *Tr.*

Heighten a Sense of Chinese Identity*

September 27, 2019

Now that Chinese socialism has entered a new era, the Chinese nation can look forward to the best period of development in history. But as we still face a complex domestic and international situation, we should unite more than ever as one and pool our strengths to ensure that our country continues to progress steadily.

All ethnic groups as one family – this is one of the fundamental guarantees for the rejuvenation of the Chinese nation. To make the Chinese Dream come true, we must focus on heightening a sense of identity of the Chinese nation, and take the cause of ethnic unity and progress as a fundamental task. We must fully implement our Party's theories and policies concerning ethnic groups, work together for common prosperity and development, and help all ethnic groups remain as closely united as the seeds of a pomegranate, so that the Chinese nation will become a more inclusive and cohesive community.

First, we must uphold the CPC leadership, unite all ethnic groups, and lead them forward on the path of Chinese socialism. Our experience shows that only the CPC can unite the Chinese nation, and only under Chinese socialism can all ethnic groups work together and achieve development and prosperity. We must uphold our Party's leadership, remember why we started, and bear in mind our mission. We must take correct approaches to addressing ethnic problems, uphold and improve the system of regional ethnic autonomy, and strengthen education on our Party's theories and policies concerning ethnic groups and ethnic solidarity. With a focus on heightening a sense of

---

* Part of the speech at the national conference commending model units and individuals for contributing to ethnic unity and progress.

national identity, we should unite people and officials from all ethnic groups in following the leadership of the Central Committee and carrying out its decisions and plans, and cultivate in all ethnic groups a growing sense of identity with the motherland, the Chinese nation, the Chinese culture, the Communist Party of China, and Chinese socialism.

Second, we must work to create a better life for all ethnic groups, and ensure that ethnic minority groups and the areas they inhabit achieve moderate prosperity and modernization together with the rest of the country. The Chinese nation is a big family; everyone in the family deserves a good life. We cannot have across-the-board moderate prosperity and modernization if ethnic minority areas are left behind. We should accelerate development of ethnic minority groups and the areas they inhabit, ensure their equal access to basic public services, and help them turn natural resources into economic gains. The achievements of reform and development should benefit more people from all ethnic groups in a fairer way, so that they will have a growing sense of gain, happiness and security. We should improve different policies for different regions, strengthen the system of transfer payments, and improve paired assistance between more developed and less developed areas. We should fully implement the plans for developing areas heavily populated by ethnic minorities and ethnic groups with smaller populations, and the action plan to bring prosperity to border areas and their residents. During the 14th Five-year Plan period (2021-2025) we should fully implement our plans for ethnic minority groups and the areas they inhabit so that all ethnic groups work together to create a better future and share the new glories and dreams of the Chinese nation.

Third, we must uphold the core socialist values in building a cultural home shared by all ethnic groups. Culture is the soul of a nation, and cultural identity is the root of ethnic unity. All ethnic groups should respect and appreciate each other's culture and learn from each other. We should work harder to promote the core socialist values among all ethnic groups. Developing sound viewpoints on the motherland, nation, culture, and history is central to building a cultural home shared by all ethnic groups and consolidating the sense of national identity. With this in mind, we should preserve and pass down ethnic cultures through updating and integration, and establish and highlight China's cultural symbols shared by all its ethnic groups and the collective image of the Chinese nation, so that people from all ethnic groups identify more with Chinese culture. We should strengthen education of all types and at all levels in areas inhabited by ethnic minority groups, strengthen the education on standard spoken and written Chinese, and give people from ethnic minority groups a better education. We should place more emphasis on patriotism in educating young people, to sow the seeds of patriotism in every child. We must seize the initiative in guiding public opinion, and make the internet a fast growing space in building a cultural home shared by all ethnic groups and in consolidating the sense of national identity.

Fourth, we must uphold the unity of the Chinese nation, and enhance communication and integration between ethnic groups. For seven decades, and particularly since 1978 when reform and opening up was introduced, China's ethnic groups have strengthened their ties in many ways and to a degree never seen before. They share the country's vast lands and live in compact communities; they also live amongst each other. This trend has intensified over time, underlined by free flow of people and more ethnic communities living together. In response to this trend, we should come up with policies, measures and mechanisms that are conducive to building an ethnically integrated society, and improve the services for and management of the migrant population of ethnic minority groups, so that all ethnic groups work together for a better home and a brighter future. We should consistently enhance ethnic unity and progress in all areas, and introduce new forms of initiative to government departments, enterprises, communities, towns and townships, schools, military units, and venues for religious activities. Han chauvinism and local ethnic chauvinism are both enemies of ethnic unity, and must be opposed.

Fifth, we must handle ethnic affairs in accordance with the law, and ensure that citizens of all ethnic groups are equal before the law. On the basis of the Law on Regional Ethnic Autonomy, we should improve laws and regulations concerning ethnic minority groups, and protect the legitimate rights and interests of all groups by law. We must treat all equally without discrimination, and pass judgments only through the law. Cases and incidents involving ethnic factors should be dealt with appropriately in accordance with the law, and citizens of all ethnic groups must enjoy their rights and discharge their obligations on an equal basis. The governance of ethnic affairs must be ruled by law. We must guard against and crack down on all forms of infiltration, sabotage and subversive activities, violence, terrorism, ethnic separatism, and religious extremism.

To improve our work in ethnic affairs in the current era, we must strengthen Party leadership in this regard. Party committees at all levels should place ethnic affairs high on their agenda, and make their ability to deal with ethnic affairs and enhance ethnic unity an important indicator in appraising the performance of officials. We should strengthen research on the basic theories and key issues of ethnic affairs, add new content to the discourse system of China's socialist theory and policy on ethnic affairs, and increase our influence and capacity to inspire internationally. To have a solid basis in addressing ethnic affairs, Party and government organs, enterprises and public institutions, other political parties, and people's organizations should all participate and work together. We should lay emphasis on developing a contingent of officials specializing in ethnic affairs, select and train officials and personnel with professional expertise from ethnic minority groups, and encourage departments handling ethnic affairs to do their job more diligently.

The rejuvenation of the Chinese nation requires all ethnic groups to stand together, to work together with one heart. Let us unite more closely around the CPC Central Committee, forge ahead with one mind, and strive for ethnic unity and progress, for the sake of the Two Centenary Goals and the Chinese Dream.

Chinese Culture

Enhance Cyber Capabilities Through Innovation*

April 20, 2018

Information technology has brought China unprecedented opportunities, which we must seize without hesitation to reinforce positive publicity online and safeguard cybersecurity. We should encourage breakthroughs in core information technologies, let IT application boost economic and social development, and increase civil-military integration in IT application. We should take the initiative to participate in international governance of cyberspace, and build China into a cyberpower through independent innovation. All these efforts will further contribute to achieving moderate prosperity in all respects throughout the country, striving for the victory of socialism with Chinese characteristics for a new era, and realizing the Chinese Dream of national rejuvenation.

Since the 18th CPC National Congress in 2012, the Party Central Committee has attached great importance to the development and governance of the internet. It has coordinated its efforts to address problems concerning cybersecurity and IT application in political, economic, cultural, social, military and some other sectors, and has made a series of major decisions and enacted important measures in this field, yielding results of historic significance. The achievements have proved that the Central Committee's decision on strengthening the Party's centralized and unified leadership over cybersecurity and IT application and its strategic planning of this work during this period are absolutely correct. Constant innovation in theory and practice has helped us to embark on a path of cyberspace governance

---

* Main points of the speech at the National Conference on Cybersecurity and IT Application.

with Chinese characteristics, and form a cyberpower strategy based on a range of new visions, ideas and concepts.

We should improve our comprehensive cyberspace governance capacity and put in place a framework in which Party committees take the leadership, government departments perform administrative functions, internet enterprises fulfill their responsibilities, the public exercise supervision, and netizens discipline themselves, while economic, legal and technical means are employed. We should strengthen positive publicity online, maintain the correct political direction, guide public opinion, advocate positive values, and unite hundreds of millions of netizens under the Thought on Socialism with Chinese Characteristics for a New Era and the decisions of the 19th CPC National Congress. We should strengthen education in ideals and convictions, promote socialism with Chinese characteristics for a new era and the Chinese Dream, and actively foster and implement the core socialist values. We should encourage innovation in concept, content, form, method, and means for online publicity, pay attention to the ideal timing, extent, and impact of publicity, and build consensus online and offline, so as to consolidate the ideological basis of the whole Party and the nation. The internet operators must take on the primary responsibility for preventing the internet from becoming a platform to spread pernicious information or rumors. Discipline should be imposed on the internet industry, with netizens and all kinds of players encouraged to be involved in governance.

Without cybersecurity we can ensure neither national security, nor economic and social stability, nor the interests of the people. We need to build a sound understanding of cybersecurity, and strengthen cybersecurity and information infrastructure protection. We will establish a mechanism and platform for coordinating cybersecurity information, increase our emergency command capability in dealing with cyber incidents, and actively steer the cybersecurity industry towards preventing problems before they start. Responsibilities for protecting critical information infrastructure should be distributed among the players: Internet companies and the industry as a whole should shoulder the main responsibility because they are the operators of critical information infrastructure, and the government departments in charge should perform the duty of supervision and regulation. We should combat cyber hacking, online fraud, invasion of individual privacy, and all other criminal acts. We must cut the profit chains of online crime and maintain a tough stance against them, so as to protect the legitimate rights and interests of the people. We should further publicize cybersecurity information to raise the public's awareness and enhance their ability to protect themselves.

Core technologies are the treasures of a nation. We need to accelerate new advances in core information technologies with determination, perseverance and targeted attention. We need to focus on building an overall industrial system and coordinate our efforts in technology, industry and policy. We need to follow the law of technological development, have a long-term vision in making plans, and concentrate on achieving major breakthroughs with best resources. We need to strengthen centralized and unified leadership, improve policies in finance, taxation, international trade, human resources and intellectual property protection, and regulate the market to better motivate all kinds of innovators. We need to create a fair market environment, strengthen intellectual property protection, and oppose monopoly and unfair competition. We need to break the barriers between basic research and technological innovation to highlight the role of the former in leading breakthroughs in application technologies.

Cybersecurity and IT application represents a new productive force and a new development trend, and should take the lead in implementing the new development philosophy. Aiming for a modern economic system and high-quality development, we should accelerate IT application, and promote new industrialization, urbanization and agricultural modernization as a whole. We should develop the digital economy and speed up digital industrialization. We should encourage innovation driven by information technology to create new industries, businesses, and models, and promote development with new growth drivers. We should advance digital transformation of industry, use new internet technology and applications to upgrade traditional industries in a comprehensive way, improve total factor productivity, and release the full potential of digitization in boosting the economy. We should fully integrate the internet, big data, and artificial intelligence with the real economy to make manufacturing, agriculture, and service industries more digital, networked and intelligent. We should help enterprises in the cybersecurity and IT application sector to grow bigger and stronger by strengthening regulation and guidance for their sound and orderly development. They should seek both economic and social benefits to better shoulder their social and ethical responsibilities. We should employ information technologies to make government and Party affairs more transparent, and build e-government and one-stop online service platforms to better address the problems of red tape that are of strong concern to enterprises and the public. We should put people first in the development of cybersecurity and IT application and make the wellbeing of the people its ultimate goal, giving people a stronger sense of gain, happiness, and security.

Cybersecurity and IT application is a key and frontier area, and also the most dynamic and promising field for civil-military integration. We need to seize the historic opportunities presented by the evolution of information technology and new military reforms, fully understand the internal relationship between productive forces and combat effectiveness, and between market and battlefield, and follow the working principles and laws behind this integration to create a comprehensive framework that covers all areas and all production factors and produces high returns.

Reforming global internet governance is an irresistible and desirable trend. It should feature a multilateral approach with multiparty participation, while leveraging the role of various players including governments, international organizations, internet enterprises, tech-savvy communities, NGOs and individual citizens. We will promote cyber governance under the framework of the UN and in the meantime bring into play the active role of non-state actors. We will take the Belt and Road Initiative as an opportunity to strengthen cooperation with countries along the Belt and Road, particularly developing countries, in internet infrastructure construction, digital economy and cybersecurity, as part of our effort to build a digital Silk Road of the 21st century.

We must strengthen the Party's centralized and unified leadership over cybersecurity and IT application to ensure it moves in the right direction. All provincial authorities and central departments should attach great importance to this work, including it at the top of their agenda and their lists of priorities, and solving new problems in new circumstances promptly. We should encourage social organizations for workers, the youth, women, and other groups to play their unique roles, and make good use of enterprises, research institutes, and think tanks, pooling the resources of all of society to improve work in cybersecurity and IT application. Leading officials at all levels and particularly senior officials need to adapt to the information age, and improve their cyber awareness and their ability to understand the rules of internet development, to guide online public opinion, to lead the development of IT application, and to ensure cybersecurity. Party and government institutions at all levels and their leaders should improve their ability to organize, mobilize, guide, and serve the public via the internet. We will regulate, operate and use the internet in accordance with the law to ensure that the development of the internet is within the bounds of the law. We will formulate an overall plan for talent development to promote institutional reforms in this regard, stimulate creativity and attract more qualified personnel. We will enhance the Four Consciousnesses, prioritize the effort to reinforce our Party's political foundations, step up efforts to build a high-quality team of Party members and enforce strict Party discipline over them, and select qualified leaders at all levels. All these efforts will give firm organizational and human resources support to developing cybersecurity and IT application.

Public Communication in the New Era*

August 21, 2018

To carry out our public communication, we must uphold the Thought on Socialism with Chinese Characteristics for a New Era and the guiding principles of the 19th CPC National Congress. We must strengthen our commitment to the Four Consciousnesses and the Four-sphere Confidence. We should uphold socialism, rally public support, foster a new generation with sound values and ethics, develop Chinese culture, and build a positive image of China. With the correct political orientation, we should lay the strategic groundwork, intensify efforts in key areas, and improve working practices and performance, with a view to enhancing our public communication. We should inspire the people to embrace shared ideals, convictions, values and moral standards, and mobilize them to contribute more to the overall interests of our Party and our country.

Since the 18th CPC National Congress in 2012, we have prioritized our public communication, and adopted a set of important decisions and measures. Under the firm leadership of the CPC Central Committee, we have worked with great resolve and achieved positive results. We have explored new ground in expanding our Party's theoretical base. Our people have embraced both socialism with Chinese characteristics and the Chinese Dream. The core socialist values and the best of traditional Chinese culture are alive in the people's hearts. Positive thinking and mainstream public opinion have been consolidated. The Chinese people have greater confidence in their own culture. China's soft power and the international influence of Chinese culture have increased significantly. There is closer unity of thinking

---

* Main points of the speech at the National Conference on Public Communication.

between Party members and the public. The decisions and plans made by the CPC Central Committee have proved effective in enhancing our public communication.

In practice, we have furthered our understanding of our public communication, and put forward new ideas, perspectives and visions:

- We must uphold CPC leadership over ideological work.
- We have two fundamental tasks in enhancing work in the realm of theoretical work – to consolidate Marxism as the guiding philosophy in China, and to cement the common ground of thinking of the whole Party and the people.
- We must strengthen the whole Party and inspire the people with the Thought on Socialism with Chinese Characteristics for a New Era.
- We must cultivate and practice the core socialist values.
- Cultural confidence is a more essential, broader and deeper confidence, and represents a more fundamental, more profound and long-lasting force that sustains a country.
- The mass media should expand their penetration, guidance and influence, and enhance credibility.
- Writers and artists should take a people-centered approach.
- We must create a clean and upright cyberspace.
- We need to tell China's stories well and have China's voice heard.

To improve our public communication, we must adhere to and further develop the above ideas.

As Chinese socialism has entered a new era, we must focus on unifying people's thinking and pulling their strength together through our public communication. On the whole, the current situation in this regard is very good. To unite and lead the people to achieve the strategic goals set at the 19th CPC National Congress in 2017, and to strive for the success of Chinese socialism, we need to be more confident and motivated, and work together with one heart. To realize the people's aspiration for a better life must always be the goal of our efforts. We should resolve both their practical problems and ideological questions, increasing public confidence, rallying popular support, gaining people's trust, and building consensus. We must better explain China's development path and China's features. At the same time, we must ensure the country's political and cultural security. We must establish the new while removing the outdated, with the former taking precedence. We must keep increasing the cohesiveness and guidance of socialist ideology. We must understand communication in cyberspace, and improve our ability to utilize and regulate cyberspace, to make the maximum use of the internet for our development.

To improve our public discourse in the new era, we must conscientiously uphold socialism, rally public support, foster a new generation, develop Chinese culture, and build a positive image of China.

Upholding socialism means championing Marxism and Chinese socialism. We must continue to educate the whole Party and the people in the Thought on Socialism with Chinese Characteristics for a New Era, and advance our work inspired by the thought. We must make a greater effort to study and understand the thought thoroughly, and firmly plant the seeds of Marxism in contemporary China and in the 21st century.

Rallying public support means making sure that public opinion stays on the right track. We must raise our voice in advocating socialism, augment positive energy, extend the influence of mainstream opinion, and bolster the morale of the Party and the people, so that they will unite as one and progress towards the goals set by the CPC Central Committee.

Fostering a new generation means cultivating educated people with sound values and ethics. We must develop a guiding socialist philosophy, inculcate the core socialist values, and put them into practice. We must enhance the public's political awareness and ethical standards, and encourage civil behavior. In this way, we will be able to foster a new generation capable of shouldering the mission of national rejuvenation.

Developing Chinese culture means orienting culture towards socialism. We must promote the creative evolution and development of traditional Chinese culture, inherit our revolutionary cultural traditions, and develop an advanced socialist culture. We must inspire the cultural creativity of our whole nation, and develop a great socialist culture in China.

Building a positive image of China means improving our capacity for international communication, so as to tell better and more accurate stories and make China's voice heard. We should project a true, multi-dimensional and all-round picture of China, and increase China's soft power and the influence of Chinese culture in the world.

The whole Party, especially our colleagues working on public communication, has a strategic task, which is to enhance the appeal of socialism to unite and inspire the people. We should improve theoretical education on Marxism, and in particular ensure a thorough understanding of the Thought on Socialism with Chinese Characteristics for a New Era through serious study and practice. The key to developing socialist ideology is to build full confidence in the path, theory, system and culture of Chinese socialism. We should consolidate the guiding role of Marxism and develop our philosophy and social sciences with salient Chinese features, style and ethos. We must maintain the right tone in guiding public opinion, strengthen the penetration, guidance, influence and credibility of the media, and promote constructive thoughts and opinion. We should improve means of communication and create new means to promote our Party's innovative theories among the people. We should establish county-level integrated media centers to better inspire and serve the people. We must hold firmly to truth and rectify misconceptions. We should urge Party committees and Party leadership groups at all levels to fulfill their duties to the letter, improve performance, and tighten accountability in the strictest sense.

The purpose of our public communication is to win over more people. Our major responsibility is to foster a new generation capable of shouldering the mission of national rejuvenation. The top priority is to strengthen our ideals and convictions, underpinned by our faith in Marxism, socialism and communism, and our confidence in the path, theory, system and culture of Chinese socialism. We should offer the people better guidance, expose them to successful practices, and provide institutional guarantees. We should see that all areas of social development are imbued with the core socialist values, and encourage the public to honor these values. As young people are in the process of developing their values, we should guide them how to "fasten the first button" of a meaningful life. Publicity is necessary to encourage the public to learn from role models, and to nurture a positive atmosphere of respecting, emulating, honoring and caring for heroes. We should promote good and up-to-date practices and trends, and raise people's moral standards. We should continue the civic morality campaign, and enhance the public's theoretical and political awareness. We should build centers for promoting ethical and cultural progress, to help our people raise their political awareness and moral standards, foster appreciation of fine culture, and enhance social etiquette and civility. To improve civility in rural areas, we should promote healthy practices in place of outdated social mores, nurturing good folk customs, cultivating fine family traditions, and encouraging virtues in individuals.

We should encourage cultural workers to produce works drawing inspiration from everyday life and the experiences of the people. We should encourage them to work hard to create fine works for this great era, works that tell the stories of our Party, our country, our people and our heroes, and works that record the historic progress of the Chinese nation. In promoting the cultural sector, we must always put social benefits first. We should see that writers and artists develop a sound understanding of history, nation, state and culture. They should cultivate refined tastes, styles and a sense of responsibility, and raise their awareness of observing state laws and regulations. Cultural workers should enhance their moral integrity and firmly resist unhealthy tendencies in literary and artistic creation. They should aim to set an example with their works and personal conduct to refine character, inspire minds, and shape social trends. They should produce more wholesome and inspiring online works.

We should ensure consistent and equal access to public cultural services. Efforts to improve cultural services should be led by the government, involve extensive public participation, be more community-focused, and encourage shared benefits through joint contribution. We should expand the coverage and applicability of our basic public cultural services. We should promote the high-quality development of cultural industries, improve modern systems for cultural industries and markets, and support the growth of cultural market players. We should develop new forms of business and new models of consumption in the cultural sector, so that the people have a stronger sense of fulfillment and happiness from enjoying refined cultural products and services. We should further structural reform of the cultural sector and continue to inspire cultural creativity.

We should increase the international influence of Chinese culture. We need to take stock of the global landscape, and take targeted measures when we present the Thought on Socialism with Chinese Characteristics for a New Era to the international community. We should find better ways to tell stories about the CPC's governance of China, about our people's hard work to realize the Chinese Dream, and about China's peaceful development through mutually beneficial cooperation, helping the international community to know more about our country. China's finest traditional culture is the cultural lifeline of the Chinese nation. Its visions, concepts, values and moral norms are the core of Chinese thinking, and they also hold invaluable references to resolving problems of humanity. We should extract the cream of traditional Chinese culture, and display those elements that are still relevant in the world today. We should improve our approach to international communication, develop innovative concepts and mechanisms, and gather more resources and strength.

We should uphold and strengthen CPC leadership over our public communication. Reinforcing our Party's political foundations should be the overarching principle. In enhancing our public communication, we must apply the Four Consciousnesses, uphold the authority of the CPC Central Committee and its centralized, unified leadership, and maintain the correct political orientation. We must improve our conduct, and oppose the practice of favoring form over substance, bureaucratism, hedonism, and extravagance, the first two in particular. Those working on public communication should absorb new learning, get to know new areas, broaden their horizons, improve their comprehensive skills, and conduct more field research. They should have the will to get down to the grassroots, and improve their ability to observe clearly, to think profoundly and to write powerfully. Our purpose is to forge a workforce, which is innovative, professional, politically upright and practical-minded.

Accelerate Media Integration*

January 25, 2019

As the information society continues to develop, new media see their influence expanding. The number of internet users in China stands at 802 million, 98.3 percent of them mobile internet users. News apps and various social media have become primary information sources for many people, especially the young. And everyone can be a source. It is said that in the past, "people looked for information". Now, "information follows people". Therefore, we are facing an urgent need to boost media integration and build a framework that covers all media.

Our aim is to strengthen mainstream opinion, so as to consolidate a common base of political philosophy for all Party members and people, uniting them and providing mental strength and public support for the realization of the Two Centenary Goals and the Chinese Dream of national rejuvenation.

I. Fully Understand the Challenges and Opportunities in the Age of Media Integration

As we all know from historical records as it is stated in *Lü's Spring and Autumn Annals*[1], "Emperor Yao set up a drum for people to beat and offer their advice, and Emperor Shun set up wooden boards for people to write down their criticisms." Their purpose was to collect public opinion. In the late Qin Dynasty (221-206 BC) Chen Sheng and Wu Guang rose in revolt.[2] They wrote a fabricated prophecy –

---

* Part of the speech at the 12th group study session of the Political Bureau of the 19th CPC Central Committee.

"Chen Sheng will be king!" – on a piece of silk and hid it inside a fish for someone to discover. They also mimicked the barking of a fox, crying "Great Chu will rise again! Chen Sheng will be king!" Over time people came to believe it and began to support them. All this shows that the ancients knew well the importance of public opinion.

No cybersecurity, no national security. I have said this on many occasions. If we fail to adapt to the internet, we will not be in power for long. As the media keep developing on all fronts, they have taken on new features characterized by up-to-the-minute reporting, multi-dimensional coverage, widespread public participation, and targeted effect, bringing about profound changes in the means of communication and posing new challenges to our communication work.

We need to understand general trends to plan and act as required by the times. We need to accelerate media integration, so that our mainstream media will have more extensive coverage, stronger guidance, higher public trust, and more influence. The aim is to create concentric circles of diffusion, online and offline, within which all the people will be united on the basis of common ideals, convictions, values, and moral standards, so that positive energy and mainstream values prevail.

II. Fully Understand the Trends and Laws of Media Integration

Since the 18th CPC National Congress in 2012, we have emphasized the importance of guiding public opinion, giving priority to mobile media, improving media content, and promoting innovation. The integration of institutions and mechanisms, policies, procedures, technology and talent has been accelerated. Positive results have been achieved in building up integrated all-media matrices and in creating cross-media products.

Traditional and new media cannot replace each other; each serves its own purpose. They complement and promote each other without the question of one being primary and strong, while the other secondary and weak. To date, China has yet to tap the full potential of media integration. We need to keep moving towards integration and move faster from media plus to media integration. By optimizing the process and building new platforms, we aim to achieve effective integration of various media resources and production factors, such as content, technology applications, platforms, terminals and means of management. We need to facilitate qualitative changes, amplify efficiency, and create new types of mainstream media that are more influential and competitive.

I have said many times our major efforts in public discourse should be devoted to people. Where there are people, where our public communication should reach. As cyberspace has become such a new place, we should make it a priority to build public consensus there. At the same time, mobile internet has become a key channel for disseminating information. With such technologies as 5G, big data, cloud computing, internet of things, and artificial intelligence, it will enter a new stage of faster development. We must give priority to mobile media, improving state-owned communication platforms, while managing and making good use of commercial and social platforms. By means of mobile communication, the mainstream media will occupy the commanding heights in guiding public opinion and mentality, promoting culture, and serving the people.

Media intelligence is developing rapidly around the world. With a stronger sense of mission and urgency in bolstering our capability to guide public opinion, we need to make breakthroughs in the independent innovation of key technologies, exploring the application of artificial intelligence in news gathering, generating, distribution, reception and feedback. The use of algorithms must be managed in accordance with mainstream values for better guidance of public opinion.

To promote media integration we must avoid a one-size-fits-all approach, differentiating between traditional and new media, national and local media, government and commercial platforms, and mass and professional media. We should work to form an all-media communication framework featuring intensive use of resources, rational structures, differentiated development, coordination, and high efficiency.

Nothing can be accomplished without rules and regulations. Whatever the form of the media, whether online or offline, "big screen" or "small screen", none is beyond the rule of law. Those in charge of administration must fulfill their responsibilities and strengthen the management of new media in accordance with the law to ensure a cleaner cyberspace.

III. Advance In-Depth Media Integration

The application of information technology has brought us a rare opportunity. We must use the results of the information revolution to build an integrated all-media communication framework at a faster rate.

I have said many times that creating positive energy is a general requirement, and exercising effective management a top priority. Now I want to add that proper application shows real competence. Media integration does not concern news organizations only. We need to turn our public resources – social, ideological and cultural, our big data on social governance, and our institutional strengths in policy-making into strengths for enhancing our mainstream opinion. We need to pay close attention to top-level design, create new types of communication platform, establish new mainstream media, and enhance the influence of mainstream values, so that the Party's voice will spread more widely and deeply.

The internet is a double-edged sword. A picture or a video can spread widely through various media in just a few hours, and significantly impact public opinion. This kind of influence will benefit the country and the people if used properly, or may result in unpredictable damage if used improperly. We must clearly keep to the correct political and value orientations, and maintain sound guidance of public opinion. In the field of information generation, supply-side structural reform must be rolled out to significantly improve the quality and level of positive communication through innovations in concept, content, form, method and means.

When accurate and authoritative information does not spread in a timely manner, false and distorted information will mislead people; if positive and sound thoughts are not promoted, negative and misguided opinions will spread unchecked. In this regard, the mainstream media should shoulder their responsibilities and do their utmost to provide authentic, objective, and timely information with a clear-cut stance, and keep hold of the initiative in leading our public discourse. The mainstream media should be bold enough to guide and be skilled in guiding public opinion, with a firm and clear-cut stance on major issues of principle.

We must ensure that all-media communication is run under the rule of law, and adopt uniform standards and exercise integrated management for both traditional and new media. The mainstream media must publish accurate and timely news and information so as to provide news sources for other qualified media. We need to comprehensively improve our capacity for cybersecurity governance with technology, regulate the use of data resources, and guard against the risks posed by new technologies such as big data.

We must be fully aware of the trend in international communication towards mobile, social and visual media, and make more effort to build a discourse system for international communication. We also need to ensure our works are easy to understand and are readily accepted by more foreign audiences, thus constantly enhancing the impact of international communication.

More members of the international community are viewing China with reason and objectivity and offering their approval. It shows we are on the right road. It also presents good historic opportunities for the mainstream media. We must persevere in sharing Chinese stories with more confidence and enthusiasm. We aim to have a stronger voice in the world that is compatible with China's international status.

In summary, integrating the media is a great task. We must make concerted efforts across the country. Party committees and governments at all levels should give greater support to this task in terms of policies, funds and human resources. Departments in charge of information services at all levels should reform and innovate administrative mechanisms, carry out supporting policies and measures, and steer media integration in the right direction. Officials at all levels must improve their ability to handle the media so as to raise their governance ability.

Notes

[1] *Lü's Spring and Autumn Annals* (*Lü Shi Chun Qiu*) was compiled by the followers of Lü Buwei (c. 292-235 BC), chief minister of the State of Qin during the Warring States Period.

[2] This refers to the peasant uprising led by Chen Sheng and Wu Guang in the late Qin Dynasty. In 209 BC, on their way to take up their border defense duties, Qin army officers Chen Sheng and Wu Guang led 900 soldiers in a rebellion against the brutal rule of the Qin Dynasty at Dazexiang, Qixian County (southeast of today's Suzhou City, Anhui Province).

A Nation Must Have a Soul*

March 4, 2019

The year 2018 was an extraordinary one for China. On the path to realize the Two Centenary Goals, we pressed forward with full confidence; we endured hardships and achieved self-fulfillment; we invested efforts and reaped harvests. The CPC Central Committee united and led the Party and the Chinese people in seeking progress while maintaining stability. As a result, China's economic growth has been within a reasonable range, the country has maintained overall social stability, and the Chinese people have attained an increasingly strong sense of fulfillment, happiness, and security. This is a prelude to the implementation of the guiding principles of the 19th CPC National Congress held in 2017. We celebrated the 40th anniversary of reform and opening up in 2018, and will mark the 70th anniversary of the founding of the PRC in 2019. Both are important occasions, not only for this era but even in terms of the entire Chinese history of thousands of years. As we summarize the accomplishments and experience gained from reform and opening up, and drive reform in all areas to a deeper level, the Party and the Chinese people become more resolved in and confident of their ability to advance reform and opening up. These achievements have been hard-won, under the firm leadership of the CPC Central Committee, and through the concerted efforts of all our people and the wisdom of all CPPCC members, including all those present today.

The CPC Central Committee has always valued literature, art,

---

* Speech at a joint panel discussion of CPPCC National Committee members from the literary, art and social science circles during the Second Session of the 13th CPPCC National Committee.

philosophy and social sciences. I presided over the Seminar on Literature and Art in October 2014 and the Seminar on Philosophy and Social Sciences in May 2016, and addressed both seminars. In recent years, our literary, art and social science circles have strengthened their commitment to the Four Consciousnesses, the Four-sphere Confidence and the Two Upholds, and have taken on the mission of upholding socialism, rallying public support, fostering a new generation with sound values and ethics, developing Chinese culture, and building a positive image of China. In literary and artistic creation, they take on the responsibility for identifying the root problems and addressing them thoroughly, keeping to the right political direction by carrying on fine traditions and facilitating innovation. They have consolidated the guiding role of Marxism and reinforced their people-centered approach. The quality of literary and artistic works is improving. Philosophy and social sciences with Chinese features are thriving and generating remarkable results. A nation must have a soul that captures our fine traditions. As cerebral undertakings, literature, art, philosophy and social sciences are creations of the soul; they are indispensable and must never go astray.

The CPPCC members in the literary, art and social science circles have done tremendous work in deliberating on how to foster and practice the core socialist values, how to strengthen confidence in the culture of Chinese socialism and better present China to the world, how to promote progress in socialist literature and art, how to improve the public cultural service system, and how to ensure a clean and decent cyberspace. In 2018, they offered proposals on how to promote the ethos of model workers and high standards of craftsmanship, how to protect and utilize resources for tourism in former revolutionary sites, and how to develop the cultural and creative industries. They have played an important role in facilitating rational decision-making and effective governance.

On the whole, for several years the literary, art, and social science circles have successfully identified their goals, followed the right path, improved their conduct, created new positive trends, produced fine works, and trained capable professionals. Their undertakings are thriving as a result of these changes.

Our work in literature, art, philosophy and social sciences, weighing high in the overall work of the Party and the country, plays a significant role in upholding and developing the Thought on Socialism with Chinese Characteristics for a New Era. At the National Conference on Public Communication held in 2018, I set my expectations of our work in these fields under the current situation. Here, I would like to share with you some of my thoughts.

First, we should keep pace with the times. As an ancient Chinese poet said, "Prose and poetry are composed to reflect the times and reality."[1] We should keep pace with and speak for our times. In 2018, we held a grand celebration for the 40th anniversary of reform and opening up, and commended 100 pioneers of reform. Among them were many writers, artists and social scientists, including Li Guyi, Li Xuejian, Shi Guangnan, Jiang Zilong, Xie Jin, Lu Yao, Fan Jinshi, Li Yining, Lin Yifu, Wang Jiafu, Hu Fuming, Xu Chongde, Du Runsheng, and Zheng Derong. They are all outstanding representatives in their fields, keeping up with and serving the needs of the times.

The new era of Chinese socialism calls for outstanding writers, artists and theorists and offers extensive space for literary and artistic creation and academic innovation. I hope we will increase confidence in our culture, keep up with the pulse of the times, and listen to the voices of the times. Our mission is to record the new era, create the new era, and extol the best of the new era. We should brave challenges and seek inspiration for innovative themes from contemporary Chinese creations. We should reflect the historic changes in our era and depict the spirit of our age. We should record the progress of this era, tell its stories, and manifest its virtues.

Second, we should adopt a people-centered approach. The people are the creators of history. All achievements come from the people, and all glories belong to the people. Looking into the future, we must rely closely on the people to overcome the challenges that confront us on our road ahead, and realize the blueprint for national development drawn up at the 19th CPC National Congress. "The roc soars not merely because of the lightness of one of its feathers; the steed gallops not merely because of the strength of one of its legs."[2] If China wants to fly high and run fast, it must rely on the strength of its nearly 1.4 billion people.

In producing literary and artistic works and conducting research in philosophy and social sciences, we must know who we are creating and speaking for. This is a fundamental issue. The people are the source of inspiration for literary and artistic creations. Only through a people-centered approach can we draw inexhaustible inspiration. Our writers and artists should look beyond their own lives and go deeper into the lives of ordinary people to tell stories about them, listen to their voices, and celebrate their merits. People working in the philosophy and social science circles should look beyond their ivory tower and conduct extensive field research to see how people live and think, then address their doubts and concerns in a way that echoes their inner world. Philosophy, social sciences, literature, and art must respond to reality and analyze social problems. Before prescribing the right solutions for our country, we must first have an idea of its health and then identify the ailments and their causes. How can we treat the ailments without a sound diagnosis?

Third, we should create fine works for the people. Great writers and scholars do not put on airs, but produce great works. Mentioning Lao Zi, Confucius, and Mencius, we recall *Dao De Jing*, *The Analects of Confucius*, and *The Mencius*.[3] Referring to Tao Yuanming, Li Bai, and Du Fu,[4] we think of their well-known poems and prose. Speaking of Plato, William Shakespeare, and Adam Smith, we remember *The Republic*, *Hamlet*, and *The Wealth of Nations*. If writers and scholars do not focus on creating fine works, but take shortcuts and seek instant benefits, they cannot grow into masters. As I mentioned at the Seminar on Literature and Art in 2014, it is fine works that count. All ostentatious activities are superficial and will soon be gone with the wind.

All cultural creations and academic research, to be valuable and meaningful, should reflect and respond to reality, address practical problems, and tackle real issues. I hope that based on China's actual conditions, you can create works that reflect our country's progress and our people's enriched lives, and demonstrate the spirit, values and strength of the Chinese nation. Originality is a characteristic shared by all fine works. Our literary and artistic creations should highlight the Chinese context and the current era. Writers and artists should increase the ethical, cultural and artistic value of their works by integrating new concepts with new approaches, and new contents with new forms. Our research in philosophy and social sciences should be grounded on the practice of Chinese socialism, and produce original theories and perspectives to build a system of disciplines, an academic system and a discourse system with Chinese characteristics. At the National Conference on Public Communication, I emphasized the need to generate the will to get down to the grassroots, and to improve the ability to observe clearly, think profoundly and write powerfully. This requirement is also the prerequisite and foundation for creating fine works. I hope CPPCC members from the literary, art and social science circles will take the lead and set a good example. In addition to releasing individual talent, we also need to gather source materials and conduct in-depth and detailed research. Success lies in the details. As screenplays and novels draw on emotive and genuine details, we need to dig deeper into real life to obtain them.

Fourth, we should build social norms by promoting virtue. According to *Zuo's Commentary on the Spring and Autumn Annals*[5], "The highest attainment is to exemplify virtue; the second highest is to perform great deeds; the third highest is to put forth noble ideas." People working in the literary, art, philosophy and social science circles have the responsibility to inspire minds, refine character, and warm hearts. You also shoulder the mission to cultivate morality and consolidate the foundations of our society through your works. As well-known public figures, you are expected to set an example for society with your lofty aspirations, sound morals and noble sentiment.

To promote virtue, we should first establish moral integrity. It requires those working in the literary, art, philosophy and social science circles to be firm in their beliefs and ideals, be responsible, aim high, and have a deep love for the country. The artistic and academic quests of individuals should be integrated into the country's future and the people's wellbeing. Accordingly, writers, artists and scholars should make their due contribution to the country and the people. They should observe professional ethics, improve professional proficiency, and be hardworking and diligent. They should practice the core socialist values and develop a strong sense of responsibility. They should reject sycophancy in favor of self-respect, and vulgarity in favor of refinement. Writers, artists and scholars with a good work ethic should demonstrate dedication and perseverance in the pursuit of their professional aspirations, and achieve their goals through assiduous and painstaking efforts.

The year 2019 marks the 70th anniversary of the founding of the PRC. Over the past 70 years, China has witnessed profound changes and achieved a tremendous transformation. The Chinese nation has stood up, become better off and grown in strength. In the history of both China and the wider world, it deserves to be written into a heroic epic. I hope you can produce fine works to reflect the hard work of our Party and our people, to explore the immanent causes of change in our country, to explain the strengths in the path, theory, system and culture of Chinese socialism behind our achievements, and to better interpret China's practices with Chinese theories, so as to stimulate the Party and the people to forge ahead.

As I said at the New Year gathering of the CPPCC National Committee at the end of 2018, the people's support is our top political priority and public consensus is our driving force for progress. To achieve the Two Centenary Goals and the Chinese Dream of national rejuvenation, we need to pool the wisdom and strength of all Chinese people, build broad consensus, and promote unity. We should be fully aware of the role of the CPPCC, which is to focus on the central tasks of the Party and the country and fulfill its duties. The CPPCC must enhance its function of democratic scrutiny, and gather all the positive energy for national rejuvenation. I hope all of you as CPPCC members will improve your competencies and capabilities, take the lead in every aspect of your work, honor your commitment, and fulfill your mission.

Notes

[1] Bai Juyi: "A Letter to Yuan Zhen" (*Yu Yuan Jiu Shu*). Bai Juyi (772-846) was a poet of the Tang Dynasty.

[2] Wang Fu: *Comments of a Recluse* (*Qian Fu Lun*). Wang Fu (c. 85-c. 163) was a philosopher and political commentator of the Eastern Han Dynasty.

[3] *Dao De Jing*, also known as *Lao Zi*, is an important philosophical work from ancient China. It is reputed to have been written by Lao Zi during the Spring and Autumn Period (770-476 BC).

The Analects of Confucius (*Lun Yu*) is one of the Confucian classics. Written by the disciples of Confucius, it records the words and deeds of Confucius, and also comprises dialogues between Confucius and his disciples.

The Mencius (*Meng Zi*) is one of the Confucian classics compiled by Mencius and his disciples. The book is a collection of anecdotes and conversations of Mencius during the Warring States Period (475-221 BC).

[4] Tao Yuanming (365-427) was a poet of the Eastern Jin Dynasty. Li Bai (701-762) and Du Fu (712-770) were poets of the Tang Dynasty.

[5] *Zuo's Commentary on the Spring and Autumn Annals* (*Zuo Zhuan*), one of the Chinese Confucian classics, is believed to have been written by Zuoqiu Ming. Zuoqiu Ming (556-451 BC) was a historian in the State of Lu during the Spring and Autumn Period.

Raise Students' Awareness of the Thought on Socialism with Chinese Characteristics for a New Era*

March 18, 2019

The key to improving our education in political philosophy is to fully implement the Party's policies on education. We must be clear about fundamental issues like the purposes, standards and approaches of education. To carry out the Party's education policies in the new era, we must follow the guiding role of Marxism, implement the Thought on Socialism with Chinese Characteristics for a New Era, keep to the path of socialism in managing schools, and take solid measures to build strong moral character. Education should always serve the people, the CPC's governance of China, the development of Chinese socialism, reform and opening up, and socialist modernization. We must base our education on our national conditions and integrate it with work and everyday life. We should push forward educational modernization and develop a strong educational sector that satisfies the people. We should ensure that the younger generations can shoulder the responsibility of rejuvenating the Chinese nation, and that they become morally, intellectually, physically and aesthetically equipped to carry on the cause of socialism.

Young people are the future of China and the hope of our nation. Our Party is committed to developing future generations of capable people – those who support the leadership of the CPC and our socialist system and are determined to devote themselves to the cause of Chinese socialism. We must take a clear stance on this matter of

---

* Main points of the speech at a seminar with teachers of political philosophy.

principle. We should work hard on the education of younger generations, beginning with children in schools. It is very important to open courses on political philosophy at primary and secondary schools and institutions of higher education. This needs to be done in steps, in a gradual way, as a fundamental prop.

Courses on political philosophy are fundamental to building strong moral character. Young people are at a crucial stage of life. Like flowers in budding which need to be watered, they should be carefully guided and educated while they grow up. In our socialist education, it is necessary to educate the students in political philosophy, equip them with the Thought on Socialism with Chinese Characteristics for a New Era, guide them to enhance their confidence in the path, theory, system and culture of Chinese socialism, and inspire their patriotism. In this way, they are encouraged to serve the country and make it stronger by carrying forward Chinese socialism, advancing socialist modernization and realizing national rejuvenation. Courses on political philosophy play an irreplaceable role in this regard, and teachers of these courses bear a great responsibility.

The Party Central Committee places high value on education. Attaching great importance to education in political philosophy, we have always followed the guiding role of Marxism, and developed a discipline of Chinese socialist system, laying foundation for developing courses on political philosophy. We have developed a deeper understanding of the laws that underlie governance by a communist party, the development of socialism, and the evolution of human society, and have learned to use them wisely. We have opened up a new realm in socialism with Chinese characteristics in both theory and practice, and our achievements have drawn worldwide attention. Our growing confidence in the path, theory, system and culture of Chinese socialism has provided strong support for the development of courses on political philosophy. Over the course of several thousand years, the Chinese nation as a whole has developed a profound and outstanding traditional culture. Our Party in particular has forged an advanced socialist culture in the course of revolution, economic development, and reform. These are the engines powering our courses on political philosophy. The successful experiences we have gained and our understanding of the regularity of the course over a long period provide an important basis for us to keep to the right track and facilitate innovation. With these in place, and with our team of trustworthy, respectable and reliable teachers who have the enthusiasm, determination and ability required, we are fully confident that we have what it takes to create better courses on political philosophy.

Teachers are the key to developing these courses, and we should give full rein to their enthusiasm, initiative, and creativity. Teachers of political philosophy should help their students sow the seeds of the true, the good and the beautiful, and guide them how to tie their shoelaces properly before embarking on their journey of life. First, they must have strong political convictions. We should let those who have faith share that faith with others, and they should have acute political awareness and keep a clear head when faced with matters of principle. Second, they should love the country and the people, care about the future of the Chinese nation, and enrich themselves by drawing on the wealth of experience from the practice of the Party and the people in the new era. Third, they should be good thinkers, learn to use dialectical and historical materialism, and be innovative in teaching, so as to let the students have a profound learning experience and guide them towards noble ideals and beliefs and sound ways of thinking. Fourth, they should broaden their vision of knowledge, the world and history. They should be able to explain complicated matters by using examples and through in-depth analyses and comparisons. Fifth, they should exercise strict self-discipline, be consistent in class and out of class, online and offline, advocate the themes of the times, and spread positive energy. Sixth, they should have an upright character, since those who have upright character are attractive to students. They should have integrity and exercise a positive influence on their students. Only if the students relate to their teachers will they believe in what the teachers teach, so the teachers should try to win the students' respect with their profound theoretical knowledge and serve as role models in studies and in life that the students like and admire.

To push reform and innovation in teaching political philosophy, we should give it more theoretical substance and make it more inspirational, appealing and targeted. We must integrate political principles with scientific rationale, responding to students' questions with thorough scientific and academic analysis, convincing them with profound theories, and guiding them with truth. We must integrate values with knowledge, guiding students to embrace the right values while acquiring knowledge. We must be both constructive and critical, advocating mainstream ideology, and confronting all erroneous ideas and trends of thought. We must integrate theory with practice, teaching theory in class, emphasizing practice in society, and encouraging students to have great ideals and work for their goals. We must integrate uniformity with diversity, adopting the same standards in the objectives, curriculum, materials and management of teaching activities, and taking different approaches according to the place, time, and audience. We must integrate teachers' guidance with students' initiative, strengthening research to help students better understand and assimilate political philosophy, and ensuring they play the primary role in learning. We must integrate imparting knowledge with inspiring thinking, guiding students to identify, analyze and dissect problems and draw their own conclusions with help from teachers. We must integrate explicit education with implicit education, and tap into the resources of other courses and methodologies, so as to involve all faculties in integrating education in political philosophy into every aspect of the entire education process.

China's success hinges on our Party. Party committees at all levels should make it a priority to develop courses on political philosophy, focus on the pressing problems hindering the effort, and take effective measures underlined by good planning, team building and support systems. Under the unified leadership of Party committees, Party and government institutions should work together to promote these courses, relevant authorities should do their part, and the whole society should join in the endeavor, so that the Party, society, teachers, and students are all involved and coordinated in their efforts. Party committees at schools must be strict in management and take effective measures. The Party secretaries and presidents of schools should have first-hand experience of courses on political philosophy, take the lead in developing these courses, and work closely with teachers. We should have adequate professionals specializing in teaching political philosophy, with the majority working full-time. We should focus on developing a holistic approach to education in political philosophy at primary and secondary schools and institutions of higher learning, and bring out its full potential. We should improve the curriculum, ensure coordination between political philosophy and other courses, and encourage eminent teachers from other courses to give lectures on political philosophy. Leading officials of local Party committees and governments should do likewise at schools.

Carry On the Legacy of the May 4th Movement, and Be Worthy of the New Era*

April 30, 2019

Under the leadership of the Party, we have opened up the path of Chinese socialism, formed its theoretical framework, established its system, developed its culture, and brought it into a new era. The Chinese people have unprecedented confidence in the path, theory, system and culture of Chinese socialism, and the prospects for national rejuvenation have never been brighter.

In the new era, the theme and direction of the Chinese youth movement and the mission of Chinese youths are to uphold the leadership of the CPC, and work along with other people to realize the Two Centenary Goals and the Chinese Dream of national rejuvenation.

Youth is the most active and energetic element among all forces in society. You are the hope and future of our country. Today, in the most promising period of the Chinese nation, young Chinese are endowed with rare opportunities to achieve things, and the mission to shoulder great responsibilities. In this new era, you should continue to carry forward the spirit of the May 4th Movement and take on your mission to realize national rejuvenation. You should meet the expectations of our Party and our people, be worthy of the trust of the nation, and live up to the demands of this great era.

First, Chinese youths in the new era should establish great ideals.

The ideals and beliefs of youths have a bearing on the future of a country. Young people with great ideals and firm beliefs are the driving force that builds an invincible nation. High ambitions

---

* Part of the speech at a conference marking the centenary of the May 4th Movement.

can stimulate your potential to forge ahead, so that you will not drift aimlessly like a boat without a rudder. It is said that "a person who aspires to be a saint will become a saint; and a person who aspires to be a sage will become a sage."[1] Young people have different life goals and career choices. But only when you integrate your goals with those of the nation and the people, advance with the times, and share the aspirations of the people will you live up to your values and realize the lofty goals of life. Disregarding the needs of the country and the interests of the people, those who are self-centered will find a narrower path ahead.

Young Chinese in the new era must have belief in Marxism, faith in Chinese socialism, and confidence in realizing the Chinese Dream. You must go out to the people, embrace the new era and the new world, and realize your ideals and beliefs in building your careers, so that the years of your youth will sparkle with innovation and creation.

Second, Chinese youths in the new era should love our country.

Dr. Sun Yat-sen said that the biggest thing for a citizen is "knowing how to love one's country"[2]. Whoever does not love their country – or even worse, deceives and betrays their motherland – is a disgrace and has no place anywhere in the world. Love of our country, the feeling of devotion and sense of attachment to our motherland is a duty and responsibility for every Chinese. It is the foundation on which young Chinese in the new era can become winners in life. In contemporary China, the essence of patriotism is loving our country, our Party and socialism all and at the same time.

Young Chinese in the new era should follow the instructions and guidance of the Party, and show concern and affection for our country and our people. You should dedicate yourself to the country and the people, demonstrate patriotism with lifelong sincerity and drive, and let the great banner of patriotism fly high in your heart.

Third, Chinese youths in the new era must shoulder your responsibilities.

The times call for responsibility, and our young people must take up the responsibility for national rejuvenation. As Lu Xun the great writer said, young people "have strength to spare; they can turn a dense forest into flat land, plant trees in the wilderness, and dig wells in the desert"[3]. In the new journey towards national rejuvenation, we need to respond to major challenges, guard against serious risks, overcome real obstacles, and resolve difficult problems. All these urgently demand the will to step forward in the face of difficulties. As long as young people are brave enough to shoulder responsibilities and fight hardships and risks, Chinese socialism will be full of vitality, potential and hope.

Young people must maintain your courage, fearing nothing and forging ahead in spite of difficulties and dangers. You should stand in the forefront and be the pioneers of national rejuvenation. There are people who are afraid to experiment and try out new things, or treat responsibilities as burdens and losses, or shirk their responsibilities and attend only to their own business. All such thoughts and acts are undesirable and those who entertain them will accomplish nothing and never be able to truly enjoy life.

Chinese youths must cherish this new era and grow with it. In the new era, you must work hard to perform on the vast stage of reform and opening up and on the journey to realizing the Chinese Dream. And you should endeavor to become morally, intellectually, physically, and aesthetically equipped to join and carry on the socialist cause.

Fourth, Chinese youths in the new era must work hard.

Hard work paints a bright backdrop for a young life. As Mao Zedong said, "Should I have 200 years to spare, I will surely swim for 3,000 *li* (1,500 km)."[4] The mission of national rejuvenation must be achieved through hard work, as must the ideals of life. Without an arduous popular struggle, carried out especially by generations of young people, there would have been neither the present new era of Chinese socialism nor a future in which we will realize national rejuvenation. Over thousands of years, the Chinese nation has suffered numerous hardships, but none of them could defeat us; instead, they have lifted our national spirit, willpower and strength. Today, our living conditions have improved, but we, especially our young people, must retain the spirit and fine tradition of hard work. There will definitely be daunting challenges and even perilous storms in the new journey towards national rejuvenation. The spirit of arduous struggle is especially needed during the process. Hard work is not just a ringing slogan; it is about doing small things, completing every task, and fulfilling every duty. The road of hard work will not be smooth, instead it will be cobbled with hardships and full of ups and downs. The strong can always rise from setbacks; they are never discouraged.

In the new era young Chinese must forge ahead as brave and devoted pioneers in the forefront of the times against all difficulties and obstacles, and work hard to blaze new trails, achieve successes and create miracles that will astonish the world.

Fifth, Chinese youths in the new era must have remarkable abilities.

Youth is a golden age for developing skills through hard work. "If you idle away your youth and achieve nothing, it's no good lamenting in old age."[5]

In this new era, knowledge updates quickly, the social division of labor is becoming more refined, and new technologies, models, and forms of business are emerging one after another. This not only provides a broad stage for young people to display your talents, but also raises new and higher requirements for your abilities. To achieve your ideals or to shoulder the mission of the times, young people must cherish and do justice to the prime of youth, study hard to acquire scientific knowledge, improve your capabilities, hone your skills, and keep up with new developments around the world in terms of thinking, vision, ideas, and level of understanding.

Chinese youths in the new era must have a stronger sense of urgency in learning, and work hard on studying the Marxist stance, viewpoint and methodology. You must master knowledge of science and culture and professional expertise. You must improve your attainment in humanities by educating yourselves and tempering your character through study. You must acquire more skills and become more professionally competent at work, so that you will be able to serve the people and make innovative and creative contributions to the country.

Sixth, Chinese youths in the new era should temper your moral character.

A person cannot succeed without virtues. This makes morality essential. The Chinese nation has been trying to attain moral qualities that repose in the heights of excellence. To build China into a strong modern socialist country, we must enrich ourselves not only materially but culturally and ethically. Cultural and ethical progress is more lasting, more profound and more powerful. Young people must integrate sound moral appreciation and conscious moral development with active moral practice, to improve yourselves and maintain moral integrity. This way you will travel further in the correct direction on the path of life.

Faced with a complex and changing international landscape, young people must differentiate between truth and falsehood and keep to the right path, and never blindly follow what others say or do. Facing temptation from the outside world, you must remain resolute, strictly abide by rules, create a better life with hard and honest work, and never be opportunistic or become conceited. While enjoying the good times, you should remember those who fought to make the present possible and work to repay them. You should be grateful to the Party, the country, the society and the people. You are expected to go through hardships, understand what life entails, get to know people's concerns and real problems, and identify the true meaning and value of life and work.

In the new era young people must nurture and practice the core socialist values, draw nourishment from traditional Chinese virtues, learn from heroes and role models of the times, and enhance your moral integrity through introspection. You should recognize illustrious virtue, follow social ethics, and restrict personal desires, while guarding against temptations such as worship of money, self-indulgence, overly self-centered pursuits, and historical nihilism. You should aim high and look far to pursue a more lofty and fulfilling life, so that integrity and vitality will prevail throughout our society.

Notes

[1] Wang Shouren: *Rules for Students at Longchang* (*Jiao Tiao Shi Long Chang Zhu Sheng*). Wang Shouren (1472-1529), better known as Wang Yangming, was a neo-Confucian philosopher and educator of the Ming Dynasty.

[2] Sun Yat-sen: "Speech at a Gathering to Celebrate the Founding of Guangdong No. 1 Female Normal School", *Complete Works of Sun Yat-sen*, Vol. VII, Chin. ed., People's Publishing House, Beijing, 2015, p. 597.

[3] Lu Xun: "Mentor", *Complete Works of Lu Xun*, Vol. III, Chin. ed., People's Literature Publishing House, Beijing, 2005, p. 59.

[4] Mao Zedong: "Annotations to Lines in *Poems of Mao Zedong*", *Collected Works of Mao Zedong*, Vol. VIII, Chin. ed., People's Publishing House, Beijing, 1999, p. 364.

[5] Quan Deyu: "A Reflection on My Life" (Fang Ge Xing). Quan Deyu (759-818) was a writer and official of the Tang Dynasty.

The People's Wellbeing

Continue the "Toilet Revolution"*

November 2017

Over the past two years the tourism sector has made a real effort to promote the "toilet revolution", a manifestation of a tangible and down-to-earth approach. Tourism is an emerging industry that is going strong. We should continue to improve services and infrastructure to give it a boost, as we have been doing with the "toilet revolution".

Toilets are not a trivial issue, but an important element in promoting urban and rural progress. The effort should extend from tourist sites and cities to every village. This should be a focus of the rural revitalization strategy – it is a weak area that needs to be remedied.

---

* Main points of the directive on progress made in the "toilet revolution" of the tourism sector.

Bring a Sense of Gain, Happiness and Security to the People*

December 2017-November 3, 2019

I

In recent years solid results have been achieved in the construction, management, maintenance and operation of roads in rural areas – those connecting rural areas, especially poor areas, to the rest of the country and bringing them prosperity. The Party has thus garnered greater support at the grassroots.

The Ministry of Transport, relevant departments, and all localities must fully implement the decisions and plans made at the 19th CPC National Congress, and make sure they understand the importance of building roads in rural areas as a component of the rural revitalization strategy and the final fight against poverty. They should focus on prominent problems, improve policies and mechanisms, and better build, manage, maintain, and operate rural roads, to provide the infrastructure that is necessary for rural people to achieve moderate prosperity and for modernizing agriculture and rural areas.

(from the directive on the construction, management, maintenance and operation of roads in rural areas, December 2017)

II

We must always place the people's interests above everything

---

* Excerpts from speeches made between December 2017 and November 3, 2019.

else, accelerate reforming our systems and mechanisms in sectors for public wellbeing, and do everything in our means to guarantee and improve people's standard of living. We should continue to improve public services, enhance social fairness and justice, and direct more public resources to communities, rural areas, and groups in need of help. Priority should be given to matters that concern the people's immediate interests.

(from the speech at a gathering celebrating the 30th anniversary of the founding of Hainan Province and Hainan Special Economic Zone, April 13, 2018)

III

The renovation of rundown urban areas concerns the life and work of millions. We cannot have cities with skyscrapers on the one side and slums on the other. We still face a daunting task in renovating rundown urban areas across the country. But as long as it is to the benefit of the people, we must try our best and do it well.

(from the speech during a visit to Hubei Province, April 24-28, 2018)

IV

Ensuring the safety of medicines is a duty that no Party committee or government at any level may neglect. We must always prioritize people's health, improve vaccine management, and hold firm to the red line of medication safety, just as we would take a heavy dose of medicine to treat a serious disease. We must do our best to protect the immediate interests of the people and ensure public security and social stability.

(from the directive on the fake vaccine case of Changsheng Bio-Technology Co., Ltd. in Changchun, Jilin Province, July 2018)

V

Myopia is a growing trend among students, particularly the younger ones. It is doing severe damage to their health, and is a major issue bearing on the future of our country. We must attach greater importance to the problem and prevent it from worsening.

In the context of deeper educational reform, all relevant authorities should come up with effective prevention and control plans and urge all local authorities and departments to ensure implementation. The whole society must act for better eyesight and a better future for our children.

(from the directive in response to the article "High Incidence of Myopia Among Chinese Students", August 2018)

VI

Couriers of express delivery services work very hard, rising early and working long into the night, regardless of the weather. They can be particularly busy on weekends and during holidays. Just like bees, they are the hardest-working people, making our lives easier. We must put employment at the top of our agenda, and create more jobs for the people.

(from talks during a visit to grassroots officials and communities in Beijing before the Spring Festival, February 1, 2019)

VII

The ancient Chinese used to say, "Filial piety is the root of morality."[1] The Chinese people have always honored filial piety and the value of family, caring for the elderly and the children of others as they care for their own. China is now an aging society. It is a matter of social harmony and stability to ensure care, support, recreation, and security for the elderly. The whole of society should respect, care for, and support the elderly, and ensure they have a happy life with more and better old-age programs.

(from the speech at a Spring Festival gathering, February 3, 2019)

VIII

Civil affairs concern people's wellbeing and can affect their attitude towards the Party and the government. They involve basic work in society and how we can guarantee people's basic needs. Party committees and governments at all levels should put people at the center of their work, intensify leadership over civil affairs, improve the capacity of grassroots agencies to render service in civil affairs, and ensure the sustainable and sound development of this sector. Civil affairs agencies at all levels should strengthen the Party, persevere in reform and innovation, pay special attention to poverty elimination, special groups and public concerns, and fulfill their duties in guaranteeing people basic living, grassroots social governance, and basic social services, so as to contribute to the building of a moderately prosperous society and a modern socialist country.

(from the directive on civil affairs work, April 2019)

IX

Garbage sorting concerns the public's living environment and resource conservation. It is also an important indicator of social progress.

The key to promoting garbage sorting lies in strengthening management, developing a long-term mechanism, and accustoming people to the practice. We should strengthen guidance in light of local conditions, take solid and concrete measures, and persevere to the end. Guidance should be given in the form of extensive education campaigns, so that people understand the importance of and necessity for garbage sorting. Through effective supervision and guidance, more people will act and take up the habit. Everybody should join the effort, work for a better environment, and contribute to green and sustainable development.

(from the directive on garbage sorting, June 2019)

X

We need to focus on the most pressing and relevant problems that are of the greatest concern to the people and the difficulties they face in their lives, and solve each and every one of them. We will do our best to achieve real results quickly to give our people a strong sense of gain, happiness and security. The Party and the government should fulfill their duties, encourage and support the participation of enterprises, people's organizations, and social groups, leverage the role of the people, and inspire their enthusiasm, initiative, and creativity, so as to create a sustainable operating framework for the city.

(from the speech during a visit to Shanghai, November 2-3, 2019)

Notes

[1] *Classic of Filial Piety* (*Xiao Jing*), a Confucian classic giving advice on filial piety.

Remove Institutional Barriers to Educational Development*

September 10, 2018

Generally speaking, our education currently conforms to the national conditions and meets the needs of economic and social development, but there still exist some prominent problems and shortcomings. These include:
- extra pressure in preschool and basic education through factors such as head-start learning and over-education, which damages the physical and mental health of students as well as increasing the financial burden and energy drain on families;
- the urgent need to improve the quality of institutions of higher learning after their rapid expansion;
- the need to take further measures to change the trend of teaching and imparting knowledge to the detriment of the all-round development of students; and
- the need to enhance the Party's leadership over education and strengthen the Party and political education.

All these problems require further reform of the education system.

Since the 18th CPC National Congress in 2012, remarkable progress has been made in education reform, but many more things need to be done as this is a prolonged campaign involving many factors and facets. Last year, the central authorities issued the "Opinions on Deeper Reform of the Education System", requiring that we follow the established practices and principles of educational development and the way students grow to create a vibrant, efficient, and more

---

* Part of the speech at the National Education Conference.

open education system which is conducive to high-quality education.

Our drive to modernize education should be socialism-oriented, maintain the nature of education as a public undertaking, ensure equal access to education as the basic national policy, and promote innovation in reforming the education system. We should make education available to every individual throughout their life and make study a habit and a lifestyle choice, so that people can study whenever and wherever they want to. We should guarantee equal access to education, trying to make good education available to everyone regardless of gender, region, and ethnicity, and whether they are rich or poor, or from an urban or rural area. We should make education adaptable to each individual's needs, enabling students with different temperament, interests, and potential to receive an education suitable to their growth. We should build a more open and flexible education system to offer more choices to students to expand their path for growth and clear the ladder to academic excellence, career advancement, and upward mobility.

First, the mechanism to promote education on values and moral integrity should be improved to correct the warped evaluation system that guides the development of education. The evaluation system determines the orientation of educational development. At present, the most salient problem in education is too much pressure on primary and secondary school students due to short-sighted and utilitarian thinking. The deeper problem is that while everyone knows it is wrong, they are trapped in conformist thinking and are dragged down deeper and deeper into this quagmire of error until it becomes a vicious spiral. The concept of education for all-round development was raised over 20 years ago. Some progress has been made in this regard, but across the regions it is unbalanced. In the final analysis, the problem is the requirement for education to foster values and moral integrity has not been fully implemented in the education system – the yardstick for education is scores and admission rates for primary and secondary schools, and research papers for colleges and universities. There is no proper place or sound evaluation system for moral education and education for all-round development, which is a long-standing problem we must solve. We should get rid of this obsession with scores, enrollment rates, diplomas, academic papers and professional titles, remove their excessive influence on the evaluation of the education system, and reverse the utilitarian trend in education. Educational institutions should fully implement the basic requirement of education on values and moral integrity, reform the ways students are cultivated and schools are run and managed, transform the support systems, and build a long-term mechanism to promote the physical and mental health of students and their all-round development.

We should support qualified colleges and universities in their efforts to grow into leading institutions. But we should not place them in a hierarchy; rather we should encourage each college or university to highlight its own strengths and strive to build first-class disciplines and facilities. The guiding principles of examination and admission systems need to be changed to ensure that students grow in a normal way, that the state selects from the talented, and that social justice is enhanced. The evaluation system for schools, teachers, students, and teaching as a whole should be improved so as to put an end to the misguided practices of evaluating teachers based solely on the rankings of their students, evaluating students based solely on their scores, and evaluating schools based solely on the enrollment rates of their graduates to higher-level educational institutions. The practice of rewarding or punishing teachers based on enrollment rates alone, and the covert practice of approving projects, allocating educational funds, and assessing performance in accordance with enrollment rates should be rectified. Reform of the national college entrance exam is of immediate relevance to many and has a bearing on the overall situation. To ensure that this high-risk reform of wide concern is carried out smoothly, Party committees and governments at all levels should assume direct responsibility to check on and supervise this work and step up efforts to coordinate different departments.

Some off-campus training organizations offer examination-oriented courses, which goes against good practice in education and the healthy growth of students. They have increased the extra burden on students and financial burden on parents, and even disturbed the normal teaching order of schools, all of which has aroused strong criticisms. An industry calling for conscience should not become profit-driven. We should regulate these training organizations pursuant to the law and make them focus on well-rounded development of students.

Second, we should drive deeper reform of school operating mechanisms and education management to fully release the vigor of education. Although our country boasts the largest education system in the world, we face a rather complicated situation – unbalanced development between rural and urban areas and varying educational needs among the people. In order to run and develop this large and complex sector well, we must further our reform in school operating mechanism and education management, modernize our capacity and raise the level of governance in education by addressing such problems as inadequacy in self-restraint and self-development of schools, excessive, deficient, improper and underperforming governance of schools by governments, and lack of social participation.

At present, people complain that the government still interferes too much and involves in excessive detail with school management, stifling the vitality of schools. At the same time, the government's role in helping schools out of difficulties is not always fulfilled. The allocation of human, financial, and material resources for schools is administered by a number of government departments, some of which simply follow age-old policies and methods. This problem must be addressed systematically. Schools have their own well-established practices and focus of work. Party committees and governments at all levels should cut unnecessary inspections and assessment; they should not ask schools to suspend classes to organize social events on campus, far less assign to schools the work of attracting investment or organizing demolition projects.

Governments can use various university rankings published by different organizations as a reference, but they should never be misled by such rankings. School management should be the responsibility of each school, and governments should delegate such powers as allocation of resources, use of funds, and performance assessment to the school itself to make it accountable for its own business.

The goal of reforming the education system is to improve the quality of education. The first focus should be improving teaching capabilities by launching reforms concerning teachers, textbooks, and teaching methodology. We should identify diverse and effective teaching methodologies and approaches to make real breakthroughs in well-rounded education. The second focus should be improving learning capabilities by promoting reforms that foster moral integrity and lofty ideals, build intellectual and physical strength, and produce the talent needed by society. We should make preschool education available to all, promote integrated development of urban and rural compulsory education, encourage diversified development of high schools by exploiting their individual strengths, bring out the full potential of higher education, raise the quality of vocational education, step up poverty alleviation efforts in education, and improve the level of ethnic minority education, special needs education, and continuing education to create conditions for everyone to grow in a well-rounded way. The third focus should be improving school administration and operation in accordance with the law. We should work out a better system and stronger mechanisms for governing schools and continuously improving education management as a whole.

Third, we should improve the capacity of education to serve economic and social development. To meet the needs of a strong modern socialist country, we should adjust the regional distribution of institutions of higher learning, optimize the structure of disciplines and the setup of academic programs, and improve the management of higher education to help universities identify their particular strengths and find different ways to excel. We should instill the idea of innovation and entrepreneurship throughout the education process, enable dynamic adjustment of disciplines and programs, build first-class universities and disciplines at a quicker pace, and promote innovation by coordinating efforts of enterprises, universities, and research institutes. By doing so, we commit ourselves to implementing an innovation-driven development strategy that focuses on cultivating innovative, interdisciplinary and professional personnel with practical skills.

We should attach great importance to vocational education by encouraging the integration of efforts of enterprises and vocational institutions, improve the mechanism which attaches equal importance to cultivating moral integrity and honing skills, and integrate work with learning. This will offer a steady supply of millions of competent individuals to our industries, and give graduates from vocational schools more opportunities for career development. We should roll out flexible and effective preferential policies, foster a culture which encourages enterprises to shoulder the responsibility of vocational education, and build a community of shared future for vocational schools and colleges, industries and enterprises.

Fourth, we should open our educational sector wider to the outside world to enhance its influence around the world. The sea and river refuse no stream. To modernize the education sector, we should be committed to the opening-up policy and strengthen mutual respect, learning and exchange with all other countries. We should promote high-level collaboration with first-class institutions around the world to introduce high-quality and much-needed resources, especially state-of-the-art technology and academic disciplines and programs that are underdeveloped, absent, or in short supply in our country. As part of our effort to train global future elites, we should develop internationally competitive education to attract outstanding students from around the world, thus making China a major world education center and a sought-after destination for international students. We should enhance the role of education in serving diplomacy, ensure the ongoing success of Confucius Institutes and Confucius Classrooms across the globe through educational exchange and cooperation, and make good friends to China of millions of people studying Chinese around the world, and tens of thousands of international students in China.

We should endeavor to train talented people with a global vision who are familiar with Party and state policies, proficient in foreign languages, adept in international rules, and skillful in negotiation and communication with foreign parties. We should target our efforts to train professional and technical personnel and management staff proficient in foreign languages ready to serve the Belt and Road Initiative, and make plans to train and encourage outstanding individuals to apply for positions with international organizations. We should move faster to build overseas international schools with Chinese features. This would help the children of staff in Chinese agencies stationed abroad, of employees in overseas Chinese companies, and of overseas Chinese businesspeople and workers to receive Chinese-language education. And this will also make it convenient for the children of overseas Chinese nationals and foreign citizens of Chinese descent to study Chinese language, history and culture.

Safeguard Political Security, Social Order and Peaceful Lives*

January 15, 2019

We must follow the guidance of the Thought on Socialism with Chinese Characteristics for a New Era, uphold the absolute leadership of the CPC over judicial, prosecuting and public security work, and adhere to the people-centered philosophy of development. We should accelerate the modernization of social governance, comprehensive and in-depth reform in the judicial, prosecuting and public security fields, and the development of a consistent, specialized and professional contingent of judicial, prosecuting and public security personnel with revolutionary spirit. Working in these fields, we must faithfully fulfill our duties, have the courage to shoulder responsibilities and do what is needed, and be keen on reform and innovation. We must fulfill our duties to ensure our country's political security, social stability, social equity and justice, and a happy life for the people. In so doing, we will open a new chapter in judicial, prosecuting and public security work.

Since the 18th CPC National Congress in 2012, the Party Central Committee has been attaching more importance to judicial, prosecuting and public security work, making a string of major decisions and implementing a series of major measures, thereby safeguarding political security, social stability and the peaceful life of the people and promoting sustained and sound economic and social development. This results from the strong leadership of the Central Committee and the concerted effort of the entire Party and all the Chinese people and

---

* Main points of the speech at the Central Conference on Judicial, Prosecuting and Public Security Work.

embodies wisdom and hard work of all those working in the judicial, prosecuting and public security systems.

We must put into practice our Party's mass line and stick to the principle that social governance is for the people. We must do well in combining the best of our Party's traditions with new technologies and new tools, be creative in improving the mechanisms for organizing and mobilizing the people and for bringing them benefits, serving them and addressing their concerns, and turn the people's wisdom and ingenuity into an inexhaustible source of innovation in social governance. We should strengthen law enforcement and the judicature in key areas concerning the people's immediate interests to ensure that our people can enjoy bluer skies, cleaner water, fresher air, safer food, convenient traffic and more harmonious social order.

We should be adept at transforming the leadership of the Party and the strengths of Chinese socialism into efficient social governance, and improve the law-based social governance model under which Party committee exercises leadership, government assumes responsibility, all sectors join the effort, and the public take part, so as to establish a social governance model based on collaboration, participation, and common interests. We should innovate and improve coordination of our efforts to ensure law and order, pool the resources of judicial, prosecuting and public security systems and relevant departments, and foster a positive environment in which problems are jointly tackled, work is coordinated, and peace and security are jointly created. Leading officials of all provinces and equivalent administrative units and central departments must implement a leadership responsibility system and fulfill their duties in maintaining local stability and safeguarding local security. We must further promote innovation in community governance and build a vigorous and efficient new system for grassroots-level governance.

We need to promote the core socialist values, strengthen political and moral education, improve the nomination and commendation of role models who act bravely for justice, and let integrity and justice prevail in the whole society. We must do everything in accordance with the law, and ensure that law-abiding people feel proud and valued and that law-breakers and unethical individuals suffer the consequences of their wrongdoing. We need to improve mechanisms for community-level self-governance, motivate the enthusiasm of urban and rural residents, enterprises, public institutions and social organizations in self-governance, and build a community of social governance in which everyone has and fulfills their responsibilities. We need to improve public psychological services and related counseling and crisis intervention, and cultivate self-esteem, self-confidence, rationality, composure and amity among our people. We need to accelerate the development of a crime prevention and control system that is multifaceted and IT-based.

Gangland forces are malignant tumors in society, causing severe disruption to economic and social order and eroding the very foundations of our Party's governance. We must unswervingly pursue the goals of the three-year campaign against organized crime, improve our strategies and measures, adjust the focus of our efforts according to specific conditions in different phases and fields, and maintain an overwhelming momentum. We need to focus on major cases of organized crime and target the gangs' financial sources, connections and protective umbrellas, make real and meticulous efforts on both prevention and punishment, address both the symptoms and root causes, and ensure that we can deliver long-term concrete results.

We need to make new breakthroughs in the reform of the judicial, prosecuting and public security systems from an overall perspective and quicken our pace in establishing and optimizing judicial, prosecuting and public security departments that collaborate to achieve high efficiency. We need to improve the allocation of the functions and powers of these departments and establish a mechanism by which the departments all fulfill their duties, fully cooperate with each other, and effectively check on each other. We need to carry forward the reform of the internal institutions of judicial, prosecuting and public security agencies, and improve their division of functions, institutional setup and staff establishment, so as to make them more efficient. We should enforce judicial accountability in all respects to enable judicial personnel to concentrate their energy on fulfilling duties and handling cases well, so as to improve judicial performance, efficiency and credibility. We should focus on issues of major concern to the public, lose no time in improving checks on and oversight over the exercise of power, and resolutely prevent lax law enforcement, miscarriages of justice, law-breaking by law-enforcement personnel, and judicial corruption. We should continue to reform the litigation system, separate complicated, major or time-consuming cases from simple, minor or easy ones, and promote wide application of big data, artificial intelligence and other new technologies in our judicial work.

As providers of various public services, judicial, prosecuting and public security bodies should work hard to provide services that are universally available, equally accessible, convenient, efficient, intelligent and targeted. We should continue to reduce the requirements on document submission for the convenience of citizens, accelerate the reform aiming to provide cross-region case filing services, and facilitate the remote and coordinated handling of cross-region cases, so as to improve off-site litigation. We should continue to build a public legal services system, accelerate the integration of legal resources including lawyers, notarization, judicial authentication, arbitration, judicial offices and mediation, so as to establish an all-encompassing legal services network that is accessible anywhere and anytime. We should work faster to build systems protecting the security and safety of overseas Chinese citizens and entities, and safeguard their lawful rights and interests.

We should take a clear stand in giving top priority to raising political awareness, and work hard to build a strong contingent of legal professionals that can be relied on by the Party Central Committee and can meet the needs of the people. We should emphasize theoretical education, and guide police officers to study and thoroughly understand the Thought on Socialism with Chinese Characteristics for a New Era. This will help them maintain their political commitment, think in terms of the general picture, follow the core leadership of the CPC Central Committee, and act in accordance with its requirements. It will give them full confidence in the path, theory, system and culture of socialism with Chinese characteristics, and ensure that they will resolutely adhere to the Two Upholds, and never waver in building and safeguarding Chinese socialism. Judicial, prosecuting and public security departments should be strict with themselves, remove all irregularities despite pains, and ferret out any rotten apples with the strongest will and the most resolute actions.

All judicial, prosecuting and public security bodies should attach greater importance to developing their professional abilities. This requires an emphasis on combat effectiveness, practical usefulness and real effects, so as to comprehensively improve the officials' ability to apply laws and policies, prevent and control risks, engage with the people, utilize technology, and guide public opinion. Among our state agencies, judicial, prosecuting and public security systems are the ones which contribute the most and sacrifice the most during times of peace. We need to treat them with special care, and encourage and support people working in these systems, ensuring their legitimate income and wellbeing, giving them humanistic care, and doing our best to help them solve their problems, so that they can fully, actively and confidently apply themselves to their work.

We need to strengthen the leadership and ranks of the judicial, prosecuting and public security systems and promote the development of primary-level Party organizations. Party organizations and leaders at all levels should support the work of judicial, prosecuting and public security departments and support them in wielding power independently and impartially. All Party committees and their commissions for judicial, prosecuting and public security affairs at various levels should give priority to steering political orientation, coordinating departments' duties, commanding judicial, prosecuting and public security work, strengthening training of officials working in these systems, supervising the performance of their duties in accordance with the law, and creating an environment for impartial law enforcement. They should improve the systems and mechanisms for supervision on political integrity, maintenance of public order, law enforcement, and discipline and conduct.

Harmony Between Humanity and Nature

Principles to Apply in Protecting the Eco-Environment*

May 18, 2018

Protecting the eco-environment is a major political issue related to the mission and purpose of the CPC; it is also a major social issue related to people's wellbeing. The Party has always attached great importance to this issue, and established resource conservation and environmental protection as a fundamental national policy, and sustainable development as a national strategy. As economic and social development proceeds, our comprehension of the overall plan for building socialism with Chinese characteristics has evolved, from the Two Progresses[1] (in the 1980s), to the Three-sphere Plan[2] (in the 1990s), to the Four-sphere Plan[3] (in 2007), and to the Five-sphere Integrated Plan today. The process represents a major practical and theoretical innovation, which has brought about a profound change in China's philosophy and model of development.

The principal challenge facing our society is the gap between unbalanced and inadequate development and the ever-growing expectation of the people for a better life. To meet the people's need for a quality eco-environment has become an important element of this challenge. The general public is looking forward to a rapid improvement. Their aspiration for a better life is the goal of our Party, and solving their most pressing and immediate concerns is our mission. The people's support is our top political priority. Therefore, we should respond to the people's opinions, hopes, and concerns, promoting environmental protection, preserving the ecosystems, and providing more quality eco-products.

---

* Part of the speech at the National Conference on Eco-environmental Protection.

Humanity is a community that rises and falls as one. Protecting the eco-environment is a common challenge and a joint responsibility for the whole world. Success in this endeavor will be good for Chinese socialism; otherwise it will become a pretext for forces with ulterior motives to attack us.

Since humanity entered the industrial age, rapid traditional industrialization, while bringing about great material wealth, has accelerated the consumption of natural resources, and broken the original cycle and balance of the ecosystems, resulting in a tense relationship between humanity and nature. Since the 1930s, a number of environmental incidents have occurred in Western countries, causing huge losses, which have shocked the world and triggered a profound reflection on the development model of capitalism.

In the process of more than 200 years of modernization, industrialization was realized in no more than 30 countries with a total population of no more than 1 billion. If we promote eco-environmental progress and build China, the largest developing country with a population of more than 1.3 billion, into a modern socialist country that is prosperous, strong, democratic, culturally advanced, harmonious and beautiful, the influence of our achievement will be worldwide.

Since the 18th CPC National Congress in 2012, our Party has put forward a series of new concepts, ideas and strategies in answering the important theoretical and practical questions of why to pursue eco-environmental progress, what the goal is, and how to achieve it. In order to succeed in this endeavor in the new era, we must adhere to the following principles:

First, we must pursue the harmonious coexistence between humanity and nature. Humanity and nature are a community of life. There is no substitute for the current eco-environment. When we use it, we take it for granted. But once damaged, it will struggle to recover. "Heaven and earth coexist with me; all things and I are one."[4] "Heaven and earth do not speak, yet the seasons change and all things grow."[5] When human beings make rational use of nature and protect it, the rewards of nature are often generous; when human beings rudely exploit and plunder nature, the punishment is bound to be merciless. It is an immutable law that harm caused by human actions to nature will eventually hurt human beings themselves. "All things must be in harmony with nature to grow, and obtain from nature to thrive."[6] There are many vivid examples. One of them is Dujiangyan, a large-scale water conservancy project on the Minjiang River near the city of Chengdu on the Chengdu Plain, in southwest China's Sichuan Province. When it was first built in the Warring States Period more than 2,000 years ago, the flood patterns of the Minjiang River and the topography of the Chengdu Plain were important factors to be considered. The project is still in use today – it has benefited generations of local residents.

In the whole process of economic development, we must adhere to the principle of giving priority to conservation, protection, and the restoration of nature. We should not think about taking from nature without giving back, developing without protecting, and consuming without restoring. We should protect the eco-environment as we protect our eyes, and cherish it as we cherish our own lives. We should lay the groundwork for long-term benefits, take concrete steps to protect nature, restore the ecosystems, and create a beautiful environment. We should make it possible for people to enjoy the natural landscape and retain their love of nature, while returning serenity, harmony and beauty back to nature.

Second, clear waters and green mountains are invaluable assets. This is an important concept of development and a major principle behind our modernization drive. It emphasizes the relationship between economic development and eco-environmental protection – this means preserving and developing productive forces. It points out a new way to coordinate development and protection. Clear waters and green mountains are not only natural and ecological wealth, but also social and economic wealth. Protecting the eco-environment means protecting nature's value and adding value to nature's capital, protecting the potential of economic and social development, and giving full play to the ecological, social and economic effects of nature.

Eco-environmental problems are after all the results of our development model and our way of life. In order to fundamentally solve the problems, we must put into practice the vision of innovative, coordinated, green, open and shared development, and accelerate the formation of spatial configurations, industrial structures, production models, and lifestyles that favor resource conservation and environmental protection. We must also keep economic and human activities within the carrying capacity of natural resources and the eco-environment, leaving time and space for nature to recuperate.

We should move faster to draw and enforce red lines for the protection of the ecosystems, the quality of the environment, and rational resource utilization. Crossing these red lines by continuing the extensive growth model and through unlimited plundering of existing resources at the expense of future generations will no longer be tolerated. To enforce these red lines, it is necessary to establish a strict and unified system to manage, with consistent standards, all major environmental spaces. By doing so, we will ensure that ecological functions will not weaken and environmental areas will not decrease – we will continue to conserve these areas. Environmental quality cannot be allowed to drop further; it must only improve. Local Party and government officials must be held accountable if their regions' ecosystems are seriously damaged and their environment deteriorates. As to resource utilization, we must ensure proper exploitation within the bearing capacity of natural resources, taking into consideration not only the needs of humans and of today, but also the needs of nature and of the future.

Third, a good eco-environment is the most inclusive form of public wellbeing. We should choose to do the things that win the approval of the people, and avoid doing things that they oppose. A good environment is part of the public's wellbeing; green mountains and blue skies bring delight and happiness to the people. Economic development contributes to improving people's wellbeing, so does eco-environmental protection. We should create more material and cultural wealth to meet the people's growing expectation for a better life, and effectively preserve the ecosystems to meet their growing expectation for a beautiful environment. We must pursue environmental benefits for the people with the emphasis on solving prominent problems that threaten their health. We must accelerate this work, provide more quality eco-products, and realize social fairness and justice.

Eco-environmental progress is a common cause that requires the participation and contribution of the general public. Its results will also be shared by the people. To build a beautiful China, we should transform our efforts into conscientious action on the part of all. Each and every individual is a protector, builder and beneficiary, and no one should be a bystander, an outsider or a critic. No one should remain aloof and pay only lip service. We must enhance people's awareness of resource conservation, environmental protection, and a healthy ecosystem. We need to cultivate eco-friendly ethics and codes of conduct, launch nationwide green environment campaigns, and encourage the whole of society to contribute to environmental protection by reducing pollution and consumption of energy and other resources.

Fourth, mountains, rivers, forests, farmlands, lakes and grasslands are a community of life. An ecosystem is an integrated natural system of interdependent and closely-related ecological chains. The lifeline of humans rests with farmlands, that of farmlands with water, that of water with mountains, that of mountains with earth, and that of earth with forests and grasslands. This community of life is the material basis for the survival and development of humanity. We should take a broad and long-term view. We must try to avoid earning a little only to lose a lot, or attending to one thing and losing sight of others. Otherwise, our actions are bound to cause systematic and long-lasting damage.

In order to seek a new way of governance from a systematic and broader perspective, we must no longer take a fragmented and palliative approach that only treats the symptoms, nor can we care for our own business and hold others back. Instead we must make an overall plan that takes all relevant factors into consideration, and adopt multiple measures simultaneously to advance eco-environmental progress in all respects. For instance, to achieve the best results in systematic control of water pollution, it is necessary to consider a comprehensive range of factors concerning a body of water – river banks on both sides, upstream and downstream, surface water and groundwater, rivers, oceans, aquatic ecosystems, water resources, pollution prevention and control, and environmental protection.

We will further integrate the protection and restoration of mountains, rivers, forests, farmlands, lakes and grasslands, carry out large-scale afforestation campaigns, and speed up the comprehensive control of soil erosion, desertification, and stony desertification. In developing the Yangtze River Economic Belt, we will strive to step up conservation of the Yangtze River, stop over-development, and prioritize environmental protection and green development. All economic activities involving the Yangtze River must be conditional on not damaging the river's ecosystem.

Fifth, we should protect the eco-environment with the strictest regulations and laws. Eco-environmental protection relies on laws and regulations. Most of the outstanding environmental problems in China result from incomplete systems, the lack of appropriate rules and enforceable laws, inadequate implementation, and ineffective punishment. We must speed up institutional innovation, put in place more regulations, improve support systems, and strengthen their implementation. Regulations must be made mandatory, so that they become a powerful deterrent. We must use rules to supervise officials and their exercise of power in protecting blue skies and increasing green coverage. We must associate power with responsibility and accountability, so as to ensure the implementation of the CPC Central Committee's policies and plans for building an eco-civilization.

A country is strong when its law enforcement is strong; it is weak when its law enforcement is weak. The power of laws and decrees can only be established through their enforcement. The efficacy of rules lies in their implementation. We have introduced a series of reform measures and related rules. They must be carried out as strictly as the central inspection of environmental protection. The binding force and authority of the institutions must be firmly established, and selective implementation and perfunctory enforcement must be banned.

It is necessary to implement the accountability system among leading officials for protecting our eco-environment, and strictly assess their performance. Those who make ill-judged decisions that cause harmful consequences must be held accountable, and for life.

We must never be lenient in punishing actions that damage our eco-environment. We will strike hard at typical cases that cause damage to the eco-environment and send out the signal that the perpetrators will be severely punished. Anyone who damages the environment – no matter where or when – shall face the consequences. The institutions must not become a "paper tiger".

Sixth, we should work together to promote a global eco-civilization. The eco-environment bears on the future of humanity. Building a green home is our common dream. Protecting the environment and dealing with climate change requires the joint efforts of all countries. No country can distance itself or remain immune from such challenges.

China has become an important participant, contributor and leader in promoting a global eco-civilization. We advocate jointly building a clean and beautiful world that respects nature and favors green development. China will be heavily involved in global environmental governance, have a bigger say and greater influence, play an active part in the transformation of the international order, and help form global solutions to eco-environmental protection and to sustainable development. We must always adopt the environment-friendly approach and play a constructive role in international cooperation on climate change. We will promote the philosophy and practice of eco-environmental progress in the Belt and Road Initiative to benefit the peoples of all countries along the Belt and Road.

Notes

[1] This refers to China's plan for material and cultural progress.

[2] This refers to China's plan for economic, political and cultural progress.

[3] This refers to China's plan for economic, political, cultural and social progress.

[4] *Zhuang Zi.*

[5] Li Bai: "Letter to Pei Kuan, Governor Secretary of Anzhou Prefecture" (Shang An Zhou Pei Zhang Shi Shu).

[6] Xun Zi: *Xun Zi*. Xun Zi (c. 325-238 BC) was a philosopher, thinker and educator in the Warring States Period.

Win the Battle Against Pollution*

May 18, 2018

In the report to the 19th CPC National Congress in 2017, I said that we must focus on priorities, address shortcomings, and shore up points of weakness, and emphasized that we must take firm steps to forestall and defuse major risks, carry out targeted poverty alleviation, and prevent and control pollution, so that we build a moderately prosperous society that earns the people's approval and stands the test of time. Now we should concentrate our strengths and enact more effective policy measures to win this tough battle.

First, we should develop a system for creating an eco-civilization. We should resolve environmental problems at this critical juncture of history. For this purpose, we must foster a culture promoting eco-values, an economy highlighting eco-friendly industries and industrialization of environmental protection activities, a responsibility system for achieving the goal of improving the eco-environment, a complete support system for ensuring eco-environmental protection through modernized governance, and a security system prioritizing well-functioning ecosystems and effective control of environmental risks.

By accelerating the pace of this work we can achieve a remarkable improvement in the quality and efficiency of China's economic development. By 2035 we will put in place a land-use planning system, industrial structure, mode of production, and way of life, all of which are resource-saving and environment-friendly. The eco-environment will be much better, the basic modernization of China's eco-environmental governance system and capacity will be achieved, and the goal of building a beautiful China will be generally realized.

---

* Part of the speech at the National Conference on Eco-environmental Protection.

By the middle of the century, we will develop China into a modern socialist country that is prosperous, strong, democratic, culturally advanced, harmonious, and beautiful. By the end of this stage, we will reach new heights in every dimension of material, political, cultural, social, and eco-environmental progress. A green mode of development and a green way of life will be established, characterized by harmonious coexistence between humanity and nature. Our national eco-environmental governance system and capacity will be fully modernized, and we will complete the task of building a beautiful China.

Second, we should push for green development across the board. Green symbolizes life and nature. A healthy eco-environment is the foundation for the better life that the people are anticipating. Green development is a key component of China's new vision of innovative, coordinated, green, open and shared development. These five concepts interact with and complement each other. Green development is a must for profound reform in all respects and for building a high-quality, modern economy. The goal is to change the traditional economic model characterized by massive production, massive consumption and massive emissions, so that resources, production and consumption are in balance. As a result, social and economic development can operate in tandem with environmental protection, and humanity and nature can coexist in harmony.

A green development model is the fundamental solution to pollution. Only by reducing pollutant discharges at source can we make significant improvements to the eco-environment. We should focus on adjusting the economic structure and energy mix, optimizing the industrial and land-use configuration, strengthening industries, and stepping up environmental protection in all respects from production to consumption. A change in the economic structure and energy mix can promote economic growth and reduce pollutant discharges. We should conduct environmental assessments of major economic policies and industrial projects, and make the best use of land and land resources by adjusting industrial development plans in regions and major river basins. We should foster stronger energy-saving and eco-friendly industries, clean production industries, clean energy industries, highly-efficient agriculture, advanced manufacturing, and modern service industries. We should encourage resource conservation and recycling across the board, and adopt circular use of resources in production and in everyday life.

Green ways of life can be applied to food and clothing, housing and transport. We encourage simple, moderate, green and low-carbon ways of life, and oppose extravagance and excessive consumption. We should launch initiatives to make Party and government institutions more conservation-conscious, and develop eco-friendly families, schools, communities and transport services. By embracing green living, we can help make our mode of production more eco-friendly.

Third, we should give top priority to addressing eco-environmental problems in improving people's lives. We shall spare no effort to do the smallest things if they benefit the people, and steer clear of even the smallest things that might harm the people. We must fight a tough battle against pollution and secure major victories, concentrating our efforts on resolving prominent environmental problems that directly affect people's lives. Severe air pollution, black, fetid water bodies, piled-up trash, and a deteriorating rural environment are major and immediate public concerns. These problems, severely disturbing people's work and life, are the source of many public complaints and can even disturb the social order. We must overcome these problems. We should leverage our strengths, rally all possible forces, and get everyone involved. In this tough battle against pollution, we need to gain one success after another with the support of the people.

To improve the air quality is our top priority. It is an earnest expectation of the Chinese people and also a promise we have made to the international community as hosts of the 2022 Beijing Winter Olympic Games. In curbing air pollution, we should first and foremost target the Beijing-Tianjin-Hebei Region and its surrounding area, the Yangtze River Delta, and the Fenhe-Weihe River Plain, focusing particularly on Beijing. A substantial improvement in air quality is an unconditional requirement. We need to reinforce a concerted effort to prevent and control air pollution, putting an end to severe pollution and bringing back blue skies.

We must restructure industries, reducing excess and outdated capacity and creating new growth drivers. We should enforce upgrading in badly-polluting sectors to achieve compliance with environmental standards, and achieve ultra-low emissions in thermal power, steel and other industries. We will tighten up regulation of enterprises that do not comply with national industrial policies or local industrial planning, have not yet acquired the approval of relevant authorities, or do not meet environmental standards. Depending on their respective conditions, some of these enterprises will be closed, some reformed and upgraded, and some moved to industrial parks.

We need to change our energy mix, reducing coal use and developing clean energy. We need to take multiple measures simultaneously in conformity with local conditions. We have resolved to provide winter heating from clean energy sources in northern China, replacing coal with natural gas and/or electricity wherever it is appropriate. We need to establish a system for the production, supply, storage and sale of natural gas as soon as possible, and optimize distribution of the sources of natural gas. We need to enhance connectivity across different gas pipeline networks, and guarantee gas supply. After replacing coal with electricity and natural gas, we need to provide subsidies and favorable prices to ensure they are accessible and affordable. We need to make greater efforts to eliminate individual coal-fired boilers, and suspend operations of outdated coal-fired power plants that are sources of serious pollution and quicken the pace of their transformation and upgrading.

We must restructure transport, reducing the use of road, increasing the use of rail, and cutting down emissions from diesel-powered freight vehicles. In order to improve their performance and efficiency, we need to upgrade, integrate and scale up freight transport businesses, and encourage "chain-store" type operations.

We should continue to implement our action plans for preventing and controlling water pollution. We will give priorities to protecting water sources, cleaning up black, fetid water bodies in urban areas, improving the Bohai Sea water through comprehensive measures, and protecting and restoring the Yangtze River ecosystem. Our goal is to guarantee drinking water safety. In water pollution control, we have many problems to resolve. One of the most pressing tasks is to improve our facilities for the collection and disposal of urban sewage. We have so much to improve in this regard. According to the reports from the Central Environmental Protection Inspection Teams, discharge of untreated sewage is still prevalent in some of the municipalities directly under the central government, in developed coastal provinces, and in special economic zones. To realize full coverage of the piped sewage network, and full collection and disposal of urban sewage, we should set a "must-reach" goal and fulfill it by all possible means. Failing this, our efforts of cleaning up would be wasted.

We should fully enforce the action plan on soil pollution control, and promulgate and implement a law on the prevention and control of soil pollution. We should target key regions, industries and pollutants to enhance soil pollution control and soil restoration and forestall risks effectively, so as to provide safe food and safe residence for the people. We will sharply reduce the variety and quantity of imported solid wastes prior to imposing a total ban on all imports of garbage. Environmental violations concerning hazardous wastes will be harshly punished, and we will stop the illegal transfer, dumping, utilization and disposal of hazardous wastes.

The rural environment has a direct impact on food and water supplies as well as on the urban environment. We should adjust agricultural input, reducing the use of chemical fertilizers and pesticides, increasing the use of organic fertilizers, and improving the recycling and disposal of plastic mulch waste. We should continue to improve rural living environments of all the villages across the country. Our main tasks are to improve garbage collection and sewage disposal, and build sufficient clean and safe toilets. By doing so, we will build the countryside into a big garden full of birds and flowers.

Eco-environmental conservation and pollution prevention and control are inseparable. The two function like a fraction, with the latter as the numerator, and the former the denominator. To better protect the environment, we must minimize the numerator by reducing pollutant discharges and maximize the denominator by enlarging the environmental carrying capacity. We should ensure that no red lines for protecting the ecosystems are ever crossed, systematically monitor the conservation of mountains, rivers, forests, farmlands, lakes and grasslands, and strengthen oversight of environmental issues at every stage. Rather than redeveloping urban land made available after the demolition of illegal structures, we should turn it into green spaces where the people can enjoy their leisure.

Fourth, we should forestall eco-environmental risks effectively. Eco-security is a key element of national security and an important guarantee for sound and sustained social and economic development. "Nip the problem in the bud when it is in the making; prepare yourself for risks yet to emerge."[1] We should be highly alert to the accumulation and spread of all kinds of eco-environmental risks, and be prepared to meet the challenges they pose.

We should bring eco-environmental risks under management on a regular basis, and build a multi-tiered risk management system covering the whole process of social and economic development. We need to impose tight controls on waste incineration and paraxylene pollution, prevent and resolve NIMBY ("not in my back yard") problems concerning projects with a significant environmental impact, and improve our emergency response capacity for environmental accidents. We need to enhance nuclear and radiation safety regulation and supervision, and improve our regulatory and supervisory mechanisms and capacity, in order to ensure absolute safety.

Fifth, we should promote eco-environmental progress through further institutional reform. This is an important part of China's deeper comprehensive reform. With the goal of resolving prominent environmental problems, we should ensure the implementation of existing measures and formulate new plans in a timely manner. We must see that our measures concerning institutional reform for eco-environmental progress are put in place and play their role. The Central Environmental Protection Inspection Teams should strengthen their authority, appoint capable personnel, and make further progress. We should explore sustainable ways to realize the value of eco-products under the guidance of the government, with the participation of business and all other sectors of society, and through market-based operation. To this end, we should launch pilot programs first to gather experience. We should improve our systems for assessing the honesty and accuracy of claims about performance in environmental protection, for ensuring mandatory release of environmental information, and for imposing severe punishments on environmental violations.

In the current round of reform involving Party and state institutions, the CPC Central Committee has decided to establish the Ministry of Ecology and Environment. We have two considerations: First, we must integrate government functions in pollution prevention and control to provide effective institutional support for this tough task. Second, in terms of environmental conservation and restoration we must strengthen unified regulation and supervision of all things above and below ground, onshore and in water, on land and at sea, and in urban and rural areas, targeting both carbon monoxide and carbon dioxide emissions, and ensure that red lines for protecting the ecosystems are not crossed.

Relevant authorities must perform their duties, formulate uniform policies, plans and standards, and work concertedly in monitoring and evaluation, in oversight and law enforcement, in inspection and in enforcing accountability. To establish unified law enforcement in environmental protection we need to reorganize law enforcement agencies responsible for environmental protection and streamline their responsibilities, in accordance with the principle of shortening their chains of command and improving their efficiency. We need to improve the mechanisms for managing the eco-environment of regions, river basins and sea bodies, accelerate our pilot programs on establishing transregional environmental protection agencies, and integrate the atmospheric environment management responsibilities of relevant central departments and local governments. We will establish regulatory and law enforcement authorities for river basin environment to achieve better synergy. We need to improve marine environmental management mechanisms by setting up regulatory institutions responsible for different sea bodies.

Sixth, we should improve eco-environmental governance. This is a systematic program that requires multiple combined approaches, involving administration, market, law and technology. We should fully leverage the market to boost environmental protection, and direct more private capital into this area. We should improve resource and environment pricing mechanisms, and include environmental costs into the cost of economic activities. We should use various means to support the cooperation between government and private capital on environmental protection. In protecting the environment, we must pay out every penny required. We must ensure that our investments in pollution control are commensurate with the level of difficulties of the tasks concerned. We should devote more effort to key scientific research projects such as identifying the causes of severe air pollution and curbing such pollution, and the comprehensive environmental governance of the Beijing-Tianjin-Hebei Region. We need to carry out specialized and forward-looking research on the control of ozone, volatile organic compounds and new pollutants. We need to conduct countermeasure studies on major environmental issues having a vital bearing on social and economic development, and encourage the application of research results, to support informed and effective decision-making, environmental management, targeted pollution control and public services.

To demonstrate that China is a major and responsible country and to build a global community of shared future, we should actively respond to climate change as a national strategy, and push for the establishment of a fair and rational global climate governance system directed towards cooperation and win-win results.

Notes

[1] Liu Xu *et al.*: *Old Book of Tang (Jiu Tang Shu)*. Liu Xu (887-946) was an official and historian during the Five Dynasties.

Build a Green and Beautiful Homeland for All[*]

April 28, 2019

Your Excellencies Heads of State and Government, and your spouses,
Your Excellencies Secretary General of the Bureau International des Expositions and President of the International Association of Horticultural Producers,
Your Excellencies Diplomatic Envoys and Representatives of International Organizations,
Ladies and gentlemen,
Dear friends,

"The land bathes in the spring sunshine, and the wind sends the aromas of grass and flowers."[1] It is apt to quote these lines from a classic poem to depict Beijing in April – spring has come back and all lives are reviving. I am pleased to be here with all of you at the foot of the Great Wall by the Guishui River to witness the opening of the 2019 Beijing International Horticultural Exhibition.

On behalf of the Chinese government and people, and also in my own name, I would like to extend our warmest welcome to all of you, and our heartfelt thanks to all friends who are supporting and participating in this exhibition.

Themed "Live Green, Live Better", the Beijing International Horticultural Exhibition aims to promote respect for the environment and a better life in harmony with nature. It is our hope that this expo park, designed to blend into its splendid surrounding landscape, will demonstrate to people in all corners of the world China's vision of green development.

---

[*] Speech at the opening ceremony of the International Horticultural Exhibition 2019 in Beijing.

Ladies and gentlemen,
Dear friends,

Home to the Chinese nation, this vast and splendid land of China has nurtured a brilliant 5,000-year civilization and its philosophy of harmony between humanity and nature.

Advancing eco-environmental progress has become part of China's overall plan for national development, and building a beautiful country continues to inspire the Chinese people. As China steps up its conservation efforts, a country with more blue skies, lush mountains and lucid waters will emerge.

The rise or fall of a society is dependent on its relationship with nature if we see it from a historical perspective. Industrialization, while generating unprecedented material wealth, has caused serious damage to nature. Development without thought to the future of the Earth is not a sustainable way to progress – like killing the goose that lays the golden eggs or draining the pond to get all the fish. Green development that focuses on harmony with nature and eco-friendly progress shows the way to the future.

Ladies and gentlemen,
Dear friends,

We see myriads of glittering stars when we look up at the night sky, but the Earth is the only home we have. We must protect this planet as we protect our own eyes, and cherish Mother Nature the way we treasure life. We must preserve what gives our planet life and embrace green development.

– We should pursue harmony between humanity and nature. Lush mountains, vast tracts of forest, blue skies, green fields, singing birds, and blossoming flowers offer more than visual beauty. They are the basis for our future development. Nature punishes those who exploit and plunder it brutally, and rewards those who use and protect it carefully. We must maintain the overall balance of the Earth's ecosystems, not only to ensure that future generations can continue to access material wealth, but also to protect their right to enjoy the wonders of the natural world.

– We ought to achieve economic prosperity through green development. Green is the color of nature. I have always said that clear waters and green mountains are invaluable assets, and that eco-environmental improvement leads to greater productivity. Healthy ecosystems promise boundless economic potential, generate steady returns, and contribute to economic and social sustainability.

– We need to foster a love of nature. Well-measured exploration and use of resources is the key to eco-environmental progress. We should encourage a healthy lifestyle that is simple, green and low-carbon, and reject extravagant and excessive practices. Additionally, it is essential to raise people's awareness of environmental and ecological protection, and develop an environmental governance system in which the whole of society participates, so that the eco-environment will become a primary focus of daily life. We need to advocate the value of green development grounded in respect and care for nature so that blue skies, green fields and clear waters will be deeply cherished by all.

– We should adopt a sound approach. In environmental governance we should follow the laws of nature, make holistic and well-informed plans, do what is appropriate in light of local circumstances, and create harmonious ecosystems in which all elements coexist in tandem with each other. Human wisdom is essential to sustaining the dynamism of the Earth, our common homeland. Although environmental governance is an arduous task, we will ultimately obtain the expected results as long as we take the right steps. We must press ahead with a sense of urgency and perseverance to achieve our goals.

– We need to join hands to meet common challenges. A beautiful homeland is the shared aspiration of humanity. In the face of environmental challenges, all countries are a community with a common stake, and no country can remain aloof. Only together can we effectively address climate change, marine pollution, biological conservation, and other global environmental issues, and achieve the UN 2030 Agenda for Sustainable Development. Only concerted efforts can drive home the idea of green development and bring about steady progress in building a global eco-civilization.

Ladies and gentlemen,

Dear friends,

Many of the guests here also attended the Second Belt and Road Forum for International Cooperation which closed yesterday. We reached an important consensus at the forum that our Belt and Road cooperation will build a road of green development, in addition to a road of open development. China is ready to work with all other countries to create a better homeland and a global community of shared future.

Ladies and gentlemen,

Dear friends,

Every generation has its own mission. Our efforts to conserve our ecosystems will benefit not only this generation, but many more to come. By acting now on our own initiative, we will pass on the baton of conservation to future generations.

I now declare the 2019 International Horticultural Exhibition open.

Notes

[1] Du Fu: "Two Quatrains" (Jue Ju Er Shou).

Major Goals for Eco-Conservation and Quality Development of the Yellow River Basin*

September 18, 2019

I have pointed out that to harness the Yellow River, priority should be given to eco-environmental conservation and the key lies in eco-environmental governance. We need to protect mountains, waters, forests, farmlands, lakes, and grasslands, and address all degradation at source in a coordinated way. We should strengthen coordination and cooperation in our work to promote high-quality development of the Yellow River Basin. Lucid waters and lush mountains are invaluable assets. We must act on this understanding, advance eco-environmental conservation as a priority, and pursue green development. We should use the water resources of the Yellow River as its capacity permits, and adopt differentiated measures appropriate to local conditions. We need to make comprehensive plans and joint efforts to protect the ecosystem along the upper and lower reaches, the trunk stream and tributaries, and along both banks of the Yellow River. We should better protect and restore its ecosystem, keep the Yellow River harnessed, promote high-quality development of the Yellow River Basin, improve local people's lives, and preserve and keep alive the Yellow River culture. By making these efforts, we can make the Yellow River deliver more benefits to our people.

To be specific, we need to do the following:

First, strengthen eco-environmental protection. We should take into account the different conditions on the upper, middle and lower reaches of the Yellow River and protect its ecosystem as a whole. In

---

* Part of the speech at the Forum on the Eco-conservation and Quality Development of the Yellow River Basin.

the upper reaches, we need to launch a number of key programs for protecting, restoring and developing the local ecosystem and improving water conservation, particularly in the Sanjiangyuan Natural Reserve in Qinghai, the Qilian Mountains area bordering Qinghai and Gansu, and the Gannan water conservation area in Gansu. In the middle reaches, we need to focus on soil and water conservation and pollution control. Conserving soil and water does not just mean digging pits and planting trees. As the Loess Plateau has less rainfall, before taking action, we should find out whether the land is suitable for tree-planting and what varieties are appropriate. Where conditions permit, more rainfed terraces and silt trap dams should be built. In some places, we need to improve natural eco-restoration, reduce human interference, and thus improve the climatic conditions there. We must step up efforts to clean up severely polluted tributaries such as the Fenhe River. In the lower reaches, the Yellow River Delta is the most intact wetland ecosystem in China's warm temperate zone. We must keep it well protected, maintain a sound river ecosystem, and increase biodiversity.

Second, keep the Yellow River harnessed. The river contains too much sediment. The imbalance in its sediment-water ratio is the root cause of complicated problems causing natural disasters along the river. Although the Yellow River has not caused many problems in recent years, we must not slacken our efforts, and we should do more to remove potential hazards. When the Yellow River is harnessed, China is serene. With this in mind, we must make every effort to adjust the sediment-water ratio of the Yellow River. We need to improve sediment monitoring and resolve the problem whereby too many government departments are involved in water management. We need to adopt a holistic approach to cleaning up the watercourses and mudflats, mitigate sedimentation in the lower reaches, and ensure safety along both banks of the Yellow River.

Third, promote efficient and economical utilization of water resources. The Yellow River's water supply is limited. Eco-conservation programs need water; economic development needs water; and people need water in their everyday lives. We must be keenly aware that water is not a limitless natural resource, and we should utilize the Yellow River as its capacity permits. We must make plans for population distribution as well as urban and industrial development in accordance with the water resources available. We must discourage unnecessary water demands, develop water-saving industries and technologies, promote water saving in agriculture, and encourage the public to save water, so as to stop wasteful water consumption and ensure efficient and economical water consumption.

Fourth, promote high-quality development of the Yellow River Basin. At the fifth meeting of the Central Commission for Finance and Economy on August 26, I emphasized the need to encourage different regions to leverage their comparative strengths and enhance the dynamics for quality development. The local governments along the Yellow River should act in keeping with local conditions, use the water and mountain resources, grow crops, and develop agriculture, industry or business as conditions permit, so as to blaze a new trail of high-quality development with distinctive local features. However, in Sanjiangyuan, the Qilian Mountains and other important eco-functional areas, priority should be placed not on industry and business, but on protection of the local ecosystem, conservation of water resources, and development of more eco-products. In the Hetao Irrigation Area in Inner Mongolia, Fenhe-Weihe River Plain and other major grain production areas, more should be done to develop modern agriculture and improve the quality of farm products, thereby contributing to national food security. Regional hub cities and other localities with better economic conditions should pursue efficient development and improve their economic and population carrying capacity. Poor areas should improve infrastructure and public services and ensure people's wellbeing. The Yellow River Basin should take an active part in the Belt and Road Initiative and pursue high-standard opening up to promote reform and development.

Fifth, preserve, promote, and keep alive the Yellow River culture. The Yellow River culture, which is an important part of Chinese civilization, is the origin and soul of the Chinese nation. We should preserve in a systematic way the Yellow River cultural heritage, an invaluable legacy from our ancestors. We need to explore the worth of the Yellow River culture in our era, promote the Yellow River culture, pass down our cultural traditions, and build stronger cultural confidence to realize the Chinese Dream of national rejuvenation.

The People's Armed Forces

Strengthen the Party's Leadership and Organizations in the Military*

August 17, 2018

Strengthening the Party's leadership and organizations in the military in the new era is a prerequisite for implementing the great new project of strengthening the Party, and for building a strong country with a strong military. The military must implement the Thought on Socialism with Chinese Characteristics for a New Era and the guiding principles of the 19th CPC National Congress in 2017, the Party's philosophy on strengthening the military, and the general requirements for strengthening the Party for the new era. The military must implement our Party's organizational principle, uphold the Party's absolute leadership, ensure the Party's full and rigorous self-governance, and focus on improving combat readiness and winning wars. The military must provide a firm political guarantee for achieving our Party's goal of building strong armed forces and fulfilling their missions in the new era.

After the 18th CPC National Congress in 2012, the CPC Central Committee and the Central Military Commission (CMC) set about strengthening the military and its political governance. In particular, the Gutian Conference on Military Political Work was held in 2014 to emphasize the need to promote our Party's full and rigorous self-governance and govern the military with strict discipline in every respect. As was decided at the meeting, we must:

- uphold absolute Party leadership over the military;

---

* Main points of the speech at a meeting of the Central Military Commission on strengthening the Party.

- enhance political education to improve Party conduct in the military;
- preserve the unity of the military through theoretical education;
- strengthen Party organizations in the military;
- set up qualification requirements for military officers;
- improve Party conduct and enforce Party discipline;
- fight corruption and punish vice;
- lead the military in maintaining our original aspiration, abandoning outdated practices, and creating new institutions; and
- ensure Party self-governance with stricter, harsher, and more punitive discipline.

Through these efforts, the Party's leadership and organizations have been strengthened, as a firm political guarantee for the historic achievements and changes required in building a strong military. We must review experience and consolidate current outcomes.

Strengthening the Party's leadership and organizations in the military is key to the long-term stability of the Party and the country. To realize the Party's goal of building a strong military in the new era, to transform the military into world-class armed forces, and to complete the mission entrusted by the Party and the people for the new era, we must make sustained efforts to resolve the problems and weaknesses in Party leadership, and do more solid work to strengthen the Party organizations in the military at all levels.

Upholding absolute Party leadership over the military is the top priority. We must strengthen the Party politically, and guide the military in upholding the authority of the Central Committee and its centralized, unified leadership, and in obeying the command of the Central Committee and the CMC. We must continue to educate our officers and soldiers with the Thought on Socialism with Chinese Characteristics for a New Era and our Party's philosophy on strengthening the military for the new era, as a foundation for maintaining the military's absolute loyalty to our Party.

We must implement the leaders' responsibility system under the unified, collective leadership of Party committees, ensuring that all work is done under the leadership of Party committees and all major issues are decided by the Party committees after discussion. We must improve the institutional framework for Party leadership in the military to make Party affairs and other political work in the military more procedure-based.

Our Party's strength comes from its organizations. The military led by strong Party organizations must be powerful. In the armed forces, the Party's organizational principle serves its political principle. The military must focus on improving its combat readiness and winning wars as its major responsibility. We must strengthen Party organizations at all levels in the military, enhance their leadership, organizational capability and performance, and try to win wars based on our Party's political and organizational strength. The military must be adapted to its reformed institutions and functions, under a new structure with the CMC exercising overall leadership, the theater commands responsible for military operations, and the services focusing on developing their capabilities. Military Party organizations at all levels must identify their functions, improve their structure, institutions and mechanisms, and their way of exercising leadership, so as to fully perform their organizational functions.

Party committees at the army level and above are important military Party organizations. They must take a clear political stance and be more capable politically. They must be better able to devise strategies, prepare for real combat, reform and innovate, give effective command, and implement decisions and plans.

Success in building a powerful military lies in capable military personnel. We need to attach greater importance to the training of officers and professionals, with a focus on training competent officers who are loyal to our Party and our people, have moral integrity, and demonstrate a keen sense of responsibility, and on using outstanding professionals who are resolved to strengthen the military and win wars. In selecting and appointing officers, we must emphasize both integrity and ability, with the former taking precedence. We must make good use of the talent needed by a strong military, and place the right people in the right posts. In accordance with the strategy of the Central Committee, we must formulate and implement plans for training outstanding young officers and give promising officers special training in the forefront of our military combat and war readiness, assigning them with urgent, difficult, dangerous, or weighty tasks.

Human resources are a source of strategic wealth for strengthening and developing the armed forces. We need to build a new system for training military personnel, which consists of military school education, field training, and professional military education, with a focus on training commanders for joint operations, new types of combat personnel, high-caliber personnel for technological innovation, and high-level strategic management. We need to improve related supporting policies and strengthen the training of civilian staff. We need to be both strict and caring, and place equal emphasis on providing incentives and imposing constraints. We need to encourage solid work and innovation, help resolve practical difficulties for military personnel, and fully arouse their enthusiasm, initiative and creativity.

We must never falter in our efforts to improve Party conduct and combat corruption in the military, with the strictest discipline in all respects and at all times. We must fight hedonism and extravagance and eliminate the practice of favoring form over substance and bureaucratism. We need to adapt our military governance, perform duties and exercise powers as prescribed by law, and carry out our work in accordance with regulations. We need to enhance discipline education and tighten discipline enforcement, exercising full and rigorous governance over the Party and the military.

The fight against corruption must go on with firm resolve. We must continue to see that there are no no-go zones, no ground is left unturned, and no tolerance is shown for corruption. We must punish both those who take bribes and those who offer them. We must improve systems to apply checks and oversight over the exercise of power. We must strengthen the confinement of power, leaving no back doors for abuse of power. We must address both the symptoms and root causes of corruption by enhancing intra-Party political education while encouraging officials to employ self-cultivation, self-discipline, and integrity in the fight against unhealthy tendencies and wrongdoing.

Improve the Socialist Military Policy Framework with Chinese Characteristics*

November 13, 2018

The military policy framework helps shape military relations, regulate military practices, and ensure military advancement. Reform of the military policy framework is highly significant for realizing the Party's goal of building a strong military in the new era, making the people's armed forces a world-class military, and achieving the Two Centenary Goals and the Chinese Dream of national rejuvenation. We need to fully appreciate the importance and urgency of this reform. To complete the task of the reform, we must develop consensus, build up confidence, take concerted actions, and implement policies to the letter.

Throughout the historical period of revolution, economic development and reform, the CPC has adapted and improved its military policy framework as times changed to meet its mission and perform the duties of the people's armed forces. These efforts have enabled the people's armed forces to maintain its nature, fulfill its mission, improve its capability to win wars, and secure continuous victories.

Socialism with Chinese characteristics has entered a new era, as has China's endeavor to upgrade its national defense and military capabilities. So we need to conduct urgent, systematic and in-depth reform of the military policy framework to adapt to the changing conditions. We should resolve deep-seated problems in the military policy framework, enhance the performance of in-depth reform of national defense and the military, usher in a new stage in strengthening

---

* Main points of the speech at a meeting of the Central Military Commission on reform of the military policy framework.

the armed forces, improve military competitiveness, and maintain a position of strength when it comes to fighting war.

To carry out the reform, we must follow the Thought on Socialism with Chinese Characteristics for a New Era and the guiding principles of the 19th CPC National Congress, and observe the Party's philosophy on strengthening the military for the new era, so as to ensure the Party's absolute leadership over the military. The sole and fundamental criterion for judging the success of the reform is combat capability of the military, so we should keep our service personnel fully motivated. Through systematic planning, proactive design, innovative development, and overall reform, we can build a socialist military policy framework with Chinese characteristics. This framework will provide a strong guarantee for realizing the Party's goal of building a strong military in the new era and making the Chinese military world-class armed forces.

We need to further reform the organizational systems of the Party in the military. To strengthen the Party in the new era, we must observe the Party Constitution, and improve military systems for reinforcing the Party's political foundations, improving the Party's theories, organizations and conduct, and enforcing its discipline.

We need to update the policy systems for using our military forces, so as to implement our national security strategies. The military must focus on how to fight and win when it is called on. To this end, we should reform the system for strategic military guidance, develop a system of laws and regulations for joint operations, and improve the system of combat readiness. Our policy systems for deploying our military forces must be based on joint operations and ensure both combat readiness in peacetime and prompt response in wartime, and this will enable our military to complete its mission for the new era.

We need to restructure the policy systems for strengthening the military. We should design a better institutional framework for the military human resources systems. This includes establishing a career-officer system, improving the system for ensuring the wellbeing of and social security for military personnel, and improving the military-honor system. We should reform in a coordinated way our policy systems concerning military training, equipment development, logistics, research, national defense mobilization, and civil military integration.

We need to advance reform of the policy systems for military management and create new strategic management systems. We should refine the defense expenditure system and ensure coordinated allocation of military resources. We should adopt military laws and regulations in an integrated way and enhance their codification. Our policy systems for military management must be precise, effective, comprehensive, procedure-based and mandatory, so as to improve the operations of our military and promote quality development of our armed forces.

The military must implement, as a major political responsibility, the decisions and plans of the CPC Central Committee and the Central Military Commission on reform of the military policy framework. To fulfill the task, we must have a stronger sense of responsibility, ensure implementation, and promote reform in a more forceful and well-planned way.

A consensus must be reached within the military on the importance of the reform. We should make officers and soldiers see that the reform is of political and strategic importance and support and embrace the reform. Military officers at all levels, especially high-ranking officers, must maintain their political commitment, think in terms of the general picture, follow the core leadership of the CPC Central Committee, and act in accordance with its requirements. Our high-ranking officers must set a good example in taking a clear political stance, acting in the overall interests, observing discipline, facilitating reform, and fulfilling duties.

We should see that all military organizations fulfill their respective responsibilities. A policy framework must be put in place and implemented in accordance with their functions and assignments. We should take coordinated steps for implementation to ensure that reform advances in the direction we have set.

We should ensure the overall planning and coordination of this reform. We must speed up the introduction of some policies, prioritizing those urgently needed in carrying out reform and enhancing war preparedness and expected by military personnel.

Promoting reform of the military policy framework is a task for both the military and the civil sectors. All central Party and government departments and local Party committees and governments should concern themselves with and support the reform. They should play their part and help strengthen joint civil-military endeavors to carry out this reform.

Be Combat Ready Under the New Conditions*

January 4, 2019

The military must follow the Thought on Socialism with Chinese Characteristics for a New Era and implement the guiding principles of the 19th CPC National Congress in 2017 and the second and third plenary sessions of the 19th CPC Central Committee in 2018. The military must act on the Party's philosophy on strengthening the military for the new era, implement a strategy for new conditions, and get ready to meet any new challenge at this new starting point.

Since the 18th CPC National Congress in 2012, in the face of a challenging domestic and international environment and shouldering arduous military tasks, the CPC Central Committee and the Central Military Commission have sized up new developments, made overall plans, and led the military in tackling tough issues with resolve. Thanks to these efforts, the performance of our military has been enhanced; new ground has been made; and landmark, pioneering and historic advances have been achieved. With determination, adaptive strategies and forceful actions, the military has safeguarded our sovereignty, security and development interests, and withstood severe and multiple tests.

A scale of change unseen in a century is unfolding in the world today. China is still in an important period of strategic opportunity for development, but it also faces increasing risks and challenges, both foreseeable and unexpected. In view of this, all our military personnel must gain a full understanding of China's underlying security and development trends, be ever ready to guard against potential dangers,

---

* Main points of the speech at a meeting of the Central Military Commission on military work.

and take solid steps to ensure that we are ready to meet any challenge and fulfill our missions entrusted by the Party and the people.

We should implement the military strategy and principles for the new era, and fulfill the command responsibilities to meet new challenges. We must be fully aware that the military is a fighting force and that its combat capability is what matters. We must devote all our efforts, strengths, and resources to this endeavor.

We should enhance war and combat capabilities to ensure rapid and effective response in case of war. We should build a joint operations command system to improve our capacity in this regard. We should develop new combat forces and create new combat capabilities. We should enhance military training under combat conditions to enhance war preparedness. We should do more to resolve problems progressively and deliver real outcomes.

All central Party and government departments and local Party committees and governments must support the development of national defense and the military, and work together to build our heroic people's armed forces into a more powerful military with stronger combat capability.

Hong Kong, Macao and China's Peaceful Reunification

Promote Development in Hong Kong and Macao as Part of China's Overall Development*

November 12, 2018

The Third Plenary Session of the 11th CPC Central Committee convened in December 1978 marked the start of the reform and opening up initiated by Deng Xiaoping. China has since embarked on a great journey. From the outset, the vitality of Hong Kong and Macao has played a key role. Over the past 40 years, compatriots in the two special administrative regions (SARs) have never failed to play a creative role and have been fully engaged in the process.

I know this firsthand. During my tenures in the provinces of Fujian and Zhejiang and in the city of Shanghai, I personally planned for and facilitated a good number of cooperation projects with Hong Kong and Macao. After I started working at the CPC Central Committee in 2007, I was in charge of Hong Kong and Macao affairs, and thereby gained a thorough understanding of them. During this time, I made many friends from the two SARs.

As I see it, our compatriots in Hong Kong and Macao have mainly played the following roles in reform and opening up:

First, a leading role in investment and starting businesses on the mainland. After reform and opening up began, our Hong Kong and Macao compatriots were the first to act, quickly heading to the mainland to make investments and develop businesses. You created a number of "firsts", including the first joint venture company, the first jointly-funded expressway, the first branch of a non-mainland bank, and the first joint venture five-star hotel. I once visited the Zhongshan

---

* Part of the speech at the meeting with delegations of Hong Kong and Macao in celebration of the 40th anniversary of reform and opening up.

Hot Spring Resort, which was co-invested by Mr Fok Ying Tung and Mr Ho Hung Sun in the city of Zhongshan, Guangdong Province in 1979, shortly after it opened. I was impressed by its facilities and services. Hotels on the mainland at the time were no comparison to it. Hong Kong and Macao compatriots not only fueled the mainland's economic development with their investments, but also caused a chain reaction – attracting a flood of international capital to the mainland. For many years, Hong Kong and Macao have remained the largest source of inbound investment on the mainland, which by the end of last year had added up to US$1.02 trillion, accounting for 54 percent of all inbound investments on the mainland.

Second, a demonstration role in market economy. In the early years of reform and opening up, when many people on the mainland were burdened by the influence of the planned economy and clung to old thinking, people of vision from Hong Kong and Macao were the first to share with people on the mainland their experience of international standards and international markets. Many of them took on the role of mentors, offering counseling opinions on the reform of enterprises and the land system. As early as 1978 Mr Leung Chun-ying gave free lectures on Western systems of land economy and management in Shenzhen, Shanghai and some other cities. In 1987 he co-authored a bidding document for land auctions in Chinese and English, which was the first such document in Shenzhen and in China too. Mr Anthony Neoh and Mrs Cha Shih May-lung helped the mainland establish a regulatory system for stock markets, with a symbolic annual salary of RMB1. Hong Kong and Macao compatriots have made important contribution to the development of a market economy on the mainland.

Third, a catalytic role in institutional reform. Hong Kong and Macao were among primary factors in the mainland's decision to establish special economic zones. In 1979 the CPC Guangdong Provincial Committee proposed to the Central Committee that Guangdong, tapping into the advantage of its proximity to Hong Kong and Macao, could take the lead in opening up and could set up trade zones in Shenzhen, Zhuhai, and Shantou – hometown of many overseas Chinese. Hong Kong and Macao compatriots were engaged in the whole process of creating these zones, from general planning to drafting relevant laws and regulations, and to the incubation and operation of individual programs.

Fourth, a bridging role in the country's two-way opening up. In the early stage of reform and opening up, Hong Kong and Macao, with access to quotas for exports to Europe and the US and some other advantages, helped the mainland obtain a large number of export orders. By the mid-1990s, more than 80 percent of manufacturers in Hong Kong had moved to the Pearl River Delta and other parts of the mainland. All this stimulated a rapid growth of the export-oriented manufacturing industry, and helped the mainland integrate into the global industrial chain. Meanwhile, Hong Kong and Macao also served as a conduit and platform for overseas financing and investment by mainland businesses. Through Hong Kong many of these businesses got to know and acclimatized to the international market, learning how to survive and thrive. Today nearly half of the companies listed on the Hong Kong Stock Exchange are from the mainland, making up close to 70 percent of the total exchange value.

Fifth, the role of a testing ground. China piloted many of its opening-up policies in Hong Kong and Macao first, gained experience and then introduced them into other parts of the country step by step. This approach allowed the country to advance opening up while effectively controlling risks. It also gave Hong Kong and Macao a head start. Take the opening up of the service market on the mainland as an example. Guangdong Province and the two SARs were the first to start free trade in services between them within the framework of the Mainland and Hong Kong Closer Economic Partnership Arrangement (CEPA), through which we gained experience for the nationwide introduction of a management system of pre-establishment national treatment plus a negative list for foreign investment. The role of Hong Kong and Macao as a testing ground is more prominent in the opening up of the mainland's financial sector. The Shanghai-Hong Kong

Stock Connect, Shenzhen-Hong Kong Stock Connect, and Bond Connect are all key steps taken by the mainland in recent years to open up its capital market. RMB internationalization also started in Hong Kong. The region is now the world's largest offshore Renminbi business hub with the greatest variety of offshore Renminbi products.

Sixth, an exemplary role in urban management. Hong Kong and Macao have a wealth of experience in urban development, management and public services, from which the mainland can learn. For instance, the Shanghai Hongqiao International Airport improved its operation soon after adopting the management philosophy of Hong Kong International Airport. In 2011 it took first place among the most improved airports in the Skytrax World Airport Awards. Beijing, Guangzhou, Shenzhen and other cities on the mainland have also learned from Hong Kong in the construction and operation of subways. The first flying service team was organized on the mainland with the assistance of the Government Flying Service of Hong Kong. By drawing upon the successful practice and experience of Hong Kong and Macao, the mainland has effectively improved its urban development and management.

An ancient Chinese said, "People drawn to each other by kindness and virtues make good friends; people who hold together with a meeting of minds make bosom friends."[1] It must be noted that Hong Kong and Macao compatriots have come to the mainland to invest and start businesses, not only because they have discerned business opportunities here, but also because they hope to see the mainland shake off poverty and China become stronger and more prosperous. You have donated to programs for the public good on the mainland, including those in education, technology, culture, health care and sports, not just for doing good and sowing virtue, but also out of your fraternal bonds with fellow countrymen on the mainland. Sir Run Run Shaw donated more than HK$10 billion to programs for the public good on the mainland; Mr Tin Ka Ping even sold his house to fund education programs on the mainland. He lived in a rented apartment in his later years. In the 2010 Yushu earthquake in Qinghai

Province, Hong Kong volunteer Wong Fuk Wing braved aftershocks to save others before he died in the earthquake. Every time the mainland is hit by massive natural disasters, our compatriots in Hong Kong and Macao would show great empathy for the victims, and have always been the first to offer help. Time and again you have offered help and assistance in times of adversity to fellow countrymen on the mainland, proving that blood is thicker than water.

In short, our compatriots in Hong Kong and Macao have both witnessed and participated in, both benefited from and contributed to China's reform and opening up over the past 40 years. Along with people of the mainland you have created a miracle. China's reform and opening up is a cause in which Hong Kong, Macao and the mainland complement each other with their respective strengths and develop together; it is a cause in which people in Hong Kong, Macao and the mainland work side by side with one heart and one mind; it is also a cause for Hong Kong and Macao to integrate into the overall development of the country, and share the glory of a strong and prosperous motherland.

"People on a long and arduous journey will not stop and opt for an easy one before reaching the destination."[2] Since the 18th CPC National Congress in 2012, we have championed reform and opening up and made unprecedented efforts to drive reforms on all fronts. We have made top-level designs and rolled out more than 1,600 reform programs in economic, political, cultural, social, eco-civilization and other fields. Many of the reforms are unprecedented and having a nationwide impact. They include the reform of the market system, the macroeconomic regulation system, the fiscal and tax systems, the financial system, state-owned enterprises, the judicial system, the education system, the ecological conservation system, Party and state institutions, the supervision system, and of national defense and the armed forces.

I have been talking about reform and opening up on every major occasion, emphasizing that we must have the courage to tackle tough issues, navigate treacherous waters, and engage in painful self-adjustment to carry reform through. At the opening ceremony of both the Boao Forum for Asia Annual Conference and the First China International Import Expo earlier this year, I reiterated China's resolve to press on with reform. My recent inspection tour in Guangdong Province was designed to send a strong message of continued reform and opening up in the new era; reform and opening up is an ongoing process with no endpoint. I also emphasized that, by continuing reform and opening up, China is to create new and greater miracles that will impress the world. The more complex the situation, the more steadfast we will be in reform and opening up. We will never regress to closed-door development. To realize national rejuvenation, China must advance with the times, and keep pressing forward. As our ancestors said, "If you can improve yourself in a day, do so each day, forever building on improvement."

Socialism with Chinese characteristics has entered a new era, as have China's reform and opening up and the practice of "one country, two systems". One of the hallmarks of this new era is our engagement in reform and opening up, in which Hong Kong and Macao still have a special position, unique strengths, and an irreplaceable role to play. I hope Hong Kong and Macao compatriots will continue to participate in reform and opening up in the pioneering spirit and the spirit of patriotism. I hope you will follow the trend of the times, make the best use of the conditions, and achieve better development of your home regions through integration with the overall development of the country. Together we will write a new chapter on the great rejuvenation of the Chinese nation.

For Hong Kong and Macao, the policy of "one country, two systems" gives you the biggest strength; China's reform and opening up set the broadest stage for your development; and national strategies such as the Belt and Road Initiative and the Guangdong-Hong Kong-Macao Greater Bay Area, present you new and important opportunities. We must fully understand and properly define the two SARs' position in China's reform and opening up in the new era. We will support you in seizing opportunities, cultivating new strengths, taking on new roles, seeking new development, and making new contributions. In this regard I would like to express my hopes for the two regions as follows:

First, I hope Hong Kong and Macao will support the country's all-round opening up more proactively. As the country opens up wider, Hong Kong and Macao will see their position and role grow stronger rather than diminish. I hope the two regions will continue to take the lead in attracting capital, technology, and talent for a quality development of the national economy and the new round of high-level opening up. In particular, Hong Kong and Macao should leverage their extensive international connections and sophisticated professional services on the one hand, and rely on the mainland's huge market, complete industrial system, and technological competitiveness on the other. In this way, Hong Kong may reinforce its status as the world financial, shipping, and trade hub and accelerate its ascension to an international science and technology innovation center, while Macao may intensify its efforts to develop itself into a world-class tourism and leisure center and to build a business and trade service platform between China and Portuguese-speaking countries. Thereby the two SARs will become the beachheads in China's two-way opening up.

Second, I hope Hong Kong and Macao will integrate their development into the overall development of the country more proactively. This integration is what the principle of "one country, two systems" and the program of reform and opening up in our times require. And it is also called for by the objective need of Hong Kong and Macao to explore new paths, create new space, and foster new drivers for their own development. Building the Guangdong-Hong Kong-Macao Greater Bay Area is a grand plan we have formulated on the basis of the overall and long-term interests of our country, and a major policy to maintain long-lasting prosperity and stability in Hong Kong and Macao. Innovation is critical for the success of this endeavor. Within the framework of the "one country, two systems" principle and the SARs' Basic Laws, we should give full play to the combined strengths of Guangdong, Hong Kong and Macao, introduce new systemic and institutional mechanisms, and boost the circulation of production factors. The Greater Bay Area spans three customs territories in one country that operate under two different social systems with three different currencies. This is unprecedented in the world. We must make bold experiments and blaze a new path. Meanwhile, Hong Kong and Macao should further improve their competitiveness and focus on cultivating new growth drivers.

Third, I hope Hong Kong and Macao will participate in national governance more proactively. Since their return to the motherland, the two SARs have become part of the national governance system. Our compatriots in Hong Kong and Macao should improve local systems and mechanisms for enforcing the Constitution and the Basic Laws in line with the "one country, two systems" principle, and enhance their capacity for and improve their performance of governance. Meanwhile, you should pay close attention to the country's overall development, safeguard the country's political system, actively engage in furthering the country's economic, political, cultural, social, and eco-environmental progress, and conscientiously safeguard national security. Having many advantages on the world stage, the people of Hong Kong and Macao may support our country's participation in global governance in various ways.

Fourth, I hope Hong Kong and Macao will promote international people-to-people exchanges more proactively. With cultural diversity, the two SARs may serve as key links in cultural exchanges between China and the rest of the world. Being international metropolises, Hong Kong and Macao may tap into their extensive connections with the outside world, spread the best of traditional Chinese culture, present China's principles and policies, and tell China's stories, including stories about the successful implementation of the "one country, two systems" principle. In doing so, Hong Kong and Macao will continue to play a special role in promoting cultural exchanges between the East and the West, facilitating mutual learning among civilizations, and building people-to-people bonds.

There are many young entrepreneurs from Hong Kong and Macao

in this room. I am glad to see you. A nation will prosper only when its young people are energetic. The young people of Hong Kong and Macao are the hope and future of the two regions; they are the new lifeblood for national development. Only when the young people of Hong Kong and Macao get strong, can the two regions and the entire country be strong. We will create more opportunities for the young people in the two SARs and help them overcome difficulties in education, employment, and in starting their own business, thereby fostering a favorable social environment for them to realize their dreams.

Today we are closer than ever before to our goal of national rejuvenation. There is much that Hong Kong and Macao compatriots can contribute in realizing this goal, and by doing so you will add new glory to your home regions. As our ancestors said, "On reaching the last leg of a journey, one is only half way there." All Chinese should work in unity, and persevere, dauntlessly and steadfastly, in reaching our target. I hope that people in Hong Kong and Macao will work together with those on the mainland to open up new prospects for "one country, two systems", to create a better life for yourselves, and to realize the Chinese Dream.

Notes

[1] Feng Menglong: *Stories to Caution the World* (*Jing Shi Tong Yan*). Feng Menglong (1574-1646) was a writer and thinker of the Ming Dynasty.

[2] Han Ying: *Han's Short Essays on* Book of Songs (*Han Shi Wai Zhuan*). Han Ying (c. 200-130 BC) was a scholar of the Western Han Dynasty.

Strive for China's National Rejuvenation and Peaceful Reunification*

January 2, 2019

Comrades,
My fellow Chinese,
Friends,

Today, we are meeting here to solemnly commemorate the 40th anniversary of the release of the Message to Compatriots in Taiwan by the Standing Committee of the National People's Congress. As a new year begins, on behalf of the people on the mainland, I extend sincere greetings and best wishes to our fellow Chinese in Taiwan.

It has been 70 years since Taiwan and the mainland were separated. Since China entered the modern era, the emergence and evolution of the Taiwan question has been inextricably interwoven with the history of the Chinese nation. The Opium War of 1840 and ensuing wars of aggression launched by Western powers plunged China into a state of anguished turmoil, with its lands torn apart. And Taiwan fell under a foreign occupation that lasted for half a century. In wave after wave, we Chinese engaged in an epic struggle to resist foreign aggression, liberate the Chinese nation, and realize the country's reunification. Our fellow Chinese in Taiwan made a huge contribution to this struggle. In 1945, together with other peoples around the world, the Chinese people won victory in the War of Resistance Against Japanese Aggression, a part of the Global War Against Fascism. Taiwan was thus recovered and returned to China. It was not long, however,

---

* Speech at the meeting marking the 40th anniversary of the release of the Message to Compatriots in Taiwan.

before the two sides of the Taiwan Straits fell into a state of protracted political confrontation due to the civil war in China and the interference of foreign forces.

Since 1949, the Communist Party of China, the Chinese government, and the Chinese people have endeavored to pursue the historic mission of resolving the Taiwan question and realizing China's full reunification. Working with our fellow Chinese in Taiwan, we have de-escalated tense confrontation across the Taiwan Straits, improved cross-Straits relations, set out on a path of peaceful development, and continually made breakthroughs in cross-Straits relations.

– Over the past 70 years, responding to the longing of people on both sides of the Taiwan Straits, we have ended the estrangement between the two sides. We have achieved overall direct two-way "three links"[1] and have initiated substantial exchanges, communication, and cooperation between the two sides. Cross-Straits exchanges and cooperation have steadily expanded and grown increasingly closer, and mutual affinity has deepened. Our fellow Chinese in Taiwan have made a major contribution to the mainland's reform and opening up, and they, in turn, have shared the mainland's development opportunities.

– Over the past 70 years, acting in a spirit of seeking common ground while setting aside differences and on the basis of the one-China principle, the two sides have reached the 1992 Consensus that "both sides of the Taiwan Straits belong to one China and will work together towards national reunification". The two sides have thus initiated consultations and negotiation and promoted cross-Straits party-to-party exchanges. We have opened up a path for the peaceful growth of cross-Straits relations and realized a historic meeting between leaders of both sides, thus elevating cross-Straits political interactions to a new height.

– Over the past 70 years, keeping in mind the changes over time in the growth of cross-Straits relations, we have proposed the policy of seeking a peaceful solution to the Taiwan question, and established the fundamental guideline of peaceful reunification based on the well-conceived principle of "one country, two systems". With this, we have responded to the call of our times in the new era, namely, to promote the peaceful growth of cross-Straits relations and unite our fellow Chinese in Taiwan to strive for our country's rejuvenation and peaceful reunification.

– Over the past 70 years, holding high the banner of peace, development, cooperation, and mutual benefit, and on the basis of the Five Principles of Peaceful Coexistence, we have forged friendship and strengthened cooperation with other countries and consolidated the international community's commitment to the one-China principle. More and more countries and people have gained a better understanding of China's position on reunification and given their support to it.

– Over the past 70 years, bearing in mind the overall and long-term interests of the Chinese nation, we have stood firm in safeguarding China's sovereignty and territorial integrity. Rallying all the Chinese people around us, we have resolutely defeated all attempts to create "two Chinas", "one China, one Taiwan", or "Taiwan independence", and have achieved major victories in the fight against separatist activities for "Taiwan independence".

As the evolution of cross-Straits relations attests, no force or people can ever change the historical fact and principle that Taiwan is part of China and that the two sides belong to one and the same China. We people on both sides of the Taiwan Straits are Chinese and share a natural affinity and national identity built of kinship and mutual assistance, a fact that can never be altered by any force or any people. The tide of our times – cross-Straits relations moving towards peace and stability and continuing to move forward – is a tide that cannot be stopped by any force or any people. The historical trend towards a stronger China, national rejuvenation, and reunification cannot be stopped by any force or any people.

Comrades,

My fellow Chinese,

Friends,

By reviewing the past, we can draw inspiration for both the present and the future. Our country must be reunified, and will surely be reunified. This is a conclusion drawn from the evolution of cross-Straits relations over the past seven decades; it is also critical to the rejuvenation of the Chinese nation in the new era. We Chinese on both sides of the Taiwan Straits, all of us Chinese at home and abroad, should jointly uphold the national interest, follow the historical trend, and work together for the peaceful growth of cross-Straits relations.

First, we should work together to promote China's rejuvenation and achieve its peaceful reunification.

The rejuvenation of the Chinese nation and the reunification of our country are a surging popular trend. They are where our greater national interest lies, and they are what the people hope to see. We face each other just across a strip of water, yet our two sides are still far apart. The fact that we have still not been reunified is a wound left by history on the Chinese nation. We Chinese on both sides should work together to achieve reunification and heal this wound. All our fellow Chinese in Taiwan are members of the Chinese nation. You should be proud of your Chinese identity, fully consider the position and role of Taiwan in China's rejuvenation, and pursue both the full reunification and rejuvenation of China as an honorable cause.

The future of Taiwan lies in China's reunification, and the wellbeing of the people in Taiwan hinges on the rejuvenation of the Chinese nation. The peaceful growth of cross-Straits relations is the right path for safeguarding peace, promoting common development, and benefiting people on both sides. Thus, the peaceful growth of cross-Straits relations is something people on both sides should jointly promote, safeguard, and enjoy. The Chinese Dream is a dream shared by both sides of the Taiwan Straits; only China's rejuvenation and prosperity can bring lives of plenty and happiness to us on both sides. As the Chinese nation moves towards rejuvenation, our fellow Chinese in Taiwan should certainly not miss out. We people on both sides should join hands to fulfill the Chinese Dream, shoulder the responsibility, and share the glory of national rejuvenation. The Taiwan question originated in a weak and ravaged China, and it is certain to end with China's rejuvenation.

Second, we should explore a "two systems" solution to the Taiwan question and enrich our efforts towards peaceful reunification.

The vision of peaceful reunification and "one country, two systems" is the best way to realize China's reunification. It embodies Chinese wisdom – thriving by embracing each other, takes full account of Taiwan's reality, and is conducive to long-term stability in Taiwan after reunification.

Difference in systems should not be an obstacle to reunification; it is certainly no excuse for separation. The principle of "one country, two systems" was proposed precisely to accommodate Taiwan's actual conditions and to safeguard the interests and wellbeing of our fellow Chinese in Taiwan. In terms of how the principle should be carried out, we will fully consider the situation in Taiwan, give full consideration to the views and proposals from all walks of life on both sides, and fully accommodate the interests and sentiments of our fellow Chinese in Taiwan. Provided that China's sovereignty, security, and development interests are ensured, after peaceful reunification, Taiwan's social system and its way of life will be fully respected, and the private property, religious beliefs, and lawful rights and interests of our fellow Chinese in Taiwan will be fully protected.

We people on both sides of the Taiwan Straits are of one family. Issues between our two sides are domestic affairs, and it is therefore natural that they should be discussed and resolved by family members. Peaceful reunification means achieving reunification through consultation and discussion as equals. The long-standing political differences between the two sides are the root cause that affects the steady growth of cross-Straits relations, but we should not allow this problem to be passed down from one generation to the next. Our both sides must live up to our responsibility, to our nation, and to future generations; we should put our heads together, be creative, reduce differences, and seek common ground. Doing so will enable us to end political antagonism at an early date, ensure lasting peace across the Taiwan Straits, and agree on a vision for China's reunification, so that our future generations can live and grow up in a shared home with peace, stability, prosperity, and dignity.

On the basis of abiding by the one-China principle, there will be no obstacles in exchanges between political parties and groups in Taiwan and on the mainland. When dialogue replaces confrontation, cooperation replaces dispute, and win-win mindset replaces zero-sum mentality, cross-Straits relations will progress steadily and move far. We are ready to engage in broad exchanges of views with all parties, groups, or individuals in Taiwan regarding political issues between the two sides and the promotion of China's peaceful reunification, in order to forge social consensus and advance political negotiations.

Here we wish to make a solemn proposal: On the common political foundation of adhering to the 1992 Consensus and opposing "Taiwan independence", representatives can be recommended by all political parties and all sectors of society on both sides, and they will engage in extensive and in-depth democratic consultations on cross-Straits relations and the future of the nation, and work towards institutional arrangements for promoting the peaceful growth of cross-Straits relations.

Third, we should abide by the one-China principle and ensure the prospects for peaceful reunification.

Although our two sides have yet to be reunified, the sovereignty and territory of China has never been severed, and the fact that the mainland and Taiwan belong to one and the same China has never changed. The one-China principle is the political foundation of cross-Straits relations. When we adhere to this principle, cross-Straits relations will improve and grow, and our fellow Chinese in Taiwan will benefit. However, if we deviate from it, cross-Straits relations will become strained and volatile, and the interests of our fellow Chinese in Taiwan will be harmed.

China's reunification is a historic trend and the right path, while "Taiwan independence" goes against the tide of history and is a path that can only lead to a dead end. Our fellow Chinese in Taiwan have a glorious patriotic tradition and share a close kinship with us. We remain committed to the principle of placing our hopes on the people of Taiwan. We will continue, as ever, to respect, care about, work with, and rely on them, and we will do our utmost to help them overcome difficulties and meet their needs. Our fellow Chinese in Taiwan, regardless of political affiliation, religious belief, social status, or origin of birth, whether civilian or military, you must clearly see that "Taiwan independence" will only bring disaster. You should resolutely oppose it and join hands with us to create the bright prospects of peaceful reunification. We are ready to create vast space for peaceful reunification; but we will definitely not leave any room for separatist activities in any form.

As Chinese, we should not fight each other. We will work with the greatest sincerity and exert our utmost efforts to achieve peaceful reunification, because this works best for the people on both sides and for our whole nation. We do not renounce the use of force and reserve the option of taking all necessary measures. This is to guard against external interference and a tiny number of separatists and their activities for "Taiwan independence". In no way does it target our fellow Chinese in Taiwan. We people on both sides should work together to pursue peace, protect peace, and enjoy peace.

Fourth, we should promote integrated development of the two sides and cement the foundation for peaceful reunification.

People on both sides of the Taiwan Straits share the bonds of kinship. Just as loved ones wish each other well, we Chinese should help each other. We treat our fellow Chinese in Taiwan as equals, and will continue paving the way for them to benefit first from the mainland's development opportunities and ensure that our fellow Chinese and enterprises from Taiwan receive the same treatment as those of the mainland, thus giving them a greater sense of fulfillment. After peaceful reunification, Taiwan will enjoy lasting peace and the people there will live in peace and contentment. Backed by a strong motherland, our fellow Chinese in Taiwan will enjoy better lives and have more opportunities for development, and they will have more confidence and a greater sense of security and dignity in the international community.

We should take active steps to institutionalize cross-Straits economic cooperation and create a common market for the two sides, so as to increase momentum for development and vitality of cooperation and strengthen the Chinese economy. We on the two sides should promote connectivity wherever necessary, including trade and economic cooperation, building infrastructure, developing energy and resources, and sharing industrial standards. We can start by supplying water, electricity, and gas from coastal areas in Fujian Province to Kinmen and Matsu, and building bridges between them. We should promote cooperation in culture, education, and health care, and the sharing of social security and public resources, and we should support neighboring areas or areas with similar conditions on the two sides in providing equal, universal, and accessible basic public services.

Fifth, we should forge closer bonds of heart and mind between people on both sides and strengthen our joint commitment to peaceful reunification.

The soul of a nation is molded by its culture. We on the mainland and in Taiwan share the same roots, culture, and ethnic identity; it is the Chinese culture that has instilled vitality in us and given us a sense of belonging. The key to kinship lies in mutual understanding. No matter what interference and obstruction we may encounter, exchanges and cooperation between our people on both sides must never be hampered, diminished, or stopped.

We people on both sides should together pass on the best of traditional Chinese culture and ensure that it evolves and grows in new and creative ways. We should engage in exchanges and mutual learning, promote dialogue and inclusiveness, enhance empathy, deepen mutual understanding, strengthen mutual trust, and increase our shared sense of identity. We should maintain our bonds of kinship and shared values, use the right approach to our history, our nation, and our country to raise the awareness of younger generations, and keep alive the great spirit of our nation. Between loved ones, there is no knot of perception that cannot be untied. With perseverance, we are sure to forge closer bonds of heart and mind between people on both sides.

Supporting and pursuing reunification is a righteous cause of the Chinese nation, and this commitment should be recognized by all of us. Our country will always stand firm behind patriots working for reunification. It is our sincere hope that all our fellow Chinese in Taiwan will treasure peace as they do the gift of sight, pursue reunification with the same zeal with which they pursue a better life, and play an active part in advancing the just cause of China's peaceful reunification.

The young are the hope of the country and the future of the nation. Young people on both sides should shoulder responsibilities, forge solidarity and friendship, and work together for a better future. Young people from Taiwan are welcome to pursue and fulfill their dreams on the mainland. We Chinese on both sides must be united and work together to seek happiness for ourselves and create a bright future for our nation.

Comrades,

My fellow Chinese,

Friends,

Over the years, our fellow Chinese in Hong Kong, Macao, and overseas have shown understanding for and supported the great cause of reunification, and have contributed greatly to this cause. I hope that you will remain committed and further contribute to the peaceful growth of cross-Straits relations and China's peaceful reunification.

Comrades,

My fellow Chinese,

Friends,

There is only one China on this Earth. The one-China principle is a generally recognized norm in international relations, and it represents a general consensus of the international community. The international community has extended understanding and support for the Chinese people's just cause of opposing separatist activities towards "Taiwan independence" and striving for China's reunification. The

Chinese government expresses its appreciation for this understanding and support. We as Chinese must decide our own affairs. The Taiwan question is an internal affair that involves China's core interests and the Chinese people's national sentiments, and no external interference in this issue will be tolerated.

China's reunification will not harm any country's legitimate interests, including its economic interests in Taiwan. On the contrary, it will bring the world more opportunities for development, and create more positive momentum for the prosperity and stability of the Asia Pacific and the rest of the world. Indeed, it will make a greater contribution to building a global community of shared future, to the cause of global peace and development, and to the cause of human progress.

Comrades,

My fellow Chinese,

Friends,

We cannot choose our past, but we can steer the current course and shape the future. The new era is an era for the Chinese nation to achieve major development and major successes; it is also an era for the people on both sides of the Taiwan Straits to pursue the same goal. The path ahead may not be always smooth, but when we stand and work together, we can surely create a promising future for the rejuvenation of the Chinese nation, and we can surely achieve the great cause of China's reunification.

Notes

[1] This refers to mail, business and transport.

Speech on the 20th Anniversary of Macao's Return to China and the Inauguration of the Fifth-Term Government of the Macao Special Administrative Region

December 20, 2019

My fellow compatriots,
Dear friends,

Not long ago, we held a grand celebration of the 70th anniversary of the founding of the People's Republic of China. Today, we have gathered here with great joy to celebrate the 20th anniversary of Macao's return to the motherland. First of all, on behalf of the central government and people of all ethnic groups, I wish to extend cordial greetings to all residents in Macao, and offer warm congratulations to Mr Ho Iat Seng, the fifth chief executive of the Macao Special Administrative Region (MSAR), all principal officials and the members of the Executive Council who have just been sworn in. I also wish to express heartfelt thanks to all fellow Chinese at home and abroad and foreign friends who have taken an active interest in Macao's development and given their support.

Twenty years ago today, Macao, having endured many years of separation, returned to the embrace of the motherland, and the Macao Special Administrative Region of the People's Republic of China was established. This marked the beginning of a historic era for Macao. Over the past two decades, with the strong support of the central government and the mainland and under the leadership of Chief Executives Ho Hau Wah and Chui Sai On, the MSAR government and people from every sector of Macao have worked closely together to usher in Macao's best period of development in its history. A shining chapter has been written in the successful application of "one country, two systems" with Macao characteristics.

– In the past 20 years since its return to the motherland, Macao has established a solid constitutional order on the basis of China's Constitution and the MSAR Basic Law and improved its governance system. The MSAR has firmly upheld the central authorities' overall jurisdiction and properly exercised its high degree of autonomy. It has smoothly completed the enactment of local legislation necessary to apply relevant national laws including Article 23 of the Basic Law and the National Anthem Law, and set up a Committee for Safeguarding National Security. The MSAR has effectively fulfilled its constitutional responsibility for upholding China's national sovereignty, security and development interests. Its executive authorities, legislature and judiciary have performed their duties in strict accordance with the law. They have properly handled their mutual relations and consciously upheld the authority of the chief executive. In so doing, they have ensured the smooth operation of the executive-led system with the chief executive at its center. As a result, the MSAR has made orderly progress in democracy, and Macao residents' extensive rights and freedoms under the law have been fully guaranteed.

– In the past 20 years since its return to the motherland, Macao has achieved phenomenal economic development and a continuous improvement in its people's lives. Steady progress has been made in establishing Macao as "One Center, One Platform, One Base"[1]. Macao's per capita GDP has jumped to the second highest in the world. Significant results have been achieved in its appropriate economic diversification. Emerging industries, such as conventions and exhibitions, traditional Chinese medicine, and Macao-specific financial services, are booming. The city has taken an active part in the Belt and Road Initiative and the development of the Guangdong-Hong Kong-Macao Greater Bay Area. Welfare benefits have risen substantially. A host of policies, including free education and health care, and two-tier social security, have benefited the whole community. Macao residents now have a greater sense of fulfillment and happiness.

– In the past 20 years since its return to the motherland, Macao has enjoyed social stability and harmony and a fusion of diverse cultures. Inadequate law and order, a problem that plagued Macao before its return, was swiftly addressed. This city is now one of the safest in the world. Close communication has been maintained between the MSAR government and citizens, between different sectors of society, and between different ethnic communities. People from all walks of life express their wishes in a rational manner through sound mechanisms of coordination. On this basis, Macao has both contributed to Chinese culture and embraced diverse cultures.

My fellow compatriots,

Dear friends,

Macao's accomplishments in the past two decades have captured the world's attention. Though limited in size, Macao plays a unique role in the practice of "one country, two systems". Four important things can be learned from Macao's successful application of the policy:

First, we must always have rock-solid confidence in "one country, two systems". Our fellow compatriots in Macao genuinely support the "one country, two systems" policy and see it as the best institutional arrangement to ensure Macao's long-term prosperity and stability. In implementing the policy, the MSAR government and all sectors of Macao have endeavored to both safeguard our country's sovereignty, security and development interests and promote Macao's long-term prosperity and stability. Firm and resolute, Macao has never wavered in the face of temporary complications or become distracted by external interference. On the contrary, Macao has excelled in seizing the opportunities brought by major national development strategies and policies. Macao has thus gained strong momentum and made tremendous progress by taking its proper place in the overall development of the country.

Macao's successful experience proves that as long as we uphold "one country, two systems" and act upon it, the viability and strength of this policy will be on full display.

Second, we must always stay on the right course of "one country, two systems". Our fellow compatriots in Macao fully recognize the "one country" principle as the premise and precondition of "two systems". They unequivocally uphold the constitutional order established by the Constitution and the Basic Law, respect the socialist system practiced in the main body of the country, and correctly handle issues concerning the relationship between the central authorities and the MSAR. The executive, legislative and judiciary branches of the MSAR have upheld the central authorities' overall jurisdiction while enjoying a high degree of autonomy. They have resolutely safeguarded the one-China principle and the authority of the central leadership and the Basic Law.

Macao's successful experience shows that the principle of "one country, two systems" must be applied without deviation or distortion to ensure its steady and long-term progress.

Third, we must always maintain a strong sense of mission and responsibility in implementing the "one country, two systems" principle. Our fellow compatriots in Macao have a sense of being the masters of their own affairs and always keep Macao's fundamental interests and the country's overall interests firmly in mind. They have made it their common mission to ensure the success of "one country, two systems", "Macao people governing Macao" and a high degree of autonomy. They see it as an integral contribution to realizing the Chinese Dream of national rejuvenation. The MSAR government has led people from all sectors of society in actively exploring a governance model and a development path that are suited to the realities of Macao. A range of policy measures have been introduced, including "consolidating the foundations and developing steadily", "comprehensively improving the quality of life of Macao residents", "preserving heritage while pursuing innovation to promote social harmony", and "standing united to achieve common goals and shared prosperity". Intensive efforts have been made to focus on economic growth, effectively raise living standards, steadfastly uphold the rule of law, progressively advance democracy, and promote social inclusiveness and harmony. These measures have made Macao young and dynamic again.

Macao's successful experience demonstrates that our fellow compatriots in Macao, as masters of their own affairs, are fully capable of meeting the challenges of our time and achieving success in governing, building and developing the MSAR.

Fourth, we must always cement the social and political foundations for "one country, two systems". Our fellow compatriots in Macao have a tradition of loving the motherland and a strong sense of national identity, belonging and pride. This is the most important reason for the success of "one country, two systems" in Macao. The MSAR government and people of all sectors of Macao are committed to carrying forward this tradition and firmly implementing the principle that Macao must be governed by Macao people with patriots as the mainstay. The MSAR governing institutions are mainly composed of those who love the country. The ranks of people who love the country and Macao are expanding and growing in strength by the day. Love for the country and Macao, as a core value, predominates in Macao. Thanks to the leadership of the chief executive, earnest efforts by MSAR government agencies and wide participation of all sectors, patriotic education is carried out with much success in all types of schools in Macao, planting the seeds of national identity and patriotism deep in the hearts and minds of the young.

Macao's successful experience teaches us the importance of continuously cementing and expanding the social and political foundations required for "one country, two systems" and of achieving the broadest possible unity based on love for the country and Macao. This provides the fundamental safeguard for continued progress along the right track of "one country, two systems".

My fellow compatriots,

Dear friends,

The journey of "one country, two systems" is long and hard. The world is undergoing a scale of change unseen in a century, and Macao is facing new internal and external dynamics. In this context, the new

MSAR government and all sectors of Macao need to stand taller and look farther, brace for potential risks even when the going is good, break new ground while keeping to the right path, and be results-oriented and hard-working. I encourage you to build on what Macao has accomplished and take all undertakings in the MSAR to the next level. For this, let me share with you four expectations:

First, keep abreast of the times and further enhance the quality of governance. The ancient Chinese understood that "those with a sound grasp of governance will leave no problems unresolved and no defects unrepaired"[2]. Macao needs to adapt to the new dynamics and requirements of modern social governance, advance reform in public administration and other systems, enhance efficacy in administration, and modernize its governance. It needs to take the rule of law as the basic principle of governing the MSAR and continue to improve the systems and mechanisms for governing Macao in accordance with the law. It needs to harness science and technology, move faster towards a smart city, and create innovative models of government administration and social governance through the application of big data and other information technologies. The objective is to improve government decision-making, and make social governance better targeted and public services more efficient.

Second, break new ground to better realize sustained and sound economic development. A long-term perspective must be adopted when drawing up development plans. With the goal of becoming "One Center, One Platform, One Base" in mind, Macao needs to develop well-conceived plans, adopt a holistic and coordinated approach, and implement the plans progressively. On the basis of Macao's realities and through rigorous feasibility studies, the MSAR needs to identify the main focus and key projects for appropriately diversifying its economy. It needs to take a multi-pronged strategy in terms of policy, human resources and financial support, and resolve the most difficult issues through synergy. Macao needs to carve out its role in national strategies, seize the opportunities provided by the Belt and Road Initiative and the development of the Guangdong-Hong Kong-Macao Greater

Bay Area, better leverage its own strengths, and sharpen its competitive edge. What is particularly important is to ensure good collaboration with Zhuhai in developing Hengqin, which will create immense space and new momentum for Macao's long-term development.

Third, continue to put people first and better ensure and improve their living standards. It must be clearly understood that the goal of development is to make people's lives better. Thus the MSAR needs to adopt institutional arrangements that are fairer, more equitable, and beneficial to all, so that the fruits of development can be shared by all in the community. To foster a better living environment and higher quality of life, Macao needs to combine its development needs with the people's needs and improve public infrastructure relating to transport, energy, environmental protection, information, and urban safety and security. The MSAR needs to actively respond to public concerns, address prominent issues in housing, health care, and care for the elderly, and scale up assistance and support to the vulnerable. It is also important to further develop education and put in place the best possible education system, so as to create a more conducive environment for children and young people to grow and live to their full potential.

Fourth, persist in an inclusive approach and further promote social harmony and stability. The core value of loving the motherland and Macao needs to be upheld and encouraged so that everyone is mobilized to contribute to Macao's development. Community organizations in Macao should be strengthened, and those that embrace the core values can serve as bridges between the government and the people. Macao's tradition of valuing unity and consultation must be preserved. Matters should be addressed through consultation and settled through coordination. Societal problems must be properly addressed for the greater good of social harmony. As a place where Chinese and Western cultures meet, Macao is well positioned to promote international people-to-people exchanges and mutual learning between cultures.

My fellow compatriots,

Dear friends,

I wish to emphasize that, with the return of Hong Kong and

Macao, the handling of affairs in the two special administrative regions is strictly China's internal business. No external force has any right to dictate to us. The government and the people of China have a rock-firm determination to uphold our national sovereignty, security and development interests. We will never tolerate any external interference in Hong Kong and Macao affairs.

My fellow compatriots,

Dear friends,

In the early 1980s when Deng Xiaoping and other leaders of his generation put forward the great vision of "one country, two systems", they were of the firm belief that it was the right policy and would work, succeed, and win public support. For the past 30 years, the success of "one country, two systems" has won widespread recognition throughout the world. Naturally, steady improvements are needed in the institutional arrangements as the policy continues to be applied. We have every confidence that we Chinese, including our fellow compatriots in Hong Kong and Macao, have the wisdom and ability to better practice and develop "one country, two systems", carry out the necessary improvements in institutional arrangements, and achieve still greater success in governing the two special administrative regions. The rejuvenation of the Chinese nation is unstoppable, and the common development and prosperity of Hong Kong and Macao together with the mainland of China can foresee an ever-brighter future.

Thank you.

Notes

[1] This refers to a global tourism and leisure center, a service platform for commercial and trade cooperation between China and Portuguese-speaking countries, and a cultural exchange and cooperation base with Chinese culture as the mainstream and the coexistence of multiple cultures.

[2] Huan Kuan: *Discourses on Salt and Iron (Yan Tie Lun)*. Huan Kuan (dates unknown) was an official of the Western Han Dynasty (206 BC-AD 25).

Meeting with relatives of late Lao leader Quinim Pholsena in Vientiane, November 14, 2017, during his state visit to Laos.

President Xi Jinping and his Russian counterpart Vladimir Putin receiving jerseys from players before a friendly match between the youth ice hockey teams of China and Russia in Tianjin, June 8, 2018.

With other leaders attending the Qingdao Summit of the Shanghai Cooperation Organization, June 10, 2018. Xi chaired and addressed the 18th Meeting of the Council of Heads of Member States of the SCO.

Addressing the Eighth Ministerial Conference of the China-Arab States Cooperation Forum at the opening ceremony in Beijing, July 10, 2018.

With South African President Cyril Ramaphosa at an exhibition of China-South Africa cooperation in scientific and technological innovation, prior to the opening ceremony of a high-level dialogue between Chinese and South African scientists in Pretoria, July 24, 2018.

Delivering a speech at the opening ceremony of the BRICS Business Forum, July 25, 2018, during the 10th BRICS Summit in Johannesburg, South Africa.

Together with foreign leaders on their way to the opening ceremony of the Beijing Summit of the Forum on China-Africa Cooperation in the Great Hall of the People, September 3, 2018. Xi gave a keynote speech at the ceremony.

Touring the exhibition hall with foreign leaders attending the First China International Import Expo in Shanghai, November 5, 2018.

Xi and his wife, Peng Liyuan, together with heads of delegations for the 13th G20 Summit and their spouses in Buenos Aires, Argentina, November 30, 2018.

At a dinner with US President Donald Trump during the 13th G20 Summit in Buenos Aires, December 1, 2018.

Xi and his wife, Peng Liyuan, on a visit to the new locks of the Panama Canal, together with Panamanian President Juan Carlos Varela and his wife, Lorena Castillo Garcia, in Panama City, December 3, 2018.

Receiving a first French translation of The Analects of Confucius, *published in 1688, offered by French President Emmanuel Macron as a gift, prior to their official meeting in Nice, France, March 24, 2019.*

Meeting with French President Emmanuel Macron, German Chancellor Angela Merkel, and European Commission President Jean-Claude Juncker at the closing ceremony of the Seminar on Global Governance co-hosted by China and France in Paris, March 26, 2019.

Xi and his wife, Peng Liyuan, held a banquet in the Great Hall of the People to welcome foreign leaders and their spouses and other guests attending the Second Belt and Road Forum for International Cooperation in Beijing, April 26, 2019.

Accompanying foreign leaders at the International Horticultural Exhibition 2019 after the opening ceremony in Yanqing District, Beijing, April 28, 2019.

With foreign leaders and other guests at the opening ceremony of the Conference on Dialogue of Asian Civilizations in the China National Convention Center, Beijing, May 15, 2019. Xi delivered a keynote speech at the ceremony.

China's Diplomacy as a Major Country

China's Diplomacy in the New Era*

December 28, 2017

Since the 18th CPC National Congress in 2012, under the leadership of the Party Central Committee and with the support of the people, we have forged ahead on the diplomatic front in the face of multiple challenges.

We have remained resolute in safeguarding China's sovereignty, national security and development interests. We have broadened our global diplomatic agenda, and played an active part in global governance. We have launched the Belt and Road Initiative (BRI) and moved it forward. We have achieved unprecedented successes, and created a favorable external environment for realizing the Two Centenary Goals and the Chinese Dream of national rejuvenation, thus contributing significantly to human progress. Our remarkable accomplishments in foreign affairs over the past five years have won plaudits from the whole Party and the people of China.

Chinese socialism has entered a new era. To improve our diplomatic work in the new era, we must get a solid grasp of the guiding principles established at the 19th CPC National Congress, and clearly identify the underlying trends of the times and international developments.

The world is undergoing momentous changes of a scale unseen in a century. Since the turn of this century, a significant number of emerging markets and developing countries have achieved rapid economic growth. The trend towards multi-polarity is gaining momentum and the configuration of international dynamics is moving towards balance. This is an irreversible trend.

---

* Main points of the speech at the 2017 Meeting for Chinese Diplomatic Envoys.

Under the leadership of the CPC and with resolve and tenacity, our Chinese nation has stood up, become better off, and grown in strength. The prospects for China's rejuvenation are bright as never before. As long as we stay true to our vision and forge ahead on the path of building socialism with Chinese characteristics, we will make China stronger and even more prosperous. Our country will move closer to the center stage of the world and make a greater contribution to humanity.

Under the strong leadership of the Party, we Chinese are marching on the path of Chinese socialism, reform and opening up with pride, confidence and commitment. We refuse to return to the old path of a rigid closed-door policy or follow an erroneous path of abandoning socialism. Instead, we have endeavored to break new ground. As a result, we have made remarkable advances in building socialism with Chinese characteristics. Our future is bright.

China now faces both unprecedented opportunities and challenges. You and all those working on China's diplomatic front must gain a full understanding of and apply the guiding principles established at the 19th CPC National Congress and the Thought on Socialism with Chinese Characteristics for a New Era. You must remain true to our original aspiration and founding mission, and press ahead with determination. You should break new ground in diplomacy that befits China's status as a major country, and further contribute to the cause of the Party and the state.

First, remain loyal to the Party and dedicate yourselves to the nation. Strong commitment to your ideals and convictions and absolute loyalty to the Party, nation and people are the root and soul of a Chinese diplomat. You should enhance the Four Consciousnesses and reinforce the Four-sphere Confidence. You should keep in alignment with the CPC Central Committee in the way of thinking, in political principles and in actions. You should firmly uphold the authority of the Central Committee and its centralized, unified leadership. You should act on the principles and policies on foreign affairs formulated by the Central Committee, and resolutely safeguard China's interests and national dignity. Our diplomats should conduct diplomacy for the people and serve them wholeheartedly.

Second, be enterprising and have a stronger sense of mission. The CPC strives for both the wellbeing of the Chinese people and the progress of humanity. You should take a holistic approach to both the domestic and international situation, develop a global and strategic vision, and pursue the interests of both China and the world. We should promote a new model of international relations and a global community of shared future. You should endeavor to pursue a broad diplomatic agenda, expand the network of global partnerships, and make more friends across the world.

You should promote BRI, boost win-win cooperation between China and other countries, and pursue common development. You should become more actively involved in global governance and multilateral affairs to uphold the interests of the Chinese and humanity. You need to tell the world China's success stories, especially those of the Party and people, to promote mutual understanding and friendship between China and other countries.

Third, pursue continuous learning and self-improvement. China's diplomacy is taking on new and broader dimensions, and conditions are changing. This has raised new tasks and missions for you diplomats, and much more is expected of you. You should have both strong political commitment and professional competence. To this end, you should take a live-and-learn approach, and gain a keen understanding of the Party's theories, principles and policies, as well as Chinese laws and regulations. You should also enrich your knowledge of a range of subjects, enhance your professional caliber, and build up your capacity so that you will be better able to fulfill your diplomatic mission.

Fourth, remain committed to the principle that the Party must practice self-discipline and be strict with its members. The power to make foreign policy rests with the CPC Central Committee, which exercises centralized and unified leadership over China's foreign affairs. Party organizations must fulfill their principal responsibilities for enforcing Party discipline and conducting strict Party self-supervision and self-governance. You must see that the Party's leadership over foreign affairs is upheld, Party organizations strengthened, and the Party's political foundations reinforced. You must strictly comply with Party political discipline and rules, and the Central Committee's Eight Rules. You should build yourselves into a vigorous contingent of diplomats who have strong political commitment, are professionally competent, and are exemplary in conduct and well-disciplined.

It is my hope that you will live up to the trust of the Party and people, faithfully perform your duties, work creatively, and make your contribution to China's diplomatic work in the new era.

Strengthen CPC Central Committee Leadership over Foreign Affairs*

May 15, 2018

Since the 18th CPC National Congress in 2012, under the strong leadership of the Party Central Committee, we have worked creatively to break new ground in our diplomatic theories and practices. We have better pursued and expanded our global diplomatic agenda. We have initiated the Belt and Road Initiative (BRI). We have been more actively involved in reform and improvement of the global governance system. We have been firm in safeguarding China's sovereignty, national security and development interests.

The Party's centralized and unified leadership over our foreign affairs has been enhanced. We have pursued a distinctive Chinese approach to diplomacy befitting a major country, and achieved historic successes.

Given the build-up of factors of uncertainty and instability in the world today, we are faced with both opportunities and challenges. We must therefore have a correct reading of the evolving international environment and the development trends in both China and the world, while being conscious of potential risks and challenges that may arise on our journey ahead. We must be prepared to address problems should they arise.

Now and in the time to come, we should pursue a broader diplomatic agenda, and see that our major initiatives are delivered as planned. We should guard against risks and dangers, and make sure that China's sovereignty, national security and development interests

---

* Main points of the speech at the first session of the Commission for Foreign Affairs under the CPC Central Committee.

will never be compromised.

BRI cooperation provides a solid platform for building a global community of shared future. In just a few years, this initiative has evolved from vision into action, a results-oriented project of international cooperation. We should follow up on the programs and projects agreed at the First Belt and Road Forum for International Cooperation, and work closely with other BRI participants to build consensus and plan for future cooperation. We should open up further and enhance dialogue, consultation, and cooperation with other parties. We should see that BRI cooperation makes solid and sustainable progress and deliver true benefits to the peoples of participating countries.

The conduct of foreign affairs at the subnational level is an integral part of the foreign affairs agenda of the Party and the government. It can make a significant contribution to international exchanges and cooperation and to reform and development of local areas.

The conduct of foreign affairs at the subnational level must be planned under the centralized and unified leadership of the Central Commission for Foreign Affairs to ensure success. The resources for foreign affairs at the subnational level should be managed centrally and used for localities with clear and specific objectives.

To advance China's foreign affairs in the new era, the Central Commission for Foreign Affairs should play its role of policy-making, deliberation and coordination. The commission should encourage and promote new breakthroughs in diplomatic theories and practices, and provide guidance in opening up new horizons.

We should strengthen top-level design and coordination, and build up our capacity to chart the right course, craft overall plans and design policies. We should advance reform of foreign affairs-related systems and mechanisms, and strengthen the training and management of officials involved.

We should ensure that priority programs are carried out through proper management, inspection and follow-up measures and that the Party Central Committee's decisions on foreign affairs are implemented in full.

Break New Ground in China's Major-Country Diplomacy*

June 22, 2018

In conducting foreign affairs, we should be guided by the thought on foreign affairs of socialism with Chinese characteristics in the new era. We must take a holistic approach to the situation both at home and abroad, focus on the goal of rejuvenating the Chinese nation and promoting the progress of humanity, and endeavor to build a global community of shared future.

We must firmly uphold China's sovereignty, national security, and development interests, actively participate in reform of the global governance system and steer its course. We should enhance our network of global partnerships, and endeavor to break new ground in pursuing major-country diplomacy with distinctive Chinese features. We hope that with these efforts, we will be able to create a favorable external environment and contribute to the building of a moderately prosperous society in all respects, and, ultimately, a great modern socialist country.

Since the 18th CPC National Congress in 2012, under the strong leadership of the Party Central Committee, we have overcome multiple difficulties in the ever-changing world and forged ahead on the diplomatic front in the face of multiple challenges. We have made remarkable progress in pursuing in a creative way major-country diplomacy with distinctive Chinese features. We have withstood the test of numerous risks, fought many tough battles, accomplished no small number of difficult missions, and made historic progress.

Reviewing these practice and experiences, we are more keenly

---

* Main points of the speech at the Central Conference on Foreign Affairs.

aware that in conducting foreign affairs, we must always take a holistic approach to the domestic and international situation, have confidence in our diplomatic strategies, maintain strategic resolve, and creatively develop and enrich our diplomatic theories and practices. We need to plan and pursue our diplomatic agenda from a strategic and global perspective and firmly safeguard our core and major national interests. We should uphold the greater good and shared interests in promoting mutually beneficial cooperation, and remain alert to risks and potential dangers.

Since the 18th CPC National Congress, based on a keen understanding of the general development trends in China and the world in the new era, we have made significant breakthroughs in our diplomatic theories and practices. It is on this basis that the thought on foreign affairs of socialism with Chinese characteristics in the new era has taken shape. The ten principles underlying the thought are as follows:

- upholding the authority of the CPC Central Committee and strengthening the Party's centralized and unified leadership over China's foreign affairs;
- pursuing major-country diplomacy with distinctive Chinese features to accomplish the great rejuvenation of the Chinese nation;
- building a global community of shared future to safeguard world peace and promote common development;
- upholding socialism with Chinese characteristics and enhancing our strategic confidence;
- pursuing the Belt and Road Initiative (BRI) under the principles of extensive consultation and joint contribution to benefit all;
- pursuing peaceful development on the basis of mutual respect and win-win cooperation;
- building global partnerships through pursuing a broad diplomatic agenda;
- steering reform of the global governance system to promote greater equity and justice;
- upholding China's sovereignty, national security, and develop-

ment interests as our core and non-negotiable position; and
- shaping China's distinctive diplomatic conduct by drawing on its best traditions and adapting to the changing times.

We must put into action the thought on foreign affairs and work continuously to create an external environment favorable for realizing the Chinese Dream of national rejuvenation and building a global community of shared future.

We need to adopt a historical and holistic approach to assessing international developments and choose the right approach to China's role.

A historical approach is to observe the unfolding international developments from a historical perspective. We need to review the past and learn lessons from history so as to gain a keen understanding of the underlying trends of the future.

A holistic approach is to look beyond individual phenomena or specifics to capture the essence of developments and see the broader picture. We must focus on the main problems and their key features, so as not to get disoriented or pursue minor interests to the neglect of fundamental ones in a fluid and ever-changing world.

The right approach to China's role is to be cool-headed in analyzing global developments. We should view China's role in the context of its relations with the rest of the world so as to clearly define its position and role in an evolving international landscape, and adopt a foreign policy that befits China's role.

Our country is now in its best period of development since the advent of modern times; and the world is undergoing momentous changes unseen in a century. Both trends are growing and impacting each other. These developments are conducive to conducting our foreign affairs for now and in the years to come.

The period between the 19th and the 20th CPC national congresses is one where the timeframes of the Two Centenary Goals converge; and this period is of special significance to achieving the rejuvenation of the Chinese nation.

World history tells us that the progress of humanity has always been driven by the interplay of interwoven events. We must make an in-depth analysis of evolving international developments as the world is going through a period of transition. This will help us to gain a keen understanding of the underlying features of China's external environment, and plan and conduct our foreign affairs accordingly.

We need to have a keen appreciation of the dynamics of the accelerating global trend towards multi-polarity, and closely follow the significant adjustments of relations among major countries.

We need to closely follow both the growing trend of economic globalization and the profound changes in the world economic landscape.

We need to recognize both the overall stability in the international environment and the complexity of interwoven international security challenges.

We also need to see both the trend of mutual learning and enrichment between civilizations and the diversity of ideas and cultures.

To successfully conduct China's foreign affairs, we should implement the overall plans and decisions of the Party Central Committee and pursue a well-considered diplomatic agenda with clearly defined priorities.

We should endeavor to break new ground in conducting foreign affairs, with a focus on historic junctures and major events on the timeline of the Party and our country. In the next five years, we will accomplish the First Centenary Goal, and start working towards the second. A series of major events are scheduled for this period. We must align our diplomatic programs with these events and junctures. We should make overall plans with clearly set priorities and adopt a phased approach to their implementation. We should move forward on multiple fronts while taking targeted measures in priority areas so as to deliver desired outcomes.

We should continue to champion the cause of building a global community of shared future, and work for greater fairness and equity in global governance.

We should continue to push forward the BRI under the principles of extensive consultation and joint contribution to benefit all, and see that BRI cooperation will achieve solid and sustainable progress, and will lift China's opening up to a new level.

We should properly handle our relations with other major countries and put in place a framework for stable and balanced growth of relations among major countries.

We should continue to pursue neighborhood diplomacy to foster a more favorable and friendlier environment in areas around China.

We should strengthen ties and cooperation with other developing countries to promote common progress and development. Other developing countries are China's natural allies in international affairs. We must pursue the greater good and shared interests, and boost solidarity and collaboration between developing nations.

We must further promote in-depth exchanges and mutual learning between China and the rest of the world.

Foreign policy epitomizes the will of a state. The power to make foreign policy is vested in the CPC Central Committee. It is important to maintain our political commitment, think in terms of the general picture, follow the core leadership of the CPC Central Committee, and act in accordance with its requirements. It is imperative to uphold the authority of the CPC Central Committee and its centralized and unified leadership, and closely follow the leadership in terms of thinking, political commitment and actions. All directives and orders of the CPC Central Committee must be executed without fail.

The conduct of foreign affairs is a systematic endeavor. It requires coordination between all actors involved, including the Party, the government, NPC, CPPCC, the military, local authorities, and non-governmental sectors. Each actor needs to have their own focus and work in concert with others. There should be a general framework of cooperation and coordination in place where the CPC exercises overall leadership and coordinates the foreign affairs programs of all the actors. This mechanism will ensure the foreign policy and strategies decided by the CPC Central Committee be implemented in letter and spirit.

A Global Community of
Shared Future

Meet the People's Expectation for a Better Life*

December 1, 2017

As the term suggests, a global community of shared future means that the future of each and every nation and country is interlocked. We are in the same boat, and we should stick together, share weal and woe, endeavor to build this planet of ours into a single harmonious family, and turn people's longing for a better life into reality.

– We should endeavor to build a world of universal security free from fear. The evolution of human civilization shows that despite our longing for lasting peace for thousands of years, the specter of war has never been far away and has continued to haunt us. As all of humanity lives on the same planet, no country should maintain its own security at the cost of another's. A threat to another country may turn out to be a challenge to your own. Unilateral action or blind belief in the use of force cannot provide an answer to increasingly complex and multifaceted security threats.

Instead, we should adopt a new common approach to security that is comprehensive, cooperative, and sustainable, and we should work together to put in place a new security architecture that is equitable, fair, and beneficial to all. We should jointly remove the root causes of war, reach out to those displaced by war, and protect women and children from the scourge of war, so that the sunshine of peace will radiate across our land and everyone will live in peace and harmony.

– We should endeavor to build a world of common prosperity free from poverty. Despite the fact that material and technological development in the world today has reached a level that would have

---

* Part of the keynote speech at the CPC in Dialogue with World Political Parties High-level Meeting.

been unimaginable to our ancestors, imbalanced and inadequate development still presents a major issue. There is a huge development gap between the North and the South; poverty and hunger remain widespread; a new digital divide is emerging; and people in many countries are still living in distress. If you follow the old-fashioned logic of winner-takes-all, or beggar-thy-neighbor, you will shut the door on others and only end up blocking your own way. Such practices can only serve to erode the foundations of one's own development and impair the future of humanity.

We should subscribe to the concept of benefiting all, and push for economic globalization that is more open, inclusive, equitable and balanced, thus creating conditions for pursuing common development of all peoples. Together, we should work for the common development and prosperity of all countries, eradicate poverty and backwardness that still plague people in many countries, and create a worry-free life for children around the world. It will enable all countries to benefit from development and all peoples to enjoy prosperity, peace and good health.

– We should endeavor to build a world that is open and inclusive, a world free from isolation. As an ancient Chinese saying goes, "All living things grow side by side without harming one another; the sun, moon and seasons rotate according to their own laws without hindering each other."[1] The flourishing of civilization and the progress of humanity will not be possible without enhancing common ground, openness, inclusiveness, exchanges and mutual learning among civilizations, and agreeing to disagree.

Different civilizations should blossom and coexist in harmony with each other, and draw on each other's strength to inspire and nourish human development – this is the call of history. We should always bear in mind that the world is a colorful one with diverse civilizations; and we should see that different civilizations enrich each other and create a splendid world. We should work together to bring down cultural barriers, reject prejudices that stand in the way of human interactions, and eliminate cultural bias that prevents people from engaging with one another. Let us work together to make sure that different civilizations coexist in harmony with each other and that everybody enjoys cultural nourishment.

– We should endeavor to build a green, clean and beautiful world. The Earth is the only shared home for humanity. Now, a few individuals are trying to find a new home in outer space, but that is still a distant dream. And in the foreseeable future, human beings still need to live on this planet. This is a fact that will not change. We should jointly protect our planet, not only for ourselves, but also for the sake of future generations. Believing in harmony between man and nature, we should cherish the environment as dearly as we cherish our own lives. We should revere, respect, adapt to, and protect nature. We should protect the irreplaceable planet Earth, our home, heal wounds inflicted on the eco-environment, and build a harmonious and livable home for humanity. This will allow the natural ecosystems to recover and regenerate themselves, and allow everyone to live in an environment of lucid waters and lush mountains.

Today, the world is changing, as are our development models. Political parties must move with the tide of the times, have a good understanding of the general trends of human progress, meet the common expectations of the people, and closely link their personal development with the development of their country, their nation and humanity. We should aim high and look far, have the courage to take up responsibilities, and shoulder the mission of the times, bearing in mind the interests of both our own countries and the world at large, and both the overall interests and long-term interests.

We should have a good knowledge of our people's conditions and translate their needs into our Party's guiding thoughts, purposes, and goals, and design concrete and practical implementation plans.

The building of a global community of shared future requires the participation of all peoples. To advance this great cause we should build consensus among people of different nations, with different beliefs and cultures, and from different regions.

To realize a great dream, it is imperative to draw on the wisdom and strength of all involved. We should try to pool ideas from multiple dimensions, different levels and different perspectives, draw on best practices, explore new ways of thinking, get inspiration, and build momentum. Political parties from different countries should enhance mutual trust, dialogue, and coordination. Building on a new model of international relations, we should explore a new model of party-to-party relations in which political parties seek to expand common ground while reserving differences, and respect and learn from each other. We should build a multiform, multilevel international network for party-to-party exchanges and cooperation. All these will work together and form a mighty force for building a global community of shared future.

A trail can be blazed only by taking steps; and a cause can be accomplished only by taking actions. Building a global community of shared future is a historic process. It cannot be completed overnight, nor will it be plain sailing. Persistent and arduous efforts are called for. To build such a community, we must make unremitting efforts. We should not give up on our dream because of the complexity of the reality, nor should we stop pursuing our ideals as they seem so far away to reach.

The CPC is a political party dedicated to the wellbeing of the Chinese people and to the progress of human society. It is the largest political party in the world. As I once said, the CPC must act in the way that a major party should. What we Chinese Communists are doing is to better the lives of the Chinese people, rejuvenate the Chinese nation, and promote peace and development for humanity. We must run our own house well, which in itself is a contribution to the building of a global community of shared future. We intend to create more opportunities for the rest of the world through our own development. We will achieve social development through our actions, and share our experience with other countries. We do not want to import models from other countries, nor do we want to export the Chinese model; still less will we ask other countries to copy our practices. We Chinese Communists will stay true to the following commitments:

First, we will continue to work for global peace and tranquility.

Nearly 100 years ago, the CPC was born when China was in turmoil. One of its founding missions was to put an end to the dire plight in which China had suffered from frequent wars and the Chinese people from destitution since the mid-19th century. From 1921 to 1949, in order to achieve peace and stability in China and enable its people to live and work in peace, the CPC rallied the Chinese people and led them in an armed struggle for 28 years, and made huge sacrifices.

Having gone through all this, we Chinese Communists know only too well how precious peace is; hence we are resolved to maintain peace. China remains committed to promoting peace, development, and cooperation, and delivering win-win outcomes. We will always pursue peaceful development, actively promote the building of global partnerships, and proactively engage ourselves in the process of political settlement of international hotspot and difficult issues.

China, a major contributor of troops and funds for UN peacekeeping operations, has cumulatively dispatched over 36,000 peacekeepers. As I am talking now, more than 2,500 Chinese peacekeepers are serving UN missions in eight mission zones, safeguarding local peace and security, regardless of the difficulties and dangers.

China will continue to actively engage in the reform and development of the global governance system, and will promote efforts to develop a more just and equitable international political and economic order. No matter how advanced China's development is, China will never seek hegemony or engage in expansion. We call on political parties in all countries to join us and become builders of world peace, contributors to global development, and defenders of the international order.

Second, we will continue to work for common development.

The CPC has its origin in the people and has relied on the people for its growth and development. It has always cared about the people, Chinese and others, and is committed to working for their wellbeing.

Over the years, China has helped many developing countries

in various ways, including providing large amounts of free aid and concessional loans, as well as technical, personnel, and intellectual support. It has helped them complete numerous projects to facilitate their economic and social development and to improve the lives of their people. Today, thousands of Chinese scientists, engineers, entrepreneurs, technicians, doctors and nurses, teachers, workers, and volunteers are working hand in hand and shoulder to shoulder with local people in many developing countries to help them change their lives for the better.

As envisaged by the CPC at its 19th National Congress in 2017, China will achieve moderate prosperity in all respects throughout the country by the year 2020. It will, by and large, realize socialist modernization by the year 2035, and will turn itself into a great modern socialist country that is prosperous, strong, democratic, culturally advanced, harmonious and beautiful by the middle of this century. This will benefit not only the Chinese people, but also the people of other countries. We propose that political parties of other countries work with us and create more cooperation opportunities to the benefit of common development and prosperity.

Third, we will continue to promote exchanges and mutual learning among civilizations.

As a Chinese saying goes, a stone taken from another mountain may serve as a tool to polish the local jade – advice from others may help remedy one's own shortcomings. The CPC always stresses the need to develop a global perspective. We have learned and drawn on the achievements of other cultures and applied them in the Chinese context. Indeed, Marxism is the solid truth we have learned from other countries. We have adapted Marxism to China's conditions, kept it current, and enhanced its popular appeal. As a result, Marxism has become the underlying theory guiding the CPC's efforts to lead the Chinese people on the march forward.

The CPC approaches the achievements of other cultures with an open mind and keen interest. We would like to engage in dialogue, exchanges and cooperation with the people and political parties of other countries, and we support increased cultural and people-to-people exchanges among different countries.

Over the next five years, the CPC will invite 15,000 members of other political parties to visit China for exchanges and interaction. We propose that the CPC in Dialogue with World Political Parties High-level Meeting be institutionalized and be made a high-level platform for political dialogue with broad representation and international influence.

More than 2,000 years ago, the ancient Chinese philosopher Confucius observed that one should make friends with people who are upright, sincere, and well-informed. The CPC is ready to build more friendships across the world. Over the years, we have maintained regular contacts with more than 400 political parties and organizations in over 160 countries and regions, and our circle of friends continues to grow.

Moving forward, the CPC will enhance exchanges with political parties of other countries to share ideas on enhancing party competence and state governance, and conduct further exchanges and dialogue among civilizations so as to improve our strategic mutual trust. Let all of us, people of all countries, join hands to build a global community of shared future and a better world.

Notes

[1] *Book of Rites (Li Ji)*.

Carry Forward the Shanghai Spirit; Build a Community of Shared Future*

June 10, 2018

Dear colleagues,

In this lovely month of June, I am delighted to welcome all of you to the picturesque city of Qingdao for the 18th meeting of the Council of Heads of Member States of the Shanghai Cooperation Organization (SCO). Over 2,500 years ago, the great Chinese philosopher Confucius had this to say, "What a joy to have friends coming from afar!"[1] It is therefore of special significance that I host my distinguished guests in Shandong, the home province of Confucius, for a summit that will chart the future course for the SCO.

In five days, the SCO will celebrate its 17th anniversary, an occasion for us to review our organization's remarkable journey and important achievements.

Over the past 17 years, guided by the SCO Charter and the Treaty of Long-term Good-neighborliness, Friendship and Cooperation Between the Member States of the Shanghai Cooperation Organization, we have forged a constructive partnership of non-alliance, non-confrontation, and non-targeting of any third party. This represents a major breakthrough in the theory and practice of international relations, a new model for regional cooperation, and a new contribution to peace and development in the region.

Today, the SCO stands as a comprehensive regional cooperation organization that encompasses the largest area and population in

---

* Speech at the 18th meeting of the Council of Heads of Member States of the Shanghai Cooperation Organization.

the world. The economy and population of the SCO member states account for about 20 percent and 40 percent of the world's total. The SCO has four observer states and six dialogue partners as well as extensive cooperation links with the United Nations and other international and regional organizations. With its rising international influence, the SCO has become a force to be reckoned with – one promoting world peace and development and upholding international fairness and justice.

Cooperation within the SCO enjoys strong vitality and momentum. In the final analysis, this can be attributed to the Shanghai Spirit, a creative vision initiated and followed through by the SCO that champions mutual trust, mutual benefit, equality, consultation, respect for diversity of civilizations, and pursuit of common development. The Shanghai Spirit, transcending outdated concepts such as the clash of civilizations, Cold War thinking, and zero-sum mentality, has turned a new page in the history of international relations and is winning increasing support from the international community.

Dear colleagues,

Mencius, another ancient Chinese philosopher, aptly observed, "When Confucius looks down from the peak of the Dongshan Mountain, the local Kingdom of Lu comes into view; when he looks down from the peak of Mount Tai, the whole land comes into view."[2] At a time when the world is undergoing major developments, transformation and adjustment, we must aim high and look far, and keep pace with the underlying trends of both the world and our times to drive forward the cause of human civilization and progress.

While hegemony and power politics still persist in this world, the call for a more just and equitable international order must be heeded. Democracy in international relations has become an unstoppable trend.

For all that traditional and non-traditional security threats continue to emerge, the force for peace will prevail – security and stability are what people long for.

For all that unilateralism, trade protectionism and anti-globalization continue to manifest themselves in new forms, in this global village of ours, where countries' interests and future are so interconnected, cooperation for mutual benefit represents a general trend.

For all that we keep hearing such rhetoric as the clash of civilizations or the superiority of one civilization over another, it is the diversity of civilizations that sustains human progress. Indeed, mutual learning between different cultures is a shared aspiration of all peoples.

Dear colleagues,

The world today faces both opportunities and challenges. The road ahead may not be smooth, but it will lead to a promising future. We should stay committed to the Shanghai Spirit, surmount difficulties, defuse risks, and meet challenges head-on.

– We should stand for innovative, coordinated, green, open and shared development, work for coordinated social and economic progress in our countries, and resolve problems caused by imbalanced development. We should bridge the gap in development and promote shared prosperity.

– We should pursue common, comprehensive, cooperative and sustainable security. We should reject the Cold War mentality and confrontation between blocs, and oppose the practice of seeking absolute security for oneself at the expense of others', so as to achieve security for all.

– We should promote open and inclusive cooperation for win-win outcomes. We must be open, farsighted and visionary, rejecting self-centered policies. We should uphold WTO rules and support the multilateral trading system so as to build an open world economy.

– We should champion equality, mutual learning, dialogue and inclusiveness between civilizations. It is important that we remove cultural misunderstandings, transcend cultural clashes, and dispel notions of cultural supremacy, through cultural exchanges, mutual learning and harmonious coexistence.

– We should follow the principle of achieving shared growth through consultation and collaboration in global governance. We should reform and improve the global governance system, and work with all other countries to build a global community of shared future.

Dear colleagues,

The Shanghai Spirit is our shared asset, and the SCO is our shared home. Guided by the Shanghai Spirit, we should work closely to build an SCO community of shared future, move towards a new model of international relations, and build an open, inclusive, clean and beautiful world that enjoys lasting peace, universal security, and common prosperity. To this end, I would like to propose the following:

First, we need to strengthen unity and build mutual trust. We should ensure a full implementation of the commitments made in the Qingdao Declaration, the Plan of Action of the Treaty of Long-term Good-neighborliness, Friendship and Cooperation, and other documents. All should respect the others' choice of development path and accommodate the others' core interests and mutual concerns. We should enhance mutual understanding by seeing things from others' perspectives, and boost harmony and unity by seeking common ground and shelving differences. This will enhance the cohesion and appeal of our organization.

Second, we need to strengthen the foundations of shared peace and security. We need to actively implement the 2019-2021 program of cooperation in combating the "three evil forces" of terrorism, separatism and extremism, continue to conduct the "peace mission" and other joint counter-terrorism exercises, and enhance cooperation in defense security, law enforcement security and information security. We need to give full play to the role of the SCO-Afghanistan Contact Group in facilitating peace and reconstruction in Afghanistan. China wishes to train 2,000 law enforcement officers from SCO member states in the next three years through the China-SCO Training Base for International Exchange and Judicial Cooperation and other platforms to strengthen capacity in law enforcement.

Third, we need to build a powerful engine to achieve common development and prosperity. We should increase complementarity in our respective development strategies, continue to advance the

Belt and Road Initiative in the context of delivering shared benefits through extensive consultation and joint contribution, accelerate the process of regional trade facilitation, and step up the implementation of the Agreement on International Road Transport Facilitation and other cooperation documents. China welcomes all member states to attend the First China International Import Expo in Shanghai in November this year. The Chinese government supports the establishment of a demonstration area in Qingdao for China-SCO local economic and trade cooperation, and a China-SCO legal service committee to provide legal support for economic and trade cooperation.

In support of these measures, I would like to announce that China will set up a special lending facility with a value of RMB30 billion within the framework of the SCO Inter-bank Consortium.

Fourth, we need to forge closer ties through cultural and people-to-people exchanges. We should actively implement the adopted documents, including the SCO concept on environmental protection, ensure the continued success of such well-recognized programs as youth exchange camps, and secure solid progress in cooperation in education, science and technology, culture, tourism, health, disaster relief and the media. In the next three years, China will provide 3,000 training opportunities for personnel from SCO member states to enhance public awareness of and support for the SCO family. China offers all member states meteorological services through access to its *Fengyun-2* weather satellites.

Fifth, we need to expand partnership networks of international cooperation. By intensifying exchanges and cooperation with SCO observer states, dialogue partners, and other countries in our region, by enhancing partnerships with the United Nations and other international and regional organizations, and by engaging in dialogue with the International Monetary Fund, the World Bank and other international financial institutions, we can contribute our share to resolving flashpoint issues and improving global governance.

Dear colleagues,

Thanks to the support and assistance of all other SCO member states over the past year, China has completed its SCO presidency and hosted this summit. Here I wish to express my sincere thanks to you all. China will maintain practical, close and friendly cooperation with other SCO member states to ensure the full implementation of the agreements reached at this summit and support Kyrgyzstan in its SCO presidency. Let us join hands to create an even brighter future for the SCO!

Thank you.

Notes

[1] *The Analects of Confucius (Lun Yu)*.
[2] *The Mencius (Meng Zi)*.

The Role of the BRICS in Building a Global Community of Shared Future*

July 25, 2018

The BRICS mechanism owes its birth and growth to the evolving global economy and international landscape. In its first decade, BRICS cooperation got off the ground and bore rich fruit. We five BRICS countries, guided by the BRICS spirit of openness, inclusiveness and win-win cooperation, have expanded our cooperation, strengthened our solidarity and mutual trust, improved the lives of our peoples, and drawn our bond of interests and friendship even closer. Indeed, our cooperation has contributed much to global economic recovery and growth.

The world is undergoing momentous changes, the scale of which is unseen in a century. This is a world of both opportunities and challenges for us emerging markets and developing countries. We should pursue BRICS cooperation in the historic process of global transformation, and we should promote the development of our own countries in the historic course of promoting the common development of both BRICS countries and other countries, thus making new advances in the next Golden Decade.

– The next decade will be crucial as new global growth drivers will take the place of old ones. A new round of revolution and transformation in science, technology and industry featuring artificial intelligence, big data, quantum information and bio-technology is gaining momentum. These are giving birth to a large number of new industries and business forms and models and will fundamentally change global development and the way people work and live. We must

---

* Part of the speech at the BRICS Business Forum.

seize this historic opportunity and promote leapfrog development in emerging markets and developing countries.

– The next decade will see faster changes in the international landscape and the world balance of power. Emerging markets and developing countries already contribute 80 percent of global economic growth. Based on current exchange rates, these countries account for nearly 40 percent of the global economic output. Growing at their current pace, these countries will see their economic output approach half of the global total in a decade. The collective rise of emerging markets and developing countries is unstoppable, and it will ensure more balanced global development and provide a stronger cornerstone for global peace.

– The next decade will see a profound reshaping of the global governance system. Despite some setbacks, the world is moving towards multi-polarity and greater economic globalization. Geopolitical flashpoints keep emerging, and the dark shadow of terrorism and armed conflict still haunts us. Unilateralism and protectionism are resurgent, dealing a severe blow to multilateralism and the multilateral trade regime. The international community has reached a new crossroads, and we are facing a choice between cooperation and confrontation, between opening up and a close-door policy, and between mutual benefit and a beggar-thy-neighbor approach. Thus, the evolution of the global governance system will have a profound impact on all nations, particularly emerging markets and developing countries, and indeed on the prosperity and stability of the whole world.

We BRICS countries need to keep abreast of the historic trend, seize development opportunities, jointly meet challenges, and play a constructive role in building a new model of international relations and a global community of shared future.

First, we need to pursue win-win cooperation to build an open economy. Opening up and cooperation provide a sure way to achieve progress in science and technology and growth in productivity. Trade wars should be rejected, because there will be no winner. Economic hegemony is even more objectionable, as it will undermine the collective interests of the international community; those who pursue this course will only end up hurting themselves.

As the world economy is going through profound transition and changes, only by opening themselves to others can different countries achieve mutual benefit, shared prosperity, and sustainable development. This should be the choice for all countries. We BRICS countries should firmly promote an open world economy, resolutely reject unilateralism and protectionism, liberate trade and facilitate investment, and jointly steer the global economy towards greater openness, inclusiveness, balanced growth, and win-win outcomes for all. We should see that economic globalization will deliver more benefits. We should help emerging markets and developing countries, African countries and the least developed countries in particular, to become fully involved in international division of labor and share the benefits of economic globalization.

Second, we need to pursue innovation and seize development opportunities. Science and technology, as the primary production forces, have provided inexhaustible power driving the progress of human civilization. Humanity had made giant leaps forward as it progressed from an agricultural civilization to an industrial civilization, a process which created both huge gains in social productivity and growing pains. The world today has once again reached a critical historic juncture. In the unfolding new round of scientific and technological revolution and industrial transformation, new things will inevitably emerge and take the place of old ones. Indeed, this will be a difficult and painful process. But if countries use these opportunities of change and transformation to their advantage, they will be able to achieve dynamic growth and bring better lives to their people.

In the face of new opportunities brought by new science and technology, every country has an equal right to development. Those who fail to keep abreast of the times will fall behind and become irrelevant. What we can and should do is to seize opportunities, increase input in innovation, focus on developing new growth areas, and replace old growth drivers with new ones. We should endeavor to advance structural reform, remove all institutional barriers to innovation, fully unlock innovation potential, and energize the market. We need to develop a global perspective, boost international exchanges and cooperation in innovation, and fully leverage each other's comparative strengths and resource endowment, so as to enable more countries and people to benefit from scientific and technological advances. At the same time, we should ease the adverse impact of IT application, automation and smart technology on traditional industries, and create new job opportunities in the process of fostering new industries.

Third, we need to pursue inclusive growth to deliver benefits to the peoples of all countries. Uneven and insufficient development is a common challenge facing all countries. The North-South gap, namely, the gap between developed countries and emerging markets and developing countries, remains huge. And there are also development gaps of varying degrees within countries.

The 2030 Agenda for Sustainable Development provides a comprehensive action plan for the international community. Basing ourselves on our actual national conditions, we BRICS countries need to follow the guidance of the 2030 Agenda as we pursue our own development strategies. We should put people first, ensure coordinated social and economic development, and protect the environment, thus giving our people a stronger sense of fulfillment and happiness. We should ensure harmony between man and nature and encourage the international community to fully implement the Paris Agreement. We should treat nature with awe and do more to foster an ecosystem conducive to green development. It is important to promote international development cooperation, urge developed countries to fulfill their promises on official development assistance, and increase support to developing countries.

Home to more developing countries than any other continent, Africa has more potential than any other region in the world. We need to strengthen cooperation with Africa, support its development and make BRICS-Africa cooperation a model for South-South cooperation. We should actively carry out cooperation with African countries in such areas as poverty reduction, food security, innovation, infrastructure, and industrialization in ways compatible with their national conditions. We should help African countries improve their economic structure, contribute to the implementation of Agenda 2063 of the African Union (AU), and thus enable Africa, an ancient continent, to grow stronger.

Fourth, we need to uphold multilateralism and improve global governance. An enabling and stable external environment is essential for any country, particularly emerging markets and developing countries, to achieve growth. The current international order is clearly not perfect. But as long as it is rule-based, equity-oriented, and facilitates a win-win outcome, it should not be discarded at will, still less should it be dismantled and rebuilt all over again.

We BRICS countries must uphold multilateralism. We should urge all parties to fully observe collectively-adopted international rules. All countries should be treated as equals regardless of their size, and issues that matter to all must be addressed through consultation. We should say no to hegemony and power politics. We need to promote common, comprehensive, cooperative and sustainable security, and be actively involved in mediation efforts to resolve geopolitical flashpoints. It is important for us to firmly support the multilateral trade regime, advance the reform of global economic governance, and increase the representation and voice of emerging markets and developing countries. When new rules are made on such issues as innovation, trade and investment, and protection of intellectual property rights, or on new frontiers including cyberspace, outer space and the polar regions, we should make sure that the views of emerging markets and developing countries are heeded, that their interests and requests are taken into consideration, and that they are offered sufficient opportunities for development.

Towards a Stronger China-Africa Community of Shared Future*

September 3, 2018

To quote a Chinese saying, "The ocean is vast because it rejects no rivers."[1] China is the world's largest developing country, and Africa is the continent with the largest number of developing countries. China and Africa have long forged a community of shared future, and we rise and fall together. China will work closely with African nations to build an even stronger community of shared future and turn it into a pacesetter for building such a community for humanity.

First, let us build a stronger China-Africa community of shared future that assumes our joint responsibilities. Let us increase political and policy dialogue at various levels, enhance mutual understanding and support on issues bearing on our core interests and major concerns, and strengthen coordination on major international and regional issues. These efforts will serve our common interests and those of other developing countries.

Second, let us build a stronger China-Africa community of shared future that pursues win-win cooperation. Let us build on the complementarity between our respective development strategies and seize the opportunities offered by the Belt and Road Initiative. We need to see to it that the Belt and Road Initiative and the AU Agenda 2063, the UN 2030 Agenda for Sustainable Development and the development programs of African countries better complement each other. With these efforts, we can consolidate our traditional areas of cooperation, expand into new areas, unlock new potential, and foster

---

* Part of the keynote speech at the opening ceremony of the 2018 Beijing Summit of the Forum on China-Africa Cooperation.

new growth areas in the economy.

Third, let us build a stronger China-Africa community of shared future that delivers happiness for all of us. A better life for our people is the ultimate goal of growing our relations, so we need to make sure our cooperation delivers tangible benefits to both Chinese and African peoples. Mutual assistance and solidarity has been the hallmark of China-Africa relations over the years. China, for its part, will do more to help African countries to alleviate poverty, pursue development, increase employment and incomes, and improve the lives of their peoples.

Fourth, let us build a stronger China-Africa community of shared future that promotes cultural prosperity. China and African nations have all created splendid civilizations that we can be proud of. We are ready to make a greater contribution to cultural diversity in the world. We will promote exchanges, mutual learning and harmony between our civilizations, and thereby invigorate our civilizations and cultures, enrich our arts, and provide rich cultural nourishment for China-Africa cooperation. With more people-to-people exchanges in culture and the arts, education, sports, and between our think tanks, media organizations, and women and young people, the bonds between the peoples of China and Africa will grow stronger.

Fifth, let us build a stronger China-Africa community of shared future that enjoys common security. Those who value peace most are those who have gone through adversity. China champions a new vision of security to pursue common, comprehensive, cooperative and sustainable security. China firmly supports African countries and the African Union as well as other regional organizations in Africa in solving African issues in the African way. China also supports the African initiative of "Silence the Guns in Africa". China is ready to play a constructive role in promoting peace and stability in Africa and supports African countries in building up their own capacity for safeguarding stability and peace.

Sixth, let us build a stronger China-Africa community of shared future that promotes harmony between man and nature. The Earth is the only place we can call home. China will work with Africa to pursue green, low-carbon, circular and sustainable development and protect our lush mountains and lucid waters and all living beings on our planet. China will strengthen exchanges and cooperation with Africa on climate change, clean energy, prevention and control of desertification and soil erosion, protection of wildlife, and other areas of ecological and environmental preservation. Together, we can make China and Africa beautiful places for people to live in harmony with nature.

Since the 2015 FOCAC Johannesburg Summit, China has fully implemented the 10 cooperation plans adopted at the summit. A large number of railway, highway, airport, port and other infrastructure projects have been completed or are under construction, as well as a number of economic and trade cooperation zones. Our cooperation in peace and security, science, education, culture, health, poverty reduction, and people-to-people interactions has deepened. The US$60 billion financing pledged by China has been delivered or arranged. These 10 plans have brought huge benefits to the African and Chinese peoples. They amply demonstrate the creativity, rallying power and efficiency of China-Africa cooperation, and lifted China-Africa comprehensive strategic and cooperative partnership to new heights.

As a step towards an even stronger China-Africa community of shared future in the new era, China will build on these 10 cooperation plans and launch eight new initiatives in close collaboration with African countries in the next three years and beyond.

First, an industrial promotion initiative. We will open a China-Africa economic and trade expo in China; we encourage Chinese companies to increase investment in Africa, and will build and upgrade a number of economic and trade cooperation zones in Africa. China supports Africa in achieving general food security by 2030, and will work with Africa to formulate and implement a program of action to promote China-Africa cooperation in agricultural modernization. China will implement 50 agricultural assistance programs, and provide

RMB1 billion of emergency humanitarian food assistance to African countries affected by natural disasters. We will send 500 senior agriculture specialists to Africa and provide training for young leaders of agricultural science and research and for young farmers who can lead others to a better life. We will support Chinese companies in Africa to forge alliances of corporate social responsibilities. We will continue to strengthen cooperation with African countries in local currency settlement and make good use of the China-Africa Development Fund, the China-Africa Fund for Industrial Cooperation, and the Special Loan for the Development of African SMEs.

Second, an infrastructure connectivity initiative. China will work with the African Union to formulate a China-Africa infrastructure cooperation plan. We support Chinese companies in participating in infrastructure development projects in African countries under an invest-build-operate or other applicable model, with a focus on cooperation in energy, transport, IT, telecommunications, and cross-border water resources. We will work with African countries to undertake a number of key connectivity projects. We support the development of the Single African Air Transport Market and will open more direct flights between China and Africa. We will facilitate bond issuance by African countries and their financial institutions in China. Following multilateral rules and procedures, we will support African countries in making better use of the financing resources of the Asian Infrastructure Investment Bank, the New Development Bank, and the Silk Road Fund.

Third, a trade facilitation initiative. We will increase imports from Africa, especially non-resource products. We support African countries' participation in the China International Import Expo. The least developed African countries participating in the Expo will be exempted from exhibition stand fees. We will continue to strengthen exchanges and cooperation on market regulation and between customs authorities, and implement 50 trade facilitation programs for Africa. On a regular basis, we will hold marketing activities for Chinese and African brand products. We support the building of the

African Continental Free Trade Area and will continue to hold free trade negotiations with interested African countries and regions, and we will set up relevant mechanisms to promote e-commerce cooperation with Africa.

Fourth, a green development initiative. China will start 50 projects for green development and ecological and environmental protection in Africa to expand exchanges and cooperation with Africa on climate change, ocean, desertification prevention and control, and wildlife protection. A China-Africa environmental cooperation center will be set up, and more policy dialogue and joint research on environmental issues will be conducted. The China-Africa Green Envoys Program will be implemented to strengthen Africa's human capacity for environmental management, pollution prevention and control, and green development. A China-Africa bamboo center will be established to help Africa make bamboo and rattan products. China will also work with Africa to raise public awareness of environmental protection.

Fifth, a capacity building initiative. China will share more of its development experience with Africa and support cooperation with Africa in planning economic and social development. Ten Lu Ban[2] Workshops will be set up in Africa to provide vocational training for young Africans. China will support a China-Africa innovation cooperation center to promote youth innovation and entrepreneurship. A tailor-made program will be carried out to train 1,000 talented Africans. China will provide Africa with 50,000 government scholarships and 50,000 training opportunities for seminars and workshops, and will invite 2,000 young Africans to visit China for exchanges.

Sixth, a health care initiative. China will upgrade 50 medical and health aid programs for Africa, particularly flagship projects such as the headquarters of the African Center for Disease Control and Prevention and China-Africa friendship hospitals. Exchange and information cooperation will be carried out on public health. Cooperation programs will be launched on the prevention and control of emerging and re-emerging communicable diseases, schistosomiasis,

HIV/AIDS and malaria. China will train more medical specialists for Africa and continue to send medical teams that best meet Africa's needs. More mobile medical services will be provided to patients for the treatment of cataracts, heart disease and dental defects, and targeted health care services will be provided to women and children of vulnerable groups in Africa.

Seventh, a people-to-people exchange initiative. China will establish an institute of African studies to enhance inter-civilizational exchanges with African nations. The China-Africa Joint Research and Exchange Plan will be upgraded. Fifty joint cultural, sports and tourism events will be organized. China welcomes Africa's participation in the Silk Road International League of Theaters, the Silk Road International Museum Alliance, and the Network of Silk Road Art Festivals. A China-Africa media cooperation network will be established. More African culture centers will be opened in China and more Chinese culture centers in Africa. Qualified African educational institutes are welcome to host Confucius Institutes. More African countries are welcome to become destinations for Chinese tour groups.

Eighth, a peace and security initiative. China will set up a China-Africa peace and security fund to boost our cooperation in peace, security, peacekeeping, and law and order. China will continue to provide military aid to the AU, and will support countries in the Sahel region and those bordering the Gulf of Aden and the Gulf of Guinea in upholding security and combating terrorism in their regions. A China-Africa peace and security forum will be established as a platform for more exchanges in this area. Fifty security assistance programs will be launched to advance China-Africa cooperation under the Belt and Road Initiative, and in law and order, UN peacekeeping missions, fighting piracy, and combating terrorism.

To make sure that these eight initiatives are implemented on the ground, China will extend US$60 billion of financing to Africa in the form of government assistance as well as investment and financing by financial institutions and companies. This will include US$15 billion of grants, interest-free loans and concessional loans, US$20 billion of credit lines, the setting up of a US$10 billion special fund for development financing and a US$5 billion special fund for financing imports from Africa. We are encouraging Chinese companies to make at least US$10 billion of investment in Africa in the next three years. In addition, for those of Africa's least developed countries, heavily indebted and poor countries, landlocked developing countries, and small island developing countries that have diplomatic relations with China, the debt they have incurred in the form of interest-free Chinese government loans due to mature by the end of 2018 will be written off.

The future of China-Africa relations lies in our young people. Many of the measures in the eight initiatives I have just announced are designed to help young people in Africa. These measures will provide young Africans with more training and job opportunities and open up more space for their development. Last October, I wrote back to the exchange students of the Institute of South-South Cooperation and Development. Most of them were from Africa. I encouraged them to make the best of what they have learned, aim high, and keep working hard to promote China-Africa cooperation and South-South cooperation. I believe they have new roles to play and new accomplishments to make in this regard.

"The red rising sun will light up the road ahead."[3] I am confident that the baton of China-Africa friendship will be passed from one generation to the next and that China and Africa, working together, will build an even more vibrant community of shared future. The day will surely come when the Chinese nation realizes its dream of national rejuvenation and Africa realizes its dream of unity and invigoration.

Notes

[1] *Guan Zi.*

² Lu Ban (507-444 BC) was a civil engineer and inventor in the Spring and Autumn Period.

³ Liang Qichao: "Young China" (Shao Nian Zhong Guo Shuo). Liang Qichao (1873-1929) was a thinker and scholar, and one of the leaders of the Hundred Days' Reform in 1898 in the late Qing Dynasty.

Define an Effective Approach to Global Economic Governance*

November 17, 2018

The scale of change we are encountering in the world today has not been seen in a century. Change creates opportunities, but more often than not, it is accompanied by risks and challenges. Humanity has once again reached a crossroads. Which direction should we choose? Cooperation or confrontation? Opening up or closing our doors? Win-win progress or a zero-sum game? The interests of all countries and indeed, the future of humanity hinge on the choices we make.

A review of modern world history clearly shows that different choices will lead the world onto different paths.

In the Asia-Pacific, the establishment of the Asia-Pacific Economic Cooperation (APEC) is a real success story. Its birth and growth echo the historic trend of opening and integration, our region's fervent desire for development, and our people's need to meet challenges through cooperation. Opening and cooperation in the Asia-Pacific has boosted its prosperity and injected vitality into the vast ocean of the global economy. Today's Asia-Pacific has the world's most dynamic and promising economies, and is widely recognized as a key engine driving global growth.

However, not all that has happened in the past has been a success story. Humanity has learned lessons the hard way. In the last century, for instance, World War II plunged the world into the abyss of calamity. Not far from where we are meeting now are the sites of the fierce

---

* Part of the speech at the APEC CEO Summit.

Battle of the Coral Sea in 1942 and the Battle of Guadalcanal between 1942 and 1943. Today, this part of the ocean has long been restored to peace and calm, but never should we forget the lessons of history.

An ancient Chinese philosopher observed that "one needs to clean the mirror before taking a look at oneself, and should learn the lessons of the past before making the decisions of today"[1]. In reviewing history, we should draw on its lessons to prevent the recurrence of past tragedies. Facing surging historic trends, we need to ask ourselves: How can we steer the right course for global economic development? How can the international community find an effective way of conducting global governance? I believe it is imperative that we focus on the following:

First, we should focus on opening up to create more space for development. Economic globalization is a sure way for human society to achieve development, and the multilateral trading system has created opportunities for us all. In today's world, countries' interests are so closely intertwined, and the global supply chain, industrial chain and value chain are so closely connected that we are all links in the global chain of cooperation; increasingly, we are becoming one and the same community with shared interests and of shared future.

This is the working of the laws of economics, a fact no one can change. We need to gain a keen appreciation of this underlying trend and view the changing world for what it is, and on that basis, respond to new developments and meet new challenges in a responsible and rule-based way. Any attempt to erect barriers and cut the close economic ties among countries works against the laws of economics and the trend of history, and runs counter to the shared desire of people around the world. This is a short-sighted approach, and it is doomed to failure.

Every era faces the problems of its day. Problems themselves are not to be feared; what truly matters is for us to take the right approach to resolving them. Resorting to old practices such as protectionism and unilateralism will achieve nothing. On the contrary, they will only add uncertainties to the global economy. Only opening up and cooperation can bring more opportunities and create more space for development. This is a clear historical fact. Those who choose to close their doors will only cut themselves off from the rest of the world and lose their direction.

APEC is a pioneer in building an open global economy. As the Bogor Goals are set for 2020, we should set our sights on post-2020 cooperation and endeavor to build a Free Trade Area of the Asia-Pacific (FTAAP). We should say no to protectionism and unilateralism, uphold the WTO-centered multilateral trading system, make economic globalization more open, inclusive, balanced and beneficial to all, expand converging interests, and share opportunities through opening up and cooperation.

Second, we need to focus on development to deliver more gains to our peoples. More than anything else, we should place our peoples' wellbeing at the top of our agenda. Every country is entitled to an equal right to development; and no one has the right or the power to stop people of developing countries from pursuing a better life. We should strengthen development cooperation and help developing countries eliminate poverty so that people in all countries will live a better life. This is what fairness is essentially about; it is also a moral responsibility of the international community.

We need to incorporate the 2030 Agenda for Sustainable Development into our national development strategies, promote coordinated advances in the social, economic and environmental fields, pursue inclusive development appropriate to our respective national conditions, and build equal and balanced global development partnerships. Developed countries should honor their commitments on official development assistance and increase support to developing countries.

We need to give priority to development in international economic policy coordination and have a clear focus on development when adopting policies and rules on trade and investment, protection of intellectual property rights (IPR), the digital economy, and other areas. By doing so, we will be able to create more opportunities and space for all countries as well as robust drivers and a stable environment for global growth. The principle of "special and differential treatment", which is a cornerstone of the WTO, is not to be challenged. Otherwise the very foundation of the multilateral trading system will be undermined.

Third, we need to focus on inclusiveness and promote harmony and mutual learning between nations. We live on the same planet. It is home to more than 200 countries and regions, 2,500-plus ethnic groups, and over 7 billion people. No attempt to erase their differences will work. Such differences are not a hindrance to exchanges, still less a cause for confrontation. Harmony in diversity and mutual learning between civilizations, social systems and paths can provide strong impetus for human progress. We should reject hubris and prejudice, treat each other with respect, stay open and inclusive, and embrace the diversity of our world. We should seek common ground while setting aside differences, draw upon each other's strengths, and pursue coexistence in harmony and win-win cooperation.

When it comes to choosing a development path for a country, no one is in a better position to make the decision than the people of that country. Just as one does not expect a single prescription to cure all diseases, one should not expect a particular model of development to fit all countries. Blindly copying the models of others will only be counterproductive, as will be any attempt to impose one's own model on others.

Fourth, we need to focus on innovation to tap new sources of growth. Breakthroughs are constantly being made in frontier areas such as information technology, life sciences, smart manufacturing, and green energy; new materials, new products and new business forms are replacing existing ones at a faster pace. Big data, 3D printing and artificial intelligence, which we read about only in science fiction in the past, are now part of our daily life. The future is already with us.

In a boat race, those who row the hardest will win. If we do not move proactively to adapt to the surging tide of new scientific revolution and industrial transformation, we risk missing valuable opportunities or even falling behind. We must lose no time in exploring new growth drivers and development paths, and removing all institutional obstacles holding back innovation. We should boost innovation and market vitality, and expand international exchanges and cooperation in innovation so as to better meet our own and our common challenges.

The sweeping new scientific revolution and industrial transformation will have a profound impact on the mode of production, way of life, and values of human society. The need to strike a balance between equity and efficiency, capital and labor, technology and employment, has become a common challenge for the international community. If not handled properly, this issue will further widen the wealth gap between the North and the South. We should gain a keen understanding of the complex dimensions of this issue and make the right decisions. This will enable us to steer the new scientific revolution and industrial transformation in the right direction.

Technological innovations should meet people's needs. Every country is entitled to benefit from such innovations, whether made through their own efforts or through international cooperation. Technological innovations should not be locked up or become profit-making tools for just a few. The IPR regime is designed to protect and encourage innovation, not to create or widen the technological divide. We should develop a policy framework that is responsive to the new scientific revolution and industrial transformation, and foster an enabling environment for international cooperation that will deliver the fruits of innovation to more countries and peoples.

Fifth, we need to focus on a rule-based approach to improving global governance. With the painful lessons of two world wars in mind, countries established the global governance framework underpinned by the United Nations and composed of the IMF, the World Bank, the WTO and other institutions. This framework, while not an ideal one, represents an important step in human history. Indeed, it has been pivotal to global peace and development in the past decades. We must strengthen rule-based global governance if we are to achieve stability and development. Rules should be formulated by the international community, not in a might-is-right manner. Once the rules are made, they should not be followed or bent as one sees fit, and they should not be applied with double standards for selfish agendas.

If the system of global economic governance is to be equitable and efficient, it must keep up with the times. Our approach to the reform of the global governance system should be one of consultation, cooperation, and benefit for all. This reform should be based on the principles of equality, openness, transparency, and inclusiveness. Developing countries should have more say and greater representation in this process. Disagreements should be resolved through consultation. Attempts to form exclusive blocs or impose one's will on others should be rejected. History has shown that confrontation, whether in the form of a cold war, a hot war, or a trade war, will produce no winners. We believe that there exist no issues that countries cannot resolve through consultation as long as they handle these issues in a spirit of equality, mutual understanding and accommodation.

Notes

[1] Chen Shou: *Records of the Three Kingdoms* (*San Guo Zhi*). Chen Shou (233-297) was an official and historian of the Western Jin Dynasty.

Endeavor to Shape the Future of Humanity*

March 26, 2019

In my speech at the United Nations Office at Geneva two years ago, I raised a question: "What is happening to the world and how should we respond?" The world today is undergoing momentous changes unseen in a century. Peace and development remain the underlying trend of our time, yet humanity is faced with many common challenges, particularly mounting instability and uncertainty.

As a French proverb goes, every man is the architect of his own fate. All countries need to demonstrate a strong commitment to their global responsibilities in the face of daunting global challenges. Indeed, they need to determine a decisive direction for humanity at this juncture. We must take action instead of simply watching as bystanders, and endeavor to shape the future of humanity.

First, we need to address the governance deficit in a fair and equitable way. Across the globe, flashpoints keep emerging. Non-conventional security threats, such as climate change, cybersecurity, and the refugee crisis, are spreading. Protectionism and unilateralism are mounting. The global governance system and the multilateral system are under assault. It is therefore important that we promote global governance that is based on consultation and cooperation and will benefit all. We should ensure that global affairs are managed by all the people through consultation; and we should work together to see that rule-making in global governance is more democratic. We should uphold multilateralism as represented by the United Nations, give full

---

* Part of the speech at the closing ceremony of the Seminar on Global Governance co-hosted by China and France in Paris.

play to the constructive role of the World Trade Organization (WTO), the International Monetary Fund, the World Bank, the Group of 20, the European Union and other international and regional multilateral mechanisms, and work together to build a global community of shared future.

Second, we need to strengthen consultation and mutual understanding to address the trust deficit. Trust is the best adhesive to bring countries together. We are seeing more competition and friction, and more geopolitical rivalry, which have eroded international trust and cooperation. We need to enhance mutual trust and respect, make full use of dialogue and consultation, and seek common ground while shelving and reducing differences. We need to engage in candid and in-depth dialogue to enhance strategic mutual trust and reduce misgivings. We need to pursue the greater public good and shared interests and build global partnerships for a shared future for all countries. We also need to promote dialogue between different civilizations so as to increase mutual understanding and appreciation, and ensure that peoples of all countries have understanding, respect and trust of each other and are close to each other. In current China-EU relations, cooperation far outweighs competition, and even such competition is benign in nature. We should trust each other and forge ahead together.

Third, we need to enhance solidarity to address the peace deficit. The current global security environment is still a source of concern. Local wars and conflicts continue, and some parts of the world are plagued by terrorism, devastating the lives of many, particularly children. We should take a new approach towards security and pursue common, comprehensive, cooperative and sustainable security. We must reject the Cold War mentality, the zero-sum game mindset, and the law of the jungle, and promote peace and security through cooperation. We should resolve disputes through peaceful means, oppose the arbitrary use or threat of force, oppose any provocation and escalation of tensions for self-interest, and reject the practice of shifting trouble onto neighbors and seeking gain at the expense of others. All countries should pursue peaceful development in a common endeavor to achieve enduring global peace.

Fourth, we need to pursue mutually beneficial cooperation to address the development deficit. Economic globalization is an engine of global growth. However, a trend against globalization is emerging, and the harm of protectionism is all too visible. Income disparity and the imbalance in development among regions are growing. They have become the most pressing issues to tackle when it comes to world economic governance. We need to pursue innovation-driven development to foster dynamic growth. We need to take a well-coordinated and interconnected approach to enhance open and win-win cooperation. We need to uphold equity and inclusiveness to promote balanced and inclusive development so that people across the world can all benefit from economic globalization. China supports efforts to carry out necessary reform of the WTO, to make the world economy more open, and to safeguard the multilateral trading system, thus enabling economic globalization to advance in the right direction. The Belt and Road Initiative enriches international economic cooperation and multilateralism; and it offers an important way of achieving global growth and common development. China welcomes France and other countries to take part in the Belt and Road Initiative.

Build a Maritime Community of Shared Future[*]

April 23, 2019

The ocean is of great significance to the survival and development of human society. It gave birth to life, connects the world, and facilitates development. It does not separate our blue planet into isolated continents; instead, it links the peoples of all countries to form a global community of shared future that remains bound together through thick and thin. Maritime peace has a bearing on the safety and interests of all countries, and thus needs to be protected and cherished by all. The Chinese people love and long for peace, and are committed to the path of peaceful development. China upholds a national defense policy that is in nature defensive, and advocates a new concept of common, comprehensive, cooperative and sustainable security. The Chinese armed forces have always followed the principle of win-win cooperation and been dedicated to creating a security environment of equality, mutual trust, fairness, justice, joint efforts, and shared interests. As the main maritime force of a country, the navy shoulders important responsibilities in maintaining maritime peace and order. With mutual respect, equality and mutual trust, we need to strengthen maritime dialogue and exchanges, increase practical naval cooperation, pursue a path of maritime security based on mutual benefit and win-win results, and join hands to respond to common threats and challenges and to maintain maritime peace.

Currently, cooperation in markets, technology, information and culture through maritime bonds is becoming ever closer. Precisely

---

[*] Main points of the speech at a group meeting with the heads of foreign delegations attending the multinational naval events marking the 70th anniversary of the founding of the People's Liberation Army Navy.

for this reason, China's initiative to build the 21st Century Maritime Silk Road aims to promote maritime connectivity and cooperation in various fields, develop the blue economy, advance maritime cultural integration, and jointly amplify ocean benefits. The Chinese military is willing to join other militaries in promoting maritime progress and prosperity.

We need to care for the ocean as dearly as we treasure our lives. China takes full part in UN mechanisms concerning maritime governance and in formulating and implementing relevant rules to achieve sustainable maritime development goals. China highly values marine eco-environmental progress, intensifies efforts to address marine pollution, protects marine biodiversity, and develops and utilizes marine resources in an orderly manner, so as to leave future generations with turquoise seas and blue skies. The Chinese Navy will, as always, enhance exchanges and cooperation with other navies, undertake international responsibilities and obligations, safeguard the security of international sea lines of communication, and provide more public goods in maritime security.

As a Chinese saying goes, "The ocean is vast because it admits all rivers." Whenever a problem crops up, countries concerned should always hold deliberations in good faith, rather than resort to the use or threat of force at will. We need to discuss issues as equals, improve consultation mechanisms to deal with crises, enhance cooperation on regional security, and work for the proper settlement of maritime disputes. As part of the ongoing multinational naval events, China will hold a high-level forum under the theme of "building a global maritime community of shared future". I hope you will pool wisdom, build consensus, and contribute to this endeavor.

Create an Asian Community of Shared Future Through Mutual Learning*

May 15, 2019

Your Excellencies Heads of State and Government,
Your Excellencies Heads of International Organizations,
Distinguished guests,
Ladies and gentlemen,
Friends,

In this lovely season of thriving green, I am pleased that our friends from 47 Asian countries and five continents are meeting here for a discussion on deeper exchanges and mutual learning among civilizations. On behalf of the Chinese government and people, and in my own name, let me express my warmest congratulations on the opening of the Conference on Dialogue of Asian Civilizations and extend a very warm welcome to you all.

The world today is moving towards multi-polarity and becoming more economically globalized, culturally diverse, and IT-driven. All this offers hope to humanity. In contrast, however, instability and uncertainties are mounting, and the global challenges faced by humanity are ever more daunting, calling for joint responses from all countries.

To meet our common challenges and create a better future for all, we look to culture and civilization to play their roles, which are as important as the roles played by the economy, and by science and technology. The Conference on Dialogue of Asian Civilizations is for this very purpose, as it provides a new platform for civilizations

---

* Keynote speech at the opening ceremony of the Conference on Dialogue of Asian Civilizations.

in Asia and beyond to engage in dialogue and exchanges on an equal footing and facilitate mutual learning.

Ladies and gentlemen,

Friends,

Asia is home to one of the earliest human settlements and a major cradle of human civilization. This vast and beautiful continent covers a third of the Earth's land mass and has two-thirds of the world's population. It has more than 1,000 ethnic groups living in 47 countries. For several thousand years before the Common Era, our forefathers living along the Tigris and the Euphrates, the Indus and the Ganges, the Yellow River and the Yangtze River, tilled and irrigated the land, made tools and utensils, and built homes to live in. Generation after generation, our ancestors in Asia, with their tireless endeavors, created a time-honored history and profound and rich civilizations. Our vast and fertile plains, beautiful river basins, broad steppes, immense deserts, mighty rivers and oceans, and lofty mountains have nourished and enriched diverse and colorful civilizations across Asia.

In building our civilizations over the course of several millennia, we the people of Asia have achieved great splendor. I think of literary classics such as the *Book of Songs*[1], *The Analects of Confucius*, the Talmud[2], *One Thousand and One Nights*[3], *The Rigveda*[4] and *The Tale of Genji*[5]; of inventions such as the cuneiform script, maps, glass, Arabic numerals, and papermaking and printing techniques; and of majestic structures like the Great Wall, the Great Mosque of Mecca, the Taj Mahal, and Angkor Wat. They all form part of the invaluable heritage of human civilization. Through interactions on this continent, Asian civilizations have enriched each other and written an epic of development.

Our forefathers in Asia have long engaged in inter-civilization exchanges and mutual learning. The ancient trade routes, notably the Silk Road, the Tea Road and the Spice Road, brought silk, tea, porcelain, spices, paintings and sculpture to all corners of Asia, and witnessed inter-civilization dialogue in the form of trade and cultural interflow. Today, the Belt and Road Initiative, together with the Two Corridors and One Belt, the Eurasian Economic Union and other initiatives, has greatly expanded inter-civilization exchanges and mutual learning. Cooperation among nations in science and technology, education, culture, health and people-to-people exchanges is thriving as never before. Thanks to exchanges and mutual learning between each other and with other civilizations in the world, Asian civilizations have grown from strength to strength.

The great Asian civilizations have a special place in the annals of world civilization, and they have added to the diversity of human civilization. Think of what Asia stands to offer in terms of religion, philosophy, code of ethics, law, literature, painting, drama, music, and even the building of towns and villages. They speak volumes for Asia's proud achievements – extensive systems of social customs, immortal classics that have endured for millennia, the fine pool of exquisite art, and diverse institutions, among others. All these offer rich choices for civilizations the world over to draw on.

As we review our past and look beyond Asia, we should have greater confidence in our civilizations. We may build on the rich heritage of our forefathers, stay engaged with other civilizations, and increase mutual learning. By doing so, we will add new glory to Asian civilizations.

Ladies and gentlemen,

Friends,

We Asian countries are closely connected and share a natural bond of affinity. We have passed through similar historical trials, and we cherish the same dreams for the future. Going forward, we need to see where the world is heading, ride the trends of the times, and turn our people's longing for a better life into reality.

– We Asian people hope to see peace and stability across Asia. Upholding peace is the responsibility of every country. When peace is interrupted by conflict or war, economic growth, decent lives, social stability and people-to-people exchanges will fall by the wayside. We the people of Asian countries wish to live and work in contentment and security, free from fear. We hope that all countries will respect and trust each other, live in harmony, and interact with each other in a manner that transcends national boundaries, time and space, as well as the differences between civilizations. We should work together to safeguard peace, something that is far more precious than gold.

– We Asian people hope to see common prosperity in Asia. Economic growth sustains a civilization, and prosperity underpins the progress of a nation. In some parts of Asia, people – women and children in particular – are still suffering from poverty, hunger, and disease. This must change. We Asian people long for a decent life free of poverty. We hope that countries will work together to promote economic globalization and make it more open, inclusive, balanced, and beneficial to all. This will enable us to eradicate the poverty and backwardness that still plague people in some countries. It will enable our children to live a carefree life and bring happiness to all families.

– We Asian people hope to see an open and better-connected Asia. Asia's rapid development over the past decades shows that it is important to open our doors to the outside world and ride the trend of global economic development. If countries choose to close their doors and hide behind them, world civilizations will be cut off from each other and lose all vitality. We Asian people hope that all countries will reject self-imposed isolation, embrace integration, uphold opening up, and promote policy, infrastructure, trade, financial and people-to-people connectivity. This way, we can jointly foster a community of shared future for both Asians and all humanity.

Ladies and gentlemen,

Friends,

Diversity spurs interaction among civilizations, which in turn promotes mutual learning and further development. We need to promote exchanges and mutual learning among countries, nations and cultures around the world, and strengthen popular support for a community of shared future for both Asia and humanity as a whole. To that end, I believe it is imperative that we take the following actions:

First, we need to respect each other and treat each other as equals.

All civilizations are rooted in their unique cultural environment. Each embodies the wisdom and vision of a country or nation, and each is valuable for being unique itself. Civilizations vary from each other only as human beings differ in terms of skin color and the language used. No civilization is superior to others. It is foolhardy to think that one's own race and civilization are superior and to insist on remolding or replacing other civilizations. To act these out will only have catastrophic consequences. If world civilizations are reduced to one single color or one single model, the world will become monolithic and a dull place to live. What we need is to respect each other as equals and say no to hubris and prejudice. We need a deeper understanding of the differences between our own civilizations and others, and we must work to promote interaction, dialogue and harmony among civilizations.

In the many places I have visited around the world, what fascinates me most is civilizations in their rich diversity. I cannot but think of the Central Asian city of Samarkand, the Luxor Temple in Egypt, Sentosa in Singapore, Wat Phra Kaew in Bangkok, and the Acropolis in Athens, to mention just a few. China is ready to work with other countries to protect Asian cultural heritage and better preserve and sustain our civilizations.

Second, we need to uphold the beauty of each civilization and the diversity of civilizations around the world. Each civilization is the crystallization of human creation, and each is beautiful in its own way. An aspiration for all that is beautiful is common to all humanity, and nothing can hold it back. Civilizations do not have to clash with each other; what is needed is to see the beauty in all civilizations with eyes. We should keep our own civilizations dynamic and create conditions for other civilizations to flourish. Together we can make the garden of world civilizations more colorful and vibrant.

The beauty of a civilization finds concrete expression in the classic works of philosophy and social sciences and works of literature, music, film and TV drama. Now, a large number of outstanding cultural works from other countries are being brought into China, and a lot of fine Chinese cultural products are being introduced to other countries. China is happy to launch initiatives with other countries to translate Asian classics both from and into Chinese and to promote film and TV exchanges and cooperation in Asia. This will help people in Asia better understand and appreciate each other's cultures and build a platform of exchanges and mutual learning for the best of Asian civilizations to spread and be better known to the world.

Third, we need to stay open and inclusive and draw on each other's strengths. All living organisms must renew themselves through metabolism; otherwise, life would come to an end. The same is true for civilizations. Long-term self-imposed isolation will cause a civilization to decline, while exchanges and mutual learning will sustain it. A civilization can flourish only through exchanges and mutual learning with other civilizations. Such exchanges and mutual learning should be reciprocal, equal-footed, diverse, and multidimensional; they should not be coercive, imposed, one-dimensional, or one-way. We need to be broad-minded and strive to remove all barriers to cultural exchanges. We need to be inclusive and always seek nourishment from other civilizations to promote the common development of Asian civilizations through exchanges and mutual learning.

People are the best bridge for exchanges and mutual learning among civilizations. Increased people-to-people exchanges and mutual learning, for that matter, are a sure way to eliminate estrangement and misunderstanding and to promote mutual understanding among nations. Over the years, in collaboration with other countries, China has established many platforms and channels for cooperation in education, culture, sports, health, and other fields. China will work with other countries to step up exchanges among youths, NGOs, subnational entities, and media organizations, to create a network of exchanges and cooperation between think tanks, to explore new models of cooperation, and to deliver more solid outcomes in diverse forms. Such efforts will boost exchanges and mutual learning among civilizations.

Fourth, we need to advance with the times and explore new

ground. To sustain a civilization, it must be kept vibrant and built on its heritage from one generation to the next. More importantly, a civilization needs to adapt itself to the changing times and break new ground. The history of world civilizations tells us that every civilization needs to advance with the times and take in the best of its age in order to progress. We need to come up with new ideas to add impetus and inspiration to our civilizations. Through these efforts we will deliver achievements for our civilizations to transcend time and space and endure.

To spur people's innovation and creativity, the best way is to come into contact with different civilizations, see the strengths of others, and draw upon them. Last year, Chinese tourists made over 160 million overseas trips, and more than 140 million foreign tourists visited China. These visits played an important role in promoting exchanges and mutual learning between China and the rest of the world. In this connection, China will work with other countries to implement a plan to promote tourism in Asia. This will further boost economic development in Asia and deepen friendship among the Asian people.

Ladies and gentlemen,

Friends,

As an inseparable part of Asian civilization, Chinese civilization, since its early days, has evolved and grown by drawing on its past achievements, exploring new ground, and adapting to changes. This represents a profound aspiration of the Chinese nation and provides a rich source of strength for its lasting development. Chinese inventions such as papermaking, gunpowder, printing and the compass, as well as China's astronomical knowledge, calendar system, philosophy and people-centered doctrine have all had a global impact and propelled the development of human civilization.

Chinese civilization, as an inclusive and integrated whole, has become what it is today through constant interactions with other civilizations. It has been enriched by the introduction of Buddhism and the confluence of Islam and Confucianism in the old days, and by the introduction of Western learning, the launch of the New Culture Movement, and the introduction of Marxism and socialism in modern times. All-round opening up of the country, starting with the reform and opening-up program, has added to its vitality today. For Chinese civilization, pursuing amity, good neighborliness and harmony is the principle guiding our interactions with other countries. To bring prosperity and security to the people is the overarching goal, to keep pace with the times through reform and innovation the abiding commitment, and to achieve harmony between man and nature the underlying philosophy.

China today is more than the country itself; it is very much a part of Asia and the world. In times to come, China will open its arms wider to embrace the world and contribute the dynamic achievements of Chinese civilization to a better world.

Ladies and gentlemen,

Friends,

The Conference on Dialogue of Asian Civilizations has a wide-ranging agenda, and I look forward to your keen perspectives and insights. By bringing our minds together, we will create an even better tomorrow for civilizations in Asia and beyond.

To conclude, I wish this conference every success.

Thank you.

Notes

[1] The *Book of Songs* (*Shi Jing*) is the earliest collection of poems in China. It contains 305 poems composed over some 500 years from the early Western Zhou Dynasty (1046-771 BC) to the middle of the Spring and Autumn Period (770-476 BC).

[2] The Talmud is a compilation of Jewish oral law.

[3] *One Thousand and One Nights* is a collection of folk tales in Arabic.

[4] *The Rigveda* is an ancient Indian collection of hymns.

[5] *The Tale of Genji* is a novel written by Japanese female writer Murasaki Shikibu in the early years of the 11th century.

Work Together for a High-Quality World Economy*

June 28, 2019

Ten years after the 2008 international financial crisis, the global economy has again reached a crossroads. Protectionism and unilateralism are spreading, and trade and investment tensions are on the rise, causing disruption to the global industrial chain and financial stability. The world economy faces more risks and uncertainties, dampening the confidence of international investors.

The G20 is the premier forum for international economic cooperation. We, as the leaders of major economies, are duty bound to recalibrate the direction of the world economy and improve global governance at this critical juncture, work together to boost market confidence, and bring hope to our people.

– We should respect the objective laws governing the economy. Economic operations have their underlying laws. Fully respecting these laws, leveraging the role of the market, and removing man-made obstacles are a sure way to raise productivity, boost trade, and revitalize businesses.

– We need to follow the prevailing trend of development. The history of human society is a transition from isolation and exclusion to openness and integration, which is an unstoppable trend. We need to open up further to embrace opportunities for development and seek win-win outcomes through closer cooperation. We need to work together to steer economic globalization in the right direction.

– We need to keep in mind our shared future. In today's world, all countries are connected, and their interests are closely intertwined. We

---

* Part of the speech on global economy and international trade at the G20 Summit.

have a high stake in each other's future. By expanding common interests and taking a long-term view, we can realize enduring peace and prosperity in the world and bring a better life to all our people. We must not allow ourselves to become prisoners of short-term interests and make irrevocable mistakes of historic consequence.

Based on these principles, I would like to propose the following:

First, we need to persevere in reform and explore new ground to create more impetus for growth. The world economy is in a transition in which new drivers of growth are taking the place of old ones. We need to vigorously advance structural reform. We need to develop a future-oriented economic structure, policy framework and management system through promoting the digital economy, strengthening connectivity and improving social security, so as to enhance the performance and resilience of our economies and strive for high-quality development. We need to capitalize on the historic opportunities brought by new technologies, industries and forms of business, to foster an enabling market environment where innovation is respected, protected and encouraged. We need to champion international collaboration on innovation and overcome geographical and man-made obstacles. When we put our heads together to resolve common challenges and spread the fruits of innovation, we can make a difference for more countries and transform their peoples' lives.

Second, we need to advance with the times and improve global governance. When economic globalization faces headwinds, we need to reflect on the important question of how best to improve global governance. The G20 should continue to take the lead in making the world economy open, inclusive, balanced, and beneficial to all. We need to strengthen the multilateral trading system and pursue WTO reform as necessary. The goal of this reform should enable the WTO to advance with the time so that it will be better able to perform its mandate of enhancing market openness and boosting development; and such reform should be conducive to upholding free trade and multilateralism and narrowing the development gap. At the same time, the G20 should also be prepared to deal with future systemic financial risks and challenges at the global level. We must ensure that there are sufficient resources for the financial safety net and see to it that the international financial architecture is more balanced in terms of representation and give better expression to the realities of the world economy. This is a matter of fairness, and it will also enhance our ability to take targeted measures to meet challenges and navigate crises when they emerge. It is also important for the G20 to implement the Paris Agreement and improve energy, environmental and digital governance.

Third, we need to rise up to challenges and break through logjams holding up development. The myriad challenges facing the world today are all caused, in one way or another, by the development gap and deficit. The gaping shortfall in financing global development means that the realization of the UN 2030 Agenda for Sustainable Development remains a daunting task. It is against such a backdrop that China launched the Belt and Road Initiative. The initiative is designed to mobilize more resources, strengthen connectivity, leverage potential growth drivers, and connect markets. It is designed to integrate more countries and regions into economic globalization and achieve shared prosperity through mutually beneficial cooperation. The success of the Second Belt and Road Forum for International Cooperation demonstrates that this initiative enjoys the broad welcome and support of the global community, as it effectively responds to the expectations of our people and the trend of our times. It is important that the G20 continue to prioritize development in macroeconomic policy coordination, scale up input in development, and promote cooperation through concrete actions. By doing so, we can live up to the expectations of developing countries and create a lasting driving force for global growth.

Fourth, we need to forge closer partnerships and resolve differences properly. The G20 is a group of major advanced economies and emerging markets, accounting for nearly 90 percent of the global economy. As G20 members are in different stages of development, it is only natural that we may have diverging interests and views on some issues. What is important is that we should promote our partnership and respect and trust each other, and in that spirit, engage in consultation as equals, manage differences while seeking common ground, and build greater consensus. If this can be achieved between major countries, it will serve not only our own interests but also enhance global peace and development.

The Belt and Road Initiative

Open a Path to Cooperation Across the Pacific*

January 22, 2018

The world is now at a stage of major development, transformation, and adjustment. All countries are interdependent and increasingly connected to each other, and humanity faces many common challenges. Although geographically distant, China and the Latin American and Caribbean states are all developing countries pursuing the common dream of world peace, prosperity, and a better life for our peoples. The Chinese people will work with the peoples of Latin America and the Caribbean in making a greater contribution to the building of a global community of shared future.

When I proposed international cooperation on the Belt and Road Initiative four years ago, China offered to work with all interested parties to build a new platform of global cooperation, to boost interconnectivity, and to add new drivers for common development. The initiative has received warm support from the international community, including many Latin American and Caribbean countries. In ancient times Chinese ancestors braved the oceans and opened up the maritime Silk Road between China and Latin America. Today, as we roll out the blueprint for the Belt and Road Initiative, we strive to forge a route for cooperation across the Pacific, in order to draw closer the two lands of abundance of China and Latin America, and open a new era of friendly relations.

Let us sail together towards a better tomorrow for China and Latin America, and a better future for humanity.

---

* Part of the congratulatory letter to the Second Ministerial Meeting of the Forum of China and the Community of Latin American and Caribbean States.

Strengthen Cooperation to Advance the Belt and Road Initiative*

July 10, 2018

Sino-Arab friendship is time-honored and strong as ever. The Chinese and Arab peoples, though far apart in distance, are close like a family. Our ancestors, merchants and diplomatic envoys alike, traveled back and forth along the overland and maritime Silk Roads. In the modern era, we fought side by side for independence and liberation. We also gave each other strong support in development, creating a splendid chapter of win-win cooperation. Past and present experiences have proved that whatever changes may take place in the world and whatever obstacles may confront us, China and Arab states have always been good partners, sharing mutual benefit, and good brothers, going through thick and thin together.

To facilitate the common prosperity and progress of interested countries, China has put forward the Belt and Road Initiative. With a commitment to the principles of extensive consultation, joint contribution and shared benefits, this initiative focuses on promoting policy, infrastructure, trade, financial and people-to-people connectivity. It has attracted wide support and active participation from the Arab world and the broader international community. As important participants and co-creators of the ancient Silk Road civilization located at the juncture of the overland and maritime Silk Roads, Arab states are natural partners in Belt and Road cooperation.

Belt and Road cooperation features prominently in the *Arab Policy Paper* issued by the Chinese government. The Arab League Council

---

* Part of the speech at the opening ceremony of the Eighth Ministerial Conference of the China-Arab States Cooperation Forum.

at the level of foreign ministers has adopted a resolution expressing the collective political will of Arab states to participate in the Belt and Road Initiative. It is expected that later during this ministerial conference, a Declaration of Action on China-Arab States Belt and Road Cooperation will be signed.

Over the past four years, China and Arab states have worked together to develop Belt and Road cooperation in the light of regional realities, to combine collective action with bilateral cooperation, and to promote development while upholding peace. Complementing each other's strengths and pursuing win-win results, we have delivered benefits to people both in our region and beyond. As various projects attest, a dynamic situation has been created and many fruits harvested in our Belt and Road cooperation.

Also over the past four years, Belt and Road cooperation has energized every dimension of Sino-Arab relations and propelled all-round Sino-Arab cooperation into a new phase. In this context, I am pleased to announce that after friendly consultation between the two sides, we have agreed to establish a Sino-Arab future-oriented strategic partnership of comprehensive cooperation and common development. This marks a new historic milestone in Sino-Arab friendship and cooperation.

As we advance the Belt and Road Initiative, China stands ready to work with the Arab side to coordinate our development strategies and actions. We must strive to uphold peace and stability in the Middle East, safeguard fairness and justice, promote common development, and learn from each other as friends do. This joint commitment will help us build a community of shared future for China and Arab states, and one for all of humanity.

First, China and Arab states need to strengthen strategic trust. A Chinese adage has it that "a just world should be pursued for the common good"[1]. The Middle East faces the urgent task of removing the barriers to peace and resolving the development conundrum. People in the region yearn for peace and development. Having formulated its Middle East policy in line with such yearnings, China is an advocate of the legitimate concerns of Arab states in the international arena and stands ready to play a bigger role for peace and stability in the region.

We must stay committed to dialogue and consultation. Many intractable issues in the Middle East must be addressed by all stakeholders together. They should not and cannot be decided by one party alone. We need to uphold the principle of sovereignty and oppose division and fragmentation. We need to champion inclusive reconciliation and stand against forced compromises. We need to fight terrorism and take well-coordinated actions to improve people's lives.

China is ready for more dialogue and consultation with Arab states on a wide range of topics such as development for peace, collective security, humanitarian assistance, shipping corridors, and a nuclear-weapon-free zone. I hereby announce that China is setting up a special program for economic reconstruction through industrial revitalization. Under this program, a credit line of US$20 billion will be extended, in accordance with commercial principles, to projects that will produce good employment opportunities and positive social impact in Arab states that have reconstruction needs. China will provide an additional RMB600 million of assistance to the peoples of Syria, Yemen, Jordan and Lebanon to meet their humanitarian and reconstruction needs. China will also discuss with regional countries the implementation of programs totaling RMB1 billion to help interested countries build up capacity for maintaining stability.

Second, China and Arab states need to help each other realize dreams of rejuvenation. The Arab world is strategically located and blessed with abundant energy resources. With our strong complementarity and converging interests, China and Arab states must synergize our development strategies in pursuit of our respective dreams of rejuvenation.

In this effort, we must stay focused on connectivity. China welcomes opportunities to participate in the development of ports and the construction of railway networks in Arab states, and support Arab efforts in building a logistics network connecting Central Asia with East Africa, and the Indian Ocean with the Mediterranean. We need to work together to build a maritime cooperation center to boost the ocean industry, enhance our ability to provide ocean-related public services, and create a "blue economy corridor". The two sides may jointly build a Belt and Road space information corridor, strengthen aerospace cooperation, and enable Arab states to access China's BeiDou Navigation System and meteorological satellite remote-sensing technology for the good of their national development.

China and Arab states need to boost cooperation in the oil and gas and low-carbon energy sectors, which are the main drivers of our energy cooperation. We will continue our "oil and gas-plus" model and intensify energy cooperation across the entire industrial chain, which includes oil and gas exploration, extraction, refinery, storage and transportation. At the same time, given the surging global energy revolution and the boom in green and low-carbon industries, we need to work more closely on peaceful uses of nuclear energy and in the solar, wind and hydro power sectors. These efforts will lead to an energy cooperation structure which is underpinned by oil and gas and reinforced by nuclear and clean energy sectors. Based on this structure, we can build a strategic partnership in energy sectors that delivers mutual benefits and fosters long-term friendship.

Financial cooperation must go in tandem with cooperation in new and high technologies. We need to explore how best new and high technologies and financial services can facilitate our cooperation and provide short- and long-term support for the Belt and Road. To this end, we must find a model that suits the needs and conditions of the Middle East.

China supports the establishment of a financial platform for industrial cooperation. The platform is expected to offer access to diverse sources of funding for the development of industrial parks and provide an enabling environment for enterprises to grow in these parks through its financial support and other services. The Chinese government supports Chinese financial and securities institutions in partnering with Arab states' sovereign wealth funds and regulatory bodies to build an international trading platform that is based in the Gulf region, serves the Middle East and North Africa, and attracts investors from around the globe. This platform can be an enabler of Belt and Road cooperation by facilitating the free flow of production factors, efficient allocation of resources and deep integration of markets. To stimulate more exchanges and cooperation between financial institutions, China will set up a Sino-Arab inter-bank association and equip it with a credit line of US$3 billion.

In relation to the medium- to long-term development plans followed by Arab states, China will pursue closer cooperation in the digital economy, artificial intelligence, new materials, biopharma and smart cities. We need to fully implement our science and technology partnership program and build joint laboratories in key areas of mutual interest. We also need to accelerate our work on a cyber Silk Road, and strive for more cooperation, consensus, and outcomes in internet infrastructure, big data, cloud computing and e-commerce.

Third, China and Arab states need to achieve win-win outcomes. With a commitment to deeper reform in all areas, to continuing its fundamental policy of opening up, and to pursuing development with its doors wide open, China is expected to import over US$8 trillion of goods and make over US$750 billion of outbound investment in the next five years. This will bring more opportunities and real benefits to Arab states. We need to fully leverage special and concessional loans in support of industrialization in the Middle East, and encourage more Chinese business involvement in the development and operation of industrial parks in Arab states to boost industrial clusters there. China looks forward to the participation of Arab states in the First China International Import Expo in Shanghai this November, and in the course of the next five years China will invite all Arab states to the Expo and its country pavilions for trade and investment. China will work for solid progress in its FTA negotiations with the Gulf Cooperation Council and with Palestine, and stands ready to explore with more Arab states the possibility of concluding comprehensive free trade agreements.

Fourth, China and Arab states need to promote inclusiveness and mutual learning. A civilization stays vibrant through constant interactions with other civilizations. The Chinese and the Arab civilizations, sharing a long history of mutually reinforcing exchanges, have all the more reason to draw wisdom and strength from each other in this day and age. I am glad to note that the Sino-Arab Research Center on Reform and Development that I proposed is operating well as an intellectual platform for experience sharing on reform, opening up and governance. I wish the center still greater success in providing more intellectual support to both sides.

We must spread the message of peace, harmony and truth. One way to do that is to make a continuing success of the Roundtable on Sino-Arab Inter-civilization Dialogue and Eradication of Extremism. Efforts should be made to clear up misunderstandings through dialogue, solve disagreements through tolerance, and foster a wholesome environment in which genuine faith and good deeds prevail. We need to delve deeper into different religions for ideas of greater harmony and positivity, and interpret religious teachings in the context of progressing times. It is important that we work together to cultivate a healthy cyber culture to oppose the spread of extremist content and hate speech through the internet.

To enhance mutual understanding between the Chinese and Arab people, China will do the following for Arab states in the coming three years: invite 100 young leaders in innovation, 200 young scientists, and 300 science professionals to workshops in China; invite 100 religious leaders and 600 political party leaders to China; provide 10,000 training opportunities; and send 500 medical staff to Arab states.

To this end, I am glad to announce the official launch of a Sino-Arab press center, a Sino-Arab e-library portal and the Fourth Arab Art Festival co-hosted by the two sides in China.

Notes

[1] *Book of Rites (Li Ji)*.

Ensure that Belt and Road Cooperation Delivers Solid Outcomes*

August 27, 2018

The Belt and Road Initiative (BRI) was launched in response to the call for reforming the global governance system. The BRI promotes partnership and a community of shared future, shared rights and joint responsibilities. It offers a new approach to reform and improvement of the global governance system.

For BRI cooperation to deliver solid outcomes to participating countries and their peoples, and contribute to the building of a global community of shared future, we need to follow the principles of extensive consultation, joint contribution, mutual benefit, and mutual learning. We need to seek the greatest common ground with countries along the Belt and Road and work together with them to strengthen mutual political trust and promote economic integration and people-to-people connectivity. And we should take one step at a time and deliver outcomes accordingly.

Since its launch in the autumn of 2013, the BRI has received warm responses from more and more countries. It provides an avenue for China to participate in open global cooperation. It offers China's approach to improving global economic governance and promoting global prosperity and common development. It is a pathway to building a global community of shared future.

Over the past five years, BRI cooperation has given a substantial boost to free trade and investment in China and helped expand overall opening up from areas along coasts and major rivers to inland and

---

* Main points of the speech at the meeting marking the fifth anniversary of the Belt and Road Initiative.

border areas. As a result, we are breaking new ground through links running eastward and westward, across land and sea.

China's trade in goods with its BRI partners has exceeded US$5 trillion, and China's foreign direct investment in these countries has surpassed US$60 billion. This has created over 200,000 new jobs. Our foreign investment has become a major engine driving the growth of FDI global.

The world today is experiencing profound transformation and change. We should view these developments in a global and strategic context. We should seize historic opportunities while guarding against potential risks and dangers, so as to steer the right course in the face of levels of change unseen in a century.

It is to further reform, opening up and sustainable development that we have proposed the BRI, and we view it as a solid platform to build a global community of shared future. The BRI gives expression to the ancient Chinese vision of universal harmony, and the Chinese nation's worldview of making friends beyond borders and seeking peace and harmony between nations. Indeed, BRI cooperation is an exemplary international venture.

The BRI is about economic cooperation, but it is also designed to improve the global development model and global governance and promote sound economic globalization.

We developing countries are accelerating our industrialization and urbanization in an effort to achieve economic independence and national revitalization. This process is gaining momentum. The BRI echoes the deep wish of the peoples of the world, especially in the developing nations, for peace and development. This explains their enthusiastic support for the initiative.

The BRI is an initiative designed for economic cooperation, not for geopolitical or military alliance. It is an open and inclusive process that does not exclude any party. It is not designed to form an exclusive bloc or a "China club". Its participation is not based on ideology, and it is certainly not a zero-sum game. Any country that wants to participate in this initiative is welcome to do so.

Thanks to five years of hard work, the groundwork of the BRI has been laid, and it has entered a stage of all-round growth. We should build on this momentum to upgrade BRI cooperation in the next phase.

We should follow the fundamental principle of pursuing steady progress and the new development philosophy. We should pool resources to launch major projects in infrastructural development and industrial cooperation, and address issues confronting some key projects, such as financing, the investment environment, risk management, and safety management, so as to deliver more solid outcomes.

Thanks to our efforts in the past few years, a general framework of cooperation has been put in place. It is like completing a drawing: The outline has been sketched; now we must fill in the fine details. And we need to do so with meticulous care.

We should move forward faster with our projects, particularly those that will meet the pressing needs of people in host countries. To this end, we need to establish working mechanisms supported by targeted measures.

We will make every effort to expand markets. We should establish more trading platforms, encourage competitive Chinese enterprises to invest in BRI countries, and develop cross-border e-commerce and other new forms and models of trade, and seek balanced trade.

We should improve financing. We should adopt policies to strengthen financing for BRI cooperation. We should continue the internationalization of the Renminbi in an orderly manner, encourage private sector investment in infrastructure and resource projects in BRI partner countries, and provide financing in foreign currencies to Chinese enterprises that operate in these countries.

We should promote exchanges in the fields of education, science, technology, culture, sports, tourism, health, and archeology, and develop aid projects under the framework of BRI cooperation to improve people's lives.

We should ensure that Chinese enterprises invest and operate in a well-regulated way and that they comply strictly with the laws and regulations of host countries and protect the environment. They should fulfill their corporate social responsibilities and become pacesetters in pursuing the BRI.

We should take overseas risk prevention and management seriously. We should improve our risk prevention mechanisms and upgrade security safeguards so as to guard against security risks.

We should strengthen the Party's leadership over BRI-related work. Local authorities, government departments and all those involved in BRI cooperation should maintain their political commitment, think in terms of the general picture, follow the core leadership of the CPC Central Committee, and act in accordance with its requirements. They should maintain firm confidence in the path, theory, system and culture of socialism with Chinese characteristics. We should pursue the BRI as an initiative that is important to the overall interests of the Party and state.

Under the guidance of the CPC Central Committee, the Leading Group for Promoting the Belt and Road Initiative should fulfill its role as the main coordinator. It should ensure BRI-related coordination among local authorities and government departments, set priorities, formulate detailed implementation measures, and assign tasks to those involved at all levels. It should adopt follow-up and supervisory measures to ensure that all the policies and plans of the central authorities are faithfully implemented without fail.

All local authorities involved should pursue the BRI in alignment with national development strategies such as those concerning the coordinated development of the Beijing-Tianjin-Hebei Region, the development of the Yangtze River Economic Belt, and the development of the Guangdong-Hong Kong-Macao Greater Bay Area.

We should boost opening up in the western and northeastern regions and encourage inland and border areas to take the lead in pursuing opening up. With these steps, we can make new advances in opening up by building connectivity both eastward and westward, across land and sea.

Promote High-Quality Belt and Road Cooperation[*]

April 26, 2019

The Belt and Road Initiative (BRI) aims to enhance connectivity and results-oriented cooperation. It is about working together to meet the challenges and risks that confront humanity, and delivering win-win outcomes and common development. Thanks to the efforts of all involved in this initiative, a general connectivity framework consisting of six corridors, six routes and multiple countries and ports has been created. A large number of cooperation projects have been launched, and the decisions of the First Belt and Road Forum for International Cooperation (BRF) have been smoothly implemented. More than 150 countries and international organizations have signed agreements on Belt and Road cooperation with China. There is greater synergy between the BRI and the plans or cooperation initiatives of international and regional organizations such as the United Nations, the Association of Southeast Asian Nations, the African Union, the European Union, and the Eurasian Economic Union, and between the BRI and the development strategies of the participating countries. From the Eurasian continent to Africa, the Americas and Oceania, Belt and Road cooperation has opened up new space for global economic growth, produced new platforms for international trade and investment, and offered new ways for improving global economic governance. Indeed, this initiative has helped improve people's lives in countries involved and created more opportunities for common prosperity. What we have achieved amply demonstrates that Belt and Road

---

[*] Part of the keynote speech at the opening ceremony of the Second Belt and Road Forum for International Cooperation.

cooperation has both generated new opportunities for all participating countries and opened up new horizons for China's development and opening up.

An ancient Chinese philosopher observed that "plants with strong roots grow well, and efforts with the right focus ensure success"[1]. Belt and Road cooperation embraces the historic trend of economic globalization, responds to the call for improving the global governance system, and addresses people's desire for a better life. As our next step, we should focus on priorities and project execution, move forward with meticulous implementation, and join together to promote high-quality Belt and Road cooperation.

– We need to be guided by the principles of extensive consultation, joint contribution and shared benefits. We need to act in the spirit of multilateralism, pursue cooperation through consultation, and keep all participants motivated. We intend to tap into all the strengths of all participants through bilateral, trilateral or multilateral cooperation. As a Chinese proverb says, "A tower is composed of many a grain of sand, and a river is formed of many a stream."

– We need to take an open, green and clean approach. Belt and Road cooperation is not about establishing an exclusive club. It aims to promote green development. We should launch green infrastructure projects, make green investment, and provide green financing to protect the Earth which we all call home. In pursuing Belt and Road cooperation, everything should be done in a transparent way, and we should have zero tolerance for corruption. The Beijing Initiative for a Clean Silk Road that has been launched is for this very purpose, and manifests our strong commitment to transparency and clean governance in Belt and Road cooperation.

– We need to pursue high-standard cooperation to improve people's lives and promote sustainable development. We will apply widely accepted rules and standards and encourage participating companies to comply with general international rules and standards in building and operating projects and in the process of procurement, project bidding and tendering. The laws and regulations of participating countries should also be respected. We need to take a people-centered approach, give priority to poverty alleviation and job creation, and guarantee that Belt and Road cooperation will deliver true benefits to the people of participating countries and contribute to their social and economic development. We also need to ensure the commercial and fiscal sustainability of all projects so that they will achieve the intended goals as scheduled.

Connectivity is vital to Belt and Road cooperation. We need to promote a global partnership of connectivity to achieve common development and prosperity. I am confident that as we work closely together, we will transcend geographical distance and embark on a path of win-win cooperation.

Infrastructure is the bedrock of connectivity – it is the lack of infrastructure that has held up the development of many countries. High-quality, sustainable, resilient, affordable, inclusive and accessible infrastructure projects can help countries fully leverage their resources, better integrate into the global supply, industrial and value chains, and realize interconnected development. To this end, China will continue to work with other parties to build an infrastructure connectivity network, one that centers on the economic corridors such as the New Eurasian Land Bridge, and is connected by major transport routes, such as the China-Europe Railway Express and the New International Land-Sea Trade Corridor, and information expressways, and is underpinned by major railway, port and gas pipeline projects and underground power and telecommunications cable network. We will continue to make good use of the Belt and Road Special Lending Scheme, the Silk Road Fund, and other special investment funds. We will develop Silk Road theme bonds, and support the Multilateral Cooperation Center for Development Finance in its operation. We welcome the participation of multilateral and national financial institutions in BRI investment and financing and encourage third-market cooperation. With the involvement of multiple stakeholders, we can surely deliver benefits to all.

The flow of goods, capital, technology and people will power economic growth and create the broad space it needs. As a Chinese saying goes, "The ceaseless inflow of rivers makes the ocean deep."[2] However, were such inflow to be cut, the ocean, however big, would eventually dry up. We need to facilitate free trade and investment, say no to protectionism, and make economic globalization more open, inclusive, balanced and beneficial to all. To this end, we will enter into negotiations with more countries to conclude high-standard free trade agreements, and strengthen cooperation in customs, taxation and audit oversight by introducing the BRI Tax Administration Cooperation Mechanism and accelerating international collaboration on the mutual recognition of Authorized Economic Operators. We have formulated the Guiding Principles on Financing the Development of the Belt and Road and published the Debt Sustainability Framework for Participating Countries of the Belt and Road Initiative to provide guidance for BRI financing cooperation. In addition, the Second China International Import Expo will be held this year to provide an even bigger platform for other parties to access the Chinese market.

Innovation boosts productivity; it makes companies competitive and countries strong. We need to keep pace with the Fourth Industrial Revolution, jointly seize opportunities created by digital, networked and smart development, explore new technologies and new forms and models of business, foster new growth drivers and explore new development pathways, and build the digital Silk Road and the Silk Road of innovation. China will continue to implement the Belt and Road Science, Technology and Innovation Cooperation Action Plan, and will work with our partners to pursue four major initiatives, namely the Science and Technology People-to-People Exchange Initiative, the Joint Laboratory Initiative, the Science Park Cooperation Initiative, and the Technology Transfer Initiative. We will actively implement the BRI Talent Exchange Program, and will, in the coming five years, offer 5,000 opportunities of exchange, training and cooperative research for talented innovators from China and other BRI participating countries. We will also support companies from various countries in advancing ICT infrastructure to upgrade cyber connectivity.

Imbalance in development is the greatest imbalance confronting today's world. In the context of the BRI, we must always take a development-oriented approach and see that sustainability features in the entire process of project selection, implementation and management. We need to strengthen international development cooperation so as to create more opportunities for developing countries, and help them eradicate poverty and achieve sustainable development. To this end, China and its partners have set up the Belt and Road Sustainable Cities Alliance and the BRI International Green Development Coalition, formulated the Green Investment Principles for the Belt and Road, and launched the Declaration on Accelerating the Sustainable Development Goals for Children Through Inclusive Development. We have set up the BRI Environmental Big Data Platform. We will continue to implement the Green Silk Road Envoys Program and work with relevant countries to jointly implement the Belt and Road South-South Cooperation Initiative on Climate Change. We will also expand cooperation in agriculture, health, disaster mitigation and water resources; and we will enhance cooperation with the United Nations to narrow the gap in development.

We need to build bridges for exchanges and mutual learning among cultures, expand cooperation in education, science, culture, sports, tourism, health and archeology, and strengthen exchanges between parliaments, political parties, NGOs, women, young people, and people with disabilities in order to facilitate multifaceted people-to-people exchanges. To this end, in the coming five years we will invite 10,000 representatives of political parties, think tanks and NGOs from BRI participating countries to visit China. We will encourage and support social organizations of BRI participating countries in jointly undertaking projects for improving people's lives. We will organize a number of environmental protection and anti-corruption training courses, and expand human resources cooperation in various fields. We will continue to run the Chinese government scholarship Silk Road Program and host the International Youth Forum on Creativity and Heritage along the Silk Roads and the

"Chinese Bridge" summer camps. We will also put in place new mechanisms such as the Belt and Road Think Tanks Cooperation Committee and the Belt and Road News Alliance to draw inspiration and pool our strengths.

Notes

[1] See note 9, p. 156.

[2] Sima Qian: *Records of the Historian (Shi Ji)*. Sima Qian (c. 145 or 135-? BC) was a historian and writer of the Western Han Dynasty.

Self-Reform of the CPC

Never Forget Where We Started*

October 31, 2017

To stay true to our original aspiration and founding mission and to continuously work hard is the only way to keep the CPC forever vigorous. As long as all Party members and all Chinese people unite as one and do solid work, the country, like a great ship braving winds and waves, will surely reach the shore of national rejuvenation.

Mao Zedong compared this site to the cradle of the CPC. It is a vivid metaphor. I see the site as an anchor of the souls of Chinese Communists. Every relic used when the Party was founded here in 1921 is invaluable; every picture gives us food for thought. We need to recall and reflect on the founding of the Party, which may help us better understand our Party's original pledge.

Our Party's history started from its First National Congress in 1921. No matter how far we have traveled, we must never forget where we started. The oath to join the Party is not long. It is easy to recite in a moment but hard to observe for a lifetime. All Party members must bear in mind the oath, always discipline ourselves in accordance with the oath, and uphold the oath all our lives.

The Red Boat[1] sparked the flame of the Chinese revolution and started the century-spanning voyage of the Party. Since the ceremony to lay the foundation for the Nanhu Lake Revolutionary Memorial in 2006, I have been longing to visit once the construction was complete. Today, I am finally here, inspired and encouraged.

When I worked in Zhejiang, I defined the Red Boat spirit as a pioneering spirit that creates from nothing, a hard-working spirit that

---

* Main points of speeches during visits to the site of the First CPC National Congress in Shanghai and the Red Boat on the Nanhu Lake in Jiaxing, Zhejiang Province.

keeps faith and fears no setbacks, and a spirit of service that honors the Party's commitment to the public good and its loyalty to the people. We should carry forward this spirit in the context of this era.

All our Standing Committee members of the Political Bureau of the Central Committee are here today to review the Party's history, particularly its founding, carry on our revolutionary traditions, follow the lofty ideals of our predecessors, confirm the heavy responsibilities on our shoulders, and sharpen our sense of responsibility and mission to achieve the objectives set at the 19th CPC National Congress.

The site of the First CPC National Congress in Shanghai and the Red Boat on the Nanhu Lake in Jiaxing are the two places where our Party set off to live its dream. It is here that our Party was born; it is here that our Party started its expedition and finally became the governing party of the whole country. This is where our Party is rooted.

"A promising cause may seem simple at the beginning, yet proves great on completion."[2] Over the past 96 years, our Party has united the Chinese people and led them to remarkable achievements. This is a source of our pride. As our cause progresses, no Chinese Communist should ever forget our original aspiration. This is the only way to honor history and our predecessors, to win popular support and uphold the call of the era, and to accomplish our deeds with indomitable will.

At its 19th National Congress, the Party set the goals and tasks for itself as well as for the country. All Party members must uphold the Party's fundamental purpose of serving the people wholeheartedly, and lead the people in creating a better life. We must strengthen our shared ideal of socialism with Chinese characteristics, and press forward towards our ultimate ideal of communism and a better future. We must maintain a modest and prudent style of work, fear neither hardship nor self-sacrifice, and work hard to realize the Two Centenary Goals and the Chinese Dream of national rejuvenation.

Notes

[1] Starting in Shanghai in late July 1921, the First National Congress of the Communist Party of China was completed on a pleasure boat on the Nanhu Lake in Jiaxing, Zhejiang Province in early August. It heralded the official founding of the Communist Party of China. The pleasure boat has since been hailed as the "Red Boat" in Chinese revolutionary history. – *Tr.*

[2] *Zhuang Zi.*

Say No to Form over Substance and Reject Bureaucratism*

December 2017 January 11, 2019

I

The manifestations identified in the article seem new, but in fact they are old problems. They show us again that the Four Malfeasances die hard. We must never falter in correcting such problems, nor should we ever stall in our drive to improve the conduct of Party members. All provincial authorities and central departments should take a close look at their performance, examine their conduct to see where they fall short of the requirements and standards. In particular, they should work out effective measures for addressing such prominent problems as unfulfilled promises, empty sloganeering, half-hearted action, and failure in implementation, and tackle them in a down-to-earth manner. Officials at all levels should take the lead and play an exemplary role. In the upcoming Aspiration and Mission education campaign, we must not favor form over substance and must ensure good results with good conduct.

(from the directive on an article of Xinhua News Agency "Be Vigilant Against New Manifestations of Favoring Form over Substance and Bureaucratism", December 2017)

---

* Excerpts from speeches made between December 2017 and January 11, 2019.

II

The 19th CPC National Congress in 2017 created an imposing blueprint for future development. To accomplish the objectives and tasks set at the congress, we must encourage research and fact-finding in the Party. Officials at all levels should take the lead in doing frequent field work. They should go to the front line and understand the general picture; they should conduct in-depth studies of problems, understand the nature and rules of different issues, and find methods and ways to solve major difficulties. They must seek truth from facts and speak that truth, whether it is good news or not. Particularly, they must avoid favoring form over substance and bureaucratism. They should never satisfy themselves with a superficial understanding through cursory observation or a smattering of knowledge on a subject, nor should they regard a part as the whole and reach hasty conclusions and judgments.

(Comments on "Promote the Spirit of Fighting Poverty and the Coordinated Development of Material and Cultural Progress in Rural Areas – Report on Poverty Alleviation in Xunwu" submitted by the Publicity Department of the CPC Central Committee, December 15, 2017)

III

The Four Malfeasances are difficult to eradicate. Therefore, we should never slacken our efforts in rectifying these problems, and there is no end to the task of improving our conduct. Favoring form over substance and bureaucratism are entirely incompatible with the nature, mission and fine conduct of our Party. They are the archenemies of our Party and the people. Members of the Political Bureau of the CPC Central Committee must take the lead in having a correct attitude towards performance in our work; they must always be honest and do solid work, and conscientiously oppose the practice of favoring form over substance and bureaucratism. They must take the lead in rejecting and fighting these ills. They should focus on outstanding problems, and understand that there are many manifestations of favoring form over substance and bureaucratism, and that they can evolve and mutate. They need to get a thorough understanding of how the two present themselves in different periods, regions, and departments, and base their work on the reality of the situation. They should solve old problems and identify new ones, address both overt and covert problems, and resolve superficial problems and deep-rooted ones. Through their efforts, good norms will be formed and lasting effect will be achieved.

(from the speech at a meeting of criticism and self-criticism among members of the Political Bureau of the 19th CPC Central Committee, December 25-26, 2017)

IV

We should also relieve officials of meaningless tasks. Currently, the management of officials is widely based on keeping record of their activities. However, it may lay too much emphasis on the activities per se and not enough on concrete results. There are numerous, frequent, and repetitive inspections and appraisals. And, once again, officials are busy dealing with piles of documents and attending one meeting after another – a problem we have addressed before. These problems consume too much time and energy and actually encourage favoring form over substance and bureaucratism. In the past, it was said that "thousands of threads of instruction come from above, but there is only one needle". Now, officials at the grassroots complain that "thousands of hammers strike from above, but there is only one nail to be driven down below", and that "thousands of swords hack down from above, but there is only one neck for the blades". This must change. The Central Committee has set requirements for solving these problems. All provincial authorities and central departments must meet the requirements and duly address the problems.

We should enhance information sharing and cannot simply evaluate the performance of the lower levels by the number of activities they have kept record of or the volume of materials they have submitted. We should not, simply for our own convenience, ask for the same data and materials every time or every year if what we already have is enough. We cannot allow any department or any person to go and ask for the same materials. We must have rules to free officials at the grassroots level from the burden of preparing endless materials. The number and frequency of evaluations and inspections by various levels should be held in check. Matters of the same category should be dealt with together where conditions permit. The purpose is to reduce the burden of officials at grassroots levels and let them have more time for work.

(from the speech at the 10th group study session of the Political Bureau of the 19th CPC Central Committee, November 26, 2018)

V

Currently, favoring form over substance and bureaucratism are prominent problems within our Party. They are our archenemies, hindering the implementation of the guidelines, principles, and policies of the Party and the major decisions and plans of the Central Committee. In reality, there are various manifestations of these problems. Some officials and departments do not stay focused, nor do they make genuine and committed efforts to implement the decisions and plans of the Central Committee. They shout slogans but take few concrete actions. They make promises that they never act upon, or start things but do not see them through. Some keep records of their every trivial action and present these as achievements. They turn targeted poverty alleviation into targeted form filling, and claim so-called results that are no more than figures on paper. Some are dilatory and perfunctory in their work, shirking responsibility when troubles come and dodging thorny problems. They like to report every trifle to their superiors for approval or directives. In doing so, they appear to be abiding by the rules but are actually avoiding responsibilities. Some make ill-considered or purely arbitrary decisions. They place themselves above the Party organization and allow no dissenting voices. Some abuse accountability mechanisms, making officials sign written pledges for the most trivial matters, and failing them in their performance evaluation should they be unable to meet a commitment. Worse still, some exploit these mechanisms to hive off their responsibilities or pass the buck.

We must view these problems from a political perspective and address them by finding the root causes and identifying the interests involved. Those who favor form over substance are obsessed with results and achievements, with a disinclination to do any real work. This stems from a failure to understand the importance of making solid efforts for tangible progress, an absence of any sense of responsibility, and a mindset that wants only the benefits of the position but not the duties that come with the post. Those with this problem satisfy themselves with superficial work, and prefer eye-catching achievements to laying solid foundations, and window-dressing to real results.

Bureaucratism comes from the obsession with official posts and power. It reflects misguided values and a distorted view of power. Those with this problem are inclined to rely too much on their own personal proclivities and subjective judgment, and distance themselves from reality and the people. These mindsets and behavior will hamper the implementation of the guidelines, principles, and policies of our Party, disappoint the expectations of our people, and erode the foundations of the Party's governing status.

(from the speech at the Third Plenary Session of the 19th CPC Central Commission for Discipline Inspection, January 11, 2019)

VI

Eradicating the practice of favoring form over substance and bureaucratism is an important task. In combating the former, we need to ensure officials make real efforts at work, urge them to foster a correct attitude towards performance, and urge them to avoid fickleness in their daily work, abandon selfishness, and avoid distractions. In opposing the latter, we need to tackle the problem of nonfeasance in safeguarding the people's interests. We must protect the fundamental and long-term interests of the people, and also effectively address their immediate and most important concerns. Party committees or leadership groups of all provincial authorities and central departments should assume their principal responsibilities, keep a close watch for any new tendencies towards or any new forms of favoring form over substance and bureaucratism, and come up with effective measures to rectify them. Leading bodies at all levels should fight these practices, and take the lead in examining and exposing their own shortcomings accordingly. Discipline inspection and supervision bodies at all levels should highlight these as pressing problems to solve, and expose and report typical cases.

(from the speech at the Third Plenary Session of the 19th CPC Central Commission for Discipline Inspection, January 11, 2019)

Strengthen Party Self-Governance as an Ongoing Mission*

January 11, 2018

To further strengthen Party self-governance now and in the future, we must implement the guiding principles of the 19th CPC National Congress held in 2017, and follow the guidance of the Thought on Socialism with Chinese Characteristics for a New Era. While enhancing our Four Consciousnesses and bolstering our Four-sphere Confidence, we must uphold and strengthen overall Party leadership, uphold the authority of the Central Committee and its centralized, unified leadership, and see the Party's political foundations reinforced, its ideological commitment buttressed, its organizations consolidated, its conduct improved, and its discipline enforced, with institutional improvements incorporated into every aspect of strengthening the Party. We must step up our efforts to combat corruption, carry on with our work to improve the Party's political environment, and strengthen its ability to innovate, its power to unite, and its capacity to deliver. These are firm guarantees for a decisive victory in building a moderately prosperous society in all respects, and for building a modern socialist China.

First, we must focus our efforts on reinforcing the Party's political foundations, and uphold the authority of the Central Committee and its centralized, unified leadership. A governing Marxist party must take a clear political stance. A multitude of facts have shown that many problems within the Party are attributed to weak political commitment and a lack of regular and sound political activities.

---

* Part of the speech at the Second Plenary Session of the 19th CPC Central Commission for Discipline Inspection.

The 19th CPC Central Committee incorporates and prioritizes the Party's political progress into its overall effort to strengthen itself – a major decision that has been made from an overall strategic perspective.

To reinforce the Party's political foundations, we must give priority to upholding the authority of the Central Committee and its centralized, unified leadership. All the political problems within the Party, in the final analysis, are ascribed to lack of loyalty to the Party. Loyalty defines the quintessential character of Communists, and numerous revolutionary martyrs have demonstrated such loyalty by sacrificing their lives. "My loyalty comes from the bottom of my heart, and it stretches all the way from the Earth to the Heavens."[1] "I shall hold to my beliefs even at the cost of my life."[2] They were dauntless and no torture could force them to yield. They would be loyal to the Party and never betray it for as long as they should live. Loyalty to the Party must be sincere and unconditional. As a measure of practice as well as a political criterion, it must be embraced in implementing the Party's decisions and plans.

When the commander in chief gives orders, all troops obey and act accordingly. All Party organizations must implement the decisions and plans of the Central Committee to the letter. Under any circumstances, Party officials must be politically firm and reliable, be loyal and honest to the Party, follow the leadership of the Central Committee, and strictly abide by the political discipline and political rules. They must remain steadfast on the right path, increase their awareness to observe discipline, keep their moral integrity, and improve their willpower to resist corruption. They must turn the Four Consciousnesses into concrete action to obey the Party's command and assume their obligations to the Party.

A political party should have faith. For the Communist Party of China, this refers to the faith in Marxism, communism and socialism with Chinese characteristics. Party officials should learn to capture the essence of the Thought on Socialism with Chinese Characteristics for a New Era. They must read more Marxist classics and classical works on adapting Marxism to the Chinese context to truly understand the Marxist stance, viewpoint and methodology, and internalize them so that they uphold faith in Marxism and persevere in pursuing their ideals with strong convictions. These ideals should be the beacon of faith for Party officials.

Political faith and ideals do not spring fully-formed into existence, and it is not easy to stick to them. We must withstand the Four Tests[3], and overcome the Four Risks[4]. We should take account of today's realities to plan for the future. We should have a deep understanding of the dialectical relationship between the long-term goal of communism and the common ideal of building socialism with Chinese characteristics. The communist ideals would be no more than empty talk without our current efforts to develop Chinese socialism and to rejuvenate the Chinese nation. But we should not avoid talking about these ideals or abandon them simply because they will take a long time to achieve. An ancient scholar once said, "We worry about the next one thousand years when we are only to last less than a hundred."[5] Our confidence in the path, theory, system and culture of socialism with Chinese characteristics can ultimately be condensed into faith in socialism and Marxism. It is a fact that we are in the initial stage of socialism, but we should aim high for the future. Our education campaign on reaffirming ideals and convictions since 2012 has proved effective and should be continued.

Irregularities within the Party over the years have all been the results of deviating from the Party Constitution, and violations of Party discipline by leading Party officials – the culmination of their indifference to the rules of the Party Constitution. The 19th CPC National Congress wrote into the Party Constitution the fresh experience and theoretical innovations in Party governance since the 18th CPC National Congress. The unity of the Party in thinking and action should first of all be embodied in understanding and complying with the Party Constitution. Reverence for the Party Constitution is the fundamental political discipline. Party organizations at all levels and all Party members should study, observe, enforce and safeguard the Party

Constitution, use it to discipline our words and deeds, and maintain a high degree of unity with the Central Committee in terms of political stance, direction, principles, and path.

Since the Fourth Plenary Session of the 18th CPC Central Committee in 2014, I have repeatedly warned of the dangers of the Seven Malpractices[6]. They are in essence political issues which can be put into two categories: first, cliques bound together by political and economic interests attempting to usurp Party and state power; second, unauthorized activities fanned by factionalism that sabotage the Party's centralized and unified leadership. We must not bury our heads in the sand in the face of these dangers; instead we should take resolute measures to prevent or curb them and remove hidden and potential troubles. We should underline political discipline and rules at all times, strictly investigate and deal with violations of rules and discipline, and allow no factions pursuing self-interest or local cliques acting on their own. We should advocate values such as loyalty and honesty to the Party, fairness and practicality in work, and integrity in our members and officials, and ensure that they strengthen their Party awareness and political ability through sound intra-Party activities and improve themselves politically and ethically. As an ancient scholar said, "We will not act recklessly if we think right."[7] Leading Party officials should be grateful to the Party and the people and hold them in reverence, never seek position or privileges, and put a cap on their desire for material enjoyment and other perquisites. "Only the gentle breeze caressing the river and the bright moonlight pouring down on the mountains are a bounty and ceaseless feast for the eye and the ear that nature offers."[8] This sentiment of Su Shi, a great writer of ancient China, as he expressed in these words, is most precious but not seen among us now. We had nothing with us when we were born and will take nothing away with us when we die. Once we think this through, we can play a model role by being clean and have integrity prevail within the Party.

Second, we must implement the Central Committee's Eight Rules on improving Party and government conduct, and maintain close ties with the people. The Eight Rules are not intended for just five or ten years – they are to be upheld in the long term. To do this we need perseverance and tenacity. We must pay attention to both their present and future effect, implement the rules strictly and earnestly, and get every Party member and all Party organizations involved so as to make this a regular practice that produces effective results. We must keep an eye on new signs and manifestations of hedonism and extravagance, particularly on festive occasions, and prevent the resurgence of such tendencies by identifying them early. Those in command need to take full responsibility for correcting the practices of favoring form over substance and bureaucratism. We need to address the issue of giving only lip service to the Central Committee's decisions and policies. We need to conduct in-depth analyses of tough issues and take practical measures based on reality and public concerns to ensure the implementation of the Central Committee's decisions and plans down to the primary level. All provincial authorities and central departments should revise anew their follow-up measures accordingly, based on what has been achieved over the past five years in implementing the Eight Rules, and release them to the public for supervision.

In improving Party conduct, we must focus on maintaining close ties with the people. The Four Malfeasances are more than specific misconduct; they represent a fundamental betrayal of our Party spirit and purpose. Many problems among primary-level Party organizations are attributed to the fact that some Party members and officials are not concerned with the people. Some are reluctant and some refuse to communicate with the people, and some just do not know how to do it. There are also a few who ignore the people's needs or dare not face them – they are struck dumb when faced with the people. Leading officials must resist the temptations of privileges in thought and in action. Mao Zedong once said, "The people choose their leaders and leadership tools from practice. It is wrong for those who are chosen to become conceited and consider themselves of great consequence, rather than serve their role."[9] His words still resonate today.

In December 2012, at a session of the Political Bureau for deliberation on the Eight Rules, I said, "Only when we are under pressure and supervision can people enjoy a more comfortable and satisfying life and have a higher opinion of us." The higher the position officials hold, the more they should connect with and serve the people, respect them and maintain closer ties with them. We must remain dedicated to the people, reach out to them, and resolve their prominent problems with solid measures. To win their trust and support we must always put people's interests first, seriously address any issues of pressing public concern, and correct any activities that damage the interests of the people.

Third, we must enforce discipline in all respects and govern the Party strictly. "When the law is effective and discipline enforced, the nation is under good governance and people's support is won."[10] Strict discipline guarantees our Party's march from victory to victory. The 19th CPC National Congress highlighted the enforcement of discipline and integrated it into the overall plan for strengthening the Party, underlining our determination to govern the Party with strict discipline.

Every Party member's effort is needed to improve conduct and combat corruption. We are all participants rather than bystanders in this campaign. Every Party official should draw lessons from those breaching discipline, be alert to potential problems, follow principles and be stricter with ourselves, so that we become immune to corruption. We should enhance education on discipline, offer education and guidance before taking disciplinary action, and use typical cases around us to send a message and shame officials into ceasing their wrongdoing. "When we see a bad example we should turn to check our own conduct."[11] In this way, we can ensure that all Party members and officials enforce self-discipline as part of their normal behavior.

We must pay more attention to checking erroneous ideas at the outset, reminding officials of their problems, and forbidding them from doing anything unethical just because it seems insignificant. We need to improve regulations on discipline, and keep our institutions up to date. Power comes with responsibility. The Party Constitution specifies the scope of power of all Party organizations including Party leadership groups for disciplinary punishment. Party committees, or Party leadership groups, at all levels must be resolute in enforcing oversight and discipline, and must take on their political responsibility for full and rigorous governance over the Party.

As an ancient scholar said, "It is easy to nip a vice in the bud but difficult to correct deep-rooted problems."[12] In recent years, we have put forward the four forms of oversight over discipline compliance[13] based on past experience and new requirements for strengthening Party discipline. In response, some officials have confessed on their own initiative their lapses and serious mistakes to the Party organization, and they have been treated leniently. Some others, on the brink of violating discipline, have returned to the right path after receiving warnings and before it was too late. Inspired by these examples, most officials hold discipline in awe and abide by principles. This demonstrates the effect of the Party's policies and methods and its full concern and care for officials. We should make a greater effort to use the first method – criticism and education – and correct minor mistakes whenever they arise. We should get general problems out in the open, straighten them out, and close the case accordingly, to help relieve officials of any concern. Party members and officials summoned by or receiving inquiry letters from discipline inspection departments should clarify their problems at meetings for criticism and self-criticism, to ensure the seriousness of intra-Party political activities. We should communicate with and warn those found in violation of discipline, to make them clarify their problems in exchange for leniency. We should educate those in serious violation of Party discipline about moral and political integrity in disciplinary review and make them realize, repent, and correct their mistakes. In the case of the very few who are unrepentant and are suspected of breaking the law, and continue to deceive the organization to the last moment while committing serious violations of Party discipline, we must thoroughly investigate and deal with them in accordance with the law and discipline as a warning to others.

Fourth, we must intensify efforts to address both the symptoms and root causes of corruption, and secure a sweeping victory. We have fought against corruption with decisive measures since the 18th CPC National Congress, and we must continue to carry it through to the end after the 19th CPC National Congress, to eliminate vice and exalt virtue, consolidate the foundation of our values, and make sure both symptoms and root causes are addressed.

To this end, we should have effective means to deal with symptoms while consolidating what we have achieved in addressing root causes. Without the deterrent effect of punishment, it is hard to achieve substantial results. We will continue to maintain our tough stance on corruption, and make no exception for any organization or individual. We will impose tight constraints for long-term deterrence, and punish those who take bribes and those who offer them. We need to resolutely deal with existing cases and curb the emergence of new ones. We need to focus on corruption cases involving interest groups formed by political degeneration and bribery; and on corrupt officials who have not restrained themselves from illegal activities, who are strongly suspected of wrongdoing, who have been repeatedly reported by the public for malpractice, and who are currently holding important offices with prospects of promotion. We must investigate and examine officials reported for political and organizational issues or corruption.

We must take out "tigers" whenever we see them and swat the "flies" that buzz around. We should combat corruption in whatever form and address even the slightest signs. "Tigers" and "flies" – major and minor corruption cases – are both to be brought under investigation. The campaign for strengthening Party self-governance should be extended to primary-level Party organizations. Corruption that directly affects people's lives must be harshly punished. We should carry out investigations in the fields of poverty relief and public wellbeing. In order to ensure that policies designed to benefit the public are implemented to their satisfaction, we should be tough in dealing with officials who embezzle disaster and poverty relief funds and supplies, who violate policies relating to land acquisition and resettlement, and misappropriate compensation funds, and who exploit their position at the primary level to take bribes, embezzle funds, and seek benefits for relatives and friends. While combating corruption, we should also eliminate criminal gangs, evil forces and illegal and criminal activities such as pornography, gambling, and drug abuse, and clamp down on individuals, families and clans who abuse or exploit their local communities. We must hunt down both gang-related organizations and the hands behind them to enhance the people's sense of gain, happiness and security.

Justice has long arms. We need to expand international cooperation on the fight against corruption, tracking down corrupt officials who have fled overseas and preventing more from fleeing. While continuing to issue Red Notices for wanted fugitives, we need to enhance international cooperation on anti-corruption law enforcement and strengthen deterrence against corrupt officials who attempt to flee abroad.

The key to addressing both the symptoms and root causes of corruption lies in action. Our Party has established the best practices of combating corruption – to ensure that the officials do not dare to be, are not able to be, and have no desire to be corrupt. We must strengthen deterrence, strengthen the institutional cage, and strengthen their vigilance. We need to break the chain sustaining abuse of state assets through reform and institutional innovation to prevent officials from falling prey to corruption. We must strengthen checks on and oversight over the exercise of power, and establish effective systems and mechanisms.

Fifth, we must improve the oversight systems of the Party and the state to increase the Party's ability to cleanse itself. As Goldbach's conjecture challenges mathematicians, self-supervision challenges countries worldwide in state governance. In seeking the solution to breaking the cycle of rise and fall[14], we must act with force and continue to improve and renew ourselves. The effort to strengthen Party discipline since the 18th CPC National Congress has proved that the mechanism to cleanse the Party is effective and we are fully capable of dealing with existing problems within the Party. We will establish an efficient oversight system with complete coverage under the Party's unified command, and align efforts in intra-Party oversight with oversight by state agencies and other political parties, judicial oversight, public oversight, and oversight through public opinion.

Discipline inspection is a strategic institutional process for scrutiny within our Party. We will intensify political inspection with a view to highlighting the Party's comprehensive leadership and strengthening the Party. The deterrent role of discipline inspection will be provided by Party self-governance and scrutiny of compliance with the Party Constitution and guiding principles of the 19th CPC National Congress. We will strengthen discipline inspection at the central, provincial, city and county levels to realize full coverage of inspection within one office term of Party committees at each level, creating a supervision network that facilitates coordination in discipline inspections among these levels. We will apply new approaches to inspection, accelerate efforts to review the effect, and adopt more flexible methods, such as randomly selecting the targets for inspection, to deter and warn potential wrongdoers. To deter misconduct and address the problem from the root, we must improve the whole discipline inspection system and ensure the results serve their intended purposes, and call to account those who fail to carry out their responsibility, fail to reach the desired effect, or act in a perfunctory manner.

Reform of the national supervision system is a major political reform bearing on the overall situation and a key measure to strengthen self-supervision of the Party and the state. We will establish supervision commissions at the national, provincial, city, and county levels in line with the schedule and roadmap specified by the Central Committee. We will create an anti-corruption working mechanism under the Party's unified leadership and an authoritative, efficient supervision system. We will develop a law on supervision, revise and improve relevant laws, form a power supervision network covering inspection, personnel dispatching, and supervision, and turn institutional strengths into effective governance.

Sixth, we must build a team for discipline inspection and supervision that is honest, clean, responsible, and loyal to the Party and the people. Since the 18th CPC National Congress, the Central Commission for Discipline Inspection and the discipline inspection and supervision departments at all lower levels have enhanced the Four Consciousnesses and maintained a high degree of unity with the Central Committee by resolutely implementing its policies and plans, upholding the Party Constitution and performing their duties with loyalty. Being selfless and fearless, and always ready to assume responsibility, they have performed their duties for the Party and the people.

As a disciplinary force within the Party, discipline inspection commissions are meant to exercise supervision and this will make some people unhappy. They should be absolutely loyal to the Party and willing to assume their responsibilities. They must have political integrity, a strategic vision, and the ability to craft overall plans and put them into practice. They must enhance supervision, enforce discipline impartially, and reinforce accountability. They must strengthen the scrutiny and inspection of compliance with Party regulations such as the Party Constitution and the code of conduct for intra-Party political activities. Their primary tasks are to uphold the Central Committee's authority and its centralized, unified leadership, and implement it in strengthening discipline, exercising scrutiny, carrying out inspections and regulating the accountability system. They should extend reform of the discipline inspection system by transforming its functions and methods to create new approaches, new initiatives and new measures. They should also strengthen the supervisory role of discipline inspection departments in colleges and state-owned enterprises, opening up a new page of discipline inspection and supervision work.

Discipline enforcers must first discipline themselves. Discipline inspection and supervision teams are bestowed with great power and carry a heavy responsibility. They are a key target of people with ulterior motives. Discipline inspection and supervision departments at all levels must discipline themselves with higher standards, observe stricter discipline, and be more resistant to corruption. Officials on the team must be reliable, responsible, law-abiding and incorruptible. Their power, granted by the Party and the people, must never be abused and must be wielded for the purposes of safeguarding justice and punishing corruption.

Notes

[1] Cai Hesen: "Ambitious Youth: Crossing Dongting Lake on the Way North", *Collected Works of Cai Hesen*, Vol. I, Chin. ed., People's Publishing House, Beijing, 2013, p. 23.

[2] Xia Minghan: "Die for My Beliefs", *Xia Minghan*, Chin. ed., People's Publishing House, Beijing, 1984, p. 1.

[3] This refers to exercising governance, carrying out reform and opening up, developing the market economy and responding to external development.

[4] This refers to lack of drive, incompetence, disengagement from the people, and inaction and corruption.

[5] *Nineteen Ancient Poems (Gu Shi Shi Jiu Shou)*.

[6] This was put forward by Xi Jinping at the second full assembly of the Fourth Plenary Session of the 18th CPC Central Committee in October 2014: In order to seek promotion and greater power, some officials, ignoring the Party's political discipline and rules, have engaged in one or more of these malpractices: (1) making appointments based on favoritism and discriminating against those who hold different views; (2) ganging together to form self-interested factions; (3) making anonymous and false allegations against others and spreading rumors; (4) buying support and votes; (5) promising high positions in exchange for favors and relying on cronyism for promotion; (6) feigning compliance while opposing in action and going their own way; and (7) failing to comply with Central Committee decisions or even making baseless criticisms of them.

[7] Zhu Xi: *The Analects of Zhu Xi (Zhu Zi Yu Lei)*.

[8] Su Shi: "Ode to the Red Cliffs" (Chi Bi Fu).

[9] Mao Zedong: "Guidelines for Electing the Seventh Central Committee of the Communist Party of China", *Collected Works of Mao Zedong*, Vol. III, Chin. ed., People's Publishing House, Beijing, 1996, p. 373.

[10] Bao Zheng: *Memorials to the Throne (Shang Dian Zha Zi)*. Bao Zheng (999-1062) was an official of the Northern Song Dynasty who was known for his integrity and impartiality in redressing injustices for the people.

[11] *The Analects of Confucius* (*Lun Yu*).

[12] Fan Ye: *The Book of Eastern Han* (*Hou Han Shu*). Fan Ye (398-445) was a historian during the Northern and Southern Dynasties.

[13] See note 18, p. 79.

[14] See note 19, p. 79.

Strengthen the Party and Its Organizational Line in the New Era*

July 3, 2018

I emphasized at the Party's 19th National Congress that of the great struggle, great project, great cause, and great dream, the great project of strengthening the Party itself plays the decisive role. To successfully carry out the great social revolution of upholding and developing socialism with Chinese characteristics in the new era, our Party must have the courage to reform itself and become stronger.

We have achieved remarkable results in strengthening Party discipline since the 18th CPC National Congress in 2012, but we still have a long way to go. We are still to go through the Four Tests and to overcome the Four Risks; they are protracted and tough. The root causes undermining the Party's pioneering nature are complex. While prominent problems such as unwholesome thinking, organization and conduct and petty politics in the Party have not yet been fully resolved, new ones continue to arise.

Some Party members and officials do not abide by political discipline and rules, groundlessly criticizing the Central Committee's major policies, feigning compliance, and practicing duplicity. Some waver in their ideals and convictions, having doubts about communism. Some lose their faith in Marxism-Leninism and instead believe in ghosts and gods, experiencing drastic changes in their worldview, their outlook on life, and their values. Some lack drive in their work, ducking responsibility and shying away from action, in order to avoid mistakes. To play safe, they neither stand in the fore to avoid the limelight, nor stay in the rear. Some have a penchant for forming

---

* Part of the speech at the CPC's National Conference on Organizational Work.

cliques and factions, cultivating connections or currying favors with higher-ups for personal benefit. Some lack resolution or commitment in addressing undesirable work practices, using artifice or taking a perfunctory approach to deal with issues such as favoring form over substance, bureaucratism, hedonism and extravagance. Some abuse power for personal gain and become corrupt and degenerate, refusing to restrain themselves in spite of repeated warnings from the Central Committee. Some grassroots Party organizations are dysfunctional, weak, ineffective or marginalized, and these problems have not been properly addressed. Some places have seen unbalanced and inadequate development of their talent, failing to unleash their potential for creativity. Some places neglect reality in bringing in high-caliber personnel, paying too much attention to their number, academic titles, and nationality. Some places and entities lack the awareness to enforce proper Party discipline, failing to fulfill their responsibilities, and even refusing or disdaining to work towards strengthening the Party.

These problems severely undermine the Party's unity and solidarity and adversely affect its cause and the people's interests.

The great social revolution is being carried out in the new era by the people under the leadership of the Party. We should be fully aware that never before has it covered such a wide range of social sectors, affected so many interest groups, touched upon so many severe problems, involved so many institutional barriers, and faced such complicated circumstances. We must enhance our risk awareness and sense of responsibility to ensure that the self-reform of the Party is carried through to the end.

Deng Xiaoping once pointed out, "The implementation of the correct political line must be ensured by a correct organizational line."[1] Our Party has always made its organizational line serve its political line. The program it adopted at its First National Congress in 1921 specified the principles for its organizational work. The concept of "organizational line" was established at the Sixth National Congress in 1928. At the Gutian Meeting held in 1929, a requirement was set to "transform Party organizations to make them capable of fulfilling the Party's political tasks"[2]. At the Sixth Plenary Session of the Sixth Central Committee in 1938, Mao Zedong pointed out, "Cadres are a decisive factor, once the political line is determined."[3] He defined "appointing people on their merits" as the key principle in appointing and promoting officials and "political integrity and professional capability" as the standards to be applied. After the founding of the People's Republic of China in 1949, in line with the needs of the socialist revolution and development, our Party emphasized that officials in all positions must be socialist-minded and professionally competent.

After the Third Plenary Session of the 11th CPC Central Committee in 1978, Deng Xiaoping said, "We must guarantee China's stability and the realization of the four modernizations by following the correct organizational line."[4] He also set forth requirements for selecting officials: They should be more revolutionary, younger, better educated, and more professionally competent.

"When the line of a fishing net is held up, all the meshes will be open. When the fundamental principles are upheld, all work will fall in place."[5] The organizational line is instrumental in upholding Party leadership and strengthening the Party and its work. I now define the Party's organizational line for the new era as follows:

- fully embrace the Thought on Socialism with Chinese Characteristics for a New Era;
- with a focus on improving the organizational system, train high-caliber officials who are loyal to the Party, have moral integrity, and demonstrate a keen sense of responsibility;
- gather talented people who are patriotic and dedicated, evaluate them in terms of both political integrity and professional competence, with priority given to integrity, and appoint people on their merits; and
- guarantee a strong organization in upholding and strengthening overall Party leadership and in adhering to developing socialism with Chinese characteristics.

The Party's organizational line in the new era is both theoretical and applicable; it must be fully implemented in the great new project of strengthening the Party and its self-governance.

Notes

[1] Deng Xiaoping: "Excerpts from Talks Given in Wuchang, Shenzhen, Zhuhai and Shanghai", *Selected Works of Deng Xiaoping*, Vol. III, Eng. ed., Foreign Languages Press, Beijing, 1994, p. 367.

[2] Mao Zedong: "Resolution of the Ninth Party Congress of the Fourth Army of the Red Army", *Collected Works of Mao Zedong*, Vol. I, Chin. ed., People's Publishing House, Beijing, 1993, p. 88.

[3] Mao Zedong: "The Role of the Chinese Communist Party in the National War", *Selected Works of Mao Zedong*, Vol. II, Eng. ed., Foreign Languages Press, Beijing, 1965, p. 202.

[4] Deng Xiaoping: "The Organizational Line Guarantees the Implementation of the Ideological and Political Lines", *Selected Works of Deng Xiaoping*, Vol. II, Eng. ed., Foreign Languages Press, Beijing, 1995, p. 200.

[5] Yang Quan: *Discourse on Truth and Matter* (*Wu Li Lun*). Yang Quan (dates unknown) was a philosopher during the Western Jin Dynasty (265-317).

Cultivate Officials with Firm Conviction, Political Commitment, Professional Competence, and Proper Conduct*

March 1, 2019

The training and selection of outstanding young officials is of great importance to the future of our Party, our country and our nation as well as the wellbeing of our people. Party officials, especially younger ones like you, should have a thorough understanding and good command of theories and strengthen your ideals and convictions through study. You should remain true to our original aspiration and founding mission as Party members, apply what you have learned in your work, acquire further knowledge through practice, improve yourselves through self-reflection, and faithfully follow our Party's principles and discipline; you should take the lead in shouldering your responsibilities by applying what you have learned to your actions. You should maintain loyalty to the Party, be grateful to the people, revere the law and discipline, and advance your career with enterprise. This means you should be firm in ideals and convictions, maintain political integrity and professional competence, and be disciplined.

Without a thorough understanding of theory, it is impossible to have a firm political stance and stay true to our Party's mission. Party officials must equip themselves with Marxist theories. Our Party governs a large country with a population of close to 1.4 billion, faces challenging domestic and international environments, and shoulders weighty mission. Without a good understanding of theory,

---

* Main points of the speech at the opening ceremony of a training program for younger officials at the Central Party School (National Academy of Governance) during its 2019 spring semester.

it is difficult to overcome risks and challenges and make continuous progress. We should thus strengthen theoretical study, master and apply dialectical and historical materialism, in particular the Marxist stance, viewpoint and methodology as applied to them, and gain a thorough understanding of the principles of governance by the Party, the established practices of building socialism, and the laws underlying social progress.

Party officials should study theory in a comprehensive, systematic and timely fashion, and apply it to practice. When studying the Thought on Socialism with Chinese Characteristics for a New Era, we should gain a full understanding of its importance to our era, to the Party's theory and practice, and to the world, and its underlying message and requirements. Our theoretical study should be problem-oriented and closely connected with our new practices in the new era, our thinking and actual work. We should reflect on what we have learned, develop an in-depth understanding of it, and know not only the hows but also the whys. The most effective way to study theory is to read the original works and articles, and fully understand the principles. We need to study, remember, and ponder over subjects of learning, conduct in-depth research, and guide our daily work with study, so that learning, reflection, and application are integrated and that knowledge strengthens faith and guides practice.

The ideals and convictions of the Chinese Communists are founded on a comprehensive understanding of Marxism and the laws governing historical development. History and experiences have time and again proved that if a party stays true to its ideals and aspirations, it will remain invincible and rise through hardships and adversity. If an official is firm in ideals and convictions, he or she will have a broader vision, keep to the correct political direction, and "remain as steadfast as a peak in the face of storm"[1]. Therefore, we should stay true to our faith, otherwise we may go astray.

The yardstick to judge whether an official has strong ideals and convictions is to see if he or she is loyal to our Party. An official should be loyal, honest, and responsible, with loyalty always coming first. Being loyal to our Party means we should enhance the Four Consciousnesses, reinforce the Four-sphere Confidence, ensure the Two Upholds, strictly observe our political discipline and rules, and follow the central Party leadership in terms of political stance, direction, principles and path. This commitment must be heartfelt and firm at any time and under any circumstance. Loyalty to the Party and faith in Marxism demand concrete actions. We should never forget to check whether we comply with the Party Constitution, rules, and discipline in terms of ideals, convictions, statements and deeds, beat the dust off our soul, and remain true Communists.

Never forget why we started, and we can accomplish our mission. The 70th anniversary of the founding of the People's Republic of China is the best time to carry out the Aspiration and Mission education campaign. All officials should bear in mind the original aspiration and founding mission of our Party, so that we can aim high and have an inexhaustible source of aspiration for our endeavors. We should hold the people dearest in our hearts. Sticking together, maintaining a close bond, and sharing weal and woe with the people – this is what enables our Party to overcome all difficulties and dangers. Without the support of the people, we can accomplish nothing. We should keep in mind that the people are the true heroes; at no time should we forget whom we serve, whom we rely on, and who we are, and we must forge a true bond with the people.

The nature of a political party or a government is determined by whom it serves and whom it relies on for support. All of our officials must adhere to the Party's commitment to building itself for the public good and exercising power for the people. We should learn from the people with humility, truly take on responsibility for the people, passionately serve the people, and sincerely subject ourselves to their scrutiny. We need to look to the people as our teachers, learn from them, stay engaged with them, and know what they are concerned about. We should conduct in-depth research to identify prominent problems and difficulties faced by the people, heed their views, and extend their good practices. We should always care for the people, work for them, and deliver benefit to them. When analyzing and addressing issues or making decisions, we should share the concerns of the people. We should help the people solve problems, cater for their wellbeing, and see that they are satisfied with what they have gained and feel secure. We should have a strong sense of political responsibility and mission, remain committed to our great struggle, great project, great cause and great dream, and advance the cause of China's prosperity and rejuvenation and the wellbeing of our people with dedication.

Self-cultivation is essential to the performance of duties of officials. An official's moral integrity and commitment to our Party do not grow simply because the years of their Party membership or public service increase, or as they are promoted to higher posts. Therefore they should strengthen self-cultivation, self-restraint and self-reform. The Thought on Socialism with Chinese Characteristics for a New Era sets out not only important guidelines for our Party's exercise of governance, but also requirements for Party members in terms of political integrity, values, ethics, and approach to work. We should remain firm in our faith, strengthen political commitment, obey political rules, and enhance our political awareness and integrity.

One's moral character demonstrates one's ethical standards. Selfless devotion and being open and above board are our defining qualities as Communists, and they are qualities that we officials should cultivate and keep. We officials should maintain high ethical standards and follow Confucius' advice: "When you meet people of virtue and wisdom, think how you should learn to equal them; when you meet people with poor moral standards, remind yourselves against such behavior." We should draw a line between public and private interests, justice and benefit, right and wrong, rectitude and evil, and hard work and hedonism. We should dedicate ourselves to our great cause rather than seeking higher posts. We should be open-minded, and we should work for the Party and the people rather than seeking promotion and personal gain.

We officials should cultivate moral integrity, act in good faith, and maintain self-respect, good conduct and a healthy lifestyle. In particular, we should strengthen self-discipline and guard against temptations. If one cannot maintain integrity and self-discipline, one is doomed to failure. We should realize that incorruptibility is a blessing and greed a curse. To remain incorruptible, one should take the right attitude towards power, position, and interests, remain sober-minded, and maintain good conduct at all times. We should adopt the right approach to our job performance. We should contribute our share to our cause without claiming credit for its success. We should hammer away until a job is done, and be down-to-earth in our approach to work.

We should arm ourselves with our Party's theories and use them to guide and enhance our work. We should study in depth these theories, gain a thorough understanding of them, and put them to good use. We must remember that empty talk harms the country, while hard work makes it flourish. We should match our words with deeds and deliver outcomes. We should take a firm stand on major issues of principle, rise to challenges and crises, accept responsibility for mistakes, and resolutely fight against unhealthy tendencies. We should be like the sturdy grass that withstands high winds and true gold that stands the test of fire. There is no easy way to cultivate these qualities. Only by facing up to the storm and exploring the new world can we officials enhance our performance. We should act rather than just uttering empty rhetoric. We should work hard to surmount difficulties, steel ourselves through hardships, and increase our capabilities through work on the ground.

The best way to test an official's commitment to the Party and performance is to see if he or she is ready to take on responsibilities. A strong sense of responsibility, the courage to confront difficulties, and more skills are what we need to accomplish the following endeavors: carry out the Five-sphere Integrated Plan and the Four-pronged Comprehensive Strategy in a coordinated manner, act on the new development philosophy, win the three critical battles against major risks, poverty, and pollution, ensure steady growth, promote reform, make structural adjustments, improve people's lives, guard against risks, and maintain social stability. We should demonstrate our loyalty to the Party and the people by completing important tasks and meeting challenges.

Notes

[1] Du Fu: "Song of the Thatched Cottage Broken by the Autumn Wind" (Mao Wu Wei Qiu Feng Suo Po Ge).

Goals of the Aspiration and Mission Education Campaign*

May 31, 2019

The CPC Central Committee has defined clear requirements, targets, tasks, methods, and a timeframe for the Aspiration and Mission education campaign. All provincial authorities and central departments need to have an accurate understanding of them, and take active, targeted and context-based measures to ensure the desired results.

First, the requirements.

The requirements of this campaign – staying true to our original aspiration and founding mission, identifying areas of improvement, and enforcing implementation – are based on the task of strengthening the Party in the new era and addressing the existing problems.

To stay true to our original aspiration, we must remember the fundamental purpose of serving the people wholeheartedly, remain true to the original aspiration with strong convictions, and remember that people's desire for a better life must be the focus of our efforts. Nourishing the aspiration with genuine compassion and concern for the people, we must never forget that our Party comes from the people and is rooted in them, and that their support is a source of inexhaustible strength propelling us to advance and gain victories. Working to make the aspiration come true as servants of the people, we must always remember that we Communists rely on the people to survive, that we must serve them and never distance ourselves from them, and that we must never make light of them, ignore them or be indifferent to their difficulties.

---

* Part of the speech at the Conference on the Aspiration and Mission Education Campaign.

To stay true to our mission, we must remember that our Party must respond to the historic challenge of national rejuvenation. We need to be bold in taking on responsibilities, act proactively, and plan for our cause under sound and practical guidelines and with foresight. We should face up to risks and challenges, know our responsibilities and fulfill them, and overcome all difficulties and barriers on our way forward with perseverance and a selfless, dauntless spirit. This way, we will be able to gain experience and wisdom, and grow stronger and more capable through trials and tribulations.

To identify areas of improvement, we must check our conduct against the Thought on Socialism with Chinese Characteristics for a New Era, against the Central Committee's decisions and plans, against the Party Constitution and rules, against the people's new aspirations, and against role models and pacesetters around us, and we must discipline ourselves by setting high standards. We need to identify areas of improvement in enhancing the Four Consciousnesses, reinforcing the Four-sphere Confidence, and ensuring the Two Upholds. We need to identify areas of improvement in having respect for discipline and upholding principles, in putting the people first, thinking in their shoes, and serving them, and in improving our political integrity, capability and competence, moral standards, and conduct. And then we should take specific and targeted measures to rectify problems and improve performance.

To enforce implementation, we must apply the Thought on Socialism with Chinese Characteristics for a New Era in all our endeavors to promote reform, development, and stability, and in strengthening the Party. We must see that in staying true to our original aspiration and founding mission, Party members and officials forge ahead with determination, pioneer our cause with solid work, and act conscientiously. To do this, we must avoid favoring form over substance and bureaucratism. We must ensure full implementation of the Party's guidelines and policies, address issues of major concern to the public, and continue to enhance people's sense of gain, happiness and security.

We must understand that these requirements are interconnected and work as a whole throughout the campaign.

Second, the tasks and targets.

In this campaign our major tasks are to gain a full understanding of and implement the Thought on Socialism with Chinese Characteristics for a New Era, forge a political character of loyalty, integrity, and responsibility, and unite with and guide all the people to strive for the realization of our great dream. The specific targets are to make sure that Party members and officials benefit from theoretical studies, enhance their political awareness, readily take on responsibilities in starting new endeavors, serve the people and address their concerns, and act as role models of clean governance. These tasks and targets embody the fundamental requirements for Party members and officials in the new era in areas of thought, political awareness, conduct, ability, and clean government.

To benefit from theoretical studies, the key is to guide Party members and officials to make further progress, and extend their understanding of the Thought on Socialism with Chinese Characteristics for a New Era and the Central Committee's guidelines and policies. We must dig deep into the theories to understand them in full, be more active and resolute in applying them, and enhance the ability to use the Party's new theories to guide our work.

To enhance political awareness, the key is to guide Party members and officials to reaffirm their faith in Marxism and Chinese socialism, and carry on the Party's legacy. We need to enhance the Four Consciousnesses, reinforce the Four-sphere Confidence, and ensure the Two Upholds. We need to stay consistent with the Central Committee in political principles, thought and action, and always remain loyal to the Party, the people, and Marxism.

To readily take on responsibilities in starting new endeavors, the key is to guide Party members and officials to be fully aware of their political responsibility and historic mission, to work hard, and to waste no time in furthering our cause no matter what difficulties lie ahead. Like a hammer driving a nail, we need to do solid work and abandon all thoughts of playing safe or muddling along, avoid token efforts, never shirk responsibilities and neglect our duties, and deliver results that are recognized by the people and withstand the test of time.

To serve the people and address their concerns, the key is to guide Party members and officials to always put the people first, seek people-centered development, forge closer ties with the people, and think and act in the people's interests. We need to focus on the people's concerns, and gain their trust by working for their benefit.

To act as role models of integrity, the key is to guide Party members and officials to serve the people and be pragmatic, clean and honest. We need to balance work and personal life, the greater good and individual interests, right and wrong, personal favors and the law, affinity with businesses and integrity of office, frugality and extravagance, work and leisure, and gains and losses. We must fight against the pursuit of privilege in any form, prevent and combat corruption, and be clean and honest in office and daily life.

Third, key measures.

This campaign is not divided into stages. This does not mean we can lower our standards. On the contrary, we must reach higher. All provincial authorities and central departments need to be creative in carrying out the campaign based on the local context. All Party members and officials need to study, research, identify and rectify problems throughout the whole campaign for the best possible effect.

Some prominent intra-Party problems are caused by ideological deficiency. All our major education campaigns since the Yan'an Rectification Movement[1] in the 1940s have prioritized ideological and theoretical guidance. In the current campaign, we need to strengthen theoretical studies, and focus on root causes of those problems. Party members and officials need to read and study works of Marxism, understand its basic tenets, examine themselves against our goals and standards, and promptly rectify any deviation. We need to set up theory study groups for leading officials and reading groups for Party members, and discussion sessions for exchanges on different topics. More means need to be employed to educate Party members and officials on our revolutionary traditions, our current situation, and our policies, and to introduce role models on the one hand and cases that can serve as a warning on the other. All this needs to be more targeted, effective and appealing. We need to tell the stories of role models who hold fast to the Party's ideals and convictions, remain true to its original aspiration and founding mission, and readily take on responsibilities, so as to encourage Party members and officials to learn from them and become role models themselves.

"There is no use in reading 10,000 books if we cannot even put one of their words into practice."[2] Party members and officials must understand people's lives and needs and keep abreast of the real situation, identify problems and their causes, and come up with feasible solutions to difficult issues. Research must produce solid results, and help us better understand the Party's new theories and maintain close ties with the people – it needs to serve and facilitate our cause. We cannot research for the sake of it. We cannot be perfunctory in research or all rush to one and the same place for research purposes, nor can we make a show of research.

The courage to face up to problems and correct mistakes is a prominent feature and strength of our Party. Party members and officials need to be bold in reforming themselves. They need to widely solicit opinions, examine their conduct, reflect on problems, and find the root causes, so as to know where to improve and how to improve. No one should brush off defects casually, downgrade the severity of problems, or avoid key issues and real problems. Problems pointed out by higher levels should not serve to mask problems discovered through self-inspection; problems of the collective leadership should not serve to mask problems of individual members; problems of other people should not serve to mask problems of our own; problems in work and professional competence should not serve to mask problems in political commitment; and problems of the past should not serve to mask the problems of today. When a problem is pinpointed, targeted measures need to be provided to address it effectively.

"It is most pitiful that one does not know one's mistakes, and those who know but do not change have no courage."[3] Rectification is key. When a problem is found, it needs to be corrected at once. A time limit needs to be set for problems that we expect to resolve quickly, and the requirements must be met before the deadline. Those that cannot be resolved soon need to be kept on the radar, and followed up with conscientious and continuous efforts directed towards targets set for different stages. Rectification cannot be a one-off process. We must be quick to take real action and avoid procrastination, empty talk, and falsification. Enforcing accountability does not mean simply blaming officials working at the community level, and no more form filling needs to be imposed on lower levels in the name of rectification. The education campaign needs to offer guidance on the placement of officials. Leading bodies and officials need to be evaluated in terms of political and theoretical awareness, conduct, and the ability to perform duties. Capable and upright officials should achieve faster promotion, and those who are disloyal to the Party, corrupt in office, or fail to fulfill their duties must be investigated or removed. We must promote the able, demote the incapable, and discharge the poorest performers.

In recent years, in response to people's concerns, we have carried out programs against such misconduct as wining and dining at public expense, using public-funded cars above one's designated grade, and putting up office buildings and other facilities without authorization. These programs have clear targets and have proved effective in solving problems. In the current education campaign, special programs are a key element and must be enforced throughout the whole process. In addition to Central Committee planning, all provincial authorities, central departments and major state-owned enterprises should make a list of their main problems and address them with force. The results of these programs need to be made public, and violations of Party discipline or the law must be dealt with.

Before the education campaign ends, leaderships at and above the county level need to have meetings for criticism and self-criticism.

Self-criticism needs to be specific about our problems and needs to touch underlying questions. When criticizing our colleagues, we need to be direct in pointing out their problems, to make them flush with embarrassment and help them scour away their ills. We must be gratified when told of our errors; we must not shy away from our shortcomings. We must accommodate different opinions and sharp criticism.

Notes

[1] This refers to a Marxist education campaign inside the CPC from the spring of 1942 to the spring of 1945. Its main aims were: to fight against subjectivism in order to improve theoretical study; to fight against sectarianism in order to improve Party conduct; and to fight against stereotype essays in order to improve writing. Through the movement the whole Party reaffirmed the practice of applying the basic theories of Marxism to the actual conditions of China's revolution. It is called the Yan'an Rectification Movement because the CPC Central Committee was seated in Yan'an at the time.

[2] Lin Hong: "Drinking" (Yin Jiu). Lin Hong (dates unknown) was a poet of the Ming Dynasty (1368-1644).

[3] Han Yu: "Five Admonitions" (Wu Zhen). Han Yu (768-824) was a writer, thinker and official of the Tang Dynasty.

Stay True to the Party's Original Aspiration and Founding Mission and Carry Out Self-Reform*

June 24, 2019

In response to the sweeping Aspiration and Mission education campaign, the Political Bureau is holding today its 15th group study session on "staying true to the Party's original aspiration and founding mission and carrying out self-reform" with a view to motivating Party members to remain true to its original aspiration, take on their responsibilities, identify areas of improvement, and enforce implementation based on a review of the historical experience of our Party and the requirements of the new era. This is also an important move the Political Bureau is taking to lead this campaign.

How will our Party, a party with a century of history, maintain its progressive nature, integrity and vigor? How will it always keep the trust and support of the people? How will our Party continue to lead the country? These are fundamental questions that we must answer and solve properly. The requirement to stay true to the Party's original aspiration and founding mission is to remind all Party members that the Party's nature, ideals, convictions, and goals manifest themselves in the aspiration and the mission. The longer our Party is in power, the more it should stick to its nature as a Marxist party, the more it should remember its original aspiration and founding mission, and the more it should carry out self-reform.

The original aspiration and founding mission of our Party are

---

* Speech at the 15th group study session of the Political Bureau of the 19th CPC Central Committee.

based on Marxism. Marx and Engels wrote in the *Manifesto of the Communist Party* that, "All previous historical movements were movements of minorities, or in the interest of minorities. The proletarian movement is the self-conscious, independent movement of the immense majority, in the interests of the immense majority." As a Marxist party, the CPC has always taken it as its original aspiration and founding mission, and made it the focus of its efforts, to work towards a happy life for the Chinese people and the rejuvenation of the Chinese nation. If it failed to stay true to the original aspiration and founding mission, it would change its nature and color, lose the support of the people, and fail to survive. Our Party will prevail so long as it adheres to its commitment to serving the public good and exercising power in the interests of the people, ensures that the Chinese people are happy, works to rejuvenate the Chinese nation, examines itself, faces up to its mistakes, and fights against all the problems that may tarnish its progressive and wholesome nature or endanger its health.

In retrospect, how could our Party flourish from small roots, survive every crucial test, surmount so many difficulties, and advance from victory to victory? The fundamental reason is that our Party is always committed to its original aspiration and founding mission whether in good or bad times and perseveres in marching towards its goal, winning wholehearted support of the people. During the revolutionary wars, in order to win national independence and people's liberation, our Party led the people to succeed in the New Democratic Revolution and establish the People's Republic of China, and made it possible for the people to be the masters of the country after years of painful struggle. After the founding of the People's Republic, in order to modernize the country, our Party led the people to establish socialism as China's fundamental system and advance socialist construction by working hard and rising to challenges.

During the years of promoting reform, opening up, and socialist modernization, our Party led the people to open up a socialist path with Chinese characteristics by freeing the mind and seeking truth from facts, and enabled the country to catch up with, and stand proud among, the nations of the world.

Now in the new era of socialism with Chinese characteristics, we are closer to, more confident, and more capable than ever before of making national rejuvenation a reality. Our achievements are impressive. This is a reason for pride, but never complacency. I have emphasized, "After achieving success it's not easy to keep the entrepreneurial drive and be mindful of possible problems; after taking power, it's not easy to stay frugal and restrained; during peacetime, it's not easy to discipline officials, and to prevent corruption and extravagant life; in the critical moments of reform, it's not easy to follow the tide and the people's aspirations." We can never allow ourselves to lose our revolutionary spirit and to indulge in complacency and pleasure-seeking amidst flattery and praise. Rather, we must remember that midstream is where the current is the strongest and the road halfway up the hill is steeper. So it is necessary to take "staying true to the Party's original aspiration and founding mission" as our eternal theme in strengthening the Party, and a lifelong task for all Party members and officials.

Staying true to the original aspiration and founding mission is not easy. It requires us to have a strong sense of self-reform. We must fulfill this mission on the new journey and reform the Party further in the new era to build it into a vibrant Marxist governing party that is always at the forefront of the times, enjoys the wholehearted support of the people, has the courage to reform itself, and is able to withstand all tests.

This year marks the 70th anniversary of the founding of the People's Republic of China, and our Party also celebrates 70 years in power. As the ancient saying goes, "One prospers in worries and hardships, and perishes in ease and comfort."[1] No external forces but we alone can beat ourselves. Our ancestors said, "It's admirable to correct one's mistakes, and it's not commendable not to make any mistakes."[2] It should be noted that as our Party has been in power for a long period of time, factors undermining its advanced and wholesome nature are ever-present, and dangers running counter to its founding mission and weakening its foundation are ubiquitous. Unless we guard against these problems or address them in time, they will accumulate into bigger and harder ones which cannot be easily solved. Some of them may even lead to disastrous consequences imperiling the whole country.

Remarkable results have been achieved in strengthening Party self-governance since the 18th CPC National Congress in 2012, winning wide acclaim from the people, but we should not be complacent about it. We should be soberly aware that prominent problems of contaminated politics, thinking, organization, and conduct in our Party have not been solved root and branch. Some problems that have been dealt with might resurface, new problems are cropping up, and the Four Tests and the Four Risks are still complex and tough. There is a long way to go for the Party to reform itself. We can never allow ourselves to slacken off. The key is not the problems themselves; it is whether we have the will and courage to confront and resolve them. It calls for the joint efforts of the whole Party to stay true to our original aspiration and founding mission. Therefore, every single Party member, and particularly every official, must engage in this education campaign while concerning themselves with the Party, shouldering their responsibility, and striving to strengthen the Party.

Marxism is an instrument to transform our objective and subjective world. As the Party worked to adapt Marxism to the Chinese context, it has developed Mao Zedong Thought, Deng Xiaoping Theory, the Theory of Three Represents, the Scientific Outlook on Development, and the Thought on Socialism with Chinese Characteristics for a New Era. They serve as powerful theoretical weapons to advance social reform and self-reform. Based on the Marxist theory of strengthening parties, our Party has developed rich theories of its self-reform such as reinforcing Party members' ideals and convictions and their Party consciousness, enforcing strict Party self-governance, being strict with intra-Party political activities and conduct, developing both regular and intensive education, carrying out regular criticism and self-criticism, strengthening internal scrutiny, accepting supervision from the public, cleansing the thinking, organization, and conduct of the Party, and keeping it in good health. As important sources of experience for the Party in conducting self-reform, they should be fully applied and developed in this campaign.

In the final analysis, this education campaign aims to solve all intra-Party problems running counter to our Party's original aspiration and founding mission. The key is to have the courage to face up to the problems. Problems are always there. So we should reflect on ourselves just as the old saying goes, "A man of virtue often examines himself as a fallible person"[3], to identify our shortcomings and have the courage to correct them.

We should be problem-oriented and settle problems in earnest. Concealing a malady for fear of taking medicine might result in incurable diseases. In fact, the outstanding problems within our Party have manifested in many ways, requiring us to make a sweep search and do all we can to address them.

To strengthen our Party politically, we need to ensure that the Party exercises centralized and unified leadership and that all its members strengthen their commitment to the Four Consciousnesses, the Four-sphere Confidence, and the Two Upholds. We need to cleanse our political environment, and remove hidden political dangers such as those brought by double-dealers to prevent and defuse political risks.

To strengthen our Party theoretically, we need to improve theoretical guidance, have firm ideals and convictions, bear in mind the Party's nature and purpose, enhance the Party spirit to combat any loss of faith and sense of purpose, and raise the awareness of the Party and Party membership.

To strengthen our Party organizationally, we need to improve the Party by consolidating its weak and slack organizations at all levels to increase their creativity, cohesiveness and ability. We need to resolutely oppose self-centered behavior, anti-centralization, disregard of the rules, the silo mentality, and sacrificing principles for selfish purposes.

We must implement in earnest the criteria for appointing good officials and rectify all unhealthy tendencies.

To improve our Party's conduct and discipline, we need to continue to address the problems of favoring form over substance, bureaucratism, hedonism and extravagance, and also resolutely correct nonfeasance and any misconduct that undermines the people's interests.

We must maintain a tough stance against corruption and eradicate the tumors endangering the health of our Party. The eight prominent problems targeted in this guidance campaign are all that might weaken the foundation and hinder the growth of our Party. They must be solved in the spirit of thorough self-reform. These problems are always visible to the public. Whether Party members and officials remain true to the Party's original aspiration and founding mission needs to be judged and evaluated in practice. We can never carry out self-reform behind closed doors. We must be receptive to the public's suggestions and willingly accept their supervision.

I expounded on how to cleanse, improve, and reform the Party at the Third Plenary Session of the 19th Central Commission for Discipline Inspection earlier this year. These measures could help to remove the tumors and enhance the health of our Party. To cleanse the Party and keep it in good shape, we must eliminate impurities and toxins and remove boils and tumors. As the ancient saying goes, "To ensure lasting peace, problems must be addressed when they arise; to enjoy eternal health, people must go to the doctor when they get ill"[4], it is necessary to prescribe medicine when confirming the diagnosis, and for some chronic ailments, a heavy dose of medicine is needed; when cancer cells are likely to spread, it even requires surgery.

We must address inadequacies, shore up points of weakness, consolidate the foundations, tackle problems at source, prevent minor problems from becoming major ones, address them when they crop up, close institutional loopholes, and improve the supervision system and the Party's long-term governance capability.

A weak person needs to build up his health and boost his immunity;

otherwise his health will deteriorate until it is too late to recover. As the saying goes, the smallest antholes in a dam must be repaired promptly, otherwise it will eventually collapse. To reform our Party, we must have a clear picture, be resolute in removing all theoretical and institutional barriers, and experiment with theoretical, practical, institutional and cultural measures. To improve the Party, we must learn from books, from practice and from the people, strengthen our Party consciousness and political ability, raise our political, theoretical, and ethical level, enhance our governance capability, and build a contingent of loyal, clean, responsible, competent, and professional officials.

To remain true to the Party's original aspiration and founding mission and to carry out self-reform of the Party, we need to deal with the following relationships:

First, we must uphold and enhance centralized and unified CPC leadership while addressing the Party's own problems. All Party members and particularly officials need to fight with extraordinary courage against any behavior by any member that weakens the Party's leadership and governance foundation, or contravenes its political discipline and rules. But we should not undermine or deny the Party's leadership and take an erroneous road of self-destruction because of the existence of those problems.

Second, we must uphold the correct path and embrace innovation. To improve the efficacy of self-reform, we must adhere to the Party's nature, purpose, original aspiration and founding mission, ideals, and convictions, and at the same time solve all problems within the Party with new methods and approaches.

Third, we must on the one hand enforce discipline on all our Party members, and on the other, show them our great care. We must improve the supervision mechanism to prevent them from practicing malfeasance. At the same time, we must also give a free hand to entrepreneurial and responsible Party members and officials, unleashing their enthusiasm, initiative, and creativity, and encouraging them to make contribution and achievements in the new era.

Fourth, we must rely on both the driving force of Party organizations and initiatives of individual members. Party organizations at all levels must be strict in requirements, education, management and supervision. Party members and officials must take the initiative to examine and cleanse themselves politically to improve their political immunity.

The key to remaining true to the Party's original aspiration and founding mission lies in Party officials at all levels and particularly high-level officials. They need to lead by example in studying the Thought on Socialism with Chinese Characteristics for a New Era, in strengthening their commitment to the Four Consciousnesses, the Four-sphere Confidence and the Two Upholds, in staying true to our original aspiration and founding mission, in carrying out criticism and self-criticism, and in upholding truth and rectifying errors. Everyone should be involved and no one should stand aside. The Political Bureau in particular needs to set a good example for the whole Party in this regard.

Finally, I would like to conclude with quotes from Chairman Mao. One is from "On Coalition Government" on April 24, 1945: "Thousands upon thousands of martyrs have heroically laid down their lives for the people; let us hold their banner high and march ahead along the path crimson with their blood!"[5] The other is from "Report to the Second Plenary Session of the Seventh Central Committee of the Communist Party of China" on March 5, 1949: "The Chinese revolution is great, but the road after the revolution will be longer, the work greater and more arduous. This must be made clear now in the Party. The comrades must be taught to remain modest, prudent and free from arrogance and rashness in their style of work. The comrades must be taught to preserve the style of plain living and hard struggle. We have the Marxist-Leninist weapon of criticism and self-criticism. We can get rid of a bad style and keep the good. We can learn what we did not know. We are not only good at destroying the old world, we are also good at building the new."[6]

Notes

¹ *The Mencius* (*Meng Zi*).

² Sima Guang: *Historical Events Retold as a Mirror for Government* (*Zi Zhi Tong Jian*).

³ *Gangcang Zi*. Gangcang Zi (dates unknown), who lived during the Spring and Autumn Period (770-476 BC), was a discipline of Lao Zi.

⁴ He Tan: *Xichou's Sayings* (*Xi Chou Chang Yan*). He Tan (dates unknown), also known as Xichou, was a scholar of the Southern Song Dynasty (1127-1279).

⁵ Mao Zedong: "On Coalition Government", *Selected Works of Mao Zedong*, Vol. III, Eng. ed., Foreign Languages Press, Beijing, 1975, p. 270.

⁶ Mao Zedong: "Report to the Second Plenary Session of the Seventh Central Committee of the Communist Party of China", *Selected Works of Mao Zedong*, Vol. IV, Eng. ed., Foreign Languages Press, Beijing, 1961, p. 374.

Remain True to Our Original Aspiration and Founding Mission – An Ongoing Campaign*

January 8, 2020

A party with over 90 million members and 4.6 million grassroots organizations that has long ruled a vast country boasting a population of 1.4 billion, the CPC gives staunch leadership in building Chinese socialism. The Party's own efforts to strengthen itself have always been a serious matter affecting the overall situation.

While today's world is undergoing changes of a scale unseen in a century, China is at the critical stage of national rejuvenation, and the CPC is leading the people in a great historic struggle with many new features. These changes that come at a staggering pace, the need to strike a balance between reform, development and stability, and the problems, risks and challenges we face – all present unprecedented tests to our Party's governance. To win constant support from the people and continue to achieve further success, our Party, with a history dating back almost 100 years, must bear in mind our original aspiration and founding mission, clear out whatever undermines the Party's progressive and wholesome nature, rid ourselves of any virus that erodes the Party's health, and guard against any danger that goes against our original aspiration and founding mission and has the potential to shake the foundations of the Party.

The past is a prologue. The whole Party must use this education campaign on our original aspiration and founding mission to commit ourselves to further self-reform. Here, I want to highlight a few points.

---

* Part of the speech at the conference reviewing the Aspiration and Mission education campaign.

First, to remain true to our original aspiration and founding mission, we must make strengthening our Party an eternal theme for all Party members and officials. Either for a person or for a party, what must be treasured most is the adherence to one's original aspirations and good qualities in the face of any hardships encountered. For our Party, its original aspiration and founding mission epitomize its nature, purpose, ideals, convictions and goals, and motivate us to stand fast and march forward. From the Shikumen building where our Party was established, to the Tian'anmen Rostrum where the founding of our country was declared, and on to the path of the new era, all of our Party's efforts, struggles and sacrifices have been dedicated to the people's wellbeing and national rejuvenation. Our original aspiration and founding mission have enabled the Party to grow and prosper in extreme difficulties, break through tight encirclements, and rise in adversity. Without them, our Party would change its nature, lose public support, and risk its future.

A nation or a party that forgets where it comes from will not grow and prosper. It should be noted that in the course of our Party's long rule, elements undermining the Party's progressive and wholesome nature are persistent, threats to our original aspiration, our founding mission, and the Party's foundation are ubiquitous, and impurities in thinking, political commitment, organization, and conduct in the Party have not been completely eradicated.

A Marxist Party will not remain progressive and wholesome automatically over time, nor will a Party member's Party consciousness deepen merely through length of service and promotion. There is a risk that our original aspiration will fade and disappear if it is neglected. It is easy to forget why we started and where we are going; it is easy to wander off track and get lost. The fundamental reason why corrupt officials break laws and infringe discipline is that they have cast aside their original aspiration. All Party members should constantly examine and analyze themselves to eradicate any impurities, negative influence, and contamination.

I have said on many occasions that Party members and officials should regularly reread the Party Constitution, their oath of admission to the Party, and the martyrs' letters to their family during the revolution. We need to check our actions against the Party Constitution to find out whether we have complied with the requirements and maintained our original aspiration, just as we tidy our rooms and polish our mirrors regularly to keep them neat and clean. We must guide all Party organizations, members and officials to examine their political thinking against the requirements of the Central Committee, scan their behavior against the Party Constitution and regulations, scrutinize their performance against the people's expectations, and compare themselves with the revolutionaries and martyrs of the older generation and with today's role models. We should constantly remind ourselves of our original aspiration, and stay true to and shoulder our founding mission. We need to nurture the aspiration and keep to the mission through innovative thinking, allow them to further motivate us by reviewing the extraordinary history of our Party, and build a deeper understanding of them as we further regulate intra-Party political activities, so that they can be a driving force for us to forge ahead, innovate and do hard and solid work.

Second, to remain true to our original aspiration and founding mission, we must unify our thinking, will and action with the latest theoretical development of Marxism in the Chinese context. The progressive nature of a Marxist party manifests itself first and foremost in its theory. It is our Party's distinctive feature, and one of its finest traditions, to highlight its theoretical development. Mao Zedong once said, "Therefore ideological education is the key link to be grasped in uniting the whole Party for great political struggles."[1] The original aspiration of Communists is based on their concern for the people, their perseverance in pursuit of truth, and more importantly, on scientific theories of Marxism. Only by improving Party members' theoretical understanding can we stay true to our original aspiration and shoulder our founding mission more conscientiously and more firmly.

The biggest enemy of theoretical study is complacency. If we want to really learn something, we must stay hungry. But we now have some Party members and officials who undervalue theoretical study and spend no time on it; some lack perseverance; some put on a show, dabbling without thorough understanding; some engage in casual and fragmented learning, choosing what interests them and ignoring what does not; many young officials are not well equipped theoretically or firm in their ideals and convictions. We need to help them adopt a serious and sound attitude, if they are to truly understand, firmly believe and actually apply the theories.

I have noted repeatedly that it is through learning that we Communists have come so far today, and it is still the weapon that we must employ as we march into the future. All Party members must keep pace with the times, casting off outdated mindsets, old routines and old practices in thought, deed and decision-making. Otherwise we will be left behind, fail to perform our duties, miss good opportunities, and ruin our work. This problem requires the highest attention from all Party members and particularly from leading officials at all levels. Advancing with the times must be more than a mere slogan; it must guide our thinking and action. We cannot blind ourselves to what is really happening out there like the people in the legendary Peach Blossom Spring[2] who cut all ties with the outside world.

Every step in theoretical innovation must be followed by education and training. All the previous education campaigns of the Party began with ideological education, to address the problems of casual study, disunity in thinking, and slow response in action. With continuous follow-up and concentrated efforts, they aimed to achieve unified thinking, political solidarity, and unison in action across the Party. The top priority should be studying, understanding and applying the Party's innovative theories. It should go together with studying the basic tenets of Marxism, and the histories of the CPC, the PRC, reform and opening up, and socialist development. This in turn must happen in the context of the efforts we have invested in the great struggle for national development, the great project of strengthening our Party, the great cause of Chinese socialism, and the great dream of national rejuvenation. We must work hard to have a good grasp of what we are learning, unify our thinking through freeing our minds, and improve our understanding of the Party's theories so as to apply them in a more proactive way.

Third, to remain true to our original aspiration and founding mission, we must have the courage to face up to problems and carry out self-reform through vigorous self-examination. "When a gentleman errs, his mistake is as visible as a solar or lunar eclipse, but when he corrects it, he is worthy of respect again."[3] Our Party's prominent strength is our ability to confront problems and correct mistakes. Vladimir Lenin once said, "Frankly acknowledging a mistake, ascertaining the reasons for it, analyzing the conditions that have led up to it, and thrashing out the means of its rectification – that is the hallmark of a serious party."[4] A strong party is forged through self-reform. In looking back at our Party's history, while carrying forward social revolutions it has always embarked on self-reform by upholding truth, rectifying its mistakes, facing problems squarely, overcoming its weaknesses, and bracing for the pain of removing the poison to heal quickly. Precisely for this reason, our Party has been able to survive every desperate situation, bring order out of chaos, and become an invulnerable Marxist party.

At present, a minority of Party members and officials lack the drive to reform themselves. They take things as they are and make little effort. Some are losing their ability to examine problems in favor of worrying about personal gains and losses, or concealing their faults for fear of criticism; some dare not air criticism, but keep themselves discreetly out of harm's way by remaining mute; some indulge themselves in corruption and extravagance – they even violate Party regulations such as the Eight Rules despite repeated prohibitions. As an ancient Chinese scholar said, "The hardest thing to do under heaven is to keep one's heart under control, and the easiest thing is to be lured by desire."[5] Once we are tempted, the will to reform ourselves will wane to the point of abandoning our original aspiration and founding mission and violating discipline, even breaking the law.

It is not hard to find the original aspiration but it is not easy to follow through. All Party members must constantly uphold revolutionary ideals, maintain high morale, and use the weapons of criticism and self-criticism to improve Party conduct, enforce Party discipline and fight corruption. We will continue to strengthen the Party's ability to cleanse, improve, reform and surpass itself. We must fight against anything that might weaken the Party's foundations and undermine the Party's undertakings, and eliminate any virus that erodes the Party's health.

Fourth, to remain true to our original aspiration and founding mission, we must maintain the resolve to fight and fulfill our duties. Our Party was born when the nation was beset by domestic crisis and foreign aggression, so it had to fight to survive, to grow and to triumph. The closer we sail towards national rejuvenation, the more we may encounter heavy seas. We must be mindful of possible dangers in time of peace and possible crisis in time of stability, remain ever-vigilant, boost morale, and be resolved to engage in the great historic struggle with many new features.

Speaking of fighting, we do not fight for the sake of it nor for personal gain; we must work hard and overcome difficulties to fulfill the people's expectation for a better life and realize the rejuvenation of the Chinese nation. To judge whether a Party member or official has the spirit to fight and the will to take responsibility, we should see whether he or she has the courage to take a stand on major issues of principle, to rise to challenges, to come forward in times of crisis, to accept responsibility for mistakes, and to fight against unhealthy trends and evil practices.

At present, among our Party members and officials, there are problems such as the lack of will, courage or ability to take on responsibilities. Some prefer to be risk-averse, avoid confrontation, or sit on the fence. They worry that "the more dishes you wash, the more likely you are to break them". They embrace ideas such as "making friends rather than enemies, and turning a blind eye to indiscretions", "rather do nothing in case something goes wrong", "taking credit for successes but refusing to accept responsibility for mistakes", and "enjoying standing in the limelight rather than working behind the scenes". They panic whenever problems and difficulties arise. This is not the conduct of a Communist! They will bring nothing but trouble or even disaster.

A towering tree will not grow in a plant pot; likewise, a great cause cannot be achieved by idlers. To become mainstays of the Party our members and officials must face the world, brave the storm, hone their skills, and enhance their capabilities. They should be men and women of courage and action, knowledgeable and ready to take on responsibilities. They should lead the charge in the face of major challenges, risks, and resistance, and distinguish themselves.

Fifth, to remain true to our original aspiration and founding mission, we must develop and improve the intra-Party systems to establish a long-term mechanism. Systemic strength is the greatest advantage of a party and a nation. Deng Xiaoping once said, "If these systems are sound, they can place restraints on the actions of bad people; if they are unsound, they may hamper the efforts of good people or indeed, in certain cases, may push them in the wrong direction."[6] Our Party suffered losses due to weak systems. Since the 18th CPC National Congress, the Central Committee has been committed to running the Party by rigorous rules, trying to develop a set of systems and institutions that are well-conceived, procedure-based, and effective. Such efforts have strengthened Party self-governance.

The Fourth Plenary Session of the 19th CPC Central Committee proposed a system for remaining true to the original aspiration and founding mission. Establishing a new system requires systematic and dialectical thinking while upholding principles so as to make it instructive, targeted and operational. In this process, we must take pragmatic and effective measures to get to grips with problems with an easy and applicable approach; we must balance the Central Committee's requirements against actual conditions and the expectations of the public at the grassroots level, keeping our eyes on the goal as well as realities; we must emphasize both breaking new ground and maintaining consistency, and make sure the new system accommodates existing intra-Party regulations and systems, determining what is to be retained, improved, established or implemented. When formulating our rules and regulations, we should not try to make them all-encompassing, nor should we overdo the detail.

Systems are to be observed and enforced. The whole Party must strengthen its will to abide by, implement and uphold our systems, and put in place an authoritative and efficient enforcement mechanism to step up supervision of their implementation. We must ensure the full and solid implementation of the system for remaining true to the original aspiration and founding mission and stamp out the practices of rule-bending, loose and selective enforcement, in case rigid restrictions become lax, and a long-acting mechanism becomes ineffective.

Sixth, to remain true to our original aspiration and founding mission, leadership organs and leading officials must make the running. Leadership organs are important bodies in state governance, and leading officials, small in number but holding key positions in state and Party undertakings, are like weather vanes for the whole Party and society. "The rulers' virtue is like wind, and commoners' virtue like grass, which always bends in the direction of the wind."[7] This means leading by example is far more effective than simply issuing orders or prodding people into action. Leadership organs and leading officials must lead the charge in this education campaign.

"If we fail to lead by example, others will neither trust nor follow us."[8] Leadership organs and leading officials have always been the first to charge forward, which is the key to our Party's success. In the years of revolutionary war, "Charge!" and "Follow me in the charge!" were two orders with a world of difference. After the founding of the PRC, thanks to a large number of exemplary officials like Jiao Yulu, Gu Wenchang, Yang Shanzhou and Zhang Fuqing, our Party is able to lead the people to make new progress in every field. Leadership organs and leading officials must fully understand the responsibilities with which they have been entrusted, keep sober-minded, and regularly examine and improve themselves.

This year will witness the end of our battle against poverty, success in building a moderately prosperous society in all respects and the conclusion of the 13th Five-year Plan. We are confronted with increasing external challenges, mounting downward pressure on the economy, and the formidable task of striking a balance between reform, development and stability. The more complicated the situation is, the more it needs leadership organs and leading officials to maintain their resolve and press forward; the more arduous the tasks are, the more it needs them to lead by example, do solid work and shoulder their responsibilities. All leadership organs and leading officials must enhance the Four Consciousnesses, improve the Four-sphere Confidence, and ensure the Two Upholds, leading the people to overcome difficulties on our way forward, and satisfying the Party and the people with good performance.

Notes

[1] Mao Zedong: "On Coalition Government", *Selected Works of Mao Zedong*, Vol. III, Eng. ed., Foreign Languages Press, Beijing, 1991, p. 265.

[2] Tao Yuanming: "Peach Blossom Spring" (Tao Hua Yuan Ji).

[3] *The Analects of Confucius* (*Lun Yu*).

[4] V. I. Lenin: "'Left-Wing' Communism – an Infantile Disorder", *V. I. Lenin: Collected Works*, Vol. 31, Eng. ed., Progress Publishers, Moscow, 1966, p. 56.

[5] Lü Xizhe: "On Nourishing Heart" (Lun Yang Xin). Lü Xizhe (1036-1114) was an educator and philosopher of the Northern Song Dynasty.

[6] See note 1, p. 142.

[7] *The Analects of Confucius* (*Lun Yu*).

[8] Tuo Tuo *et al.*: *History of the Song Dynasty* (*Song Shi*). Tuo Tuo (1314-1355) was an official of the Yuan Dynasty.

Strengthen Discipline and Scrutiny over the Exercise of Power*

January 13, 2020

We must uphold the Thought on Socialism with Chinese Characteristics for a New Era, and follow the guiding principles of the 19th CPC National Congress and the second, third and fourth plenary sessions of the 19th CPC Central Committee. We must exercise full and strict governance over the Party, improve Party and state supervision, strengthen discipline and scrutiny over the exercise of power, and ensure the implementation of the Party's guidelines, principles and policies, to provide a strong guarantee for securing a decisive victory in achieving moderate prosperity and eliminating poverty.

Since the 18th CPC National Congress in 2012, we have shown unprecedented courage and resolve in advancing full and rigorous governance of the Party, and have made historic and groundbreaking progress that will have a profound and comprehensive influence. In our effort to lead a social revolution through the Party's self-reform, we have strengthened and improved the relevant systems to fix problems such as the weakening of Party leadership, a failure to strengthen the Party, and inefficiency in Party self-governance in some fields, so that the Party continues to exercise strong leadership in building socialism with Chinese characteristics. In our effort to strengthen the ideals and convictions of all Party members with progressive theories, we have enacted institutions conducive to realizing our original aspiration and founding mission. We have armed the whole Party with the Thought on Socialism with Chinese Characteristics for a New

---

* Main points of the speech at the Fourth Plenary Session of the 19th CPC Central Commission for Discipline Inspection.

Era, inspired our people, and directed our work accordingly; we have made ideological education a regular and institutionalized practice so as to gather ideological strength for realizing the Chinese Dream of national rejuvenation. In our effort to reinforce unity and solidarity within the Party, we have ensured the Two Upholds, improved the systems for upholding the authority of the CPC Central Committee and its centralized, unified leadership. We have improved the system of the Central Committee's leadership over major programs, and unified our will and action to safeguard the Party's unity and solidarity, so as to strengthen the Party's ability to lead politically, to guide through theory, to organize the people, and to motivate the public. In our effort to improve Party conduct, enforce Party discipline and fight corruption to unite the Party, the military and the people, we have taken firm measures to combat corruption, correct misconduct, eliminate negative elements undermining the Party's progressive nature and integrity, and improve the systems of governance for the people and supported by the people, so that the people always remain a mighty force supporting the CPC's governing status and Chinese socialism.

Since the 18th CPC National Congress, we have sought out a path to resolve problems rooted in the Party's long-term governance so as to avoid the historical cycle of rise and fall, and we have built a set of effective systems for scrutinizing the exercise of power and for enforcing Party discipline and state laws. We must uphold, strengthen and develop our path and systems. At the Fourth Plenary Session of the 19th CPC Central Committee in 2019, strategic plans were laid to uphold and improve the socialist system with Chinese characteristics and to modernize the state governance system and capacity. Accordingly, discipline inspection and supervision organs should undertake the relevant work.

We should enforce political oversight and guarantees, and raise political awareness of the Two Upholds. Supervision and inspection should be strengthened to ensure the implementation of the guiding principles of the Fourth Plenary Session of the 19th CPC Central Committee, and to uphold and consolidate the fundamental, basic and major systems supporting the socialist system with Chinese characteristics. The Central Committee's major decisions and plans must yield substantial results, particularly in achieving moderate prosperity and eliminating poverty, so supervision must be strengthened this year to motivate Party organizations at all levels to do their best and complete their tasks. In terms of strengthening Party self-governance, responsibilities should be specified for each position in each Party organization, and should be assumed, observed and fulfilled accordingly, so as to strengthen grassroots Party leadership and oversight. Power must be exercised appropriately, under the principle of democratic centralism, based on sound decision-making, effective implementation, and forceful oversight, with impartiality and integrity, and in accordance with the law.

We should uphold a people-centered approach, and follow our fine traditions to secure a decisive victory in achieving moderate prosperity and eliminating poverty. Under an explicit institutional framework, officials should eradicate the malpractices of favoring form over substance and bureaucratism, work in a realistic and practical manner, and demonstrate honesty and integrity. Officials should be trained and tempered at the forefront of major programs or major battles, with an encouraging environment for them to grow and stand out from the crowd. Problems that damage the people's interest in poor areas and are of pressing public concern must be properly addressed, and efforts should be made to eliminate the malpractices of favoring form over substance and bureaucratism in targeted poverty alleviation, with a focus on enhancing scrutiny over performance, particularly poverty elimination in designated poor counties. The fight must go deeper against "micro-corruption" that undermines public welfare, against "protective umbrellas" that shelter criminal gangs and evil forces, and against the "stumbling blocks" that hamper the implementation of policies benefiting the public. With this goal in mind, grassroots Party organizations must be strengthened.

We should continue to catch "tigers" as well as "flies", and focus on punishing violations of Party discipline and state laws that occurred despite repeated warnings after the 18th CPC National Congress. We must be fully aware of the severe, complex, long-lasting and arduous struggle against corruption, guard against potential corruption, and increase the efficiency of our fight against corruption. We must severely punish corruption occurring after the 18th CPC National Congress that hampers the implementation of the Party's theories, guidelines, principles and policies, and undermines the Party's governing foundations. We must investigate and prosecute cases of corruption that cause harm; we will make greater efforts to combat corruption in financial institutions and state-owned enterprises, improve the management of state-owned resources and assets, and identify the hidden corruption in local government debt risk. We must punish insurance fraud by medical institutions and set up an effective long-term supervision mechanism. We must improve the supervision of overseas state-owned assets. We must implement the Eight Rules on improving Party and government conduct, remain determined and principled, and prevent old problems from resurging, new problems from emerging, and small problems from growing. We must enhance oversight over those in command at all levels, improve the mechanisms of avoiding work-related conflict of interest, implement regular job rotation and end-of-tenure auditing, and conduct proper criticism and self-criticism.

We should improve Party conduct and build clean government, and ensure our officials do not dare to be, are not able to be, and do not want to be corrupt. This is the fundamental guideline for battling corruption, and also a major strategy for strengthening Party self-governance in the new era. The awareness, ability and resolve to resist corruption are an integral whole, and must be reinforced together in a coordinated way. Strict enforcement of Party discipline and state laws helps strengthen the institutions, improve the institutional structure, and form an effective oversight system. In addition, we must also help Party members develop firm ideals and convictions, enhance Party consciousness, and strengthen their commitment to the Party's founding mission. Strict enforcement will remain a long-term principle, while distinctions between the three pairs of errors[1] should be made, as our measures should both respond to people's concerns and motivate officials to assume responsibility. We should make full use of the four forms of oversight over discipline compliance[2], resolving existing problems with effective measures and preventing potential offenses through strengthened oversight, so as to achieve sound political, legal and social effects.

We should improve Party and state supervision, and comprehensively reform the discipline inspection and supervision system. Institutions and systems should be further developed and improved, fitting with the Party's leadership system and merging into the national governance system; this way, they will help turn China's institutional strengths into effective governance. We should integrate overall oversight by Party committees or Party leadership groups, specialized oversight by discipline inspection commissions and supervision commissions, functional oversight by Party organs, regular oversight by grassroots Party organizations, and democratic oversight by Party members. We should focus on internal Party scrutiny, and coordinate the scrutiny by people's congresses, other political parties, administrative organs, the judiciary, auditing and accounting bodies, statistical institutions, the general public, and the media. Discipline inspection commissions and supervision commissions should play their due role in the Party and state supervision system, and facilitate and implement the institutional reform of discipline inspection and supervision.

We should protect our systems through strict discipline, and strengthen compliance and enforcement. Supervisory mechanisms for enforcement should be improved to cover all areas, and to reinforce regular supervision and targeted inspection. Enforcement results should be included in officials' performance evaluation, to motivate them to fulfill their duties and achieve results. Effective accountability helps strengthen enforcement; abuse of power and dereliction of duty should both be punished, applying to both the person directly responsible and his/her superior.

Upholding the authority of our systems and ensuring their

enforcement are important duties of discipline inspection and supervision organs. They should take the lead in reinforcing our Party's political foundations, maintain absolute loyalty to the Party, have moral integrity, demonstrate a keen sense of responsibility, dare to confront difficulties, and be capable of overcoming obstacles. The CPC Central Committee has enacted rules on supervision and discipline enforcement and approved regulations on supervision and law enforcement, which discipline inspection and supervision organs must implement to the letter. Party committees at all levels must strengthen leadership and oversight over discipline inspection commissions and supervision commissions at their corresponding levels, to ensure the exercise of power in Party discipline and law enforcement is subject to supervision and constraint. Discipline inspection and supervision organs should set an example in enhancing self-supervision and self-discipline, raise awareness of the need to uphold the rule of law, follow procedures and produce evidence, carry out their work within their jurisdiction and in accordance with regulations and standard procedures, and launch greater efforts to strengthen the ranks of inspection and supervision personnel.

Notes

[1] Distinctions should be made between the following cases: mistakes due to a lack of experience in pushing pilot reform programs, and deliberate violations of the law and Party discipline; mistakes due to trying out things not specifically banned by higher-level authorities, and violations of the law and Party discipline with full knowledge of the prohibitions; unintentional mistakes for the good of development, and violations of the law and Party discipline for personal gain. This was first raised by Xi Jinping in January 2016 at a study session on implementing the decisions of the Fifth Plenary Session of the 18th CPC Central Committee, attended by officials at the provincial and ministerial level.

[2] See note 18, p. 79.

Index

A

Acropolis, 544
Afghanistan, 513
Africa, 519-527, 559, 560, 566
African Continental Free Trade Area, 525
African Union, 522, 524, 566
Agenda 2063 of the African Union (AU Agenda 2063), 520, 521
agricultural modernization, 3, 23, 219, 302, 309, 359, 523
All-China Federation of Industry and Commerce, 139
Analects of Confucius, The, 378, 541
Angkor Wat, 541
Arab League Council, 556
Arab states, 556-561
artificial intelligence (AI), 32, 140, 238, 258, 283, 287, 290, 360, 371, 411, 516, 532, 560
Asia-Pacific, 529
Asia-Pacific Economic Cooperation (APEC), 8, 241, 250, 529, 531
Asian Infrastructure Investment Bank, 8, 271, 524
Aspiration and Mission education campaign, 124, 132, 211, 578, 603, 607, 614
Association of Southeast Asian Nations, 566
Athens, 544

B

Bangkok, 544
Basic Law of the Hong Kong Special Administrative Region, 328
BeiDou Navigation System, 559
Beijing, 35, 274, 317, 319, 329, 428, 434, 462
Beijing Summit of the Forum on China-Africa Cooperation, 241
Beijing-Tianjin-Hebei Region, 244, 284, 318, 427, 432
Belt and Road Initiative (BRI), 3, 8, 37, 64, 221, 231, 241, 242, 244, 259, 271, 275, 284, 296, 310, 317, 360, 407, 423, 440, 464, 479, 483, 489, 491, 493, 494, 496, 498, 499, 514, 521, 526, 537, 542, 550, 555-557, 562-566, 568-570
big data, 32, 140, 283, 290, 360, 371-373, 411, 483, 516, 532, 560
bio-technology, 516
Boao Forum for Asia, 239
Boao Forum for Asia Annual Conference, 464
Bohai Sea, 429
Book of Songs, 166
BRICS, 241, 250, 516-520
Buddhism, 546
bureaucratism, 9, 71, 94, 118, 368, 448, 579-583, 588, 598, 608, 619, 634

C

capital market, 36, 180, 230, 244, 462
Central Commission for Discipline Inspection, 594, 619
Central Commission for Finance and Economy, 440
Central Commission for Foreign Affairs, 494
Central Commission for Further Reform, 155, 313
Central Conference on Economic Work, 182
Central Conference on Rural Work, 182
Central Military Commission (CMC), 7, 100, 445-447, 452, 454
Changchun, 323
Chengdu, 317, 419
Chengdu-Kunming Railway expansion project, 178
China-Africa cooperation, 241, 522, 523, 526, 527
China-Africa relations, 522, 527
China-EU investment agreement, 241, 250
China-EU relations, 536
China-Gulf Cooperation Council FTA, 250
China International Import Expo (CIIE), 230, 235, 236, 240, 244, 245, 464, 514, 524, 560, 569
China-Japan-Republic of Korea free trade area (China-Japan-ROK FTA), 241, 250
China (Shanghai) Pilot Free Trade Zone, 243, 245
Chinese Dream, 1, 5, 6, 12, 19, 26, 31, 45, 59, 75, 76, 86, 93, 102, 118, 155, 168, 253, 256, 263, 342, 348, 351, 354, 357, 358, 362, 367, 369, 380, 387-389, 441, 450, 467, 471, 481, 489, 497, 576, 633

Chinese People's Political Consultative Conference (CPPCC), 39, 40, 64, 100, 113, 341-349, 380, 499
Chui Sai On, 478
city clusters, 34, 317-320
civil service examination, 145
clash of civilizations, 511, 512
climate change, 6, 62, 63, 296, 423, 432, 436, 523, 525, 535
cloud computing, 371, 560
Cold War mentality, 63, 512, 536
common development, 62, 76, 220, 221, 239, 296, 471, 485, 491, 496, 504, 507, 508, 511, 513, 516, 537, 545, 555, 557, 562, 566, 568
common prosperity, 12, 20, 25, 30, 43, 63, 88, 89, 113, 159, 215, 221, 282, 306, 351, 503, 513, 543, 556, 566
common security, 25, 522
Communist, 1, 47, 67, 92, 96-98, 121, 162, 214, 216, 264, 506, 507, 575, 576, 585, 602-604, 607, 625, 626, 629
Communist Party of China (CPC), 1, 11, 14, 15, 17, 21, 42, 43, 47, 62, 75, 89, 91, 92, 96, 102, 112, 117, 144, 146, 148, 151, 152, 175, 198, 200, 213, 218, 247, 263, 300, 303, 329, 332-335, 337, 341-343, 345, 347, 349, 351, 352, 367, 382, 387, 408, 417, 450, 469, 490, 491, 499, 506-509, 575, 585, 615, 623, 626, 633
community-level self-governance, 23, 410
compulsory education, 48, 184, 188, 189, 405
Conference on Dialogue of Asian Civilizations, 540, 547
Confucianism, 547
Confucius, 166, 509-511, 604
Confucius Classrooms, 406
Confucius Institutes, 406, 526
Constitution, 7, 24, 40, 41, 59, 146, 147,

165, 327-331, 334, 335, 341, 342, 349, 466, 479, 481
Constitution Day, 327, 331
coordinated development of the Beijing-Tianjin-Hebei Region, 3, 35, 248, 274, 317, 565
coordinated regional development, 227, 282, 318-320
coordinated regional development strategy, 29, 34, 219
core socialist values, 5, 24, 45, 94, 120, 218, 303, 315, 335, 349, 352, 358, 362-364, 366, 376, 380, 391, 409
corruption, 9, 10, 27, 65, 66, 72, 93, 115, 121, 185, 222, 260, 314, 332, 411, 446, 448, 567, 584, 585, 589, 591, 592, 595, 610, 616, 619, 627, 628, 633, 635
CPC (Party) Central Committee, 2, 8, 11, 68, 76, 87, 91, 94, 100, 105-108, 114, 129, 130, 132, 134-137, 143, 175, 183, 185, 195, 199, 209-212, 233, 256, 257, 269-272, 292, 306, 327, 328, 339, 342, 343, 345, 354, 362-364, 367, 375, 383, 411, 412, 431, 440, 445, 452, 454, 459, 489-491, 493-496, 498, 499, 565, 579, 585, 587, 594, 599, 607, 629, 632, 633, 637
CPC in Dialogue with World Political Parties High-level Meeting, 509
CPC('s) leadership, 101, 107, 108, 150, 151, 178, 179, 264, 300, 335, 351, 363, 367, 620
criticism and self-criticism, 71, 590, 612, 617, 621, 628, 635
Cultural Revolution, 135, 148
cultural soft power, 5, 30, 47
cyber governance, 360
cyber Silk Road, 560
cybersecurity, 201, 357-361, 370, 373, 535

cycle of rise and fall, 72, 592, 633

D

Dalian, 323
Dao De Jing, 378
Decision of the Central Committee of the Communist Party of China on Upholding and Improving the Socialist System with Chinese Characteristics and Modernizing the State System and Capacity for Governance, 134, 143
democratic centralism, 27, 67, 125, 196, 346, 634
Deng Xiaoping, 115, 135, 147, 198, 459, 485, 598, 599, 629
Deng Xiaoping Theory, 19, 21, 97, 216, 617
developed countries, 149, 230, 283, 289, 519, 531
developing countries, 12, 64, 220, 361, 489, 499, 507, 508, 516-521, 527, 531, 534, 550, 555, 563, 570
digital divide, 504
digital economy, 3, 238, 290, 359, 361, 531, 549, 560
digital Silk Road, 361, 569
discipline inspection, 121, 201, 593
discipline inspection and supervision departments (organs/bodies), 583, 594, 633, 637
discipline inspection and supervision system, 636
discipline inspection system, 593, 594
Doing Business Report 2020, 249
Du Fu, 378
Du Runsheng, 377
Dujiangyan flood control and irrigation system, 166

E

e-commerce, 176, 239, 525, 560, 564

eco-civilization, 6, 25, 54, 56, 144, 151, 220, 272, 303, 422, 425, 463
eco-environment, 6, 19, 184, 264, 266, 271, 272, 285, 417-420, 422, 423, 425, 426, 432, 436, 505
eco-environmental conservation, 6, 430, 438
eco-environmental governance, 425, 426, 432, 438
eco-environmental progress, 29, 30, 159, 196, 286, 304, 418, 421-423, 426, 430, 431, 435, 436, 466, 539
eco-environmental protection, 176, 205, 206, 218, 320, 321, 419, 420, 422, 423, 425, 438
eco-functional areas, 440
eco-security, 430
economic and trade cooperation zones, 523
economic globalization, 23, 62, 63, 221, 228, 231-233, 235, 236, 238, 246, 247, 250, 271, 498, 504, 517, 518, 530, 531, 537, 543, 548-550, 563, 567, 569
Egypt, 544
Eight Rules, 9, 71, 492, 587-589, 627, 635
18th CPC National Congress, 83, 85, 115-117, 119, 120, 130, 139, 141, 149, 150, 182, 196, 260, 269, 275, 300, 317, 322, 327, 331, 332, 342, 357, 362, 370, 401, 408, 418, 445, 454, 463, 489, 493, 495, 496, 586, 591, 592, 594, 597, 617, 629, 632, 633, 635
emerging markets, 489, 516-520, 550
energy security, 275, 296
Engels, Frederick, 97, 215, 294, 344, 615
environmental incidents, 418
environmental protection, 6, 25, 54, 55, 176, 249, 274, 275, 313, 320, 417, 420-422, 425, 426, 431, 432, 484, 514, 525, 570
ethnic minority areas, 352
ethnic minority groups, 352-354
Euphrates, 541
Eurasian Economic Union, 542, 566
Europe, 270, 304, 461, 568
European socialism, 145
European Union (EU), 304, 536, 566
exchanges and mutual learning among civilizations, 504, 508, 540, 545
extensive growth model, 420
extravagance, 9, 55, 71, 94, 118, 368, 427, 448, 588, 598, 610, 619, 627

F

Fan Jinshi, 377
favoring form over substance, 448, 579-581, 583, 588, 608, 634
favoring form over substance, bureaucratism, hedonism, and extravagance, 9, 71, 94, 118, 368, 598, 619
Fengyun-2 weather satellites, 514
Fenhe River, 439
Fenhe-Weihe River Plain, 427, 440
Fifth Plenary Session of the 18th CPC Central Committee, 136
First Belt and Road Forum for International Cooperation, 8, 494, 566
First Centenary Goal, 29, 88, 175, 498
First China International Import Expo, 230, 464, 514, 560
First CPC National Congress, 576
First Five-year Plan, 316
First Plenary Session of the CPPCC, 341
First Plenary Session of the 19th CPC Central Committee, 87
fitness-for-all programs, 5, 47
Five Principles of Peaceful Coexistence, 62, 470

Five-sphere Integrated Plan, 3, 20, 130, 175, 200, 273, 342, 417, 605
Fok Ying Tung, 460
food security, 34, 140, 275, 440, 520, 523
Forbidden City, 166
foreign direct investment, 271, 563
foreign trade, 4, 37, 258, 271
founding mission, 1, 16, 68, 92, 101, 164, 211, 214, 490, 507, 575, 601, 603, 607, 608, 611, 614-621, 623-625, 627-630, 632, 635
Four Cardinal Principles, 13, 217
Four Consciousnesses, 94, 105, 107-110, 115, 116, 118, 185, 214, 255, 256, 260, 264, 345, 361, 362, 367, 376, 490, 584, 585, 594, 603, 608, 609, 618, 621, 631
four forms of oversight over discipline compliance, 71, 590, 636
Four Malfeasances, 118, 578, 579, 588
Four Principles of Deference, 107
Four-pronged Comprehensive Strategy, 3, 20, 22, 130, 200, 219, 273, 304, 342, 605
Four-sphere Confidence, 109, 110, 214, 255, 256, 260, 345, 362, 376, 490, 584, 603, 608, 609, 618, 621
14th CPC National Congress, 135
14th Five-year Plan, 322, 352
Fourth Plenary Session of the 18th CPC Central Committee, 327, 587
Fourth Plenary Session of the 19th (CPC) Central Committee, 212, 248, 629, 633
France, 537
free trade areas, 64
free trade port, 37, 228, 233, 234
Fujian, 459, 475
functional zones, 56, 319, 321
functional zoning, 6, 319

G

Ganges, 541
Gansu, 439
garbage sorting, 399, 400
gender equality, 50
global community of shared future, 8, 21, 26, 63, 65, 89, 101, 220, 228, 239, 244, 250, 254, 295, 337, 349, 432, 437, 477, 491, 494-498, 503, 505, 506, 509, 513, 517, 536, 538, 555, 562, 563
global eco-civilization, 423, 437
global economic governance, 241, 244, 249, 271, 520, 534, 562, 566
global environmental governance, 55, 423
global governance, 64, 239, 337, 466, 489, 491, 498, 512, 514, 520, 530, 533, 535, 548, 549, 563
global governance system, 8, 62, 64, 220, 228, 236, 493, 495, 496, 507, 513, 517, 534, 535, 562, 567
global growth drivers, 516
global peace, 8, 477, 507, 517, 533, 537, 551
global security, 536
Grand Canal, 166
grassroots self-governance, 218
Great Mosque of Mecca, 541
Great Wall, 166, 434, 541
green development, 6, 27, 54, 272, 282, 422, 423, 426, 434-438, 519, 525, 567
green energy, 532
Group of 20 (G20), 8, 241, 250, 536, 548-550
Gu Wenchang, 630
Guangdong, 60, 460, 461, 464, 465
Guangdong-Hong Kong-Macao Greater Bay Area, 60, 244, 249, 275, 284, 317, 464, 465, 479, 483, 565
Guangzhou, 317, 462

Guangzhou-Shenzhen-Hong Kong Express Rail Link, 328
Gulf Cooperation Council, 560
Gulf of Aden, 7, 526
Gulf of Guinea, 526
Gutian Conference on Military Political Work, 7, 445
Gutian Meeting, 114, 598

H

Hainan, 233, 234
Hainan free trade port, 233, 241, 248
Hamlet, 378
Han Fei Zi, 166
Han Zheng, 87
Hangzhou, 8, 317
Harbin, 323
harmony between human (humanity/man) and nature, 25, 435, 505, 519, 522, 547
health care, 10, 51, 52, 184, 259, 462, 475, 479, 484, 525, 526
hedonism, 9, 71, 94, 118, 368, 448, 588, 598, 604, 619
higher education, 49, 309, 383, 405
Ho Hau Wah, 478
Ho Hung Sun, 460
Ho Iat Seng, 478
Hong Kong, 7, 11, 26, 59-61, 101, 264, 328, 348, 459-467, 476, 484, 485
Hong Kong International Airport, 462
Hong Kong Stock Exchange, 461
Hu Fuming, 377

I

Implementation Plan for In-depth Institutional Reform in Science and Technology, 292
independent foreign policy of peace, 63
Indian Ocean, 559

Indus, 541
industrialization, 23, 149, 219, 299-301, 309, 359, 418, 425, 435, 520, 560, 563
information technology, 74, 201, 259, 309, 322, 357, 359, 360, 372, 532
Inner Mongolia, 440
innovation-driven development, 3, 29, 32, 219, 227, 241, 250, 296, 314, 318, 406, 537
innovative, coordinated, green, open and shared development, 160, 219, 420, 426, 512
integrated development of the Yangtze River Delta, 244, 317
intellectual property rights (IPR), 205, 229-231, 520, 531, 533
international cooperation, 6, 37, 64, 221, 231, 241, 246, 249, 284, 296, 423, 494, 514, 533, 555, 592
international financial crisis, 237, 269, 548
International Monetary Fund (IMF), 271, 514, 533, 536
international order, 27, 62, 228, 236, 247, 423, 511, 520
international political and economic order, 507
international relations, 21, 62, 64, 220, 228, 476, 491, 506, 510, 511, 513, 517
internet, 5, 32, 45, 74, 140, 233, 257, 283, 287, 290, 353, 357, 358, 360, 361, 364, 369-372, 560, 561
Islam, 546

J

Jangar, 166
Japan, 270
Jiang Zilong, 377
Jiao Yulu, 630
Jiaxing, 576

Jordan, 558

K
King Gesar, 166
Kyrgyzstan, 515

L
Lao Zi, 166, 378
Latin America, 555
Latin American and Caribbean states, 555
law-based governance, 2, 4, 20, 23, 24, 38, 39, 41, 59, 74, 140, 201, 218, 229, 266, 327, 330-336, 339
law-based government, 24, 41, 331, 334
Leading Group for Financial and Economic Affairs under the CPC Central Committee, 269
Leading Group for Further Reform under the CPC Central Committee, 269, 271
Leading Group for Promoting the Belt and Road Initiative, 565
Leading Group of Poverty Alleviation and Development, 189
Lebanon, 558
Lenin, Vladimir, 198, 627
Leung Chun-ying, 460
Li Bai, 378
Li Guyi, 377
Li Keqiang, 87
Li Xuejian, 377
Li Yining, 377
Li Zhanshu, 87
Liaoning, 328
liberalize and facilitate trade and investment, 221
life sciences, 287, 532
Lin Yifu, 377
Loess Plateau, 439
Long March, 116

Lu Xun, 217, 388
Lu Yao, 377
Luxor Temple, 544
Lü's Spring and Autumn Annals, 369

M
Macao, 7, 11, 26, 59-61, 101, 264, 348, 459-467, 476-485
Macao Special Administrative Region (MSAR), 478-484
Mainland and Hong Kong Closer Economic Partnership Arrangement (CEPA), 461
major-country diplomacy, 8, 21, 495, 496
Manas, 166
Manifesto of the Communist Party, 96, 615
Mao Zedong, 96, 100, 114, 115, 206, 316, 329, 347, 389, 575, 588, 599, 625
Mao Zedong Thought, 19, 21, 97, 216, 617
maritime governance, 539
maritime peace and order, 538
market economy, 65, 148, 260, 460
Marx, Karl, 145, 329
Marxism, 5, 21, 22, 24, 28, 44, 85, 92, 96-98, 144-148, 151, 215, 216, 261, 263, 266, 276, 336, 363-366, 376, 382, 383, 388, 508, 547, 585, 586, 602, 603, 609, 610, 615, 617, 625, 626
Marxism-Leninism, 14, 19, 21, 96, 97, 216, 597
mass line, 8, 22, 113, 118, 161, 162, 215, 409
May 4th Movement, 387
medical insurance, 50, 52, 188, 189, 205
Mediterranean, 559
Mencius, 166, 378, 511
Mencius, The, 378

micro and small enterprises, 311
Middle East, 557-560
middle-income group, 6, 30, 49, 309
Ministry of Ecology and Environment 202, 431
Minjiang River, 419
moderately prosperous society in all respects, 1, 2, 12, 20, 28-30, 76, 93, 112, 135, 173, 256, 272, 345, 495, 584, 631
modern corporate system, 315
Mo Zi, 166
multi-polarity, 62, 489, 498, 517, 540
multilateral system, 535
multilateral trading system (multilateral trade regime), 64, 221, 235, 241, 244, 247, 249, 512, 517, 520, 530-532, 537, 549
multiparty cooperation and political consultation under the leadership of the CPC, 23, 218, 342, 343

N

Nanjing, 317
nanotechnology, 238
National Conference on Development-driven Poverty Alleviation, 182
national defense, 7, 26, 57-59, 63, 117, 138, 149, 196, 214, 221, 264, 265, 322, 450, 452, 455, 463, 538
National Health Commission, 189
National Healthcare Security Administration, 189, 202
National People's Congress (NPC), 100, 147, 329, 341, 342, 468, 499
national reunification, 15, 19, 26, 59, 112, 196, 469
national security, 6, 11, 19, 25, 53, 57, 201, 217, 253-255, 257, 258, 266, 291, 292, 319, 358, 370, 430, 451, 466, 489, 493, 495, 496, 498

National Security Commission, 253, 254
national supervision system, 5, 73, 329, 332, 593
negative list, 35, 37, 229, 233, 240, 246, 249, 320, 331, 461
Neoh, Anthony, 460
New Culture Movement, 547
New Democratic Revolution, 15, 146, 615
New Development Bank, 524
new development philosophy, 3, 74, 88, 244, 250, 273, 276, 278, 359, 564, 605
new model of international relations, 491, 506, 513, 517
NGOs, 360, 545, 570
1992 Consensus, 7, 26, 60, 348, 469, 473
19th (CPC) National Congress, 1, 83, 91, 92, 106, 114, 116, 121, 129, 136, 141, 159, 173, 182, 195, 209, 217, 227, 228, 232, 256, 277, 288, 299-301, 358, 362, 363, 375, 378, 396, 425, 445, 451, 454, 489, 490, 508, 576, 579, 584, 586, 589, 591, 593, 597, 632
NPC Standing Committee, 327-329, 468

O

October Revolution, 14
old revolutionary base areas, 34, 69
"On Coalition Government", 621
"On the Ten Major Relationships", 206, 316
one-China principle, 7, 26, 60, 348, 469, 470, 473, 476, 481
"one country, two systems", 7, 19, 26, 59, 60, 101, 152, 328, 348, 464-467, 470, 472, 479-482, 485
One Thousand and One Nights, 541

Opium War, 14, 468
original aspiration, 1, 92, 93, 101, 162, 211, 214, 446, 490, 575, 576, 601, 603, 607, 608, 611, 614-616, 618-621, 623-625, 627-630, 632

P

Palestine, 560
Paris Agreement, 519, 550
Party (CPC) Constitution, 5, 8, 9, 27, 66, 68, 107, 108, 451, 586, 589, 593, 594, 603, 608, 625
Party('s) leadership, 4, 5, 16, 21-23, 26, 38-40, 44, 65, 66, 71, 74, 106-108, 113, 116, 117, 126, 129, 131, 133, 139, 140, 142, 144, 151, 195, 196, 199-201, 213, 214, 218, 222, 263, 264, 272, 332, 339, 342, 347, 351, 354, 401, 445-447, 492, 565, 584, 589, 599, 603, 620, 632, 634, 636
Party leadership groups, 152, 153, 155, 365, 590, 636
Party organizations, 69-71, 108, 109, 117, 125, 154, 176, 304, 306, 412, 446, 447, 491, 492, 585, 586, 588, 589, 591, 598, 620, 625, 634, 636
Party self-governance, 65, 180, 266, 446, 584, 591, 593, 600, 617, 629, 632, 634, 635
Pearl River Delta, 60, 317, 318, 461
people-centered philosophy of development, 20, 88, 205, 272, 408
people-to-people exchanges, 466, 484, 509, 514, 522, 542, 545, 570
People's Armed Police Force, 101
people's congresses, 23, 39, 40, 64, 112, 200, 218, 327, 328, 339, 636
People's Liberation Army, 101
People's Republic of China (PRC), 14, 15, 28, 83, 85, 88, 92, 93, 100, 102, 115, 134, 148, 149, 159, 165, 263, 300, 328, 329, 341, 347, 375, 380, 478, 599, 603, 615, 616, 626, 630
people's status as masters of the country, 148
pilot free trade zone, 37, 233, 241, 248
Plato, 378
Political Bureau, 87, 106, 114, 118, 134, 138, 139, 141, 143, 269, 576, 579, 588, 614, 621
Potala Palace, 166
poverty alleviation, 10, 25, 29, 51, 162, 175-180, 182-187, 227, 273, 405, 425, 568, 581, 634
private sector, 274, 310, 311, 314, 348, 564

Q

Qingdao, 510, 513, 514
Qinghai, 439, 462
Qu Yuan, 290
quantum information, 287, 516

R

real economy, 10, 31, 32, 36, 279, 282, 283, 289, 290, 360
real estate market, 257
Red Army, 116
reform and opening up, 11, 16, 17, 28, 65, 83, 85, 88, 92, 115, 135-137, 146, 148, 149, 159, 197, 198, 203, 210, 213-217, 219-223, 238, 241, 243, 244, 248, 260, 263, 269, 273, 293, 300, 301, 310, 316, 328, 337, 375, 377, 382, 389, 459-461, 463-465, 469, 490, 547, 626
reform of Party and state institutions, 112, 113, 129, 130, 132, 133, 195, 198-202
Regional Comprehensive Economic Partnership, 241, 249
regional economic development, 316

regional ethnic autonomy, 23, 218, 351, 354
Regulations for Political Activities Within the Party in the New Era, 119
"Report to the Second Plenary Session of the Seventh Central Committee of the Communist Party of China", 621
Republic, The, 378
resource conservation, 54, 399, 417, 420, 421, 427
Rigveda, The, 541
Roundtable on Sino-Arab Inter-civilization Dialogue and Eradication of Extremism, 561
rule of law, 4, 5, 13, 19, 20, 23, 24, 29, 34, 41, 52, 58, 74, 83, 130, 151, 152, 222, 261, 305, 327, 329, 331-336, 339, 372, 373, 481, 483, 637
Run Run Shaw, 462
rural revitalization, 140, 227, 284, 299, 300, 303-307
rural revitalization strategy, 29, 33, 184, 219, 299, 301, 303-306, 395, 396

S
Samarkand, 544
Scientific Outlook on Development, 19, 21, 97, 216, 617
scientific socialism, 12, 92, 97, 98, 145, 148
SCO Inter-bank Consortium, 514
Second Belt and Road Forum for International Cooperation, 437, 550
Second Centenary Goal, 29, 88, 264, 316
Second China International Import Expo, 245, 569
Sentosa, 544
Seven Malpractices, 587
Seventh CPC National Congress, 115
Shakespeare, William, 378

Shandong, 510
Shanghai, 230, 243, 245, 317, 319, 459, 460, 514, 560, 576
Shanghai Cooperation Organization (SCO), 241, 510, 511, 513-515
Shanghai Hongqiao International Airport, 462
Shanghai Stock Exchange, 243, 246
Shantou, 461
Shanxi, 329
Shenyang, 323
Shenzhen, 317, 460-462
Shi Guangnan, 377
Sichuan Province, 178, 419
Silk Road, 541, 555, 556, 568, 570
Singapore, 544
Sino-Arab Research Center on Reform and Development, 561
Sixth Plenary Session of the Sixth Central Committee, 599
small and medium-sized enterprises, 33, 311
smart manufacturing, 532
Smith, Adam, 378
social governance, 6, 25, 30, 47, 48, 52, 53, 70, 151, 218, 259, 302, 372, 399, 408-410, 483
social stability, 15, 99, 117, 133, 138, 149, 154, 203, 217, 256, 258, 259, 265, 358, 375, 397, 408, 480, 542, 606
socialism with Chinese characteristics, 1, 2, 4, 5, 11, 12, 14, 16-18, 19-24, 27, 30, 43-45, 65, 67, 68, 76, 83, 85, 87, 91, 92, 94, 97, 101, 110, 112, 116, 134, 136, 146, 150, 159, 168, 212-214, 216, 217, 227, 254, 256, 261, 263, 275, 277, 281, 303, 330, 342, 345, 358, 362-365, 367, 377, 382, 383, 408, 411, 412, 417, 445, 446, 450, 451, 454, 464, 490, 495, 496, 565, 576, 584-586, 597, 599, 602, 604, 608, 609, 616, 617, 621, 632

socialist consultative democracy, 4, 23, 40, 218, 343, 346
socialist market economy, 31, 35, 151, 203, 204, 284
socialist modernization, 2, 18, 20, 29, 31, 83, 137, 147, 173, 203, 210, 215, 221, 278, 299, 300, 342, 382, 383, 508, 615
Songs of Chu, 166
South-South Cooperation, 527, 570
Soviet Union, 148, 316
special economic zones, 316, 429, 460
State Council, 100, 189, 292
State Council Leading Group of Poverty Alleviation and Development, 189
state governance system, 88, 136-138, 140-144, 146, 147, 149, 150, 152, 155, 212, 343, 633
state-owned enterprises, 35, 177, 312, 314, 322, 463, 594, 612, 635
state-owned sector, 35, 274, 322
state system and capacity for governance, 134, 143
Su Shi, 153, 587
Sun Yat-sen, 290, 388
Sun Zi, 166
supply-side structural reform, 3, 31, 219, 227, 243, 257, 266, 270, 273, 274, 279, 283, 289, 307, 310, 311, 372
sustainable development, 25, 29, 37, 135, 184, 204, 219, 308, 400, 417, 423, 518, 523, 563, 567, 570
Syria, 558

T

Taiwan, 7, 8, 11, 60, 61, 264, 349, 468-477
"Taiwan independence", 7, 61, 349, 470, 473, 474, 476
Taiwan question, 60, 468, 469, 471, 472, 477
Taj Mahal, 541
Tales of Genji, The, 541
Talmud, 541
Tao Yuanming, 378
targeted poverty alleviation, 29, 162, 178, 180, 186, 227, 273, 425, 581, 634
Theory of Three Represents, 19, 21, 97, 216, 617
Third Plenary Session of the 18th CPC Central Committee, 132, 135, 137, 210-212
Third Plenary Session of the 11th CPC Central Committee, 137, 210, 342, 459, 599
Third Plenary Session of the 19th CPC Central Committee, 129, 136
thought on the economy of socialism with Chinese characteristics in the new era, 275
thought on foreign affairs of socialism with Chinese characteristics in the new era, 495, 496
Thought on Socialism with Chinese Characteristics for a New Era, 19-21, 44, 67, 85, 97, 110, 216, 217, 256, 261, 342, 345, 358, 362-365, 367, 377, 382, 383, 408, 411, 445, 446, 451, 454, 490, 584, 585, 599, 602, 604, 608, 609, 617, 621, 632
Three Guarantees, 183, 188-190
Three Guidelines for Ethical Behavior and Three Basic Rules of Conduct, 8, 27, 94
Three-sphere Plan, 417
Tigris, 541
Tin Ka Ping, 462
top-level design, 58, 137, 140, 183, 201, 204, 212, 222, 293, 306, 307, 329, 372, 463, 494
trade protectionism, 511

trade war, 517, 534
traditional Chinese medicine, 52, 479
21st Century Maritime Silk Road, 539
2019 Beijing International Horticultural Exhibition, 434
2030 Agenda for Sustainable Development, 238, 247, 436, 519, 521, 531, 550
2022 Beijing Winter Olympic Games, 47, 427
Two Assurances, 183, 188, 190
Two Centenary Goals, 26, 29, 31, 83, 85, 86, 88, 102, 116, 134, 155, 200, 253, 263, 264, 281, 342, 344, 345, 354, 369, 375, 380, 387, 450, 489, 497, 576
Two Upholds, 109, 110, 124-126, 214, 256, 260, 264, 345, 376, 412, 603, 608, 609, 618, 621, 631, 633

U

UN Charter, 247
UN peacekeeping operations, 507
united front, 4, 19, 23, 42, 201, 218, 341, 343, 344, 347
United Nations, 64, 238, 250, 511, 514, 533, 535, 566, 570
United States (US), 126, 270, 304, 461
Universal Declaration of Human Rights, 337
urbanization, 3, 23, 219, 275, 299-301, 305, 309, 359, 563
utopian socialism, 148

W

Wang Huning, 87
Wang Jiafu, 377
Wang Yang, 87
War of Resistance Against Japanese Aggression, 468
Wat Phra Kaew, 544
Wealth of Nations, The, 378

West Kowloon terminus, 328
Wong Fuk Wing, 463
World Bank, 249, 514, 533, 536
World Trade Organization (WTO), 241, 244, 249, 512, 531-533, 536, 537, 549
World War II, 529
WTO Government Procurement Agreement, 230
Wuhan, 317

X

Xi'an, 317
Xie Jin, 377
Xiongan New Area, 35
Xu Chongde, 377

Y

Yan'an Rectification Movement, 610
Yang Shanzhou, 630
Yangtze River, 243, 422, 429, 541
Yangtze River Delta, 244, 246, 249, 317, 318, 427
Yangtze River Economic Belt, 3, 35, 244, 249, 274, 284, 317, 422, 565
Yellow River, 438-441, 541
Yellow River Basin, 249, 317, 438, 440
Yellow River Delta, 439
Yemen 558

Z

zero-sum mentality, 473, 511
Zhang Fuqing, 630
Zhao Leji, 87
Zhejiang 329, 459, 575
Zheng Derong, 377
Zheng Xie, 150
Zhengzhou, 317
Zhuang Zi, 166
Zhuhai, 461, 484
Zuo's Commentary on the Spring and Autumn Annals, 379

图书在版编目 (CIP) 数据

习近平谈治国理政. 第三卷 : 英文 / 习近平著 ;
英文翻译组译. – 北京 : 外文出版社, 2020.6
(2023.3重印)
ISBN 978-7-119-12411-7

I. ①习… II. ①习… ②英… III. ①习近平 – 讲话
–学习参考资料 – 英文②习近平新时代中国特色社会主义
思想 – 学习参考资料 – 英文 IV. ① D2-0 ② D610.4

中国国家版本馆 CIP 数据核字 (2023) 第 035404 号

习近平谈治国理政
第 三 卷

© 外文出版社有限责任公司
外文出版社有限责任公司出版发行
（中国北京百万庄大街 24 号）
邮政编码：100037
http://www.flp.com.cn
文畅阁印刷有限公司印刷
2020 年 6 月（小 16 开）第 1 版
2023 年 3 月第 1 版第 4 次印刷
（英文）
ISBN 978-7-119-12411-7
08000（平）